Political Parties and
Interest Groups

Political Parties and Interest Groups

Shaping Democratic Governance

edited by
Clive S. Thomas

LYNNE
RIENNER
PUBLISHERS

BOULDER
LONDON

Published in the United States of America in 2001 by
Lynne Rienner Publishers, Inc.
1800 30th Street, Boulder, Colorado 80301
www.rienner.com

and in the United Kingdom by
Lynne Rienner Publishers, Inc.
3 Henrietta Street, Covent Garden, London WC2E 8LU

© 2001 by Lynne Rienner Publishers, Inc. All rights reserved

Library of Congress Cataloging-in-Publication Data
Political parties and interest groups : shaping democratic governance /
   Clive S. Thomas, editor.
      p. cm.
   Includes bibliographical references and index.
   ISBN 1-55587-978-0
   1. Political parties. 2. Pressure groups. 3. Democracy. 4. Comparative
government. I. Thomas, Clive S.
JF2051.P569   2001
324.2—dc21

00-062629

British Cataloguing in Publication Data
A Cataloguing in Publication record for this book
is available from the British Library.

Printed and bound in the United States of America

The paper used in this publication meets the requirements
of the American National Standard for Permanence of
Paper for Printed Library Materials Z39.48-1984.

5 4 3 2 1

To my aunt Peggy and
the memory of Alice, my grandmother,
both of whom helped imbue me with the love of learning

Contents

Preface ix

1 Studying the Political Party–Interest Group Relationship
  Clive S. Thomas 1

PART ONE: THE TRADITIONAL DEMOCRACIES

2 Britain: Change and Continuity Within the
  New Realities of British Politics
  Grant Jordan and William A. Maloney 27

3 France: Party-Group Relations in the Shadow of the State
  Andrew Appleton 45

4 Sweden: Weakening Links Between Political Parties
  and Interest Organizations
  Anders Widfeldt 63

5 The United States: The Paradox of Loose Party-Group
  Ties in the Context of American Political Development
  Clive S. Thomas 79

PART TWO: THE POST–WORLD WAR II DEMOCRACIES

6 Germany: The Continuing Dominance of Neocorporatism
  Winand Gellner and John D. Robertson 101

7	Italy: The Erosion and Demise of Party Dominance *John Constantelos*	119
8	Israel: The End of Integration *Yael Yishai*	139
9	Japan: Strong State, Spectator Democracy, and Modified Corporatism *Ronald J. Hrebenar*	155

PART THREE: THE TRANSITIONAL DEMOCRACIES

10	Spain: Changing Party-Group Relations in a New Democracy *Kerstin Hamann*	175
11	The Czech Republic: Party Dominance in a Transitional System *Robert K. Evanson and Thomas M. Magstadt*	193
12	Poland: Parties, Movements, Groups, and Ambiguity *David Ost*	211
13	Argentina: Parties and Interests Operating Separately by Design and in Practice *Diane E. Johnson*	229
14	Mexico: The End of Party Corporatism? *Jonathan Rosenberg*	247

PART FOUR: CONCLUSIONS

15	Toward a Systematic Understanding of Party-Group Relations in Liberal Democracies *Clive S. Thomas*	269

List of Acronyms	293
Further Reading	297
Notes	307
References	313
The Contributors	335
Index	339
About the Book	353

Preface

One of the paradoxes of political science around the world, particularly in liberal democracies, is that broad agreement exists on the importance of the relationship between political parties and interest groups but little research has been conducted on that relationship. By drawing on the experiences of thirteen countries—old established democracies, new ones, and some in transition to democracy—this book provides the first general analysis of the party-group relationship in liberal democracies.

Some studies have been conducted on specific aspects of party-group relations within particular democracies and across Western countries, mainly on the competition between parties and groups for members and on the decline of major parties in the face of expanding numbers of interest groups, social movements, and third parties. But virtually no studies explain the various elements and assess the significance of the party-group connection within individual liberal democracies, and no comparative study exists of the relationship across Western countries. This book seeks to provide a holistic understanding of the party-group relationship, both within individual democracies and across the Western world.

Within this general, holistic objective, four specific goals can be summarized: (1) Why do some interest groups have relations with political parties while others do not, and for those that do, what determines the type and extent of the relationship? (2) What various forms do party-group relations take in democracies, and can these be developed into a model that includes, among other relationships, the close ties of socialist parties with labor groups, the lack of connection of most groups with parties, and situations where groups and parties conflict? (3) How does the party-group relationship, or lack of it, affect the political system, particularly policymaking and representation? (4) Do general patterns exist across countries that explain the party-group relationship and its consequences in liberal democracies and that can perhaps be developed into a general theory? The party-group relationship across liberal democracies has been in flux for several decades. Thus, an explanation of the past, present, and likely future party-group connection will be helpful in understanding trends in democracies in general, as well as the politics of individual countries, and in providing general background and a context for an understanding of more specific aspects of the party-group connection.

In essence, this comparative analysis draws on scholars who are experts in the party-group relationship in particular democracies and synthesizes their findings to determine general patterns and practices. To ensure that the general analysis—the theoretical synthesis—was as representative as possible, a broad range of democracies was identified for the study. The criteria on which they were chosen included such factors as population size and diversity; federal and unitary systems; two-party and multiparty systems; those with neocorporatist experiences; and well-established, post–World War II, and transitional democracies—those having recently emerged from authoritarian rule. In reaching beyond the Anglo-American and Western European democracies, the analysis provides new insights into the party-group relationship and some indications of likely future developments as more countries move to democracy and existing democracies go through major transitions in the relationship between their parties and interest groups.

As a starting point for the study, Chapter 1 reviews existing knowledge on the party-group connection in liberal democracies, explains the methodology of the study and how the project sought to facilitate comparative analysis, and provides guidelines for approaching the analysis in each country chapter. The country chapters are divided into three sections. Part 1, "The Traditional Democracies," includes Britain, France, Sweden, and the United States. Part 2, "The Post–World War II Democracies," examines Germany, Italy, Israel, and Japan. Part 3, "The Transitional Democracies," considers Spain, the Czech Republic, Poland, Argentina, and Mexico. Based on the analyses in these country chapters, the conclusion returns to the book's four main questions and summarizes the findings with a view to assessing the accuracy of existing explanations of the party-group connection and providing some theoretical basis for a more in-depth understanding of past, present, and future developments in the relationship.

* * *

At the top of the list of those I would like to thank for making this book possible are the fifteen contributors. Yael Yishai (University of Haifa, Israel) first got me interested in undertaking this project and provided many of the ideas underlying its direction and research approach. Neil Mitchell

(University of New Mexico) reviewed the entire manuscript and made several helpful suggestions. Grant Jordan (University of Aberdeen, Scotland) made valuable suggestions on an early draft of Chapter 1. Beatrice Franklin of the University of Alaska Southeast Library was of tremendous help in locating sources and helping me verify references and citations. Dan Eades and Leanne Anderson of Lynne Rienner Publishers were very helpful and supportive throughout the writing and publication process. And my former dean, now Chancellor John Pugh of the University of Alaska Southeast, was, as usual, very supportive of my efforts, as was Jean Linthwaite, his assistant.

Most important, I thank my wife, Susan, who is a great sounding board for ideas, as well as a wizard with the English language, and whose support and encouragement were so important during times when this project wasn't going quite the way I'd planned.

Clive S. Thomas

1

Studying the Political Party–Interest Group Relationship

Clive S. Thomas

In virtually all countries, especially liberal democracies, political parties and interest groups are among the most important institutions that define the character of the political system and serve as the principal links between citizens and their government. Few political scientists would disagree with this assessment, even though in recent years increasing scholarly attention has been paid to the role of social movements as an important form of citizen-government linkage. Several scholars have identified the dynamics of the political party–interest group relationship as central in shaping the structure and nature of democratic government (for example, Schattschneider 1942, 1960; Almond 1958; Duverger 1972, 1; Panebianco 1988, 269–270; Lawson 1980; Lawson and Merkl 1988, chapter 1; Zeigler 1993, chapter 7; Morlino 1998). Despite this assertion, for the most part the literature has treated parties and groups separately and, where it examines the connection between them, has focused mainly on party-group competition. In this book we take a broader look at the interrelationship of parties and groups (in some cases party-group–social movement relations) to more accurately assess the significance of the connection to democratic government.

Although there are a host of references in scholarly journals on the party-group relationship, as well as some chapters on the connection (for example, G. Wilson 1990, chapter 6; Cigler 1993; Berry 1997, chapter 3), plus several books combining the study of parties and groups (for example, Duverger 1972; Ippolito and Walker 1980), there is a lack of systematic research and theory on the fundamentals of their interrelationship. Thus, the importance of the party-group connection has long been taken for granted, falling largely into the realm of intuitive axioms. Some of these may not be true, however, or elements of them may vary from system to system. For instance: Do all interests, or even a majority of them, have connections with political parties? Are the ways in which parties and interests relate similar in old, established democracies and newer ones—including those in transition from authoritarian to democratic rule—or are they different? Are there differences between the party-group relationship in two-party systems, common in Anglo-American countries, and that in multiparty systems, commonly found in other democratic systems? Does an interdependent, symbiotic relationship always exist between major parties and major interests representing business and labor? And indeed, is the party-group relationship as important in all democracies as scholars of American politics have claimed it is in the United States?

In fact, even a cursory knowledge reveals that the relationship of parties and groups differs between countries, sometimes markedly. Compare, for example, the close relationship of many socialist parties with labor organizations, as has traditionally been the case in Sweden, with the much looser, more pragmatic relationship of the Democratic Party with labor in the United States. In addition, wide variations in the party-group relationship exist within countries. Britain, for instance, is generally viewed as having close party-group ties. Although a close alliance has existed between the Labour Party and trade unions, particularly blue-collar unions, and between the Conservative Party and business, not all unions, particularly white-collar unions, are closely allied with the Labour Party or all business with the Conservatives. Furthermore, organizations like the British Legion (ex-military personnel) and Royal Society for the Prevention of Cruelty to Animals (RSPCA) are avowedly nonpartisan and have virtually no contact with parties or strenuously try to maintain a balance. In fact, by deduction from existing studies, the vast number of interest groups in any society likely have no or very little contact with political parties and seek political influence through other channels.

Such distinctions, virtually unmentioned in the existing literature, were a major impetus for this study. There is much we do not understand about this apparently fundamental relationship—the forms it can take, its consequences for politics and policymaking, and its effect in enhancing or undermining the democratic process. By drawing on the experiences of thirteen countries—old, established democracies, new ones, and some in transition to democracy—this book elaborates on the variations noted here and provides the first comprehensive analysis of the party-group relationship between major parties and major interests in liberal democracies. As a starting point for the study, this introductory chapter reviews existing knowledge on the party-group connection in liberal democracies, explains the methodology of the study and how the project seeks to achieve coherence and consistency in the subjects covered in each country chapter to facilitate comparative analysis, and provides guidelines for approaching the analysis in each country chapter.

THE BOOK'S FOCUS AND GOALS

When parties and interests interact, they can do so in several ways within the political system. Interaction could simply occur on an informal level, such as when a group or its members help an individual party candidate during an election. Group representatives could approach party leaders in the parliament or executive to lobby them on an issue. Or the party in power could try to bring several groups together on an ad hoc basis to deal with an issue such as developing an incomes policy. However, the main focus of this book is on a longer-term aspect of the party-group relationship: the extent to which major political parties and major interests have related in the past and continue to relate or interact at the organizational level. That is, to what extent have parties and groups had formal organizational ties, cooperated in elections, or worked in concert on developing and even implementing policies, among other things? Or has the pattern of party-group organizational relations been conflict-ridden, or simply one of separation? Or has it alternated between or among some or all of these forms of interaction? If, however, the group or interest has no institutional relationship with a party or parties, we are interested in finding out what other relationships, long or short term, it has with parties. We want to identify any contact parties and groups might have, including the informal ones listed earlier.

Within this general focus of analysis of the party-group connection at the organizational level, the book has four specific goals, best stated in the form of four questions. First, why do some interest groups have relations with political parties while others do not, and for those that do, what determines the type and extent of the relationship? Second, what are the various forms that party-group relations take in democracies, and can these be developed into a model that includes, among other relationships, the close ties of socialist parties with labor groups, most groups' lack of connection with parties, and situations where groups and parties conflict? Third, how does the party-group relationship, or lack of it, affect the political system, particularly policymaking and representation? Based on these three sets of findings, the fourth question is, can general patterns be identified across countries that explain the party-group relationship and its consequences in liberal democracies and that can perhaps be developed into a general theory? Thus, this book seeks to provide a holistic understanding of the relationship in contrast to focusing primarily on one or more narrow aspects of the connection, such as the various aspects of party-group competition and its consequences.

A general explanation of past, present, and likely future party-group relationships will be helpful to students of politics trying to understand trends in democracies in general, as well as the politics of individual systems. In addition, although it is not a specific goal of this project to directly address the contemporary debate about party-group competition and the decline of major parties and the consequent rise of interest groups, social movements, and third parties, the book throws light on these subjects. Besides being important elements of the party-group relationship, as we will see later, this party decline–interest group rise and the broader element of party-group competition form the bulk of the existing literature on the party-group connection.

To be sure, this book does not fill all the gaps in our understanding. As with many research projects, this one may raise more questions than it answers. It does, however, move our understanding of this important relationship between parties and groups to a higher level. In so doing it provides a baseline of information and offers directions for further research on the subject for both comparative politics and the politics of individual countries.

DEALING WITH DEFINITIONAL QUESTIONS: A WORKING SOLUTION

There is an ongoing debate, stretching back to the early 1950s, about the distinction between a political party and an interest group. More recently, with the major socioeconomic and political changes in Western society, some scholars have extended this debate to include social movements. Burstein (1998) even goes so far as to say that no meaningful analytical distinction exists among parties, groups, and social movements. Although this is true in a few cases, as Chapter 12 on Poland argues in regard to Solidarity, and although the three organizations share similar functions and thus have some similar attributes, in most cases they also have distinct characteristics. No one can provide watertight distinctions among the three organizations, but we can develop practical and meaningful operational definitions to facilitate analysis. As the focus of this book is on the party-group relationship, we concentrate on a working distinction between these two organizations. But as several chapters, of necessity, refer to social movements in their treatment of the party-group connection, we also provide a working distinction among party, group, and social movement.

The Political Party–Interest Group Definitional Debate

The debate over the distinction between a party and an interest group has recently intensified. Although scholars have seen parties and groups as performing both distinct and overlapping functions, what were long considered the major distinctions between the two organizations (for example, Schattschneider 1960; Key 1964; Duverger 1972, 1–2; Rose 1985) no longer seem to hold, if indeed they ever did. The three most important distinctions were that (1) the major goal of a political party is to win formal control of government to implement its program, whereas an interest group does not wish to win formal control of government but simply desires to influence public policy in its areas of concern; (2) parties have an avowedly public purpose as broad coalitions that facilitate compromise and governance in a society as a whole, whereas interest groups are narrow concerns that focus and aggregate their members' interests and articulate them to government; and (3) parties run candidates in elections, whereas interest groups do not (see, for example, Almond and Powell 1966; Rose 1985; Walker 1991).[1] Several scholars (for example, Yishai 1995; Burstein 1998) have argued that these and other distinctions often do not exist in practice. This is often true not only in multiparty systems, they assert, where certain political organizations take on the guise of both party and interest group, but also in some two-party systems where the conventional wisdom—that parties and groups are clearly differentiated—does not hold. For instance, in Israel's multiparty system the religious parties, with their narrowly focused platforms, undermine all three of these "fundamental" distinctions between parties and groups. This is also true of newly formed organizations in two-party systems like the Countryside Alliance in Britain, which promotes rural values.

Yishai developed the useful designation *interest party* to refer to groups that straddle the fence between an interest group and a party. Specifically:

> When an interest group joins the electoral arena and races for public support it becomes an "interest party" rivaling established parties. An interest party is an interest group that runs candidates for legislative elections. It is not a full-fledged party, but at the same time is no longer merely an interest group. It assumes the title and activities of a party yet remains focused on the quest for private benefits and/or on a single issue. (Yishai 1995, 6)

We will return to this important category at several points in this book.

A "Big Player" Definition of Political Party

Although we clearly recognize that these problems of differentiation exist in some instances, they have only a minor bearing on our purposes here, for three reasons. First, although in certain instances a blurry line exists between party and interest group, the number of groups in the interest party category constitutes a very small percentage of the groups in a society. Second, in the past and to a large extent in contemporary democracies, the major interests—particularly business, labor, and agriculture—have defined the nature of the party-group connection (or lack thereof), and these interests rarely fall into the interest party category. Third, because the resource limitations of this project made it impossible to consider the relationship between *all* parties and *all* groups in each of the thirteen countries comprising the study, the focus is on what Maloney and Jordan (1998) call the "big players"—the major parties and, with some qualification, the major groups and interests (see the next subsection). Using the big player definition in this book is a practical way to deal with the boundary questions between certain parties and groups and, at the same time, focus on the core influences—the major parties and interests—that have shaped the party-group relationship in the past, appear to be doing so at present, and are most likely to do so in the future.

A big player political party is relatively easy to delineate. Such parties can be identified in terms of their ability to win a certain percentage of votes or a number of seats in a legislature or parliament, leading to the likelihood of their being the governing party, a member of a governing coalition, or a significant opposition party. The big player distinction is clear-cut in two-party systems like the United States (Democrats and Republicans) and in Britain (New Labour and Conservatives), even when we include two significant third parties—Liberal Democrats and the Scottish Nationalists. The distinction is also clear in what might be termed modified two-party systems like Germany with its Social Democrats, Christian Democrats, and two significant third parties in the Greens and the Free Democratic Party. It is also a practical distinction in multiparty states. For instance, although over thirty parties contested the May 1999 elections in Israel, only half won seats in the Knesset and only five, led by the Labor Party, formed a government.

A Working Definition of Interest Group and Interest

Not only is it difficult to determine with accuracy what is and what is not a big player interest group, there is also the perennial problem of defining exactly what constitutes an interest group. Certainly, some obvious big players are found among interest groups in all liberal democracies—particularly business, labor (both blue-collar and professional), and agriculture. Beyond this, however, big players become harder to identify. As Maloney and Jordan (1998, 5–6) have pointed out, interest groups are far more numerous than parties, and there is no reasonable means to screen out marginal categories. Given these problems with identifying big player interest groups beyond the major business, labor, and agricultural interests, this project defined interest group very broadly (discussed later in this subsection) and let the chapter authors determine the important groups and interests to study in their respective countries regarding their effect on the party-group relationship over the years as it relates to the big player definition of political parties. A major reason experts on each country wrote the chapters was to employ their expertise to ensure that important players in both the party and group arenas were not ignored.

Turning to the definition of an interest group and the terms used to designate such groups, Baumgartner and Leech (1998, 22–30) point out that the lack of a common definition (and, by implication, the terms to designate groups) has inhibited the accumulation of knowledge in interest groups studies. Most studies make clear a particular definition of interest group and, in some cases, clarify the use of terms such as *interest* and *lobby*. Of necessity, that is the approach used in this book.

There are many ways to define an interest group (Baumgartner and Leech 1998, 25–30). Different scholars emphasize different elements of group activities and functions depending on their needs and perspectives. Generally, it has been held that groups provide a mechanism through which citizens who have a *shared attitude* or a *shared interest* can come together and channel their collective resources into political action. Zeigler (1992, 377–380) defines an interest group as "a formal organization seeking to influence public policy in democratic polities" and dissents from the "shared attitudes," "cohesion," or "representation" elements. Jordan and Maloney (1992) coined the term *policy participant* to better designate Zeigler-type policy-influencing organizations. Salisbury (1984) also uses this policy participant definition, emphasizing that many organizations that are interest groups are not membership organizations but are institutions like universities, cities, and corporations. Walker (1991, chapter 1) sees interest groups more as functioning associations open to membership.

For convenience of research, some scholars in the United States use a purely legal definition of interest group, focusing only on those having to register by law and excluding those that do not (for example, Gray and Lowery 1996; Hunter, Wilson, and Brunk 1991; Schlozman and Tierney 1986). Such a definition obviously excludes many policy participants including major government entities that lobby, such as the military and major government departments. It also excludes informal groups, such as influential citizens forming ad hoc groups to deal with problems like crime or education. Salisbury (1994) argues against narrow definitions of interest group as overly restrictive, resulting in the exclusion of some important players in the policy process.

To avoid such restrictiveness, in their ongoing study of interest groups in all fifty U.S. states, Thomas and Hrebenar (1999a) use a broad definition of interest group that goes beyond the purely legal definition and embraces the policy participant, membership, and organizational components prominent in other definitions of interest group and allows for the shared attitudes and shared interests elements, if appropriate. Specifically, their definition is: "An interest group is an association of individuals or organizations, usually formally organized, that attempts to influence public policy" (Thomas and Hrebenar 1999a, 114). This is the definition of an interest group used in this book. It is a catchall definition, but that is its major advantage given the broad range of democracies and party-group connections covered here in an attempt to develop common denominators of patterns of the relationship. The definition allows the entire range of interests in the old and new democracies to be included—from the traditional interests of business, labor, and agriculture to new interests, such as environmentalists and other public interest groups, to the so-called third sector of voluntary organizations mainly concerned with social welfare issues to government at all levels. The definition also enables the military to be included in Argentina and Mexico, which a more restrictive definition might exclude and thus preclude an accurate assessment of the party-group relationship in these countries.

Finally, we need to address the problem of designating an interest group. So far the terms *interest group* and *interest* have been used interchangeably, a consequence of the terminology problem in interest group studies. Its cause is twofold. First, within a particular sector, such as business, there are several individual interest groups—peak associations, trade associations, individual firms, and so on. The term commonly used to designate this broader political concern is the generic term *interest* and sometimes the equally generic term *lobby*—the business interest, the business lobby, the agricultural interest, the agricultural lobby, and so on.[2] Second, a formal interest group, particularly broad-based organizations like business and labor peak associations, sometimes act and are perceived as representatives not only of their official membership but of the broad sectoral interests with which they are identified. This is particularly true in neocorporatist negotiations where business and labor are seen as representing their entire sector, including nonmembers of their organizations, but it is also true at a lesser level. For instance, formally organized antitax groups in Denmark and the United States are perceived as representing general antitax sentiments in these nations. The term *interest* is also often used to designate this aggregation of group member and nonmember attitudes within a sector or an area of political concern.

To deal with these problems, particularly the distinction between an individual interest group and the broader organized political groupings represented by the terms *interest* and *lobby,* and (by implication) to delineate this from the broader nonmembership use of the term *interest,* one study of interest groups suggested the term *organized interests* instead of simply *interest group* (Schlozman and Tierney 1986, 9–12). This term is indeed more accurate. However, as the authors who developed it admit, it is rather clumsy, and the term *interest group* is more commonly used and accepted. For this reason, and bearing in mind our broad definition of the term *inter-*

est group in this book, most of the contributors to this project use the terms *interest group, interest,* and sometimes *lobby,* with the use of a particular term made clear by its context.

A Working Definition of Social Movement

Like interest groups, social movements display a wide range of diversity depending on their degree of organizational and strategic cohesiveness and the extent of their antiestablishment status. At one end of the scale are organizations like the Countryside Alliance in Britain, a federation of establishment-type groups promoting rural values that is well financed and has well-orchestrated activities (Maloney and Jordan 1998). At the other end are loose-knit organizations with poorly coordinated strategies that are decidedly antiestablishment in their "membership" and leadership, like the peasant movement in Chiapas, Mexico. Falling in the middle are organizations like the Civil Rights movement in the United States in the 1960s, with a defined leadership, a loose organizational structure, and a mixed record of coordinated strategy. Furthermore, with the broad definition of interest groups and interests used in this book, it could be argued, along the lines of Burstein (1998), that social movements are simply a loose-knit form of interest group. Certainly, there is overlap at the margin. For instance, whether the Countryside Alliance is an interest group or a social movement is a moot point. The interest group–social movement distinction is compounded by the fact that many social movements develop into traditional, often establishment interest groups, as has the environmental movement across the Western world since the 1960s. Sometimes social movements even make the transition into parties, as with the Greens, Populists, and Progressives at the turn of the twentieth century in the United States and Solidarity in Poland.

Despite this overlap, for analytical purposes some widely accepted attributes of social movements can be identified that distinguish them from traditional interest groups, the distinction we adopt in this book. Combining and paraphrasing the work of McCarthy and Zald (1977), Tilly (1984), Eyerman and Jamison (1991), and Ost (Chapter 12 in this volume), social movements manifest all or most of six elements. They (1) represent people outside established political institutions or who feel a low level of political efficacy in affecting those institutions; (2) seek to change elements of the socioeconomic and political structure, make visible public demands for changes in the distribution or exercise of power in society, or both; (3) employ collective political action that uses, in whole or in large part, noninstitutional channels such as protests, sit-ins, passive resistance, and sometimes illegal means such as violence; (4) hold a strong antipolitics stance, particularly in their formative period, manifesting as an antiestablishment, antigovernment attitude that sees power as located not in the state but in civil society; (5) have a loosely defined, often amorphous organizational structure; and (6) usually either lack a clearly defined leadership or have a charismatic leader like Ghandi or Martin Luther King. By these criteria the vast majority of traditional interest groups—particularly business, labor, and agricultural groups, which form the bulk of interests in Western countries—would be excluded as social movements; by the same criteria, most social movements will not qualify as traditional interest groups.

PERSPECTIVES ON THE PARTY-GROUP RELATIONSHIP IN THE EXISTING LITERATURE

An extensive literature across the Western world deals with political parties and interest groups in liberal democracies.[3] Most of this, however, focuses on parties and groups in individual countries, particularly the United States. And this literature deals mostly with parties and groups as separate entities. Consequently, only a small body of scholarship exists on the party-group relationship both within individual countries and comparatively. Interestingly, much of the literature on the party-group connection has been produced by scholars of the U.S. political system, a system where party-group ties are generally considered much weaker than in the social democracies of northern Europe. Where it exists, the individual country chapters in this book review the literature on the party-group connection specific to their respective countries. In this section we briefly review the scholarship that has general implications for understanding the party-group relationship within and across countries. What does it tell us?

Political Science Perspectives on Party-Group Relations

In terms of the ways the party-group relationship has been viewed by political science over the years, we can identify five perspectives, the first three of which draw on an analysis by Yishai (1995). First, for most pluralists, groups and parties are distinct, performing separate functions in the political process. This is particularly true for a two-party system, which "makes for a sharper functional differentiation between parties and interest groups" (Epstein 1967, 278), but is valid for multiparty systems as well. Thus, most pluralists have treated parties and groups separately and been little concerned with the connection between them.

Second, neocorporatists have largely ignored the question of group-party relations because their focus is mainly on the tripartite relations of government, business, and labor. Therefore, implicitly at least, in this perspective party is used synonymously with *governing* party and not with parties in general. Consequently, a good argument can be made that this focus has caused neocorporatists to underestimate the role of parties in the political process, including the lead-up to tripartite negotiations and agreements. In fact, important accounts of corporatism have totally ignored parties as political actors (for example, Cawson 1986; Williamson 1989).

A third general approach to the group-party relationship is that in which political parties play a decisive role in the political process, which Yishai refers to as the partisan model. Here, interest groups are not distinct from political parties (pluralism), nor are they oblivious to them (corporatism). Rather, interest groups branch from political parties, are subservient to them, or both. LaPalombara (1964) described the Italian scene in terms of partisan predominance. In party-dominated systems like Germany and Japan, however, for many years interest groups eluded the attention of political scientists. Even with the establishment of a committee of the American Political Science Association in the late 1950s to study interest groups in various countries and comparatively—including party-group relations (Almond 1958) and work by Finer (1958) revealing the behind-the-scenes importance of interest groups in Britain—it took some time for political scientists to pay serious attention to the role of interest groups in parliamentary systems, including those in British politics.

The fourth and fifth perspectives on party-group relations have come largely from scholars of American politics, although they imply that their perspectives have application beyond the United States. The fourth is a product of the so-called responsible party model, which argues that the "sovereign majority" can rule only through strong political parties that meet the basic criteria of responsible government. In the absence of strong parties, interest groups undermine majority rule, developing close ties to politicians and party factions in ways that allow them to prevail over the will of the majority. The strongest advocates of this view were Schattschneider (1942) and a report by the American Political Science Association's (APSA) Committee on Political Parties (APSA 1950). To some extent the work of Lowi (1979) and Olson (1982) reflects this view, although their emphasis was on the increasing power and effects of interest groups and less on the importance of parties. Olson explained many post–World War II problems in Western Europe in terms of sclerosis caused by interest groups. Ironically, Olson demonstrated that interest groups are often strong even in strong party systems, which tended to undermine the argument of the responsible party model advocates. These advocates were extensively criticized (for example, Kirkpatrick 1971), and later research—mainly on the U.S. system—by rational choice scholars (for example, Rohde 1991; Aldrich and Rohde 1997–1998) shows that strong legislative coordination can be developed among parties to dominate political agendas and constrain interest groups.[4]

The fifth general perspective—which includes work by pluralists, those championing elitist theory, and a few rational choice scholars—is committed less to any perspective on party-group relations than to the belief that these relations, or the lack of them, matter in shaping power relationships, policy processes and outcomes, campaign funding, and political recruitment, among other things, in a political system. We can call this the party-group political system determinant model. These scholars have mainly been those interested in U.S. state politics and the party-group relationship at that level, including Gray and Lowery (1996), Key (1964), Morehouse (1981, 1997), Thomas and Hrebenar (1999b), Zeigler (1983), Zeller (1954). But they also include scholars of U.S. national politics such as Berry (1997), Cigler (1993), Paddock and Cigler (1997), and Yonish (1998). Whether these findings on party-group relations have applicability outside the unique U.S. political system is unclear.[5]

Specific Studies

Regarding treatments comparing specifics of the party-group relationship across countries, as indicated earlier, the bulk of the small body of literature focuses on party-group competition and its consequences. One study based on secondary sources (G. Wilson 1990), one based on original research (Selle 1997), and two studies that combine original research and secondary sources (Thomas and Hrebenar 1995; Yishai 1995), however, attempt to look at the relationship across Western democracies and have general implications in this regard.

Interestingly, the literature on party-group competition is not a product of an interest in party-group relations per se, but is largely a by-product of a concern about party decline. As Strøm and Svåsand (1997, 4) have commented, research on party decline has been a growth industry. This literature originated in the United States in the late 1970s (see, for example, Crotty 1984; Scott and Hrebenar 1984; Cigler 1993) and then moved to Europe and other democratic systems (see, for example, Berger 1981, 1–23; Lawson 1980; Ware 1988; Lawson and Merkl 1988: Merkl 1988; J. Richardson 1995). The rise of interest groups is by no means the only explanation for party decline in the Western world, but for several scholars it is a major reason.[6] Interest groups are seen as competing with parties mainly as agents of representation—or linkage—between citizens and government. This can be seen more specifically as competition over gaining the ear of policymakers, competition over delivering political benefits, competition for members, and competition for funds. Many scholars see major, mass parties as the losers in this competition—with the consequent rise of interest groups, social movements, third parties, small splinter parties, and "interest parties"—because major, mass parties have failed to meet the demands of a new Western public in articulating and particularly in aggregating interests (Lawson 1980, chapter 1).

One aspect of party-group competition that has become embedded in

U.S. political science and that G. Wilson (1990, 156–157) claims can be extended to liberal democracies in general is their power relationship. From the early 1940s onward, it was believed that an inverse power relationship existed between parties and interest groups: when parties are strong, groups will be weak, and when parties are weak, groups will be strong, and various combinations of the two (Schattschneider 1942; Key 1964, 154–165; Zeigler 1983, 111–117; Zeller 1954, 190–193). It has since been demonstrated (Thomas and Hrebenar 1999a, 121) that this relationship does not necessarily hold (see Chapter 5 in this volume). Furthermore, judging by the lack of literature, as scholars of other political systems have never been concerned with this party-group power relationship, the value of its application to studying party-group relations in democracies beyond the United States has yet to be demonstrated.

We can assess the four general studies by Wilson, Selle, Thomas and Hrebenar, and Yishai as follows. By extrapolating from a synthesis of work on parties and groups, G. Wilson (1990, chapter 7), among other things, offers both a typology of the party-group relationship and a framework for understanding what shapes the connection, including the nature of the state and the group's objectives. One of Wilson's major conclusions is that "there is no single pattern of relationships between interest groups and political parties either between or within countries" (G. Wilson 1990, 159).

The work by Selle (1997), based on interviews with the heads of the offices of Norway's seven major parties, assessed the formal and informal contact between parties and voluntary organizations (that is, interest groups) today and how this may have changed since the early 1980s. The caveat, of course, is that his study applies to only one country. However, it examines the overall relationship of parties and groups, and his findings reflect those that, prior to this research project, appeared to be occurring in many Western countries; as such, the work provides a baseline for conducting studies on other countries and assessing general patterns.

The work by Thomas and Hrebenar (1995), drawing mainly on original research on party-group relations in the United States and secondary sources from other systems, produced a conceptual framework of the various forms of the party-group relationship and the factors that influence that relationship in an attempt to move toward a more general understanding of party-group relations in Western democracies. Yishai's (1995) goal was similar. She, however, was more concerned about why some groups align with parties and other do not: Is this based solely on a cost-benefit calculation, or are other factors at work? She also developed a typology of the various forms the party-group relationship takes in Western democracies.

In presenting the guidelines for analysis in the final section of this chapter, I draw on some implications of this existing research, in particular that by Wilson, Selle, Thomas and Hrebenar, and Yishai.

Gaps in the Literature

This brief review of the major research on the party-group connection reveals that only a sketchy understanding of the relationship exists across Western democracies. This is not surprising, given that most of the work has not focused on the party-group relationship directly as an important element of democratic governance but is a by-product of other studies. Methodologically, much of the research focuses on the system level and not on the sector or individual party-group level, resulting in broad generalizations that have limited value in understanding the specifics of the party-group connection. A further methodological problem is that the important distinction between party-group relations and *governing* party-group relations is often unspecified.

The answers to the four major questions of the study set out earlier will provide a comprehensive understanding of the party-group relationship. Using those questions, we can identify the gaps in our knowledge as follows:

1. Why do some interest groups have relations with political parties while others do not; for those that do, what determines the type and extent of the relationship? Other than the speculative work by G. Wilson, Thomas and Hrebenar, and Yishai, we have little to go on. We have the competition literature, but questions such as why some groups relate to certain interests and not to others and how and why this situation changes over time need more extensive analysis.
2. What are the various forms party-group relations take in democracies? Again, there is the speculative work by G. Wilson, Thomas and Hrebenar, and Yishai. But a more complete typology based on research of various countries needs to be developed.
3. How does the party-group relationship, or lack of it, affect the political system, particularly policymaking and representation? Here we have numerous fragments of information on power relationships, party-group leadership and membership overlap, financial connections, and so on. What is missing is a systematic identification and analysis of the major elements of the relationship that affect policymaking and democracy and how they do so.
4. Can general patterns be identified across countries that explain the party-group relationship and its consequences in liberal democracies and that can perhaps be developed into a general theory? As has been made clear several times in this chapter, nothing of this sort exists in the literature.

PROJECT METHODOLOGY AND FORMAT OF THE BOOK

The project methodology was designed to deal with as many of these shortcomings in the literature as possible. The purpose was to provide a set of findings that could act as a starting point for future studies of the party-group relationship across liberal democracies, as well as provide benchmark studies on the relationship in several individual countries. The core of the approach was to draw upon scholars who are experts on the party-group relationship in particular democracies. To ensure that the general analysis—the theoretical synthesis—was as representative as possible, a broad range of democracies was identified for the study. The criteria on which they were chosen included such factors as population size and diversity; federal and unitary systems; two-party and multiparty systems; those with neocorporatist experiences; and well-established, post–World War II, and transitional democracies—those having recently emerged from authoritarian rule. In reaching beyond Anglo-American and Western European democracies, the analysis provides new insights into the party-group relationship and some indications of likely future developments as more countries move to democracy and existing democracies go through major transitions in that relationship. To ensure integration of the analysis, chapter authors were asked to follow a set of guidelines that included the four major questions explained earlier.

To provide a framework in which to analyze the individual country chapters and place the party-group relationship in a comparative context, the final section of this chapter sets out some initial guidelines for analysis. The country chapters are divided into three sections. Part One, "The Traditional Democracies," includes Britain, France, Sweden, and the United States. Part Two, "The Post–World War II Democracies," considers Germany, Israel, Italy, and Japan. And Part Three, "The Transitional Democracies," examines Spain, the Czech Republic, Poland, Argentina, and Mexico. Based on the analysis in these country chapters, the final chapter returns to the four main questions of the book to synthesize the findings with a view to assessing the accuracy of existing explanations of the party-group connection and providing some theoretical basis for a more in-depth understanding of past, present, and future developments in the relationship.

INITIAL GUIDELINES FOR ANALYSIS

In this final section of the chapter we set out guidelines for analyzing the individual country chapters in the rest of the book. These guidelines, gleaned from existing research, form the first steps in developing a more extensive explanation of the party-group relationship across Western democracies. The guidelines fall into six categories: (1) factors shaping party-group relations, (2) forms of the relationship, (3) recent trends in the relationship, (4) the defining role of political parties and national experiences, (5) the level and focus of analysis, and (6) the complex and dynamic nature of the relationship.

Box 1.1 Preliminary Listing of Factors Determining the Relationship Between Political Parties and Interest Groups in Liberal Democracies

Political System and Subsystem Development, and Political Ideology

1. Political System and Subsystem Development

Explanation: The extent of these developments centers around such questions as: Did the system develop with strong ideological cleavages? Did a major gulf exist between capital and labor, and were strong class distinctions present? Was the society characterized by major economic and social upheaval?

Significance: Strong ideological cleavages in a society are likely to cause groups to ally more with certain parties. Less class rigidity and less conflict between capital and labor lead to less of an "opposing camps" type of producer group configuration.

2. Political Culture and Political Ideology

Explanation: Political culture is a shared set of knowledge, attitudes, and symbols that help to define the procedures and goals of politics. *Conservative/liberal/socialist ideology* denotes specific attitudes toward the role of government.

Significance: Skepticism toward government can adversely affect the relationship between parties and groups, particularly the governing party and groups (especially economic groups), whereas a more positive attitude toward government may enhance that relationship. The strength of ideological commitment in a society will affect the strength or weakness of political parties and thus the relationship of groups to parties.

Political Structures and Organizations and Their Operation

3. Centralization/Decentralization of Government and Policymaking

Explanation: Two factors are of particular importance: (1) whether the system is parliamentary or based on the separation of power, and (2) whether it is federal or unitary.

Significance: Parliamentary systems, particularly if accompanied by strong parties, will tend to encourage certain groups, particularly producer groups, to ally with parties in order to achieve their goals. At the same time, the categorical nature of government in such systems (government with all the power, the opposition with none) will lead other groups to take a neutral or pragmatic stance. A very important factor in determining party-group relations is

(continues)

Box 1.1 Continued

which party is in power in a parliamentary system. Groups may have different relations with the same party in and out of power. Changes in control of particular branches of government can have a similar, although usually less extensive, effect in the U.S. system of separation of powers. Unitary systems close avenues open to groups in regional and local areas. Thus, less variety of patterns of party-group relations is found in unitary systems than is often the case in federal systems.

4. Nature of the Party System

Explanation: If the party system is strong in terms of discipline, it will determine the policy agenda and the enactment and implementation of policy.

Significance: Strong party systems, which also tend to be those with historically sharp ideological cleavages, tend to encourage closer ties of certain groups, particularly producer groups, with certain parties—labor to liberal and left-wing parties, business to conservative parties. The weaker the party system, the more neutral or pragmatic these groups can be in their relations with parties.

5. Political Party Dependence on Interest Groups

Explanation: This centers around the extent to which a country's parties are dependent on groups for financing, campaign support and technical information, policy enactment, and similar factors.

Significance: The more dependent particular parties are on groups, the more they will cultivate a relationship with groups. Public funding of elections, for example, tends to reduce parties' need for group contributions.

6. Encompassing Characteristics of the Interest Group System

Explanation: This relates to the extent to which interest groups pervade or embrace the society and the level of unification of group representation: the percentage of people belonging to groups, and the concentration or fragmention of the group system in representing various sectors of society.

Significance: The greater the interest group membership density (the percentage of people belonging to groups), especially producer groups, and the greater the sector concentration (the smaller the number of groups representing business, labor, and other sectors), the greater is the possibility for neocorporatist intermediation at the macro (national) level. Thus, the greater is the likelihood of the existence of peak associations and their ability to engage in policy implementation on behalf of government. Such societies will exhibit close relations between producer groups and parties.

(continues)

Box 1.1 Continued

Interest Group Development, Goals, Characteristics, and Leadership

7. Interest Group Development

Explanation: This concerns the impetus for group development: Did the group develop under the auspices of a party? Were its origins based on ideology or technical considerations?

Significance: Origin and historical development have an important influence on a group's attitude toward and association with parties. Most labor groups were closely allied with radical movements and, often, socialist parties, and these traditions continue despite differences of outlook. Most professional groups and many trade associations were founded to improve occupational or commercial conditions and had no ideological origins, and they maintain a neutral or pragmatic approach to party relations.

8. Present Group Goals and Ideology

Explanation: This factor involves such questions as: Are the group's current goals political, technical, or a combination of the two? Does the group have a particular ideological stance, or do its goals place it in a particular ideological category?

Significance: If the group's goals have a strong ideological content, it will likely work with parties of that persuasion; or the perception of the group will force it to do so, and it will be less positively received by parties with other ideological stances. If the group's goals are entirely or largely technical, it will have more options of which parties to work with or may pursue a nonpartisan approach.

9. Group Leadership

Explanation: Leadership is vitally important to the policymaking and day-to-day functioning of a group. Many groups and organizations are viewed through the perspectives of their leadership, and skillful and enterprising leaders can often dominate the operations of a group.

Significance: Leaders may align themselves with a particular party even though that party may not be supported by the majority of its membership. Another leader of the same group at a different time may take a more neutral stance. Thus, changes in leadership and the perspective of group leaders can determine the extent of interaction, or lack thereof, with political parties.

Source: Thomas and Hrebenar (1995).

Preliminary Listing of Factors Shaping the Party-Group Relationship

According to Yishai (1995), if a cost-benefit calculation were the only influence on the ties between parties and groups, the two would be an "odd couple" as groups stand to gain much more from the relationship and parties very little. Thus, she concludes that there is more to party-group relations than simply historical experience, political mores, and so on. G. Wilson (1990) and Thomas and Hrebenar (1995) concur on this point. Box 1.1 sets out a preliminary list of factors that appear to be fundamental in shaping party-group relations in Western democracies based on a synthesis of research and an examination of secondary sources by Thomas and Hrebenar. It provides initial insights into the following questions: What factors in a democracy—government structure, socioeconomic development, and political culture—produce certain forms of relationships between particular parties and groups? Why are certain groups attracted to specific types of political parties? Why do some groups have long-term relations with political parties while others have short-term relations and some have none at all?

Forms of the Relationship

By drawing again on work by Yishai (1995), G. Wilson (1990), and Thomas and Hrebenar (1995), we can develop a preliminary typology of the forms party-group relations take in liberal democracies.[7] This is set out in Box 1.2. The box identifies five specific forms that can be viewed along a spectrum from integration through noninvolvement to conflict, which in some cases may manifest itself in confrontation. As part of the spectrum, nothing is watertight about any specific form—one often merges with its adjacent forms in the practicality of day-to-day party-group relations. The forms of the relationship are based on one or more of the following: (1) ideological affinity or adversity, (2) organizational linkage or lack thereof, and (3) similarities or differences in strategy.

Recent Trends in Party-Group Relations

To identify recent trends in the party-group relationship, we can draw on the work of Selle (1997). His research produced five main conclusions. First, formal overlap between parties and groups is not extensive and has likely declined. Second, there is a tendency toward autonomy for the specialized organizations that are part of the party apparatus, such as educational and women's organizations. Third, ties are loosening between "value organizations" that have certain ties to political parties. Most important here are the loosening relationships between socialist parties and trade unions and between conservative parties and business. Fourth, formal con-

> **Box 1.2   Preliminary Classification of Types of Political Party–Interest Group Relationships in Liberal Democracies**
>
> ### Integration/Strong Partisan Model
>
> Here the political party and the interest group are virtually identical or very close organizationally, perhaps because the interest group was created by the party, or vice versa. The basis of this integration is often the result of a very close, often identical ideological affinity, and a consequent common strategy exists between the party and its affiliate group or groups. The relationship of many labor organizations, both individual unions and union peak associations, with socialist and particularly social democratic parties was the classic example of this form.
>
> ### Cooperation/Ideological Model
>
> In this situation a strong connection exists between a political party and an interest group, but it is not a relationship of integration. The connection is likely to be based on ideology, policy orientation, and historical circumstances. Except for the integration of party and group, it represents the most stable and long lasting party-group relationship. This is often the case with business and many professional groups, conservative parties, farmers' organizations, and rural parties.
>
> ### Separation/Pragmatic Involvement Model
>
> Here the group is independent of any party. It has no particular partisan attachment and perhaps only a weak, if any, ideological attachment to any particular party. Consequently, it is willing to work with any party in or out of power to promote its goals. Thus, involvement with a party occurs on an ad hoc basis determined largely by political pragmatism. Some professional groups fall into this pragmatic category—particularly those with highly technical, nonideological goals, such as architects and airline pilots—as do many social issue and public interest groups, such as children's rights groups and antismoking and anti–drunk driving groups.
>
> ### Competition/Rivalry Model
>
> When a party and a group compete with each other as vehicles of representation or in delivering political benefits, competition for members and funds often results. The upshot is sometimes intense rivalry between the party and the group. Although this form can develop into the next model
>
> *(continues)*

Box 1.2 Continued

(Conflict/Confrontation), it is fundamentally different and manifests itself in different ways. It most often involves parties and groups with a similar ideology or policy goals. Examples are Green parties and environmentalists—particularly when the party is in power and cannot meet all the demands of the interest group—and new socialist parties and labor unions as in Sweden and Britain. It is from this type of intraparty competition that interest parties are born.

Conflict/Confrontation Model

In this form open conflict and sometimes confrontation occur between a party and a group. Usually, this results from ideological cleavages or major disagreements over policy. Most often it involves parties and groups at opposite ends of the political spectrum, but it can involve a party and group that have closer ties but disagree over a policy or its implementation. Conflict and the use of confrontational tactics, such as strikes, boycotts, sit-ins, and street violence, by outsider interests and radical groups are the extreme manifestations of this model. Examples include the long-term relationship of many labor organizations, both individual unions and union associations, with conservative parties over issues such as public-sector versus private-sector provision of services and, more recently, deregulation; and confrontation between outsider interest and social movement—like extreme animal rights groups, antinuclear groups, and immigrant workers' groups—and the governing party.

Source: Developed by the author from Yishai (1995), Thomas and Hrebenar (1995), and G. Wilson (1990).

---

tact between parties and organizations is very low. Few parties contact groups, and vice versa. However, informal contact between the elites (leaders) of parties and groups has increased. Fifth, all parties are aware of the increased importance of voluntary organizations. The parties do not see this trend as a threat, however, and have adapted to it (Selle 1997, 164–165).

Overall, Selle concludes that the party-group relationship is moving toward increased autonomy rather than increased integration of both types of organizations. In terms of its direct effects on the policy process and on representation, "The weakening of ties with 'old organizations' close to certain parties has increased party competition, supporting conclusions emphasizing the decline of integrative and expressive functions of parties" (Selle 1997, 165). In other words, mass parties have become catchall parties.

The Defining Role of Political Parties and National Experiences

Two particularly important influences in shaping party-group relations stand out from the existing literature. It will be interesting to see if they are confirmed by the thirteen case studies in this book. One is that in Western democracies and their various subgovernments, like the American states, the party-group relationship seems very much determined by the organizational capacity and the ability and willingness of political parties to perform political functions. When parties are strong and fully use their capacity, as in Sweden and Mexico, they can determine the way interest groups relate to them and to the policy process. This does not mean interest groups are weak but that their activities are simply more constrained. In other countries like the United States and Argentina, parties have often been less able or willing to perform many political functions generally performed by parties in other democracies and so have given interest groups more leeway to perform many of those functions. So a pertinent question to pose regarding what shapes the party-group relationship in a particular country is, what factors lead to party organizational and political capacity and the extent or lack of ability and willingness of the party system to determine party-group relations?

The second influential factor is national experiences. Existing research suggests that some common denominators exist in party-group relations in Western democracies and that these should be pursued and investigated further. Yet evidence also indicates the importance of the local circumstances—including history, political culture, and short-term political circumstances—of a country and a political subdivision in shaping this relationship. If true, this would have implications for the content and general applicability of an explanatory theory regarding party-group relations across Western democracies.

The Level and Focus of Analysis

Here three sets of distinctions are important. First, all indications are that the system-level unit of analysis is too generic to be very useful in understanding party-group relations. Thus, attempting to categorize countries overall as having a certain type of party-group relationship is of little value, although a categorization that includes only major parties and major groups can be more meaningful. Expanding to include at least two other units of analysis, the party–interest group sector level (even given its definitional problems) and the individual party–individual group level, can be particularly instructive either as a separate analysis or when combined with other units of analysis.

Second, relations sometimes exist between groups and parties in general or particular parties not in government, and group relations are sometimes with the governing party or a coalition of parties. It is often important to make this distinction, as even the closest parties and groups can have different relations when the party is in government than they do when it is not. Partly for this reason, a third analytical distinction is often important, that of party-group relations in the long term versus those in the short term. In the long term, say, over the course of a generation or two, a party and group can have close relations; but in the short term, particularly when the party is in government, differences and even conflicts may arise over policy and strategy.

The Complex and Dynamic Nature of the Relationship

As noted earlier, much research and speculation on the party-group connection views many elements of this relationship in a two-dimensional, either/or context. For instance, when parties are strong, then groups are weak, groups compete with parties for members, and both compete for the ear of public officials. The reality is that the party-group relationship in all its aspects is likely much more complex. These relationships are multidimensional and are best characterized in shades of gray rather than in black and white.

Using these six general guidelines for analysis, we now examine the specifics of the party-group connection in individual countries. Then, in the concluding chapter, we draw on these specific experiences to evaluate the accuracy of these six implications of existing research and move toward a comprehensive understanding of the party-group relationship across Western democracies.

Part 1

The Traditional Democracies

2

Britain: Change and Continuity Within the New Realities of British Politics

Grant Jordan and William A. Maloney

For much of the twentieth century, particularly from the 1920s to the late 1970s, relations between the two major political parties and the major interest groups in Britain were patterned on a right-wing–left-wing division. The Labour Party had close ties with trade unions including the peak union association, the Trade Union Congress (TUC), and some ties with left-of-center groups such as antinuclear groups and, later, environmental interests. The Conservative Party was close to business as represented by the Confederation of British Industry (CBI), professional groups, and, to some extent, farmers as represented by the National Farmers Union (NFU). Since 1985 and particularly since 1995, major changes have occurred in this pattern of party-group relations, however. Under Tony Blair, the Labour Party has been de-emphasizing its links with the trade union movement and increasingly embracing business, a change highlighted by renaming the party New Labour. Although not to the same extent, Conservative Party relations with interest groups have also changed, in part precipitated by New Labour making inroads into its interest group base.

Yet, although change has taken place in party-group relations in Britain, which is one factor shaping the new realities of British politics, this change has not had significant consequences for the way major interest groups, particularly economic interests, attempt to influence public policy. Major interest groups work through the bureaucracy and the government in office to achieve their goals rather than through the various sectors of a party—its central organization, annual conference, parliamentary representatives, and so on—and the bureaucracy continues to be their main avenue of access and influence. For this reason, this chapter focuses exclusively on relationships between the British Conservative and Labour Parties and interest groups. The first-past-the-post method of selecting members of Parliament (MPs) means that only the Labour and Conservative Parties have any realistic chance of forming a national government. Labour has won seven of the fifteen general elections since 1945, and the Conservatives have won eight. Although interest groups may interact with other parties, such as the third-party Social and Liberal Democrats, they are likely to devote most of their resources to relationships with potential British governing parties.

Despite the well-known past links between Labour and the unions and Conservatives and business, the party-group relationship in Britain has been understudied, both empirically and conceptually. Treatments of both British parties (for example, McKenzie 1955; Fisher 1996; Garner and Kelly 1998) and British interest groups (such as Alderman 1984; Grant 1990) deal with the relationship only incidentally and do not assess its significance in the policymaking process, perhaps in part because these and other scholars do not see this relationship as significant. Even so, the party-group relationship is worth studying because its significance or lack thereof tells us much about the politics of a country and the dynamics of changes in those politics. With this in mind, we provide a general explanation of these relations from several perspectives, including organizational, parliamentary, and financial links. In addition, we place party-group relations in Britain in a conceptual context that emphasizes the importance of the bureaucratic and governmental focus of the strategy and tactics of major groups.

RECENT CHANGES IN BRITISH PARTY POLITICS: AN OVERVIEW

The Labour Party emerged from the trade union movement around 1900. As a consequence, trade unions in Britain have traditionally held a central position "inside" the Labour Party. This symbiotic relationship has been maintained because the party receives great human and economic benefits from trade union affiliations. Trade unions can mobilize members and others from the predisposed public to vote for the party, provide substantial sums of money for organizational and campaign purposes, and provide a pool of potential Labour activists. As of 1999, affiliated trade unions were distinct legal entities yet still important power brokers within the Labour Party, with significant voting rights.[1] In fact, some trade unions not affiliated to the party have significantly greater power—albeit reduced from what it was previously—within the Labour Party than do many internal party groups. The contemporary party is in an advanced stage of organizational and ideological change, however, and New Labour's relationship with the trade unions is dramatically different from that of the 1920s or even the 1960s.

The Conservative Party is also undertaking major organizational change. Primarily, more transparent and formal democratic procedures have been introduced for the election of the leader and the development of policy.

This process of ideological and organizational change within the two governing parties has had a significant impact on their relationships with interest groups, most notably the weakening of ties between trade unions and the Labour Party. Although traditionally the two-party system encouraged partnership with either business or trade unions, the trend toward "catchall" parties has generated a tactical logic that tends to reduce reliance on simple links. Parties are reluctant to commit to any cause that is likely, or that has the potential, to reduce their electoral appeal. And in general, groups are reluctant to develop too close an association with one major party because of the strong probability that in the short to medium term the parties in government will alternate, and the cost of too cozy relationships could be future ostracism.

New Labour is now more clearly a catchall party that is keen to de-emphasize its historical association with the trade union movement and that has successfully appealed to various segments of society, most notably the middle classes and business. Otto Kirchheimer argued that catchall parties underwent a change process that involved (1) a reduction in the party's ideological baggage and a focus on general issues of concern to large segments of the population; (2) increased party reliance on interest group influence, and "the transformation of collateral, religious, trade-union organizations, etc., into interest groups with weaker and less regular party ties"; (3) de-emphasis of rank-and-file political activism; (4) a strengthening of the leaders' organizational power, and a greater dependence on external organizations for funding; and (5) no longer being "linked to strong social settlements and to solid and unified political sub-cultures" (cited in Panebianco 1988, 263).[2] This process is well advanced in New Labour and is clearly illustrated in the foreword to the 1997 *Labour Party Conference Guide* in which Tony Blair demonstrated his catchall credentials, stating, "We are breaking down the barriers between different sections of society, standing at the centre and reaching out to all. We are showing that the politics of the future will embrace wealth creation as well as equal opportunity, that we can be strongly pro-business at the same time as leading an active government on welfare reform, health and education."

With changes in the social structure of Britain since the early 1970s—including the decline of the heavily unionized manufacturing sector and the growth of service-sector trade unions—and arguably most important, the impact of Thatcherism, affiliation with the trade union movement has proven electorally unpopular. This began to develop in a major way following the industrial strife of the 1970s, most notably the miners' strike in 1973 and the so-called Winter of Discontent in 1978. The cumulative effect of these developments pushed New Labour's relationship with the trade unions away from integration toward separation.

With these changes in mind, we now examine the traditional ties between the two governing parties and interest groups in Britain, trace changes in the relations, and assess the political significance of the party-group connection, past and present.

PARTY–INTEREST GROUP LINKAGES: TRADITIONAL PATTERNS, CHANGING TIES

Organizational Structure of Governing Parties

The two major British parties have different organizational structures that affect their relationships with interest groups. The Conservative Party is effectively a leader-dominated party; power is highly centralized (McKenzie 1955). In theory, the party leadership and the parliamentary party are independent of the other parts of the Conservative Party such as the National Union of Conservative and Unionist Associations and the Constituency Associations, which together, in effect, constitute the party membership. The leader drafts the party manifesto (platform) and has direct control over the organizational center of the party, Conservative Central Office. Unlike the Labour Party (discussed next), the Conservatives' annual conference has no formal policymaking powers. The National Union convenes the conference but constitutionally has a purely advisory role. The Constituency Associations have three main roles: campaigning for the party in local and national elections, raising funds, and selecting parliamentary candidates. For groups wishing to influence party policy, the main target is the parliamentary leadership (Garner and Kelly 1998).

The Labour Party has six main organizational elements: the leader, the Parliamentary Labour Party (PLP), the party headquarters, the National Executive Committee (NEC), the Joint Policy Committee (JPC), and the annual conference. Until 1997 the two key institutions were the NEC and the leader, with most policy proposals emanating from the NEC (constitutionally the NEC has joint responsibility for drafting the manifesto), although affiliated trade unions and constituency parties may put forward motions for debate at the annual conference, which lasts five days. Delegates from the various sections and branches of the party discuss organizational and policy matters. Although the constitutional position holds that the conference is the "supreme policymaking body," the political reality is that the key institutions are the NEC and the newly established JPC, chaired by the leader and composed of an equal number of members from the NEC and the government (Garner and Kelly 1998, 135). As Coxall and

Robins (1998, 119) noted: "The JPC directs an expanded National Policy Forum which consists of representatives from all sections of the party and reviews all party policy on a two-year rolling programme."

Organizational changes carried out under the leadership of Tony Blair have reduced the power of the conference, and the NEC can now be more accurately characterized as a partner of the New Labour government rather than a competing voice in the party. A significant aspect of the changes has been a move away from trade union involvement on the NEC toward more involvement by the ordinary membership. More generally, the power trade unions wield within the party has been reduced considerably at all levels. This includes the introduction of one member/one vote for selecting parliamentary candidates and members of the NEC, reduction in the size of the trade union bloc vote entitlement at the conference from 90 percent to 50 percent, a reduced role in the selection of parliamentary candidates, the rewording of Clause IV of the party constitution, and a reduced role in funding the party. The rewording of Clause IV, which has great symbolic importance, and changes in funding have been particularly significant.

The original formulation of Clause IV committed the party to the socialist objective to "secure for the producers by hand and by brain the full fruits of their industry, and the most equitable distribution thereof that may be possible, upon the basis of the common ownership of the means of production and the best obtainable system of popular administration and control of each industry and sector." The reformulation is a clear and explicit rejection of the previous socialist principles:

> The Labour Party is a democratic socialist party. It believes that by the strength of our common endeavour we achieve more than we achieve alone, so as to create for each of us the means to realise our true potential and for all of us a community in which power, wealth and opportunity are in the hands of the many not the few; where rights we enjoy reflect the duties we owe and where we live together freely, in a spirit of solidarity, tolerance and respect.

Regarding funding, until the mid-1980s trade unions provided over 75 percent of the Labour Party's central income and general election funds, but by the mid-1990s that figure had fallen to approximately 50 percent. The shortfall has been made up with income from a significantly increased membership and very large donations. Party membership increased from 280,000 in 1994 to 425,000 in 1997, although 75,000 members left the party between the 1997 general election and 1999 (*Sunday Telegraph*, 5 September 1999). Although these developments demonstrate the decline of trade union influence within the Labour Party, trade unions remain important. For example, they contributed £11 million to New Labour's 1997 general election campaign (Coxall and Robins 1998).[3] Changes in funding as they affect party-group relations in both major parties are covered in more detail later.

The Party Conference

The most transparent point of contact between political parties and interest groups in Britain occurs at the annual party conferences at which over 150 organizations have exhibitor stands. The Labour Party conference in 1995 had 165 exhibitor stands; there were 209 in 1996 and 199 in 1997. At all three conferences well over 200 organizations were represented, either directly or through joint exhibitions or peak associations. The organizations represented at these three conferences were a catholic collection of bodies including Sainsbury's and Tesco stores (both food retailers), Amnesty International, the Police Federation, Royal College of Nursing, Age Concern, Oxfam, the Bingo Association, the Scotch Whisky Association, British Telecom, British Gas, the Post Office, and the government of Gibraltar (Table 2.1 lists only those exhibitors that attended all three conferences).

As indicated earlier, however, the influence of major interests (mainly the trade unions) on party policy through the conference has been reduced considerably. Interest groups clamor to be seen at the conferences, but we should not confuse visibility with influence.

Contacts with Parliament

Parties and groups are also linked through direct contact with MPs. Groups attempt to persuade MPs to ask parliamentary questions, which can be asked and answered either orally or in writing and are effective for gathering information. Groups are also linked to parties in Parliament through the "outside interests" of MPs. In Britain many influential parliamentarians have outside interests or connections with external organizations, particularly through their membership on bipartisan parliamentary select committees. MPs are appointed not to deliberate on details of proposed legislation but to discuss specific issues assigned by the House of Commons, such as the Public Accounts Committee, which scrutinizes public expenditure. A 1990 newspaper survey (*Independent on Sunday,* 13 May) found that eleven of the twenty-two chairs of select committees were involved with companies or organizations that dealt directly or indirectly in the areas for which their committees were responsible. Three Labour chairs were trade union–sponsored MPs, and four Conservative chairs had commercial connections that came within the purview of their committees (chairs of select committees are shared between parties). These activities are likely to be reduced for the foreseeable future with recent controversies over political

Table 2.1   Exhibitors at the 1995, 1996, and 1997 Labour Party Conferences

Action for South Africa
Advertising Association
Age Concern
Amnesty International
Audit Commission
Brewers and Licensed Retailers Association
British Airports Authority
British Airways
British Nuclear Fuels Limited
British Telecom
Cable Communications Association
Charter 88
Coalfield Communities Campaign
Compassion in World Farming
Co-op Bank
Co op Party
DHL
Disability Daily
European Parliamentary Labour Party
Falkland Islands government
GMB (trade union)
Government of Gibraltar
Health Education Authority
Institute for Public Policy Research
League Against Cruel Sports
Local Government Information Unit
Low Pay Unit
Luton Airport
Manchester Airport
MARI Group Limited
Merck, Sharp, and Dohme
Mines Advisory Group
The Mirror Group
MSF (Manufacturing Science Finances)
National Association of Citizens Advice Bureaux
National Union of Teachers
NSPCC (National Society for Prevention of Cruelty to Children)
One World Action
Oxfam
Police Federation
Post Office
QED
Refugee Council
Royal College of Midwives
Royal College of Nursing
RSPB (Royal Society for the Protection of Birds)
RSPCA (Royal Society for the Prevention of Cruelty to Animals)
Scope

(continues)

Table 2.1   Continued

Scotch Whisky Association
Sky
Socialist societies[a]
T&G
Tesco
Trade Union Congress
UNISON (public section union)
Unity Trust Bank
USDAW (shop workers union)
War on Want
Water Services Association
Wateraid
Women's National Commission

Source: Compiled by the authors.
Note: a. Socialist societies include the Christian Socialist Movement, Fabian Society, Labour Housing Group, Labour Irish Society, Labour Students, National Union of Labour and Socialists Clubs, Poale Zion, Socialist Education Association, Socialist Environment and Resources Association, and Society of Labour Lawyers.

"sleaze" that have led to publicly funded investigations and the creation of committees of inquiry into "Standards in Public Life," such as the Nolan and Neill Committees.

Interest groups also maintain parliamentary links through all-party subject groups within the House of Commons, which are unofficial cross-party groups made up of MPs, peers (members of the House of Lords), and sometimes nonparliamentarians. These groups consider issues that are generally not politically contentious. They function as liaisons with ministers and can exert pressure to modify policy proposals or influence legislation. These committees are part of the official consultation process in which government seeks views from both inside and outside of Parliament. Interest groups are active in these arenas, and some group representatives who are not MPs act as secretaries of the committees. For example, in 1996 the administrative secretary of the Chemical Industry All-Party Group was Jonathon Peel of Chemical Industries Association Limited; his counterpart on the All-Party Motor Industry Group was David McConnell of the Society of Motor Manufacturers and Traders; and the Human Genetics All-Party Group was contactable through the Genetics Interest Group.

Funding Connection

In Britain the two governing parties have traditionally relied upon distinctly different sources of funding, with the Labour Party receiving substantial sums of money from the trade union movement and the Conservative Party receiving the bulk of its funds from the business community. As indicated earlier, though, these patterns are changing.

Conservative Party funding contributors are difficult to identify because until recently the party had a policy of nondisclosure. However, the available evidence suggests that approximately 75 percent of Conservative Party funds come from a relatively small number of individuals, some of whom live overseas. The Conservatives raised £50 million over two years (1995–1996 to 1996–1997) and spent £28.3 million in the thirteen months leading up to the 1997 general election. Like New Labour, however, the Conservatives are sensitive to the funding issue and are keen to avoid criticisms of "sleaze" in obtaining funding for favors. William Hague, the Conservative Party leader, promised to match the Labour Party's stance of naming all those who give over £5,000 and of refusing overseas donations. This move may affect the total level of funding by deterring the very wealthy who have previously donated to the party in secret. Thus, the Conservative Party's current mass membership drive is likely to assume even greater importance as a source of funding if the wealthy shy away because of the publicity that may surround massive donations. The Conservatives may also be forced to follow Labour, which is now soliciting funds through direct-mail marketing techniques pioneered in part by interest groups.

In 1993, 54.4 percent of the Labour Party's total income (£6.9 of £12.7 million) came from trade unions. In fact, this percentage was low when compared with trade union contributions of 71.1 percent in 1988, 68.8 percent in 1989, 68.6 percent in 1990, and 63.3 percent in 1991 (Fisher 1996, 79). In addition to reducing trade unions' organizational and funding role, New Labour has had some success in attracting funds from the business community, from individuals who were Conservative Party donors under the Thatcher government.

New Labour has received large individual donations from David Sainsbury (food retailer), who made substantial donations to Labour's £20 million 1997 election campaign; from the late Matthew Harding, Chelsea Football Club director (£1 million); and from Bernie Ecclestone, vice president of the Formula One (motor racing) Association (£1 million).[4] Tables 2.2 and 2.3 provide a list of those individuals and companies that contributed more than £5,000 to the party, including Christopher Haskins (chair, Northern Foods), Michael Montague (chair, Montague Multinational), Pearson Media Group, Sun Life Corporation, and Tate and Lyle.

Funding for the Scottish division of the Labour Party may point to the future Blair envisaged. In Scotland during 1996–1997, the combined

Table 2.2 Labour Party Donors, 1996–1997

Robin Ashby, R. Executive Limited
Lord Attenborough, Film Makers
David J.B. Brown, businessman
Ceramic and Allied Trade Union
Cooperative Party
Creation Records
Currie Group, motor dealerships
Bernie Ecclestone
Martin Emery
Evans Hunt Scott, direct marketing firm
Richard Falkner, MD, Westminster Communications Brigades Union
Ernst Fraenkel, director, Institute of Contemporary History
Robert Gavron, chair, Guardian Media Group
GMB (trade union)
Philip Gould, Labour strategist
Graphical Paper and Media Union
Martin Green
P. B. Green
Greer Associates, defunct parliamentary lobbying company
Paul Hamlyn, publisher
Matthew Harding, vice chair, Chelsea FC
Christopher Haskins, chair, Northern Foods
Ian Holland
Iron and Steel Trades Confederation
Jeremy Irons, actor
Geraldine and Philip Jeffrey, founders, FADS-DIY chain
KFAT, footwear and clothing company
Littlewoods, football pools company
Michael Montague, chair, Montague Multinational
Joan Morgan
Lord Paul, founder, Caparo Group, steel company
Pearson Media Group
Political Animal Lobby
Lord Putnam, filmmaker
Alec Reed, founder, Reed Publishing
Lady Rendell, author
Geoffrey Robinson, MP
Lord Sainsbury, chief executive, J. Sainsbury
Leslie H. Silver, chair, Leeds United Football Club
Sir Sigmund Stern Berg, businessman
Sun Life Corporation, insurance
David Swift
Tate and Lyle, sugar refiners
Robin Thompson and Partners, solicitors
Titan Travel
Transport and General Workers' Union
Transport Salaried Staffs Association
TU Fund Managers

(continues)

Table 2.2 Continued

UNISON, public-sector workers' union
USDAW, shop workers' union
Stuart Westwater, businessman
Willis Corroon, risk management solutions

Source: Sunday Times, London, 21 September 1997.
Note: Donors are individuals and organizations making financial donations to the party ranging from very small sums of money to substantial amounts.

Table 2.3   Labour Party Sponsors, 1996–1997

British Gas
Co-operative Wholesale Society
Eastern Group (electric company)
GMB (trade union)
GPMU (trade union)
Greater London Enterprise (venture capital group)
Kingfisher (stores group)
Mirror Group (newspaper publishers)
Northumbrian Water
TGWU (trade union)
Trade Unions for Labour (Wales)

Source: Sunday Times, London, 21 September 1997.
Note: Sponsors, usually organizations as opposed to individuals, sponsor party events—such as having an exhibitor stand at the party conference, paying for conference documentation, and so on—and their company or product will be directly associated with the party event.

donations from two individuals—Brian Dempsey, a builder, and Alan McGhee, owner of Creation Record Company—totaling £150,000, was greater than the total donated by the trade union movement. The Labour Party Business Plan emphasizes funds from individuals rather than institutions and has resulted in a successful diversification of fund-raising activities. The plan was instituted in 1989 and by 1993 accounted for 18 percent of the party's total income.

As the foregoing review suggests, funding of political parties in Britain is controversial. For example, the Political Animal Lobby, which opposes foxhunting, donated £1 million to the Labour Party in its last years as the main opposition party and £100,000 in the first two years of the New Labour government. The political controversy over such donations has been fueled by the government's commitment to ban foxhunting as an apparent "reward" to the group for financial support. As part of a major public inquiry into the Standards in Public Life, the funding of political parties was examined in detail (see *The Funding of Political Parties in the United Kingdom*). The committee recommendations included proposals for the reform of party funding, such as full public disclosure of donations to political parties of £5,000 or more, and a maximum general election campaign expenditure of £20 million.[5]

PERSISTENCE OF BUREAUCRATIC LINKS FOR MAJOR INTEREST GROUPS

Notwithstanding the time-honored connections in party-group relations, as we argue in the introduction to the chapter these connections were never that significant for most interest groups in Britain, and they are even less so given the recent changes in party-group ties outlined earlier. The bureaucratic link has been and remains most significant to many major interests. Samuel Finer, in his classic text on British interest groups, recognized this reality back in 1958:

> The influential groups are the interest groups. Now the first characteristic of these is that they are, pretty well, all "domesticated" (they work, and are expected to work closely with the Ministries [note ministries, not ministers], and it would be both impolite and imprudent of them to agitate publicly. . . . For the interest groups, dealings with government departments take up far the greatest of the total time they devote to contact with government, and the vast bulk of it deals with minor detail. (Finer 1958, 130)

On the role of Parliament, Finer said: "Parliament goes about its business like a sleep-walker (or better still, as *The Times* correspondent has put it), like a pianola . . . mechanically rendering tunes composed jointly by departments of state and whatever organised interests happen to be affected" (Finer 1958, 141). More recently, leading British political consultant Charles Miller, writing on the many myths connected with "dealing with government," argued that one of the greatest misconceptions is that Parliament is all-important:

> Do not be confused by the emphasis of the media on Parliament or by the current vogue for "Parliamentary Consultants." Parliament is one component of the power structure with the ability to assert itself only when governments have precarious majorities or where a considerable amount of work is done to persuade large numbers of MPs and Peers to oppose or change Government policy. . . . *It is very rare, therefore, that Parliament would be placed at the hub of the wheel of influence* [emphasis added]. (Miller 1987, 133)

This lack of importance of Parliament is also emphasized by Jordan and Richardson (1987, 287–288). They ask rhetorically: "whether the House [of Commons] contributes more to the policy process or to the tourist trade is a difficult question." Thus, traditional insider politics is likely to be more effective on a wider range of issues than simply the issues that attract substantial public or media attention and are the staple diet of politicians in Britain. This can be further substantiated with empirical evidence.

Table 2.4 shows that for many organizations attempting to influence public policy, political parties are seen as the least effective means. Only 6.7 percent of respondents ranked "one political party in particular" first in influencing policy, and 4.9 percent ranked "political parties generally" first. Taking the policymaking process in its totality, the party channel is seen as a low contribution insurance policy, less fruitful than the bureaucratic arena. Members of Parliament and parliamentary parties are given top priority only by groups that lack privileged access or that are active on conscience issues (abortion, capital punishment, foxhunting, and so on) decided by a "free vote" (no party directive) in the House of Commons. For example, an internal Oxfam (a third-world charity) publication, *Trends in Advocacy*, which reviewed the likely successful strategies and tactics in influencing policy outputs, makes little mention of direct contact with political parties or of lobbying Parliament. It focuses on influencing policymakers through insider-style politics and the media, although it goes to great pains to argue that use of the media should not jeopardize Oxfam's insider status.[6]

Table 2.4 Sources Influencing British National Government Policy

	Percentage Placing First	Rank Order[a]
Civil servants/government departments	28.5	1
Ministers	31.6	2
The media generally	20.6	3
Parliament	7.6	4
Particular sections of public opinion	10.2	5
Public opinion generally	9.5	6
Other pressure or interest groups	5.6	7
Political parties generally	4.9	8
One political party in particular	6.7	9

Source: Rush 1990, 272.

Note: a. Calculated by scoring each ranking 1 for first, 2 for second, and so on, the lowest total indicating first and the highest ninth. Twenty-seven respondents (10.7% of the total) were "don't knows," and sixteen (6.3%) said the ranking varied with the issue.

On the surface, the changing ideological orientation that came with the Thatcher government (1979–1990) appeared at first to be moving to change this long-standing cozy relationship between major interest groups and the bureaucracy. Interest groups were generally denigrated as a largely unnecessary evil. They were seen as causing "pluralistic stagnation" (Beer 1980) and were held to have been largely responsible for the British decline (Olson 1982). The Conservative government ended tripartism (consultation in the economic policy field involving business, labor, and government) and, if only rhetorically, challenged many established professional interests such as those of doctors, lawyers, and teachers.

However, this did not end the involvement of those interests in bureaucratic accommodation. In fact, ironically, consultation during the Thatcher years increased significantly. For example, as Table 2.5 shows, 63 consultation documents were issued in 1979; that number rose to 140 in 1985 and to 267 in 1990. In this vein, Baggott (1995, 123) argues that although the Thatcher administration viewed organizations such as right-wing think tanks (the Adam Smith Institute and the Institute of Economic Affairs, among others) and business groups in a more favorable light, "there was, it seems, a degree of continuity between the Thatcher government and its predecessors. The evidence suggests that in a large proportion of cases the relationship between groups and the executive neither improved nor deteriorated." Given the success of the Thatcher government in changing many aspects of British economic and political life, major interest group–bureaucratic contact seems firmly entrenched in British politics as the most significant avenue of access and influence for interest groups.

CONCEPTUALIZING PARTY-GROUP RELATIONS IN BRITAIN

Box 1.2 identifies five types of group-party relationships along a spectrum from the Integration/Strong Partisan Model at one end to the Confrontation Model at the other. These relationships are conditioned by three variables: ideology, organization, and strategy. To what extent do these apply to the British case? In other words, how useful are they in encapsulating party-group relations in Britain, past and present?

The Integration/Strong Partisan Model is a type of parentela relationship characterized by interest groups and political parties sharing a joint ideology, organizational linkage, and consensual strategy. Accordingly, interest groups are effectively "intra-party groups and operate as full-fledged or quasi-party factions" (Yishai 1995, 2). Integration is indicated by factors such as group members being affiliated with a political party, an interest group selecting or electing a candidate for a political party's list, or an interest group leader being a member of a party central committee. As

Table 2.5 Consultative Documents Issued by the British Government, 1976–1990

Year	Number
1976	11
1977	27
1978	48
1979	63
1980	85
1981	76
1982	76
1983	112
1984	146
1985	140
1986	191
1987	208
1988	288
1989	276
1990	267

Source: Hansard Society 1993, appendix 8.

was shown earlier, in Britain trade unions have taken part in each of these activities within the Labour Party; as we have also seen, however, this prime example of integration in the British case is very much on the wane and now falls more into the Cooperation/Proximate Ideology Model. In addition to this prime example, as in other democracies many small outsider groups in Britain seek to integrate themselves or become involved in a cooperative relationship with political parties to compensate for a lack of other political resources. For example, as highlighted previously, in recent years the Political Animal Lobby in Britain made several significant financial contributions to New Labour's election funds, seeing this as the best way to influence party policy and consequently to affect public policy in its area of concern.

The Cooperation/Ideological Model represents a loose partnership predicated on a similar ideology and strategic collaboration. In this arrangement groups seek to influence party programs. In Britain a good example is the relationship between business groups and the Conservative Party in the past and, to a large extent, today, although business groups do not limit their interaction to Conservatives but seek access to all parties with which they are likely to interface. This is true, as we have seen, in regard to New Labour's appeal to business groups. Yael Yishai (1995, 4–5) argues that one element of cooperation would be demonstrated by an interest group's successful appeal to a political party to include a plank in its election manifesto or, alternatively, by a political party's appeal to an interest group for assistance. For example, from 1975 to 1977 the Labour government entered into a so-called social contract with the trade union movement that permitted the government to "intervene centrally in wage fixing without recourse to legislation. . . . In effect the TUC negotiated norms for increases with the government and then enforced them on a voluntary basis" (Henig 1979, 222, 244).

Separation means that interest groups do not attempt to influence party decisions and seek to place distance between themselves and political parties to maintain their "independent" reputations. The group views partisan affiliation as detrimental to its political standing. For example, as Self and Storing (1962) show, prior to World War II the National Farmers Union had close links to the Conservative Party. But when the NFU was faced with a Labour government keen to expand food production after the war, the NFU became convinced that it should and could work with both governing parties and "separated" itself from the Conservatives.

As we have seen, in Britain a well-developed consultative machinery involves interest groups in policy development: groups are much more likely to focus on the bureaucratic arena to affect public policy outcomes. Thus, participation in the depoliticized arena of policy network politics is highly sought. Many professional associations pursue a separation strategy, relying on their technical expertise to deliver influence within bureaucratic arenas. Thus, separation is probably the most prevalent typology of party-group relations for major groups in Britain and, in the changing scene of British politics, is likely on the rise. However, a need may exist in Britain, and likely in other Western democracies as well, to distinguish between groups that generally keep separate from parties but that may from time to time, for pragmatic reasons, work with one or more of them, such as the case of the NFU mentioned previously, and groups that never get involved with political parties and pursue a permanent strategy of noninvolvement.

With rivalry, interest groups join the electoral competition and become what Yishai terms an interest party, which is neither a fully fledged political party nor a straightforward interest group. It calls itself a party and engages in party-type activities in pursuit of "private benefits and/or a single issue" (Yishai 1995, 6). For example, in the 1997 general election in Britain, the putative clear-cut distinction between parties and interest groups was decidedly blurred. The Pro-Life Alliance put up 53 candidates. More successfully, the Referendum Party spent £20 million, put up 547 candidates, gained 811,827 votes (it averaged 3.1 percent of the vote in those seats it contested; 2.6 percent overall), and achieved "the best ever performance by a 'minor' party in a general election" (Carter et al. 1998, 162; Coxall and Robins 1998). The party was established simply to force a referendum on Britain's future role in the European Union and was described by its creator, James Goldsmith, as "a single-issue biodegradable party which will be dissolved once we have achieved our aims" (the *Times*, 25 October 1995, quoted in Carter et al. 1998, 162). Such parties can clearly be labeled "single issue interest parties" (Yishai 1995).

Confrontation views groups and parties as opponents. Groups advance an aggressive antiparty message, and parties respond by highlighting the threat such groups represent to the established political order. The British peace movement's "relationship" with Conservative governments in the early and mid-1980s is a good example. The goal pursued was nonbargainable/zero sum: a government either has nuclear weapons and accepts deterrence theory or it does not. Confrontational tactics usually occur outside the electoral arena with groups pursuing high-profile media-based strategies to alter public perceptions and problem definition. Britain in recent years has witnessed a growth of direct action protest over matters such as calf (veal) exports, runway construction at Manchester Airport, road building in numerous locations, animal rights protests, and so on (see Ridley and Jordan 1998) that seek to use the media and public opinion to pressure parties (usually the governing party) to change their priorities. This technique assumes that parties will respond to public opinion and that changing public opinion is therefore an effective instrument to secure specific policy changes.

Groups embroiled in these activities aim to influence policy outcomes through high-profile media stunts for three main reasons. First, they are ideologically opposed to insider-type politics. Second, they have failed to gain entry to the insider circle. And third, their claims on the political system are too controversial to be processed bureaucratically (see Maloney, Jordan, and McLaughin 1994). Essentially nonpartisan activism seeks to draw attention to the issues and raise public concern and consciousness. Groups can pursue some of these links in parallel. A group may want to be rather apolitical in its relationship with the bureaucracy (separation), but it might also attempt to be confrontational in relation to parties. However, some strategies are mutually exclusive: a group involved in rivalry is not likely to have access through the bureaucracy.

CONCLUSION

In British politics today, ideology is less important to both business and labor. In the current climate, pragmatism has been elevated to new heights and is likely to continue to climb, with the major parties vigorously and aggressively pursuing catchall strategies. Furthermore, group influence in party policymaking is limited today as it has always been.

In terms of big player parties and interests, the Labour Party's traditional relationship with the trade union movement could be characterized as integrative in that there was a shared ideology, organization, and strategy. The relationship is moving along the continuum toward a more cooperative relationship: the bloc vote has been reduced, and the party is aiming to widen its membership base and operate on a one-member one-vote system. The Conservative Party has maintained a cooperative relationship with business, although it now faces a challenge from New Labour for funds from that source. In fact, in the contemporary climate business is as likely to fund the Labour Party as it is the Conservative, and formal contact between groups and parties is low. Thus, the most visible changes in party-group relations in Britain in recent years have been the decline of integration and the rise of confrontation, albeit still with a characteristic emphasis on separation.

These findings on Britain mirror much of what Per Selle (1997) identified in Norway: that the group-party relationship is becoming less integrated and more autonomous and that no extensive overlap is found between parties and groups. At least in Britain, the explanation for such developments seems clear. If we accept the basic definition of an interest group as an organization wanting to influence public policy outcomes while not wishing to govern, the bureaucratic arena will almost always hold more appeal for groups in a country like Britain, characterized by a highly centralized political system with an executive-dominated Parliament. Interest groups will continue to do what they have found most advantageous in the past—place greater emphasis on influencing government through insider tactics rather than through direct links with political parties.

3

France: Party-Group Relations in the Shadow of the State

Andrew Appleton

In the history of France there have always been, in one form or another, feudal fiefdoms. Today . . . these fiefdoms are in the political parties, the trade unions, in certain sectors of business . . . of the press, the bureaucracy, etc. Those who represent this new feudalism never like a state that does its job and which, as a consequence, is able to dominate them. (General de Gaulle, quoted in F. Wilson 1987, 13)

Here Charles de Gaulle summarized one of the axioms of the modern French political system. On the one hand, interest groups and political parties flourish along with the ambitions of those in the political elite and those who aspire to join it. On the other, these flourishing groups are often treated with suspicion and even disdain by agents of a state considered above all free from sectional preferences. The theme of this chapter is centered around this paradox and the ambiguous relationships among the state, interest groups, and political parties that it produces. Accordingly, we argue that the institutional structures of the French Republic and the political culture of the system actually promote associational life within a very particular view of the role of both state and associations. Where associations act as intermediaries between state and society—in other words, where groups act in a classical pluralist fashion—those associations find themselves in difficult circumstances. Where these groups seek preferential relationships with the state and in some instances with political parties, their role is often facilitated and encouraged.

Little literature focuses explicitly on the party–interest group connection in France. One exception, although rather dated, is the treatment by Meynaud (1962) in which he proposes a five-category scheme for conceptualizing relations between parties and groups. In his comparative approach, Meynaud suggests that the most common party–interest group relationship is one where groups are appended to parties as auxiliary units (the term coined by Duverger 1951). More recent studies have produced interesting reappraisals of the relationship between groups and parties, including work by Suleiman (1987) and F. Wilson (1987) referred to later in this chapter. No one, however, has produced an overall appraisal and explanation of the party-group relationship in France, past and present, that facilitates comparison of its similarities and differences with other Western countries.

KEYS TO UNDERSTANDING PARTY-GROUP RELATIONS IN FRANCE

In some ways the contemporary French party and interest group systems, the recent developments of those systems, and the ways in which parties and groups relate have elements in common with other liberal democracies, particularly those of Western Europe. As in many of those countries, ideological ties between voters and parties are weak, despite the apparent transformation of the French party system in the era of the Fifth Republic, and a certain fluidity marks the contemporary party system. The main parties today in terms of being able to win large numbers of seats in the National Assembly and to contest presidential elections (and thus the major parties of concern in understanding French party-group relations) are the conservative Gaullists (Rasemblement pour la République—RPR); the less conservative Centrists (mainly the Union pour la Démocratie Française—UDF); the Socialists (mainly the Parti Socialiste—PS) and their allies in the smaller socialist and radical parties; and, to a lesser extent, the Communists (Parti Communiste Français—PCF). As is also true in other Western European countries, the PS has recently moved in the direction of a catchall party, and the Communists have moderated their platform.

France also has a wide range of interest groups, both traditional and of more recent vintage, including trade union, employer, business, education, women's, and recreational organizations, among many others. Like most of the Western world, France has experienced an advocacy explosion since the early 1970s as a plethora of new groups—from environmentalists to human rights to community groups—has emerged to represent new and hitherto unrepresented causes. The development of local and community organizations is particularly evident. As in other member countries of the European Union (EU), the focus of many French interest groups has necessarily shifted toward Brussels, although the often statist stance of the French government at the European level has perhaps mitigated this effect. In addition, French interest groups, whatever their ideological proclivities, often regard the French state as a protection against the supranational challenges of the EU.

Party-group relations in France also manifest some similarities with other democracies. There has been a connection, although uneven among parties and over time, between parties of the left and the trade unions and a recent distancing of those relations. Political parties in France have a long history of using interest groups and voluntary associations (at both local and national levels) for their own strategic purposes; the reverse has also been true. Of particular note, Suleiman (1987) pointed out the extraordinary number of nonpartisan groups, and F. Wilson (1987) noted that the majority of interest groups in contemporary France are neither national in scope nor political in aim. In other words, in the language of Chapter 1 and as is common in all democracies, most groups in France follow a separation or noninvolvement strategy with parties.

Yet if we delve deeper into the French party and interest group systems, especially the party-group connection, we find some important contrasts with other democracies, particularly those of Anglo-America and northern Europe. For instance, for the most part France does not have the close ties between conservative parties and business organizations common in countries like Britain, the United States, and Germany. And rather akin to Italy, France has a fragmented interest group system and lacks the dominant peak associations of northern Europe, particularly in the labor sector. These and several other differences can be traced to elements of the political, cultural, and historical heritage of France, which stunted or gave a different complexion to the development of many aspects of party-group relations prevalent in other democracies. This legacy is so deep-rooted and all pervasive that it continues today, working to shape contemporary party-group relations. As is evident from the comparisons with other systems earlier, this is not to argue French exceptionalism in all aspects of the party-group connection. At the same time, it does mean that many key elements of this relationship and its development are peculiarly French.

The essence of this peculiarity is the paradox between the long-standing existence and activities of groups and the suspicion and disdain of them by certain elements of the state. To be sure, such a paradox is common in other countries, especially the United States. The difference in France is that the inability of parties to control the state and the power of the bureaucracy means that this suspicion and disdain are given teeth to the extent that the state can not only channel interest group demands but in doing so very much shapes party-group relations. In short, the party-group relationship in France is determined by the triangular relationship of parties, groups, and the state.

Yet this is not a classic case of neocorporatism. The links between the state and organized interests are much more ambiguous than those posited by the neocorporatist model. Indeed, studying party-group relations in France helps us understand where the neocorporatist model falls short in explaining and predicting the impact of organized interests on the policy process. It may be that the fragmentation of the interest group system and the relative weakness of parties precluded the type of corporatist arrangements that have been possible in countries like Germany, Austria, and Switzerland where there are strong peak associations and stronger parties.

FRENCH POLITICAL CULTURE AND PARTY-GROUP RELATIONS

In their importance in shaping party-group relations, two features of French political culture stand out. The first is a deep distrust of intermediary organizations in the political process, organizations that intervene in the relationship between citizen and state. The second is the propensity of the French to achieve political transformation through direct action.

The distrust of intermediary institutions in the political process stems from the thought of Jean-Jacques Rousseau. In elevating the General Will to the summit of political community, Rousseau rejected the notions of representative democracy and institutionalized interests. He argued that none could stand as a representative of other citizens—the only embodiment of their interests could be the General Will. In addition, Rousseau stood against institutionalized interests, which he condemned as a tilt toward a fragmented body politic. As Hall (1990, 78) pointed out, such thinking was rooted in the experience of the ancien régime "with the corporate bodies that seemed bastions of privilege." Thus, Rousseau laid out a line of thought that argued against organized parties and interests as core elements in the democratic process (Wright 1981, 27).

The second relevant strand in French political culture is the tendency of the French over the centuries to make public policy *dans la rue* (in the streets). Almond and Powell (1988, 68) observed that "particularly where organized groups are absent or where they have failed to obtain adequate representation of their interests in the political system, smoldering discontent may be sparked by an incident or by the emergence of a leader and it may suddenly explode in unpredictable and uncontrollable ways." These so-called anomic interest groups have little or no structure, are ephemeral, yet may have a profound transformational effect on the political system. The modern French political system, with its roots in the revolution and the triumph of popular action, has always been susceptible to the ever-present threat of mass protest.

Hence, French political culture took a profoundly different course from the pluralism and liberalism of the Anglo-Saxon world. Here the Rousseauian world of indivisible sovereignty and the General Will contrasts sharply with the economic liberalism of Adam Smith and the limitations on constitutional power of John Locke, and the unitary character of the French state embodied in the thoughts and deeds of the Jacobins stands in stark contrast to the pluralism of James Madison. The Jacobins saw the state as the instrument of the General Will, freeing innately good men from the grip of those who would use political power for their own ends. For Madison, the selfish and self-serving nature of man led inexorably to the pluralized world of organized interests, with the state acting as neutral arbiter.

As Suleiman pointed out, the cumulative effect of these complex strands of French political culture has been to dissociate the French conception of *corporatisme* from the well-known political science term *corporatism*. In the language of political science, corporatism is a system of interest mediation in which the state manages a set of privileged relationships between monopoly associations. For the French, *corporatisme* is "a variant of individualism" (Suleiman 1987, 20) that actually describes the defense of narrow sectoral interests. The term is pejorative, and for many in contemporary France, it denotes a system where the state is rendered impotent by the activities of interest groups seeking to protect *les droits acquis* (special privileges). The conception of *interest group*, then, is viewed as inherently conservative and as a force that inhibits the modernization of the state. Ultimately, interest group activity is regarded in this optic as "unwholesome" and "a negation of national union and solidarity" (Suleiman 1987, 22). This perspective has been reflected in the attitude of the French state toward interest groups and political parties and thus has affected party-group relations.

DEVELOPMENT OF PARTY-GROUP RELATIONS

Legislation

From the onset of the revolution to the present, the organization and activity of both parties and interest groups have been tightly circumscribed by law. In 1791 the Le Chapelier law was promulgated, which regulated much group activity for almost a hundred years. The intent of the law was to remove the *corporations* (guilds) from the position of power and privilege that they had occupied under the ancien régime. However, the law retarded the development of trade unions and other associations in France compared with European nations such as Britain and Germany. Some artisan groups survived the revolutionary period; these associations, called *compagnonnages*, were more the equivalent of medieval guilds and "were to complicate the task of forming modern trade unions" (Wright 1981, 171).

The major law governing the right to associate in France was passed in 1901. This law, which created the French equivalent of not-for-profit associations, included two important elements. The first was a formal acknowledgment of the right to free association, recognized by the preamble to the Constitution of the Fourth Republic, ratified in 1946, as a constitutional right and further recognized in the Fifth Republic Constitution in 1958. The second important element of the law was the requirement that all voluntary associations register with the Ministry of the Interior. This law, which has governed the legal and financial status of associations in France since its passage, applies equally to interest groups, trade unions, and political parties.

Four Waves of Development

The development of associations in France since 1800 has occurred in four waves. The first wave mainly involved the emergence of trade unions and occupational groups, culminating in the repeal of the Le Chapelier law in 1884. With the brief exception of the Second Republic in 1848, little formal union organization took place until the 1860s. Under pressure, Napoleon III granted French labor the right to strike in 1864 and in 1868 allowed the creation of the first official French trade unions despite the formal prohibitions remaining in the legal code.

The oldest, and consistently the largest, trade union in France has been the Confédération Générale du Travail (CGT), formed in 1895. The framework for relations between political parties and trade unions in France was set by the CGT shortly after its formation. With the Charter of Amiens of 1906, the CGT took a formal step to reject a tight strategic alliance with the French Socialist Party (Section Française de L'International Ouvrière—SFIO, created in 1905). The charter foreswore the parliamentary route to gains for organized labor and instead placed the onus on direct action (Tilly 1986, 315). In 1920–1921 about two-thirds of the SFIO membership opted to defect to the newly formed PCF. In the wake of its creation, the PCF formed its own rival to the CGT, the Confédération Générale du Travail Unitaire—CGTU. Despite having its own trade union, the PCF continued to try to co-opt the CGT, with little success, until after World War II.

The fragmentation of the labor movement in the 1920s and 1930s can be gauged by the inability of organized labor to define a common agenda for workers' rights, which had its origins in this first wave of development. Tilly (1986) shows that during the turbulence of February 1934, organized labor proved incapable of mobilizing resistance to what was widely perceived as a threat to the Republic from fascist and extreme right-wing groups. Division within the union movement was felt most acutely during the period of the left-wing antifascist Popular Front government in 1936. Unlike Britain, where the Labour Party acted mainly in concert with the unions to promote more rights for workers, the Popular Front government found itself confronted by massive labor unrest and strikes when it rose to power. The gains that did accrue to labor resulted from pressure exerted on a left-wing government through direct action. To a degree, this pattern of a left-wing governing coalition faced by disruptive direct action from labor is true of relations between trade unions and the parties of the left in today's France.

The second wave followed the 1918 armistice and the rebuilding of French society, when there was a "proliferation of important interest groups representing almost every sector of society and of the economy" (Wright 1981, 351). The main employers' organization in France to this day, the Couseil Nationale du Patronnat Français (CNPF), was created in 1919. Since its inception the CNPF has organized the largest businesses in France and is considered ideologically close to the parties of the right, although formal ties between the CNPF and those parties have not been the norm. An attempt to organize farmers into one large interest group that same year failed, and a number of smaller groups representing individual sectors of the farming economy were created. These groups, particularly the sugar-beet growers, became disproportionately powerful under the Third and Fourth Republics. The union movement was further divided with the creation of the Catholic French trade union Confédération Française des Travailleurs Chrétiens (CFTC). The most powerful interest groups formed during this period, however, were those representing war veterans. Again, the pattern of development was one of diversity rather than unity, with several large groups representing several million veterans.

The third wave of interest group development occurred in the wake of the formation of the Fourth Republic in 1946. The explosion of group activity during this period can be attributed to two factors: the recasting of the party system and the institutional environment in which that took place. The party system of the Fourth Republic was spawned by an electoral law (modified proportional representation) that encouraged a large number of parties competing in a multiparty system. However, the principal problem was the exclusion of parties of the left and right from the process of governance. The system became characterized by fragile coalitions of moderates constantly assailed by attacks from the nongoverning left and right parties. The situation was exacerbated by a weak executive beholden to a powerful National Assembly and unable to impose any discipline on the legislature. The best characterization of party-group relations during this period is that of weak and ideologically diluted parties (with the exception of the Communists) beholden to special interests, both local and national, to gain resources and compete for office.

The fourth wave of interest group formation has occurred since the 1970s. F. Wilson (1987) presents detailed figures gleaned from opinion polls and official statistics of the Ministry of the Interior. In 1977 a poll suggested that 52 percent of respondents claimed membership in a voluntary association, compared with 41 percent in a similar poll conducted in 1951. Regarding membership in specific kinds of groups, 24 percent of respondents in the 1977 poll belonged to a trade union or professional association, and 6 percent reported membership in a political party. The rate of group formation also increased markedly. The ministry reported 17,450 new associations in 1965 but 32,877 in 1977. In 1981 an estimated 39,000 new groups were created. Thus, by both membership and rate of group formation, interest groups in modern France appear to be flourishing and bely the traditional view of associative life in the Republic as weak and underdeveloped. However, the underlying reasons for the seemingly paradoxical creation of such groups during the institutionally insulated Fifth Republic reveal much about the relations between associations and parties and among parties, associations, and the state.

During this recent period of growth, the European Union has also emerged as a major political force, with profound consequences for domestic politics. Little has been written about the impact of the EU on the organization of interests within the domestic arena; however, recent studies have clearly shown that Euro-lobbies have become important players in EU policy processes (see, for example, Greenwood 1997). We can only speculate whether this will stimulate or retard the growth of interests within the French system, and the implications for relations between interest groups and political parties are even less clear. Nonetheless, it is difficult to imagine that the growth of Euro-lobbies can occur without some impact on and reconfiguration of the organization of interests at the domestic level. For example, the French Department of Agriculture has less and less control over French agricultural policy as more and more policy in this area is made in Brussels. This has changed the role of French farmers in domestic politics as their interest groups focus more on Brussels and less on Paris. It also means the well-publicized mass public protests by farmers are less likely to have a policy impact on the French government than they did in the past.

DEMOCRATIZATION AND PLURALIZATION

The flowering of associative life in the modern era cannot be divorced from two attendant processes that have had a major effect on recasting the interest group universe in France. First is the emergence of the rationalized party system of the Fifth Republic, in particular the development of the modern Socialist Party as what Duverger (1972) termed a party of mass integration. Second, the process of decentralization of the activities of the state has been an almost incalculable stimulus to the growth of association life at the local level. Together these two aspects of the modernization of the French polity have fundamentally transformed the character of local political life and the environment within which citizens participate in associative life.

The institutional arrangements of the Fifth Republic, buttressed by a revised electoral system (constituency based, two ballot, first past the post), quickly forced a rationalization of the party system. Over the life of the Fifth Republic, party competition has crystallized to the point where the first ballot can be seen as a "primary" among the parties on the left, on the one hand, and among the parties on the right, on the other, to determine which party from left and right will carry the ideological standard in the second round. The main beneficiaries of this system have been the Socialist Party on the left (reborn as the PS in 1971) and the Gaullist movement on the right (reincarnated as the RPR in 1977). In both cases these parties have built a base of active local party organizations.

Prior to its national victory in 1981, the PS made enormous advances in local politics during the 1970s. Particularly in the wake of the municipal elections in 1977, in which the left as a whole made spectacular gains, the PS adopted a strategy of using its control over local councils to provide resources and a platform for its national ambitions. On a programmatic level, the party was committed to the concept of *autogestion* (self-government, perhaps more liberally interpreted as citizen involvement), and the party platform was replete with references to citizen participation and local democracy. As a result, municipalities controlled by the PS and its allies saw a big increase in the number of officially recognized and sponsored groups. Not to be outdone, the conservative right attempted to match the organization of the left at the grassroots, and this plan gained momentum following the RPR's loss of power in 1981. Also, the Communist Party had consistently pursued a strategy of sponsoring associational life within the municipalities it controls, to the point where it is almost possible to live a highly active civic life within organizations and associations all controlled by the party (Schain 1985).

The second feature of the modernization of the political system stimulating interest group activity has been the move to decentralize many functions of the state. Traditionally viewed as a very centralized state, France has undergone profound changes in the distribution of executive and political functions over the life of the Fifth Republic, culminating in the Deferre reforms in 1981–1983. These reforms have altered the local political landscape in numerous ways: twenty-two regions were created, each with directly elected councils; municipalities have gained important fiscal and financial powers (including powers of taxation); local councils have gained new powers; the practice of multiple office holding has been curtailed; and resources have been redirected to regional and local areas as never before.

New resources and powers at the local level have opened up new opportunities and new points of access for associations and interest groups. Direct election of the regional councils has fundamentally changed what Schlesinger (1966) called the political opportunity structure, and this has as much bearing on the organization of interests as it does on the consolidation of political parties. Local councils at all levels—municipal, departmental, and regional—have become arenas of distribution and as such have attracted the activities of new forms of local groups rarely seen in France prior to these reforms. In addition, the decentralization of the state has encouraged new kinds of cooperation between local councils, with the law providing for several kinds of associations between institutional partners including development zones, enterprise zones, water provision, and environmental quality.

The decentralization of the state and the emergence of this new kind of local participatory politics clearly stand at odds with some of the more established aspects of the interest group universe described previously. Thus, we revert to the notion of the ambiguity of relationships among the state, interest groups, and political parties with which this chapter began. The state must be understood as a complex, multilayered set of institutions in which a variety of practices and relationships exist. The reform of the state described earlier has opened a new political space at the local level for interest group action and yet has not substantially altered the political culture that has circumscribed interest groups in the French polity.

THE PARTY–INTEREST GROUP CONNECTION IN CONTEMPORARY FRANCE

In analyzing the relationships between political parties and interest groups in France today, four preliminary observations will place things in perspective. First, the majority of voluntary associations have no formal links to political parties; nor do they have an overtly political agenda. Second, the institutional environment of the Fifth Republic, as discussed earlier, places the executive branch at a tactical advantage in determining the points of access available to interest groups in the political arena. This tends to diminish the need for strong party–interest group linkages and pushes groups to pursue accommodation with the state. Third, where they do exist, party-group relations are uneven across parties or sectors, and wide variance is found in those linkages (Capdevielle and Moriaux 1991). And fourth, the formal statements concerning such relationships often mask a more complex reality, one that is hard to measure in a quantitative fashion.

Occupational Interest Groups and Political Parties

Traditional trade unions and the major white-collar organization. The organization of trade unions in France, despite the nonpartisan roots of syndicalism embodied in the Charter of Amiens of 1906, has been rife with partisan and ideological differences. Since the takeover of the CGT by the PCF in 1947, relations between these two organizations have been perhaps the tightest of those between any political party and trade union (Daley 1992; F. Wilson 1987). A CGT representative sits on the Central Committee of the PCF, and there are tight links at the level of departmental (provincial) federations. An estimated 10 percent of rank-and-file members of the CGT are in fact members of the PCF, and the union has always had a visible socialist minority. Nonetheless, at the policy level divergence rarely occurs between the PCF and the CGT, although recent internal debates within the PCF about the future of the communist movement have perhaps heralded an era of more autonomy for the CGT.

The second major union in contemporary France is the Force Ouvrière (FO), formed when the CGT was taken over by the PCF and with a marked anti-Communist character. The FO has been vociferous about its commitment to the principles of the Charter of Amiens and stays independent of official party affiliation (F. Wilson 1987). However, in spirit and temperament it has always been relatively close to the socialist party of the moment (Daley 1992). F. Wilson (1987) has attributed the comparative well-being of the FO, given declining union membership and the crisis of unionism, to its rejection of overtly political or partisan action. For example, the FO refuses to endorse candidates in elections, and it rejects political strikes aimed at governments of particular ideological persuasions. Rather than supporting militant anticapitalism, the FO focuses on what Daley (1992, 58) terms "bread and butter unionism." In 1981 the FO distanced itself from the new Socialist government by criticizing the inclusion of communists in that government, all the while participating in negotiations at the table (Daley 1992, 64).

A third union is the Confédération Française Démocratique du Travail (CFDT), originally a Catholic union. The CFDT was animated by principles of social Catholicism that cast a negative light on capitalism, but it officially shed its confessional character in 1964. For the next decade the CFDT remained close to the Parti Socialiste Unifié (PSU) until the latter became incorporated into the newly renovated PS in 1974. During this period the CFDT formed a close alliance with the CGT, cooperating in strikes and collective bargaining. The CGT was oriented more toward the development of disciplined and responsible "class actions," while the CFDT sought to provoke more spectacular kinds of labor conflict (Daley 1992). The CFDT was highly influenced by the *autogestionnaire* (self-management) ideas of the New Left and thus moved closer to that wing of the PS in the 1970s. The defeat of the left in the 1978 elections, when it was widely expected to win, led the union to reconsider its close links with the PS, and for a while it pursued a strategy of *recentrage* (recentering) on the premise that the left could not achieve power in the short term (Daley 1992; Groux and Moriaux 1989; F. Wilson 1987).

Groux and Moriaux (1996, 176) present various estimates of the membership of these three major unions. In the largest of these estimates (for 1989) the CGT has no more than 600,000 members, the FO 450,000, and the CFDT 470,000.

Two other unions are important to mention. The CFTC, noted earlier, groups the remnants of the CFDT that refused secularization in the 1960s. The CFTC has generally acted as a much more moderate union, inspired by the social Catholicism that was so important in Europe in the immediate postwar years. Before the split in 1964, the CFTC had been close to the social Catholic Movement Républicain Populaire (MRP). This party was one of the mainstays of Fourth Republic governments but did not survive the transition to the Fifth Republic for long, as social Catholicism became a rather spent force in French politics. Although officially nonpartisan, the CFTC has relatively close ideological sympathies with the small Centre des Démocrates Sociaux (CDS), the spiritual heir of the social Catholic tradition. Finally, the Confédération des Syndicats Libres (CSL) is a relatively small union that has often been seen as a deliberate attempt by management to challenge the primacy of the big three. In recent years the CSL has been close to the very right-wing party Front National (FN) and it has been accused of using strong-arm tactics to undermine labor actions by the other unions.

When the Socialist government came to power in 1981, it was widely seen in the union movement as heralding a new era of union-friendly legislation, and the expectation was that the big three unions—the CGT, FO, and CFDT—would work closely with the new government. Indeed, it was partly this expectation that led François Mitterrand and the PS to invite the PCF to participate in that government as a coalition partner. However, the experience of that government and subsequent socialist governments has demonstrated the limits to the union-party linkage in France. Although the new government set about introducing a program of legislation, known as the Auroux laws, that reformed and modernized the position of organized labor in the economy, the unions adopted a more independent stance than anticipated. Indeed, the new government found itself facing pent-up demands from both organized and unorganized labor that taxed the relationship between party and unions.

Ironically, the Auroux reforms, although granting important privileges to organized labor on the shop floor, may have in the long run weakened the bargaining power of unions (Howell 1992). Kesselman (1996a, 1996b) has suggested that the reforms did not eliminate the free rider problem that has traditionally bedeviled labor unions' efforts to increase their memberships in France and that they have probably created more pressures for labor unions at a time when unions are undergoing a profound crisis. The experience of government triggered a crisis of ideological values on the left and cemented the institutional weakness of the National Assembly in the legislative process that had been growing over the life span of the Fifth Republic.

Groux and Moriaux (1996, 178) argued that the party-union relationship has weakened in recent years, pointing to the key factor of this decline as the breakup of the Socialist-Communist coalition in 1984. The failure of the coalition and the sharp turn in economic policy signaled the end of the fiction that the left could govern as a broad, participatory coalition of parties, unions, and other *autogestionnaire* associations and revealed the triumph of the institutional logic of the Fifth Republic.

White-collar workers (*cadres*) are organized into the Confédération Générale des Cadres (CGC), which has tended to chart a relatively moderate course. As F. Wilson (1987) pointed out, the CGC has generally operated on a pragmatic basis with all parties and has negotiated limited electoral agreements with both socialists and Gaullists. In recent years the union has also tended to forge closer relationships with other unions, except for the CGT.

Business interests. These are primarily organized in the CNPF—known simply as *le patronnat*—which acts as a peak association. F. Wilson (1987) explored the complexity of employers' associations in France and argued that in reality, much of the lobbying done by business actually occurs outside of these associations. Relations between political parties of the right and the business community have generally been restrained by, first, the rather skeptical approach to capitalism incorporated into the Gaullist tradition and, second, the more dominant links of background and education that have created a French politico-technocratic elite. The former was generally most manifest in areas such as state planning and regulation, where successive French governments pursued policies diametrically opposed to unrestrained free markets. In this atmosphere, relations between the business community and the state operated predominantly through informal personal relationships among members of the technocratic elite rather than through the channel of institutionalized interests, further evidence of the ambiguity among parties, groups, and the state.

The business community was nervous about the socialist victory in 1981, officially proclaiming that the PS and its allies were incapable of governing. In fact, the *patronnat* was fearful of a disruption of the corporatist/statist patterns of policymaking and the substitution of a more participatory style of governance. When Mitterrand demonstrated that under conditions of economic crisis he would ultimately abandon the latter and opt for the former, the business community was relieved and has generally had fairly cozy relations with the socialist elite ever since. The revelations of the Elf-Aquitaine/Roland Dumas scandal still unfolding in France at the time of writing (where Dumas, former foreign minister, has been implicated in an elaborate scheme of bribes to influence the sale of naval frigates to Taiwan) demonstrate the degree to which the socialist elite maintained cozy and even corrupt relations with the business community.

During this same period, however, changes have begun to take place on the political right, and a diluted neoliberalism has appeared on the political scene. Privatization of state firms is now on the political agenda and with it a subtle shift toward closer relations between business and the parties of the right. It is perhaps too early to say if this shift will translate into more pluralist relations among interest groups, parties, and the state, but it certainly chips away at the monopoly of the politico-technocratic elite described earlier.

Nonoccupational Groups and Political Parties

Turning to the nonoccupational sector, the predominant feature of the majority of groups is that they are local rather than national in organization and ambition and therefore have little prominence on the national political scene. In some sectors attempts have been made to create national umbrella organizations, but generally these attempts to federate have been unsuccessful. At the national level the organization of interest groups in the nonoccupational sector illustrates the fragmentation of the burgeoning world of associational life in France. Here we review four areas of the nonoccupational group sector that have significant relations with parties: veterans' affairs, student groups in higher education, parent-teacher associations, and the women's movement. In each of these, the durability of the organization coexists with highly marked partisan and ideological differences that run through the interest group universe and often render concerted action impossible.

Veterans' groups. This point is typified by the manner in which veterans' interests have been represented by the Union Française d'Associations de Combattants et Victimes de Guerre (UFAC). With a small staff and limited resources, UFAC acts as an umbrella group that brings together over fifty national organizations with interest in veterans' affairs. Most of these constituent organizations have close relations with political parties, which creates constant friction between groups and within UFAC that at times has become so intense that groups have splintered off from UFAC. For example, in 1977 several conservative groups left to form their own coalition. F. Wilson (1987, 53) concluded that UFAC's range of action is severely limited by the plurality of interests and ideological leanings of its constituent associations and that the group is often forced to abstain from debates on veterans' affairs to maintain a semblance of unity.

As far as political parties are concerned, veterans' affairs occupy an important place in the national psyche (despite a declining number of veterans), and successive governments have maintained a Ministry of Veterans. However, the formation of the new government under socialist prime minister Lionel Jospin in 1997 saw the demotion of veterans' affairs, with no cabinet-rank minister appointed. The Communist Party has maintained its own organization for veterans' affairs, perhaps the most explicit linkage between party and interest group in this sector. On the other end of the ideological spectrum, in recent years the FN has attempted to recruit and organize among certain veterans' groups.

Student groups. The pattern of ideological divisions and partisan leanings is also reflected among student groups. Prior to the Fifth Republic, students were organized into one large association, the Union Nationale des Etudiants de France (UNEF), which was quite effective in the policy process. However, the events of May 1968 led to a major rift between authorities and student associations, many of which were disbanded by government proclamation. The reform of higher education that followed created elected consultative bodies, and in the wake of this move UNEF eventually broke into several parts that have close ties to political parties. These ties, however, are more ideological than organizational; student associations depend on the state for resources rather than on the parties to which they are close. In turn, all major political parties have active youth associations on college and university campuses. These youth movements typically organize so-called summer universities where representatives of student associations mingle with party members akin to their organization's ideology.

Parent-teacher associations. The role of the Catholic Church in education has been one of the most divisive issues in France since the formal separation of church and state in 1905. The array of parent-teacher associations reflects this divide. The largest parent-teacher associations are the Fédération des Conseils des Parents d'Elèves (FCPE), representing parents with children in secular public schools, and the Union Nationale des Associations de Parents d'Elèves de l'Enseignement Libre (UNAPEL), which organizes those with children in Catholic schools. The FCPE is close to the Socialist Party and is a virtual offshoot of the socialist-leaning teachers union, the Syndical National des Instituteurs (SNI).

The equivocation of successive governments on the issue of public subsidies to private schools has resulted in many ways from the opposition to reform by these groups. When the Socialist-Communist government came to power in 1981, it vowed to end the links between state and private education and initially proposed the absorption of subsidized schools into the public sector. Negotiations by the education minister, Alain Savary, produced a compromise that was acceptable to Catholic associations, only to be dismembered in parliament by the more militant secularists. UNAPEL played a major role in subsequent opposition to the amended legislation, helping to bring close to a million people into the streets in June 1984 to protest the government plans (Ambler 1996). The government proposals were withdrawn, which testifies to the power of *blocage* wielded by associations such as UNAPEL in the French system.

The relationships UNAPEL fostered during the early years of the Fifth Republic placed it close to the loci of political decisionmaking. F. Wilson (1987, 59) reported that UNAPEL had used an association of parliamentarians from conservative parties to ensure that its voice was heard in debates over education policy in parliament. Although the parliamentary process under the constitutional arrangements of the Fifth Republic allows only a limited direct role in shaping legislation, UNAPEL concerns were represented indirectly but very effectively by sympathetic members of parliament. The reality of party grouping and party affiliation provided a key transmission belt for this mode of representation, allowing deputies and senators to be heard in the corridors of government ministries. Once the right lost its parliamentary majority in 1981, UNAPEL was forced to adopt more public tactics, although it attempted to avoid confrontation with the government. It was successful in keeping the ear of Savary, the first socialist minister of education, but it failed to dampen the enthusiasm of the socialist and communist deputies in the National Assembly who were wedded to ending public subsidies of any kind.

Women's groups. The arena of women's rights is one where the more corporatist tendencies of the French state have been confronted in recent years by genuine grassroots organizations demanding access to the system. It is also an arena where the politicization of women's rights since the 1960s has resulted in political parties taking an active role. As they have done for students, the major parties have established women's sections within their organizations. The largest trade union, the CGT, has also constituted a very active women's section. However, these auxiliary organizations have sometimes been criticized by women within the political parties as largely impotent. The criticism continues that they simply act as mechanisms for coopting women within the parties and preventing their voices from being heard loudly (Appleton and Mazur 1991). During the 1970s women in the Socialist Party attempted to form a women's faction, and in 1978 many women in the party backed the effort by a feminist group, Choisir, to field women candidates independent of the party organization. Relations between women activists and party organizations remain tense in most parties (Appleton and Mazur 1991), although the discontent is rarely voiced openly in the more conservative RPR.

CLASSIFYING AND SUMMARIZING
PARTY-GROUP RELATIONS IN FRANCE

Can party-group relations in France be summed up along the continuum proposed in Box 1.2 of this book? The answer is yes and no.

Particularly in the occupational sector, parties and interest groups have fairly strong links (either the Integration or Cooperation Model). In this regard the continuum does reflect certain party-group relationships in France, even though they are highly variable depending upon sector and ideology. Close, integrative party–interest group relationships have generally been found on the communist left, where the PCF has created a network of associations and paraparty institutions. Outside the communist left, sectors of French life that have traditionally been politicized, such as education and agriculture, tend to exhibit cooperative party-group relations. But again, separation or noninvolvement is the norm for most groups in France. Furthermore, as some of the evidence presented earlier suggests, the latest wave of associational life in France is forcing a recasting of the predominant models of relations between parties and interest groups and likely means more examples of the noninvolvement model will be seen in the near future.

Yet even where we can classify groups as having integrative or cooperative connections with parties, the policy consequences of these relationships are not as great as might be expected because of the limited role afforded to political parties and their related interest groups by the institutions of the system. In France, parties do not control the state as is the case in Britain, Germany, or Sweden. In fact, parties remain vehicles for elite ambitions, and the party organizations suffer from their inability to transcend the ambitions of their leaders. Even on the left, where the PS was structured—in theory—to stimulate internal democracy, the party has come to a position of malaise and internal conflict. Parties serve as channels of recruitment and to elect leaders to office; once they're there, party and party affiliation count for much less than background and personal contact networks. As to interest groups, where they refuse to play the game and do not achieve legitimization by the state, they are reduced to tactics such as the National Day of Solidarity that in all except rare cases expose and underscore their weakness.

CONCLUSION

In this environment one cannot suggest that the party-group relationship as presented in Box 1.1 is key to the policymaking process. Hence the paradox of interest group–party relations in modern France emerges in sharp relief.

Strong party-group relationships exist alongside a limited policy impact with the ambiguity of relations between the institutions of the state and the party–interest group universe.

As noted earlier, however, some significant recent developments have occurred in French party-group-state relations. In particular, although both parties and trade unions are undergoing a crisis of organization and identity, associational life in France is flourishing. Democratization and pluralization of the state have also occurred with the decentralization reforms that have caused interest group life to burgeon at the local level. Do these reforms mean an end to the paradox of party-group relations in the shadow of the state, perhaps closer party-group relations in France, or even the pluralization of French policymaking along the lines of the United States? Although modifications in the party-group-state relationship may occur, a major change is unlikely, in part because there is little sign that political parties are becoming more potent forces within the system. After the initial promise of opening up local political space to more organized and disciplined parties, the decentralization reforms have tended to reproduce the phenomenon of politico-technocratic networks found at the national level. Associations and even party organizations in many cases remain dependent upon the resources and recognition afforded by the institutions of the state, whether at the national or local level. The state, in the French version of corporatism, continues to legitimate and recognize associational actors in all sectors of French life, with the institutions of the state and the political culture maintaining parties and groups in a situation of organizational weakness. This situation is likely to continue in the foreseeable future.

4

Sweden: Weakening Links Between Political Parties and Interest Organizations

Anders Widfeldt

More than 90 percent of adults in Sweden belong to one or more associations or organizations. This adds up to over 30 million memberships in voluntary organizations in a population of 9 million (Petersson 1994, 156f). Membership in trade unions is particularly high, with more than nine in ten employees unionized (Lane and Ersson 1994, 95). Other organizations with large memberships include sports clubs, consumer cooperatives, and housing organizations. At the same time, political parties are very important. Sweden is generally regarded as a country with strong political parties and a high degree of party government, or "partyness of government" (R. Katz 1986; Pierre and Widfeldt 1994). And in a manner common in countries with a Social Democratic heritage, connections of varying degrees between parties and organized interests have ranged from close ideological and organizational ties to separation to noninvolvement.

At the system level the characteristics of party–interest organization relations in Sweden have been shaped largely by the long-standing link between the Social Democratic Party and the Swedish Trade Union Confederation (Landsorganisationen—LO). The electoral size and government dominance of the Social Democrats, coupled with the organizational strength and dominant position of the LO, have meant these two Goliaths of Swedish politics were major players in political development during the twentieth century. The main conclusion of this chapter—that the link between parties and interest organizations in Sweden has weakened since 1970—is based largely on changes in relations between the LO and the Social Democrats.

Unlike much of the literature on party-group relations in other Western democracies, scholars deal with these relations in Swedish politics largely from a neocorporatist (henceforth referred to as corporatist) perspective (for example, Hermansson 1993; Lewin 1992, 1994; Öberg 1994). Part of the recent changes in party-group relations in Sweden can indeed be explained by the decline of corporatism since around 1990. The corporatist focus tells only part of the story, however. A comprehensive understanding of party–interest organization relations in Sweden in the past and, in particular, of the recent loosening of those ties requires that the corporatist perspective be supplemented with other explanations. Accordingly, in addition to corporatism, this chapter examines three types of party–interest organization links: financial, organizational, and political and ideological. The major focus is on the period from the late 1960s to the late 1990s, which covers the major changes in Swedish politics that have affected relations between parties and interest organizations. Before examining these links we first explain some key elements of Swedish government and politics and outline the development of organized interests and parties and their historical ties or lack of ties, as the case may be.

SWEDISH POLITICS AND THE DEVELOPMENT OF INTEREST ORGANIZATIONS AND POLITICAL PARTIES

Swedish Government and Politics

Sweden is a unitary state, and the political system has traditionally been highly centralized. The policymaking process has been described as consensual, slow, and deliberate (see Elder, Thomas, and Arter 1988, 184; Särlvik 1983). Until the 1980s the party system was stable and consisted of five parties that could be separated into two ideological blocs—the left, or socialist bloc (Social Democrats and Communists) and the moderate right, or nonsocialist bloc (Liberals, Center Party, and Moderates). As indicated earlier, an important characteristic of Swedish politics has been the dominant role of the Social Democratic Party, with its close links to unions.

In recent years, however, Swedish politics has changed in some important respects. The party system has become more fragmented (Arter 1999b) with the arrival of the Environmental Party, or Greens (Miljöpartiet de Gröna—MP), and the Christian Democrats (Kristdemokraterna—KD) and the brief entry of the populist New Democracy Party (Ny Demokrati—NYD). The Social Democrats remain the strongest party but have suffered electoral setbacks and been out of government for the longest spells of any period since the early 1930s. Sweden remains a unitary state, but there has been a decentralization of power from central to local government (Petersson 1994, 122ff). At the same time, Sweden's entry into the European Union in 1995 has changed the parameters and power centers of political decisionmaking (Arter 1999a, 335f).

Development and Relations of Organized Interests and Political Parties

The organization of Swedish society has roots back to the late nineteenth and early twentieth centuries. Six major popular movements trace their origins to this period.

The Labor movement. Political groups and trade unions with socialist ideas began to form in the 1880s, and the Social Democratic Party (Sveriges Socialdemokratiska Arbetareparti—SAP) was formed in 1889. With much involvement from SAP, in 1898 the blue-collar LO was formed. Links between SAP and the unions were close from the outset. Today the LO is the peak association for twenty-two national trade unions, and its membership totals over 55 percent of the Swedish labor force. In 1917 a group defected from the SAP and formed the Communist Party, which in 1967 changed its name to the Left Party–Communists and in 1990 to the Left Party (Vänsterpartiet).

The Free Church movement. This movement began to grow significantly during the second half of the nineteenth century. As a result of their adversary position against the state Church of Sweden, the Free Churches tended to ally with groups that challenged the political and social order of the time, especially the People's Party Liberals (Folkpartiet Liberalerna—FP). As its name suggests, the FP represents a wide and electorally volatile constituency including businesspeople, workers, intellectuals, free thinkers, and, as mentioned later, prohibitionists. The party has tended to oppose increased government and centralization of the economy.

The Farmers' movement. Interest groups on behalf of farmers and the rural population emerged around 1910. Initially, the party link was very close. The Agrarian Party was formed as an amalgamation of two different agricultural interest groups in 1921. In 1958 the party changed its name to the current Center Party (Centerpartiet) and adopted a more broad-based program, including economic decentralization and a more humane urban environment (Hancock 1998, 465). In 1929 the Rural People's Federation (Riksförbundet Landsbygdens Folk) was formed, which, after a merger with the Swedish Agricultural Association (Svenska Lantbruksförbundet) in 1971, became the current National Association of Farmers (Lantbrukarnas Riksförbund—LRF). The LRF is a unique organization, combining both the union and cooperative elements of the farmers' movement. There were links between the LRF and the Center Party, but the formation of the former was independent of the already existing party. Informal contacts existed from the beginning, but no formal and organized links were formed.

The Women's movement. The Fredrika Bremer Association (Fredrika

Bremerförbundet), named after author Fredrika Bremer—which still exists—was formed in 1884 with women's right to vote high on its agenda. However, political parties began to form their own women's organizations after the turn of the twentieth century, which could explain why nonpartisan women's pressure groups had little significance for many years. New women's groups began to form in the late 1960s, but their memberships are not large, and they have not been integrated into the policy process. They have sympathetic but unformalized relations with the Left and Green Parties, neither of which has a separate women's organization.

The Temperance movement. The antialcohol lobby became powerful in the early twentieth century, and in 1922 prohibition was rejected by a very narrow majority in a popular referendum. The Liberal Party had links to the temperance movement, but as with the Free Churches, the ties were informal.[1]

The Sports movement. This movement began quietly around 1900. It has built up an impressive membership but has little contact with political parties.

There are other interest groups, which cannot be said to have a movement background but are still important. In 1902 the Swedish Employers' Confederation (Svenska Arbetsgivareföreningen—SAF), the peak organization for private employers, was formed in response to the organization of the labor movement. In practice, many of SAF's ideas, interests, and demands are similar to those of the Conservative Party, renamed the Moderate Party (Moderata Samlingspartiet) in 1969. The party offers a clear alternative to the Social Democrats, emphasizing, among other policies, tax reductions, deregulation of private enterprise, and the partial privatization of education (Hancock 1998, 466). To some extent, SAF has also shared a common philosophy with the People's Party Liberals. However, both of these parties and SAF have been careful to keep their independence, and no formal links have been formed.

There are two main white-collar peak associations: the Swedish Confederation of Professional Employees (Tjänstemännens Centralorganisation—TCO), formed in 1944, which is the white-collar union peak association; and the Swedish Confederation of Professional Associations (Sveriges Akademikers Centralorganisation—SACO), formed in 1947, which is the peak association for professional groups such as doctors, lawyers, and academics. The members of TCO and SACO have traditionally tended to support nonsocialist rather than socialist parties, but that has become less marked over time. The organizations themselves have always claimed political independence.

THE FINANCIAL LINK

In a study published in 1966, Birger Hagård analyzed trade union financial support of the Social Democratic Party, concluding that at both the central and local levels SAP received substantial amounts from the LO, as well as from the separate LO unions. As an example, unions provided 94 percent of Social Democratic campaign expenditures in the 1964 election (Hagård 1966, 68–109). Trade unions have also made donations to the Left Party and its predecessors, but they have never been substantial because the LO and its unions have, with brief and isolated exceptions, been loyal to the Social Democrats.

The Moderate and Liberal Parties were highly dependent on private donations. Before 1965 the Moderate Party's central organization did not require membership dues from its local branches, which meant that almost all of its income came from private donations (Albinsson 1986, 52–58). The Liberal Party did charge membership fees, but private donations amounted to over 97 percent of central party income in the early 1960s (Pierre and Widfeldt 1992, 825). There is no evidence, however, that SAF or its member organizations made any donations to these parties; the money came directly from private companies and businesses. Likewise, the Center Party's accounts show no sign of money being transferred to the party from farmers' organizations, and there is little evidence of business donations. As a consequence, the Center Party's national organization had a very small annual income in the early 1960s compared with other parties (Pierre and Widfeldt 1992, 825; 1994, 347).

In 1965 the Swedish Parliament enacted state subsidies for political parties. The subsidies quickly grew in size and were soon supplemented by regional and local government subsidies (Gidlund 1991). In 1997 over SEK 213 million (about $26 million) was paid to central party organizations and parliamentary groups (*Riksdagen i siffror* 1996/1997, 24). And according to other figures produced by Parliament (*Riksdagens Faktablad* 1994/1995), in 1992 the combined total of local subsidies was SEK 252 million (about $31 million) and regional subsidies were SEK 139 million (about $17 million). This reform radically changed the financial condition of established parties. They could employ more staff, increase their research capacity, and reduce their dependence on outside donations.

In the late 1960s fierce criticism was leveled against business donations to the Liberals and Moderates. The two parties responded by ceasing to accept such donations, the Liberals in 1971 and the Moderates in 1977 (Pierre and Widfeldt 1994, 339, 346f). Despite Conservative and Liberal skepticism regarding the introduction of state subsidies, the parties soon discovered that subsidies gave them more security and facilitated long-term planning, luxuries that unpredictable donations from business and other sources had never allowed.

The Social Democrats continued to accept money from unions despite criticism from the other parties. However, the introduction of state subsidies to parties substantially reduced the significance of union donations. Furthermore, circumstantial evidence indicates that the relative importance of union donations also declined after 1965. According to Olivecrona (1968, 176), just over 30 percent of SAP's income in 1968 consisted of donations from unions. Since then, amounts under the heading Donations in published party accounts (transfers from unions are included here, but the proportions are not specified) have increased in nominal as well as current prices, but their proportion of the party's income has declined. In the late 1970s and early 1980s, union donations amounted to over 20 percent of SAP central party income in election years and between 13 and 18 percent in nonelection years. In the 1990s donations were below 10 percent of party income in both election and nonelection years.[2]

Thus, there is little doubt that the Social Democratic Party's financial dependency on unions has declined. However, the findings of Ljungberg (1991, 168) and his collaborators appear to contradict this conclusion somewhat. They argue that a good estimate of SAP-LO dependency can be reached only if LO's own activities related to promoting SAP and the use of LO staff in election campaigns are included. Yet the Ljungberg study is based on only the 1988 election campaign, and its findings do not contradict the main conclusion that the financial link between SAP and the unions has declined. In other parties financial dependence on interest organizations has rarely, if ever, existed.

ORGANIZATIONAL LINKS

As indicated in the introduction to this chapter, interest organizations in Sweden enjoy substantial membership. Table 4.1 provides an overview of patterns of membership in the major national organizations since World War II.[3] The only case of a formal membership overlap between parties and interest organizations has been between LO unions and Social Democrats. When the LO was formed in 1898, all local LO unions had to affiliate all of their members to the Social Democratic Party. Two years later collective party membership was made voluntary, with local LO union branches deciding whether to participate (Thermeanius 1933, 74; Widfeldt 1999, 104). Individual members could opt out of collective membership, but they had to do so every year (Hagård 1966, 36).

Social Democratic membership figures that distinguish between individual and collective members are hard to come by. From the limited

Table 4.1 Membership Strength of Selected Swedish Interest Organizations, 1945–1997 (in millions)

	1945	1967	1976	1984	1990	1997
LO total (peak, blue collar)	1.11	1.61	1.96	2.24	2.23	2.13
Metal industry workers' union	0.19	0.34	0.46	0.45	0.45	0.42
Municipal workers' union	0.06	0.19	0.37	0.62	0.64	0.63
TCO (peak, white collar)	0.20	0.50	1.01	1.02	1.28	1.23
SACO (peak, white collar)	0.03	0.12	0.18	0.27	0.33	0.43
Farmers' organizations	0.52	0.38	0.15	0.16	0.14	0.12

Sources: LO Annual Reports, Stockholm, 1945, 1967, 1976, 1984, 1990, 1997; Elvander 1967, 49; Faxed letter from Lizette Wahlberg (LRF), 21 June 1999; Larsson 1993, 324; Fredriksson and Gunnmo 1978, 205ff, 1985, 280ff, 1992, 185ff; http://www.tco.se; http://www.saco.se.

information available, it appears that between 34 and 39 percent of total LO membership was collectively enrolled in the Social Democratic Party between the end of World War II and the mid-1970s. These collectively affiliated LO members accounted for about two-thirds of total SAP membership during that time (Hagård 1966, 22; SAP 1975, 28; SAP and LO Annual Reports). Collective membership was subject to much debate. The main criticism was that it was antidemocratic—the party enrolled members without asking their permission. The right to opt out was limited in practice because of fear of harassment and the practical difficulty of having to renew the opt-out status every year. The LO and the Social Democrats defended collective membership, arguing that it was always subject to democratic majority decisions in the unions and that critics of collection membership were politically motivated. For instance, at the 1984 party congress, SAP party secretary Bo Toresson argued that the critics' real intention was to weaken the labor movement (Gidlund 1989, 300).

For many years the nonsocialist parties sought to legislate against collective membership, but they were blocked by the Left Party Communists. But in 1986 the Communists hinted that they might reassess their position. Facing the threat of legislation, SAP reacted quickly, and the 1987 party congress abolished collective membership. The gradual dismantling of the system was completed at the end of 1990 (Gidlund 1989, 301; Bäck and Möller 1997, 111f). Instead, a new organizational link between SAP and the unions—so-called organizational membership—was introduced in which local LO union branches can join the Social Democratic Party. This type of membership has also been criticized, but there is no immediate threat of legislation. Only those union members who apply for party membership on an individual basis become SAP members.

Besides obligatory membership arrangements there is voluntary joint membership in a party and interest organization. Table 4.2 compares the proportions of party members who were also members of a union or other vocational organization in 1968 and 1994. Interestingly, the proportion of joint party/organization membership did not decline during that period. The percentage of individual party members who were members of an organization, in fact, increased by 8 percent. In the Social Democratic Party the increase among individual members was 16 percent. In the other parties the low numbers of cases mean that none of the changes were statistically significant. There were signs of a decline in joint party–interest organization membership in the Center and Moderate Parties but a possible increase in People's Party Liberals.

If the figures are broken down by different organizations (not presented in the table), the data provide more specific insights. Not surprisingly, LO membership dominated among Social Democratic members. In 1994, 52 percent of SAP members were also LO members, an increase in individual members over 1968. Such a comparison is misleading, however, as the existence of collective membership meant that many collective members who might have joined the party individually if that had been the only option were already party members by default. The largest SAP membership overlap with an individual union in 1994 was with the Municipal Workers' Union, which accounted for 16 percent of the party's members. Members of white-collar unions who were members of SAP stood at 20 percent for the TCO and 4 percent for SACO. The Center Party's link with farmers' organizations is certainly supported by the data. In 1968 over 50 percent of Center Party members were also members of a farmers' organization, although by 1994 the proportion had dropped to 27 percent. Meanwhile, membership in trade unions appeared to have increased somewhat. Among Liberal and Moderate Party members, the most common interest organization membership was in white-collar unions.

The data in Table 4.2 do not suggest a substantially weakening voluntary membership link between parties and interest organizations, although the existence of collective membership in the Social Democratic Party in 1968 makes comparisons over time difficult. The fact that SAP has abolished collective membership does, however, suggest a decline of the organizational link. The other parties have had no or little change in terms of joint membership. Even so, the significance of collective membership was such that its abolition has had important implications for party–interest group organizational links.

Besides membership, organizational links can take the form of repre-

Table 4.2 Joint Membership in Parties and Unions or Vocational Organizations

	1968 (%)	1994 (%)
Total party members[a]	69 (458)[b]	No collective members
All individual party members	58 (317)	66 (236)
Social Democrats (total)[a]	83 (240)	No collective members
Social Democrats (individual)	64 (99)	80 (122)
People's Party Liberals	51 (45)	59 (17)
Center Party	57 (97)	49 (41)
Moderate Party	50 (62)	43 (37)

Source: Swedish Election Studies 1968, 1994.
Notes: a. Includes collective and individual memberships.
b. Figures in parentheses indicate the number of cases for the percentage base of each category.

sentation on party bodies. In a study that included six European countries, Poguntke (1995) found several cases of external representation on various bodies. Furthermore, he found that this form of representation had increased between 1960 and 1989. In Sweden, however, such links have been and continue to be virtually nonexistent (Pierre and Widfeldt 1992, 808–817). The only partial exception is the Social Democrats, who in 1984 gave SAP representatives on the Federation of Swedish County Councils and the Swedish Association of Local Authorities the right to send one delegate each to the party congress (Pierre and Widfeldt 1992, 813). It should be emphasized that the representational right was given to SAP's own representatives in these organizations, not to the organizations as such. No other party has given interest organizations any guaranteed representation, although the LO has extensive representation at all levels of the Social Democratic organization. Indeed, the strongest LO unions can in practice claim "their" representation on party bodies, as well as during party candidate selection at the constituency level. This de facto representational right, however, is confined to the union members who are also members of SAP. Further, the relationship between SAP and the LO has declined on the central level, in that since 1984 there has been no overlap of personnel between the Social Democratic parliamentary group and the central committee of the LO (Hansson 1999).

On the local level, most parties have special party branches for white- and blue-collar union members, in some cases divided into separate branches for different workplaces. These branches are particularly important in the Social Democratic Party, where they are called Social Democratic union clubs (Socialdemokratiska fackklubbar). Formally, these clubs have the same status as other party branches, but they have many more members, which gives them a powerful position in the organization. This power, however, is facilitated by the strength of their membership, not by special organizational status. During the days of collective membership, the membership advantage of the union clubs was even more accentuated. To many in the party concerned about the disproportionate influence of union clubs, SAP's move and eventual decision to abolish collective membership was a way to reduce the strength of the clubs relative to other party branches (Gidlund 1989, 302f). Thus, even though the de facto influence of LO unions in the Social Democratic Party remains strong, development during the 1990s suggests that the link has weakened.

POLITICAL AND IDEOLOGICAL LINKS

The formation of Sweden's major interest organizations strongly reflected the same cleavages as those that shaped the party system. Thus, much of the conflict within the party system has mirrored conflicts and debates among these major interest organizations. These cleavages and conflicts have lessened in recent years, however. Accordingly, in this section we argue that political and ideological links between parties and interest organizations have declined in importance but by no means disappeared. Essentially, two main developments have caused this decline: changes in the labor market and changes in class structure.

The Swedish labor market has undergone profound changes since the end of World War II. In particular, the growth of the public sector has been important. Since the early 1970s the size and role of this sector have become important and hotly debated issues, especially whether health, child care, care of the elderly, and a host of other services should be run by the private or public sector. One problem that has often been difficult is that Social Democratic politicians, through SAP's strength in central as well as regional and local government, often find themselves in the role of employers of public-sector employees. This dual role, where party representatives often have to administer cuts and keep wage increases within limits to control inflation, has led to unrest within the party.

Open conflicts within the LO involving publicly versus privately employed member unions surfaced in the 1980s. One source of conflict has been the wage structure; public employee unions claim to be lagging behind the private sector to an unacceptable extent. Private employee unions argue that they are subject to market competition and thus do not enjoy the same security as public employees. The debate is also ideological, with public unions arguing against market solutions and emphasizing the societal value of the jobs done by workers in hospitals, old people's homes, day care centers, and so on. This conflict in part reflects a change in the balance of power in the LO. Traditionally, the LO was dominated by unions organizing workers in private industries. In 1978, however, the Municipal Workers Union overtook the Metal Industry Workers Union as the largest LO union, producing a shift in the power balance not only within the LO but also, if indirectly, in the Social Democratic Party. The Municipal Workers Union consists primarily of local government employees, a large proportion of whom work in services, and over 80 percent of its members are women. The union makes important financial contributions to SAP but in recent years has been noted for criticizing Social Democratic governments.[4]

Today the conflict between the private and public sectors is as intense as ever and also affects the white-collar unions, which are split into negotiation "cartels" for private and public employees. Inevitably, the conflict has affected SAP. Social Democratic governments have pursued policies regarding the public sector that have been severely criticized by public-sector employees. Welfare cuts, measures to curtail the growth of the public sector, and attempts to keep wage and salary increases at bay are among SAP policies that have alienated many public-sector employees. This "War of the Roses" (referring to the SAP symbol) is, however, a crosscutting conflict and not solely a matter of public versus private sector. The debate is also about issues such as the welfare state in general and the redistribution of wealth. A division exists between "traditionalists" and "renewers"; the latter want to reassess traditional Social Democratic policies. This split is deep and is causing unrest within the SAP, in the LO, and between the two (see Arter 1994).

The second development affecting relations between parties and interest organizations involves changes in the class base of the parties. Class voting in Sweden remains high by international standards, but it has clearly declined over time, which means political parties have less easily identifiable core groups of supporters than previously (Gilljam and Holmberg 1995, 98ff). Given that the explanatory value of social class as an indicator of voting has declined, it is reasonable to expect a similar development in party preferences of members of the main interest organizations. This, in fact, appears to be the case. For example, although Social Democrats still enjoy a dominant position among LO members, that support has declined over time, dropping from 76 to 57 percent between 1968 and 1994. The decline was also clear in the two largest LO unions, the Metal and Municipal Workers Unions. The proportion voting for the Left Party increased, but not sufficiently to explain the SAP decline. Voting for the Social Democrats remained stable in the white-collar TCO unions and increased significantly for SACO. Fifty-five percent of the members of farmers' organizations voted for the Center Party in 1994, a decline of 14 percent compared with 1968. The People's Party Liberals enjoy relatively strong support among members of white-collar unions and business organizations, but the level decreased between 1968 and 1994. The Moderate Party increased its support in business organizations and lost support in SACO, but the main feature remained the same—namely, that most of the party's interest organization support comes from members of white-collar unions and business organizations.[5]

Overall, in recent years the party loyalty of members of the most important interest organizations in Sweden has weakened. Between 1968 and 1994 the proportion of members of major economic interest organizations who did not support any party increased. This development can also be observed in party–interest group relations in the noneconomic sphere. For instance, the People's Party Liberals' link with the Free Churches has weakened. In 1956, 56 percent of members of the Free Churches voted Liberal; in 1991 the proportion had declined to 9 percent. Such a shift in party allegiance of a large group is unique in Swedish politics (Hagevi 1994). A partial explanation is the emergence of the Christian Democratic Party, which has a substantial base in the Pentecostal Church.

There are also signs of decline in connections with other parties. The Center Party has lost much of its electoral support since its major successes during the 1970s and is hanging on to its core support groups in rural areas, which might suggest that its links with the LRF have tightened, but little evidence supports this assumption. Indeed, a recent study by Hansson (1999) showed that the overlap of personnel between the national committee of the LRF and the parliamentary faction of the Center Party has disappeared completely in the 1990s.

Links between SAF and political parties are difficult to determine. Until the late 1970s, for long periods SAF pursued a pragmatic approach toward Social Democratic governments. But around 1980 SAF launched an ideological campaign that soured relations with both the LO and SAP. This campaign was in part a response to demands for collective wage earners' funds by the LO and the Social Democrats, a proposal that, at its most radical, would have taxed employers to create a huge investment fund to promote the interests of wage earners and to further the LO and SAP's goal of socializing the economy (Lewin 1988, chapter 9). SAF also decided to challenge what it saw as leftist dominance in the media, academia, and public debate in general.

As a result of the conflict with the LO and Social Democrats this "ideological offensive" produced, SAF and the Moderate Party moved closer, although they never developed the same close bonds as those between the LO and SAP. Perhaps because of these looser ties, although SAF was not happy with every detail of the policies of the Moderate-led government between 1991 and 1994, the conflict was never as intense as that sometimes seen between SAP and the LO. The People's Party Liberals, who were on the same side as SAF during the heated debate over the development of the Swedish economy in the late 1940s (Lewin 1988, chapter 6), have recently distanced themselves from SAF. If anything, developments in the 1990s, in which Liberals often played the role of nonsocialist critics against what they saw as inhuman liberal market policies by SAF and the Moderates, widened this gap between the Liberals and SAF.

EFFECTS OF CHANGES IN CORPORATISM ON PARTY–INTEREST ORGANIZATION RELATIONS

The degree of corporatism in a political system is determined primarily by relations between interest groups and the state, in particular, the tripartite relationship among business, labor, and government. In a country like Sweden, however, with a high degree of "partyness of government," political parties play a very important role in determining the nature and extent of corporatism. Indeed, Sweden can be seen as a case of corporatism through political parties (Pierre and Widfeldt 1994, 333). In many respects the government in these tripartite relations is the party or coalition in power. Thus, changes in corporatism strongly affect party–interest organization relations.

For many years the close cooperation between interest groups and governments—mainly SAP governments—not only facilitated a consensual policymaking process in Sweden but was also conducive to the successful implementation of reforms (Rothstein 1996). For these reasons Sweden has often been seen as an exemplary corporatist state. The Swedish model of corporatism has been based on four elements: (1) the consensus and centralized bargaining process of the labor market, (2) government consultation with the main labor market organizations, (3) interest organization involvement in the commissions of inquiry that precede most important legislation, and (4) interest organization representation on the boards of public agencies.

All four factors began to change in the 1980s. The centralized wage bargaining process between the LO and SAF disappeared in 1984 and has been replaced by separate deals between individual unions and SAF member organizations (Faxén, Odhner, and Spånt 1989, 418ff; Petersson 1994, 164). Regular summit-level consultations between the government and the main labor market organizations had their heyday from the 1950s until the 1970s. These consultations sometimes contained elements of informal bargaining in which the government offered reforms in return for wage restraint (Milner 1990, 91f). Since the 1980s, however, such consultations have become less frequent and less significant.

The involvement of interest organizations in commissions of inquiry has also declined in significance. The commissions are a key part of the policymaking process because their proposals are often important in the drafting of government bills (Elder, Thomas, and Arter 1988, 184ff). Because these commissions have traditionally included representatives from political parties as well as interest organizations, they have been a very important forum for contacts between the two groups. However, Petersson has argued that the role of commissions of inquiry is diminishing (Petersson 1994, 163). Restrictions on their size and in the length of time before their reports must be submitted have contributed to this development.

Finally, representation of interest organizations on boards of public agencies is declining. Such representation has been criticized because it gives organized interests influence in decisions that should, in theory at least, involve the faithful implementation of parliamentary and government directives (Ljungberg 1991, 139f). SAF decided in 1991 to withdraw all its representatives on the boards of public agencies and has maintained this policy (Petersson 1994, 162). The Moderate-led coalition government of 1991–1994 introduced legislation that further reduced the significance of interest representation on public agencies (Bäck and Möller 1997, 217).

There is a consensus among scholars that corporatism in Sweden is declining. Certain elements could still be interpreted as corporatist, such as the involvement of interest groups during the referral stage of commissions of inquiry; the trend, however, is that corporatism is on the retreat (Lewin 1994; Petersson 1994, 164; Larsson 1993, 329). This, in turn, means that an important link between parties and interest organizations is declining in importance. The elements of corporatism have, to a varying extent, provided contacts between established interest groups and political parties. In some cases, such as interest group–government consultations and interest group representation on the boards of public agencies, the contacts have occurred exclusively between interest groups and government parties. In the commissions of inquiry, however, contacts have also occurred with opposition parties. Therefore, the decline of corporatism in Sweden has meant an overall decline in contacts between interest groups and parties.

CLASSIFYING PARTY–INTEREST GROUP LINKS IN SWEDEN

The information presented in this chapter shows that the weakening link between parties and interest organizations since 1970 has resulted largely from changes in the relations between Social Democrats and the LO. The distancing between SAF and the Social Democrats has also been a contributing factor. Traditionally, SAF, the LO, and Social Democrats were all on speaking terms. Indeed, Rothstein (1998) spoke of a "trustful relationship" between organized labor and capital and between those two and the state—in effect, Social Democratic governments. This relationship first showed signs of strain in the early 1970s and broke down completely in the 1980s with the ideological confrontation between SAF, on the one hand, and the LO and the SAP on the other. This has led to a change in the nature of party–interest organization relations in Sweden. During the heyday of the "Swedish Model," when governments and the main interest organizations had friendly relations, policymaking was comparatively consensual. The political climate became more confrontational in the 1980s, and even if the level of conflict has not remained constant, the traditional consensual Swedish Model is history. Furthermore, the relationship between other parties and interest organizations has also changed. By using the typology of party-group relations presented in Box 1.2, the development in Sweden can be summarized as follows.

The relationship between SAP and the LO has changed from the most intense form, the Integration/Strong Partisan Model, to the Cooperation/Ideological Model. Organizational and financial links have been weakened, with the abolition of collective membership the most important change. The ideological and strategic elements have become more distanced from each other, and tensions between unions and the party have increased. Members of the Center Party and the LRF have for many years been careful to avoid being seen together in public, although their loosening of ties has not reached the level of increasing tension that exists between SAP and the LO. It is a matter of judgment whether the Center Party–LRF relationship has moved from the Cooperation/Ideological to the Separation/Pragmatic Involvement Model or remained stable. On the whole, however, the relationship is weaker than that between SAP and the LO but is stronger than that between SAF and the Moderates and Liberals. The latter relationship is best described as the Noninvolvement Model. The two groups may agree about many things, but they stay at arm's length. They have never, as have the LO and SAP, portrayed themselves as gallantly fighting the same battle on different fields. The Moderates and Liberals have never received money directly from SAF or organizations connected to SAF, and they stopped accepting business donations in the 1970s.

The overall picture, then, is that traditional links and contacts between parties and interest organizations have declined, as has corporatism. Even though the Social Democratic government made some attempts to revive elements of the corporatist model after returning to power in 1994, the situation in the late 1990s was very different from what it had been before 1970. Organized interests can no longer count on being invited to the loci of power as they were before. New approaches, such as lobbying and opinion formation, are taking over from traditional and institutionalized channels of influence. Thus, we can argue that the relationship between parties and interest organizations has, at least in relative terms, become more conflictual, less structured, and less integrated.

CONCLUSION

Continued change and increasing fluidity in party–interest organization relations in Sweden are likely to continue for three major reasons. First, factors such as the entry of new parties into politics, the relative decline of government dominance by the Social Democrats, and the blurring of traditional left and right ideological party blocs as traditional class boundaries and ties between classes and parties weaken have destabilized the party system and made parties a less reliable channel of influence for interest organizations. Second, increasing decentralization of policymaking, especially policy implementation, from central to local government means that the tradition of sending delegations to meet with central government officials or members of Parliament has become, and will continue to be, less important. And third, an influence that is still difficult to assess fully is Swedish entry into the European Union. The attention of the main interest organizations is now focused on Brussels as much as on Stockholm. Thus, policymaking in Sweden is moving simultaneously toward the local and the supranational levels. Interest organizations have had to adjust their strategies to meet this dual challenge. Therefore, we can expect the changes in party–interest organization relations to continue.

5

The United States: The Paradox of Loose Party-Group Ties in the Context of American Political Development

Clive S. Thomas

Political development in the United States produced a situation where political parties and interest groups have been largely separate, independent entities. Consequently, only a token equivalent exists to the integrative relationships based on organization and strong ideological affinity found between some major parties and groups in many other Western democracies. The party-group connection in the United States has largely been dominated by pragmatism. And bearing in mind that, as in all democracies, the vast majority of groups in the United States have no involvement with parties, for those groups that do the most common modes of interaction are the Cooperation and Separation Models set out in Box 1.2.

These generalizations mask some differences, however. The connection has varied over time—between the national and state levels, according to the type of interest group, and with fifty-one major political systems (the nation plus fifty states). Thus, there is no single dominant American model of party-group relations and, consequently, no single explanation of the effect of the party-group relationship on policymaking and the democratic process.

Yet, although no dominant model exists, this chapter argues that the history and present status of party-group relations in the United States are prime illustrations that these relations are determined by the organizational capacity and the ability and willingness of political parties to perform political functions. In the United States not only have parties been less able or willing to perform many political functions—such as candidate recruitment, campaign financing, and policy development—generally performed by parties in other Western countries, but since the early 1970s their ability to do so has been undermined legally and, to some extent, by their own party rules. As a consequence, interest groups have been given more leeway to perform these functions.

Approaching an examination of party-group relations in the United States is fraught with more problems of delineating the subject matter than in perhaps any other country considered in this book, mainly because what exactly constitutes a party in the United States is less easily defined than the clearly identifiable, often highly centralized organizational structures of many Western European parties. Further, the relationship of many interest groups occurs directly with elected party officials (legislators, governors, and so on) as individuals, particularly in campaigns and lobbying, and not with parties as organizations. Given these problems, three things are important to understand about the focus of this chapter.

First, the focus is not the relationship between *all* parties and *all* groups in the United States. It is the connection between the two major parties—the Democrats and Republicans—and the major traditional interest groups such as business, agriculture, labor, and the professions, as well as some of the major new interests like environmentalists and social issues groups such as women's, minority, and gay rights groups. This relationship between the major parties and major interests has given the party-group connection in the United States its main characteristics. Second, when we refer to the Democratic Party or the Republican Party, we mean their organizational entities as represented by their national or state committees, their congressional or state legislative organizations (such as a party caucus or a party campaign committee like the U.S. Senate's Republican Campaign Committee), and the party as represented in the federal or state executive branch. Sometimes these various entities cooperate and sometimes they do not, but they more or less constitute the organization of the party. Third, although considerable overlap is found between interest group relations with individuals elected as Democrats and Republicans and the two parties as organizations, technically relations with an individual elected official— such as to lobby him or her or provide campaign support through workers and money for that official's personal benefit—are not party-group relations. Therefore, these are excluded from this chapter in favor of focusing on the relations of parties as organizations with interest groups.

EXISTING LITERATURE

As if mirroring the independent, separate nature of the party-group organizational relationship, there has been a division among scholars who study American political parties and interest groups. There are party scholars and there are interest group scholars but rarely scholars who integrate both. As Berry (1997, 44) has noted, this lack of focus on the party-group connection is likely a product more of academic training than of its importance to American politics. The result has been extensive work on political parties, an increasing literature on interest groups, but relatively little work on the essentials and importance of the party-group relationship itself. Even so, with the possible exception of Italy, more is written about aspects of party-group relations as they affect American politics than on any other country in this book.

A review of the major texts on political parties since the mid-1960s reveals that although most touch on interest groups as they affect elections and policy and some address the philosophical/ideological connection, only a few delve deeper into the party-group relationship.[1] Only Key (1964, 154–561) and Cigler (1993) attempt a general treatment of this relationship, although Maisel (1999, chapter 6) gives some attention to groups in the electoral process. A review of the major texts on interest groups reveals a similar story.[2] Parties are touched on as interest groups interact with them in the electoral process and policymaking, but only Berry (1997) focuses explicitly on the party-group relationship and attempts to assess its significance. Even books that combine parties and interest groups pay scant attention to their interrelationship (Ippolito and Walker 1980), although like Maisel and his colleagues (1999, chapter 11) they devote some space to party-group relations in the electoral process.

Of the literature that does exist on the party-group relationship, much has come from work not on the national level but on state politics. After all, the states offer fifty different systems to compare and contrast. Yet attention to the party-group relationship at this level has come much more from the interest group literature than from party literature. Works on state parties deal scantily with the relationship (Mayhew 1986; Jewell and Olson 1988; Bibby and Holbrook 1999). In contrast, much of the work on state interest groups has paid considerable attention to this relationship. Here the major works are by Zeller (1954), Zeigler (1983), Zeigler and van Dalen (1976), Zeigler and Baer (1969), Morehouse (1981, 1997), Hrebenar and Thomas (1987, 1992, 1993a, 1993b), Thomas and Hrebenar (1999a, 1999b), Gray and Lowery (1996), Lowery and Gray (1995), Baer and Dolan (1994), and Wiggins, Hamm, and Bell (1992).

In terms of the substance of the party-group connection, the literature has identified four major elements in the relationship. The first is the cooperative, symbiotic relationship between parties and groups. The focus is principally on cooperation in elections (most notably the financial connection and the rise of political action committees—PACs), in the policymaking process, and to some extent on the philosophical, sometimes ideological level in developing party platforms and policy positions.

The second element is competition between parties and groups, mainly in supporting candidates, recruiting members, and gaining access to policymakers. Although some state politics scholars, particularly those of interest groups, have been concerned about competition, most of this work has been conducted by scholars of national parties and interest groups. In fact, this competition, particularly for funds and members, and its consequences for the changing fortunes of parties in the face of the rise of interest groups since the late 1960s have been the dominant focus of scholars of American national politics concerned with party-group relations. Invariably, their focus is at the institutional level. A slightly different tack is taken by Yonish (1998) and Paddock and Cigler (1997), who although still concerned about party-group competition and party decline approach them from the perspective of the relationship and attitudes of interest group members and leaders and party elites.

The third and fourth elements have been almost the exclusive domain of state interest group scholars. Third is party control of government and competitive versus one-party systems and how they affect politics and policymaking. Fourth is the identification of an inverse power relationship between groups and parties: when parties are strong, groups are weak, and vice versa. From this relationship different party-group systems have been identified in the United States.

What does not exist in the literature is an explanation of party-group relations that synthesizes the existing research. To produce such a synthesis is one of the three purposes of the rest of this chapter. The second is to integrate into this synthesis the recent findings on the four elements of existing research to more fully understand the effects of party-group relations on the U.S. policymaking process and representation. The third purpose is to explain the current relationship by identifying the major factors that have shaped the party-group connection and to trace these influences over time. In combination with the chapter theme of party capacity, these three purposes enable us to provide a comprehensive treatment of the party-group relationship in American politics. Most of the analysis focuses on the connection at the system level, although several references are made to the relations of individual parties and groups.

FACTORS SHAPING PARTY-GROUP RELATIONS IN THE UNITED STATES

Five main factors have shaped the party-group relationship in the United States: the political culture, the government framework, the nature of the American party system and organization, statutory provisions and regulations, and the campaign financing system.

Political Culture

The emphasis in the American political culture—buttressed by the Constitution—on individual rights, as opposed to the more communal political culture of other Western democracies, has had a major influence on the party-group relationship. For example, it is at the root of the party-group financial connection and has stymied attempts to effectively restrict campaign costs and to stem their rapid rise. Individualism, together with other peculiarly American circumstances, helped inhibit the development of any strong ideological cleavages in American society and, in particular, helped undermine the development of a socialist, strong left-wing ideology. Whether this was caused by or a reflection of a weak labor movement is a moot point. But with a low level of American labor belonging to unions (never more than 25 percent and in 1999 about 15 percent, compared with countries such as Sweden with figures close to 80 percent) and business interest fragmented, with no major peak associations, the encompassing nature of American interest groups has always been low compared with Western Europe. Thus, neocorporatist arrangements have been impossible in the United States (Salisbury 1979), which has reinforced the general characteristic of the separate, nonintegrative party-group relationship, at least on a formal basis. As we will see later, however, this separateness has not meant a lack of informal political dependence between parties and interest groups.

Two other elements of the broader American culture that influence the political culture and provide important insights into party-group relations are the all-pervasive effect of the free enterprise system and the American love affair with legalism, stemming again from the nation's largely constitutional, nontraditional origins. The free enterprise system pervades politics perhaps more than in any other Western democracy through the creation of a sort of political marketplace where pragmatism and entrepreneurship among party and group leaders dominate. The almost obsessive American belief in law and regulation as a cure-all for economic and political problems has, as we will see later, been particularly evident in shaping the party-group relationship.

Government Framework

This formal separate, nonintegrative party-group relationship is also in part a product of certain aspects of the government framework, particularly the separation of powers and federalism. The separation of powers system provides many more points of access for interest groups than a parliamentary system and can help foster iron triangles (interest group–legislative committee–government agency integration) that develop their own power bases often independent of party.

The strong position of the states in the American federal system led to a federated party system—fifty-one distinct party systems. This resulted in fifty-one separate party-group systems. Related to this, the political economy of American federalism had a major influence on shaping party-group relations. As James Madison pointed out in the *Federalist,* Number 10, the nation was so diverse—so pluralistic—in terms of interests that no one interest was likely to dominate. Thus, no one interest was likely to control a party and have the whip hand. This was not the case in many of the states that were dominated by one or a few economic interests such as railroads, mining, or forestry. In these places a few interest groups ran the state, and parties were dominated by them.

Nature of the American Party System and Organization

The two major political parties in America were the original "catchall" parties in Western democracies. As such, they have always been vote maximizers as opposed to policy maximizers. Combined with the fact that the two parties are broad, loose coalitions of national and state organizations almost exclusively concerned with gaining and maintaining office, this makes them vulnerable to influence by interest groups that are policy maximizers (Berry 1997, 47). In part, this vulnerability stems from the entrepreneurial orientation of party leaders who constantly seek the aid of those who can get their party into office through electoral support, including campaign contributions.

This was less a problem for parties when there were few interests and the cost of getting elected was relatively low. But the increase in the number of interest groups after the turn of the twentieth century and their mushrooming numbers in the 1960s and 1970s seriously undermined the capacity of parties. In particular, when issue or cause groups—for example, environmentalists such as the Sierra Club and family values groups such as the Christian Coalition—infiltrate and sometimes control a party, they can reduce that party's general electoral appeal because as a policy maximizer less concerned with getting votes than with pushing its own policies, the group forces the party to adopt its issue position and thereby alienate some party supporters. The control of a party by one or a few groups undermines that party's countervailing role in relation to groups in society at large.

Statutory Provisions and Regulations

From the Progressives era of the early 1900s—which, among other things, sought to limit the influence of the railroads by outlawing free railroad passes to legislators and to curb the power of party bosses by the introduction of the primary election to the campaign finance reforms and lobby law legislation since the 1970s—parties and groups have been increasingly subject to statutes and regulations. As a consequence, American parties and interest groups are subject to more legal provisions and regulations than is the case in any other Western democracy (see Ryden 1996, chapter 1; Thomas 1998; Ridley and Greenwood 1998). In particular, in a host of ways, laws and regulations very much define the relationship between American parties and groups, both directly and indirectly. An example of a direct effect is that limitations placed on financial contributions by individuals, interest groups, or both to parties reduce party capacity to fund their candidates and those candidates seek money from elsewhere—particularly interest groups—thus undermining the strength of the party and increasing the influence of groups with party elected officials. An example of an indirect effect is that state primary laws can strengthen or weaken parties vis-à-vis interest groups, with closed primaries tending to increase party control and capacity, and open and blanket primaries tending to undermine them.

This regulation of parties and groups is an element of the American belief that laws can even the political playing field by, among other things, curtailing political corruption and constraining the power of strong political forces like business and labor and, in so doing, enhance the nature of democracy. A good case can be made, however, that in some ways this mass of legal provisions has had unforeseen consequences by undermining the capacity of political parties to perform their essential roles necessary to a healthy democracy.

The Campaign Financing System

Of all the factors shaping contemporary party-group relations in the United States, none is perhaps more important than the nature of the campaign finance system. With the exception of presidential elections, American policymakers have generally eschewed public financing of elections, and through the usual American public policy mode of incrementalism a system has emerged that is a curious combination of the free enterprise ethic and extensive government regulation, particularly involving limits on campaign contributions. Yet although the system limits contributions, it has been unable to stem the rapidly rising cost of campaigns and has been unwilling to place—arguably, constitutionally restricted from placing—limits on campaign expenditures. The consequence has been enormous pressure to find ways around the regulations to meet the increasing costs. In particular, it has produced one of the most prominent phenomena in recent American politics—the political action committee (PAC), an organization usually attached to an interest group whose purpose is to provide funds to get candidates elected. As we will see, the rise of PACs and their use by groups and parties tell much of the story of party-group relations in the United States in recent years.

A BRIEF HISTORY OF PARTY-GROUP RELATIONS

A brief history of how party-group relations developed in the United States will help illustrate the influence of the factors just considered. Although there are common threads in the development of these relations at the national and state levels, there are also some major differences. Therefore, it is useful to consider the two levels separately.

The Pattern of National Party-Group Relations

Down to the New Deal of the 1930s and even as late as the 1960s, parties and groups functioned more or less independent of each other. Parties concentrated on the electoral arena and interest groups on the policy arena (Cigler 1993, 407). This did not mean parties and groups did not interrelate. Farm groups worked within the Democratic Party to get William Jennings Bryan nominated in 1896, and labor leader Samuel Gompers moved labor toward the Democrats around the turn of the twentieth century. Following on Gompers's lead, labor became very close to the Democratic Party (or at least the northern wing of the party) as a result of Franklin Roosevelt's support of many labor issues, and this has proven to be perhaps the longest-standing connection between a party and a group in American politics. Most contact that occurred between parties and groups before the 1960s was delineated in terms of function. With the exception of farmers in the late nineteenth century, for the most part groups did not encroach on the parties' dominance of the electoral process but cooperated with parties to achieve their policy goals.

Despite this delineation, as early as the 1940s some commentators perceived a serious threat to American democracy from what they saw as a major imbalance in the party-group relationship because of a lack of responsible parties and the increasing power of interest groups. These critics contended that when parties are weak the power vacuum is filled by interest groups. In this situation, the argument went, groups undermine majority rule and develop close ties to politicians and party factions, allowing them to prevail over the will of the majority. The strongest advocates of this perspective were Schattschneider (1942) and a report by the American Political Science Association's Committee on Political Parties (APSA 1950). Although controversial (see a critique by Kirkpatrick 1971), the concerns expressed by these commentators reflected an increasing public disaffection with parties and an increasing association with interest groups. From the heyday of parties in the half century following the Civil War, by the late 1960s many Americans believed parties had failed to keep pace with the changing realities of American economic, social, and political life, particularly as represented in the opposition to the Vietnam War and the rise of issue politics. One indication of this was a decline in party affiliation and membership.

This pattern of party decline and a concomitant rise of interest groups was accelerated by two watershed events: the debacle at the Democratic

Party Convention in Chicago in 1968 and the Federal Campaign Act of 1971 and its amendments in 1974, 1976, and 1979. As a result of the first event, the Democratic Party instituted several reforms within the party and in delegate selection for the national convention, including taking power to choose delegates away from state central committees and increasing representation based on gender, race, and age. Although the Republicans did not enact the same reforms, they became more sensitive to representation issues (Cigler 1993, 416–417). Of the many provisions of the Federal Campaign Act, of most interest here is that it provided for public funding of presidential elections and placed limits on campaign contributions to U.S. House and Senate races.

The combined effect of these reforms in party rules and funding considerably altered the balance between parties and interest groups to the extent that from the mid-1970s until the late 1980s, many commentators foresaw the demise of parties and the dominance of American national politics by interest groups (see, for example, Lowi 1979; Crotty 1984) or, at the least, saw parties being reduced to the status of interest groups (Frantzich 1989). Two developments particularly undermined the effectiveness of parties because they involved interest groups seriously encroaching on the nomination and electoral roles of parties.

One development was the increased role of interest groups, particularly issue groups, in party affairs and in the run-up to the national convention. In the Democratic Party these were groups like environmentalists and gay rights activists. The Republican Party had groups from the religious right, like the Christian Coalition and the Moral Majority, which were able to exert an enormous influence on the party's platform and to take over some state Republican parties as did the Christian Coalition in Texas (Berry 1997, 54). In many ways Schattschneider's worst fears had been realized— the parties had become just a collection of interest groups. The second and perhaps more important development was the phenomenal rise of PACs. The number of federal PACs rose from 608 in 1974 to 4,200 in 1990 and accounted for about 40 percent of the cost of all U.S. House races and 25 percent of the cost of U.S. Senate races (Cigler 1993, 420). This accelerated the trend toward candidate-centered elections at the national level and decreased reliance on parties by candidates. Parties seemed less and less relevant to American life (Berry 1980), and this was reflected in the attitudes of Americans, particularly the young, who saw interest groups as much more politically efficacious than parties (see Table 5.1).

But the two national parties did not die—they fought back. In many ways they did so by becoming interest groups of their own. They reformed party rules to give party leaders a greater say in nominations and rule making. They began to court PACs to give money to them rather than to individual candidates, a course of action aided considerably by the loophole of

Table 5.1 Interest Groups and Political Parties as Representative Organizations

Question: Which kind of organizations best represent your political interests—organized groups concerned with specific issues such as business, labor, environmental, and civil rights groups or the two major political parties?

Age Group	Interest Groups (%)	Political Parties (%)
All	45	34
18–24	56	21
25–34	56	27
35–44	44	41
45–65	41	40
65+	27	42

Source: "Why Junior and Granddad Don't Talk Politics," *National Journal*, 10 March 1984, 492.

so-called soft money—contributions made directly to the party for party-building efforts that are not subject to the limitations that apply to individual candidates. As a result of these developments, there was a party resurgence in the 1990s, most clearly illustrated by the Republican congressional victory in the 1994 elections and their ability to affect the national policy agenda. Even before this victory, however, research by several scholars (for example, Rohde 1991; Aldrich and Rohde 1997–1998) demonstrated that strong legislative coordination can be developed within parties to dominate political agendas and constrain interest groups.

The Incremental Pattern of Changing State Party-Group Relations

The development of party-group relations at the state level did not exhibit the same short-term transformation that occurred in the 1970s at the national level. The state pattern is one of long dominance by interest groups with some increased pluralization in the states since 1970 that in some states has included an increase in the role of parties.

The lack of economic diversity in all states at some point in time meant they all went through eras in which one or a few interests dominated state politics. During the late nineteenth and early twentieth centuries, all forty-eight contiguous states experienced politics dominated by railroad interests. In California it was the Southern Pacific; in North Dakota, Montana, Idaho, and Washington the Northern Pacific and the Great Northern; in Kentucky the Louisville & Nashville Railroad; and in Maryland the Baltimore & Ohio. As late as the 1950s Texas politics was dominated by the big four—oil, chemicals, the Texas Manufacturers Association, and, again, the railroads. Maine's politics was long dominated by the big three—electric power, timber, and textile and shoe manufacturing—while Iowa's politics was heavily influenced by agriculture and agribusiness interests (corn and hog farmers and farm implement manufacturers), truckers, and the insurance industry. The oil industry was dominant in Louisiana and Oklahoma; the Farm Bureau, county courthouses, and utilities in many southern states; salmon canneries, mining, forestry, and shipping interests in Alaska.

These circumstances led several scholars to classify states according to the strength of their interest group systems and the corresponding weakness of their party systems (Zeller 1954, 190–193; Morehouse 1981, chapter 3; Zeigler 1983). The general consensus was that the South had the strongest groups and weakest parties, followed by the West and the Midwest, with groups less powerful in the Northeast and parties the most effective. Relations between parties and individual groups ranged from virtually no interaction between groups and the almost nonexistent parties of the southern states to informal but close ties between labor and Democrats and business and labor in states like Illinois, Massachusetts, and New York.

Beginning in the late 1960s and early 1970s, a confluence of factors worked to pluralize state politics, including an increase in the number and range of interest groups—such as environmentalists, women's advocates, and public employees, among many others—reflecting major changes in the socioeconomic life of the states. Then, following the Watergate scandal in 1973–1974, there was a wave of enactments of lobby laws across the states, including disclosure of group expenditures and restrictions or prohibitions on contributions by certain groups (Thomas 1998). These developments have meant that although some states still have one or more prominent interests—the Mormon Church in Utah, Boeing in Washington State, the coal companies in West Virginia, for example—the days of states being dominated by one or a few interests are likely gone forever. A time series study stretching from the mid-1980s to the late 1990s verifies the overall reduction in states dominated by interest groups but also shows the continued strength of interests relative to parties in most states (Thomas and Hrebenar 1999b).

Thus, until the Republicans swept into power at the national level and across the states in the 1994 elections, the diluting of interest group power in most states did not mean an increase in party influence or parties playing a greater role in the policy process as aggregators of the general interest. The political capacity of most state parties remained low, although with the rise of the Republicans in the South, both Democrats and Republicans established viable organizations in the region and its states. Part of the reason for the continued weakness of parties was that, like national parties, those in the states were also hit by increased campaign costs and began to rely increasingly on PACs for funds as the number of those organizations also mushroomed in the states. In many states such as New York and Washington, PACs and interest groups are the major source of campaign funds, and more and more states are falling into this category (Craine, Haven, and Horner 1995). As at the national level, however, state parties have also used PACs and taken advantage of soft money. The Republican victories in 1994 and since have given legislative parties more strength and coordination, and to that extent there has been a resurgence of the GOP in many states.

Yet as stated earlier, this does not necessarily reduce the power of certain groups but probably gives those with long-standing close ties to the GOP—like business and certain right-wing social issue groups—more influence. It has also caused traditional allies of the Democrats, like the National Education Association's affiliates in the states, to become more pragmatic in their campaign support (Thomas and Hrebenar 1999a). This reinforces a long tradition in the states of groups being pragmatic and playing both sides of the political fence even though they may have policy or even ideological leanings toward one party. As at the national level, a good case can be made that many state parties are in fact vote-maximizing interest groups.

THE ROLE OF THE PARTY-GROUP CONNECTION AND ITS EFFECTS ON THE POLITICAL SYSTEM

With the information presented in the last two sections, we can now assess the role and effects of the party-group relationship on American politics. Generalizing about this role and its effects, particularly on policymaking and representation, is difficult, in part because little direct research is available but also because, by extrapolation from the existing literature and based on my own research, the effect appears to be different in different places. However, we can first make some general observations and then examine and offer some reassessments of the four major areas of concern in the existing literature—party-group cooperation, party-group competition, party control of government and the effect of competitive party systems, and the power relationship of parties and groups.

General Observations

Although parties and interest groups did not lay the groundwork for the fragmented nature of the American political system, their lack of an integrated organizational relationship, among many other factors, helps to perpetuate this fragmentation, which is perhaps the major hallmark of the American system. Much of the paramount importance of money in politics in the United States can also be traced to the party-group relationship, particularly the rise of PACs and parties' increasing dependence on groups in elections. The often pragmatic, entrepreneurial nature of this relationship, as opposed to a more philosophical/ideological one, has also helped give the American political system its political marketplace character.

When parties and major interest groups are well integrated as a result of their mutual organizational strength and ideological affinity, it produces a smoother policy process and parallels the situation in many parliamentary democracies. On the other hand, when tension exists between the parties and interest groups, when one dominates the other, or when they essentially go their separate ways, the policy process is stymied. The latter situation has historically been the norm in the United States, and this tension between the two organizations has been at the root of much of the policy deadlock associated with the American political system.

To put things in perspective, however, much of the policy process in the United States—federal and state—is unaffected by the party-group relationship or is only one part, often a minor part, of the larger strategy of many groups. The power bases of individual legislators and their electoral and ideological relationship with groups are probably more important for determining the role of interests in the policy process. This in turn has led to the legislative committee–interest group–agency connection (the so-called iron triangle), which is likely more important overall to most groups than their relationship with parties.

Given this fact, in terms of the classification of party-group relations set out in Box 1.2, most of the estimated 150,000 interest groups that exist at the national and state levels would fall under the Separation/Pragmatic Model. However, some of them may never have contact with parties while others may have some contact, even if rarely, but remain essentially separate, so it is useful to distinguish between a Separation and a Noninvolvement category.

Of those groups that do have contact with parties, no tradition has ever existed that makes the Integration category, as set out in Box 1.2, an important one. Certainly, there are examples of the Integration Model from the past such as in 1828, when labor leaders in Philadelphia formed the Workingman's Labor Party; when farmers, through the Grange and other organizations, formed the Greenback-Labor Party and the Populist Party (Cigler 1993, 411); and today, with the Christian Coalition using the Republican Party as a means of advancing its policies through infiltration. But it is clear that the Cooperation/Ideological and Separation/Pragmatic Involvement Models best encapsulate the interaction of American parties and groups.

Three Major Aspects of Party-Group Cooperation

One major specific aspect of the party-group connection in the United States is the symbiotic element that leads to cooperation, if sometimes uneasy cooperation. Cooperation occurs in three major ways: through the electoral connection, in policy development and promotion, and through philosophical affinity.

Electoral cooperation. Although many groups that have relations with parties provide campaign workers and other forms of nonfinancial electoral aid to parties and candidates, as we have seen, the financial connection is paramount in the party-group electoral relationship in terms of overall effect on the political process. As we have also seen, business and the professions, labor, and increasingly new interests such as environmentalists, through financial contributions—particularly by establishing PACs—have become a major source of campaign funds at both the federal and state levels since the 1970s. Although in many cases PAC funds are given directly to candidates and not to parties, their aggregate effect is to elect one party or the other to Congress and state legislatures and to elect a president as well as chief executives and other executive officers in the states. Groups give money for three main reason: to secure access to policymakers in the policymaking process, for philosophical reasons, or a combination of the two. With increased competition among groups for the attention of public officials, the trend is for more and more groups to establish PACs and engage in the electoral process.

The upshot is an extreme form of a symbiotic relationship—one in which there is increasing dependence between parties and groups, perhaps more so than at any time in U.S. history. Parties and candidates have an increasing appetite for funds as campaign costs soar. Groups need public officials and party support to promote their policy agendas, and gaining access to a party in the electoral process has proven very effective as a foundation for pursuing a policy agenda. This increasingly important electoral-financial connection is probably the most important bonding factor between parties and groups in the United States today.

Policy development and promotion. It is an obvious, though not to be forgotten, fact that as parties control government and American interest groups do not seek to do so, groups need parties to support and promote their policy goals. This is also a major bonding force between parties and groups. Some groups attempt to get their policies into party platforms (Berry 1997). But party platforms are often only window dressing in the United States, so it is more effective to work closely with a party during the policy process to secure group objectives. Here we can identify some broad relationships in that business groups tend to work more with Republicans and labor and social issue groups with the Democrats, but that is not always the case and the situation varies from state to state, if less at the national level. It is evident that more important in this policy connection are the financial relationship during the preceding election, political pragmatism, and—something not often considered in the party-group relationship—party competition and control of government. The influence of party competition and control is considered in the next section.

Philosophical affinity. Although an obvious affinity exists between certain groups and the two major political parties in the United States, this is also subject to political pragmatism and ad hoc circumstances in the policy process. The nature of American parties as broad coalitions, geared more to winning elections than to implementing a philosophy, and the divisions within party ranks, such as the long-standing cleavage between southern and northern Democrats, does not in practice lead to a high degree of philosophical and ideological loyalty. The fact that divided government often occurs (Republicans controlling one branch, the Democrats the other) also negates strong philosophical affinity. Such affinity occurs mainly at the ends of the political spectrum—for example, the right-to-life and other family values groups aligned with the right wing of the Republican Party. As with party-group cooperation in the policy process, cooperation resulting from philosophical affinity is also affected by party competition and party control of government, as we will see later.

In sum, it is argued here that the actual level and extent of cooperation will vary from system to system (nation and states) depending on the organizational capacity and political role of parties. Further evidence of the claim that party-group relations are shaped primarily by the organizational capacity and political functions parties are able and willing to develop and perform is provided by examining the effects of party competition and control of a legislature and executive at the national and state levels.

Party-Group Competition or Complementary Roles?

Although the relationship of the two major parties to major groups is one of cooperation, considerable attention has been given recently to what has been viewed in the literature as competition between them. Scholars have identified three elements of competition between parties and groups that result from their overlapping functions: as vehicles of political representation and influence in securing policy objectives, which manifests itself mainly in competition for members; as providers of information, both technical and political, to public officials; and from their role as sources of electoral support, particularly as providers of campaign funds. The relatively homogeneous constituency and narrowly defined goals of interest groups often make them more effective agents of representation for specific interests than parties. Parties have been less effective because they are essentially broad coalitions of interests, are often rather factionalized, and tend to pursue broad issues and policies as opposed to the concerns of small and narrow group interests. Consequently, those seeking specific policy goals at the national and state levels (particularly in the South and West) have been more likely to use an interest group rather than a political party. The obvious success of interest groups in this regard since the 1970s had led many scholars to argue that parties were in serious decline (Crotty 1984), although others have been less pessimistic (Maisel 1990).

But in reality, is there really competition between parties and groups in these three overlapping functions? Do parties and groups see themselves as rivals here? Do policymakers see this as an either-or choice? Does the public see party or group membership and the roles of each organization as mutually exclusive? Evidence suggests that much of what has been viewed as competition is really complementary activity. Over the years the narrower constituency and policy focus of interest groups have enabled them to adapt more easily and quickly than parties to changes in the political environment. The loose-knit and low-budget organization of most state parties has meant they have not been geared up to provide information on issues, whereas this has been a primary purpose of interest groups. In these and other circumstances, interest groups often fill the political void left by parties. That is, groups often take over roles and functions, like funding elections and recruiting candidates, when parties cannot or will not perform them. And parties and groups often share the function of seeking benefits. In short, groups adapt to the organizational and political activities of parties.

One reason for the belief that increased competition exists between parties and groups and that groups have "won" this battle is that group activity has spiraled in recent years and more and more people are joining groups. But we must remember that the vast majority of interest group activity, as Stanley Hoffmann's well-known characterization conveys, falls under "low politics," involving low-profile work on regulations and other minutiae that affect groups but are of little interest to anyone else, including political parties. So most interest group activity in the policy process is nonpartisan and technical and does not occur at the expense of parties.

Although an element of competition no doubt is found between parties and groups, especially for members, the most accurate assessment is probably that the party-group relationship has gone through a major transition since 1970. Even though parties may have declined in power and as vehicles of representation since the late 1960s, they are not going to disappear; the symbiotic relationship between parties and groups and the unique functions of parties—such as organizing legislatures—will dictate that. What has happened, however, as in other periods of U.S. political history, is that the party-group relationship has undergone change at the national level, across the states, and within particular states. And this involves more than just the increasing power of interest groups. For instance, the move toward the Republicans in Washington, D.C., and across the states since the mid-

1990s has triggered a party reassertion of power—at least for the GOP—in relation to many interest groups.

Party Control of Government and Competitive Party Systems

Party control of government and competitive party systems affect interest group activity in rather contradictory ways—by creating policy uncertainty in some instances and clear policy direction in others (Morehouse 1997). When moderate or liberal Democrats control a legislature or an executive, their heterogeneity in terms of the groups within their ranks and their support for reform policies often cause policy uncertainty and increased group activity. Party control is also important in giving certain groups an advantage in access and influence. Moderate and liberal Democrats and sometimes moderate Republicans favor certain groups, which usually include unions and liberal causes. These interests lose out when strong conservative Republicans or conservative Democrats are in control. Since the national and state Republican victories in 1994, business and pro-development interests and those favoring privatization of many government services have risen in prominence at the expense of traditional and public-sector unions and liberal causes (Thomas and Hrebenar 1999a).

For many years it was argued that party competition was evidence of strong party cohesion, and this stifled group activity (Key 1964, 154–165; Morehouse 1981, 116–118, 127; Zeigler 1983, 111–117; Zeigler and van Dalen 1976, 94–95; Zeller 1954, 190–193). Recent work belies that assumption, however. With changes in party control, all types of groups may find their vital interests adversely affected, so more groups mobilize to protect their cause. Party competition also increases the number of groups by raising the chances of political success for certain interests and makes public officials, particularly legislators, more attentive to a wider range of interests. This is not the case in a noncompetitive party environment. In this situation groups associated with the minority party have little chance of success, while those associated with the majority party or coalition are successful most of the time (Lowery and Gray 1995; Gray and Lowery 1996, 204, 244). Consequently, party competitive states often produce a nonpartisan or bipartisan lobbying community. In this situation the entrepreneurial skill of lobbyists and group leaders is crucially important. They need to support each party, not to the extent that they antagonize the other party but enough to ensure access after an election.

The Party-Group Power Relationship: A New Perspective

Observing what they considered to be a competitive element in the party-group relationship, several scholars concluded that an inverse relationship exists between party strength and group strength within a political system such as the nation or a state. That is, strong parties, such as in the Northeast, dictate weak interest groups, and weak parties, such as in the South, result in strong interest groups (Key 1964, 154–165; Morehouse 1981, 116–118, 127; Zeigler 1983, 111–117; Zeigler and van Dalen 1976, 94–95; Zeller 1954, 190–193). This power relationship is complex, however, and evidence suggests that it is not as directly inverse as once believed. In fact, viewing it primarily as a power relationship is rather misleading. Generally, the stronger the party, the more control it has in determining the policy agenda and ensuring its passage. Strong parties also control the access of interests and interest groups to the policymaking process. The weaker a party, the more leeway other elements of the political system have to fill the power vacuum. Because of the close linkage between parties and interest groups and particularly their overlapping functions, this vacuum is filled largely by interest groups.

Although there is clearly some form of power relationship between American parties and groups and an inverse relationship may once have existed and may continue in some form today, recent evidence suggests that the theory needs serious revision and perhaps discarding. Often (but not always) weak parties do produce strong interest groups, as in parts of the South and West; but strong parties often go hand in hand with strong interest groups, as New York, Illinois, and Michigan attest. Several lines of research have undermined this simple two-dimensional, inverse relationship theory (if, indeed, it was ever valid), including a greater understanding of the relationship and access of individual groups to parties, the fact that strong and effective party organization is not necessarily a constraint on access and influence and for certain groups may even enhance them, and the fact that other factors—such as a strong executive or a political culture—may affect this party-group power relationship or fill power vacuums. For example, both South Dakota and Vermont have moderate to weak interest group systems, which according to the old theory would lead to the conclusion that they have strong parties. This is not the case: South Dakota has a weak party system and Vermont a moderate one with increasing party competition. In South Dakota a strong governorship fills this void, and Vermont also has a strong executive plus a socially oriented political culture (Mayhew 1986, 153, 168; Hrebenar and Thomas 1993a, chapter 13; 1993b, chapter 12).

This aspect of party-group relations is best viewed not as a power relationship, which leads to either a group power or party power dichotomy, but as one of different types of access and influence patterns that can exhibit elements of cooperation, some complementary elements, some competition, or a combination of all three. In essence, then, this "power relationship"–access patterns relationship is another aspect of groups' adaptation to the organizational capacity and political role of parties.

CONCLUSION

One observer of the party-group connection in the United States has described the relationship as "competitive, yet symbiotic" (Cigler 1993, 407). Bearing in mind that most groups in the United States do not have relations with parties, for those that do in this chapter we have gone further and claimed that this symbiotic relationship is one of increasing dependence. At first glance this may seem to contradict the fact that the United States has had only a token history of the Integration form of party-group relations usually associated with dependence. Indeed, the separate organizational origins of parties and groups and the Cooperation and Separation forms under which most party-group relations fall would lead to a prediction that these relations would be more autonomous than those in countries with a history of an Integration relationship of parties and groups.

However, the nature of American political development has produced a much different situation. In particular, the lack of ideology and the consequent emphasis on extreme political pragmatism, the free enterprise ethic extended to politics, and the American belief in law and regulation as a cure-all for perceived political ills, among other things, combined to produce a unique situation in which parties have often had less desire and capacity to shape their relationship with groups. Thus, although the situation varies from time to time, from nation to states, and among states, parties have often been weak and vulnerable to group infiltration and control and dependent on groups for electoral support, particularly money. Consequently, the paradox is that loose formal ties—the Cooperative and Separation modes of relationship—mask increasing dependence based on the circumstances of American politics, particularly the election process. Further, the closer groups get to parties, the more the countervailing role of parties is undermined. And a constant fear is present in the United States that a campaign finance system based on PAC money undermines democracy.

Yet, although American parties have generally been weak and lacked the will or capacity to shape the party-group relationship, they have proven very resilient, in part by becoming interest groups of their own with the goal of vote maximization and by aggressively pursuing PAC funding for the party and funneling it to their candidates. But even without such entrepreneurial leadership, parties would not have been totally eclipsed because, as in all democracies, parties and groups are not completely interchangeable as political institutions and perform many different, as well as some overlapping, functions. Combining a reinterpretation, as presented earlier, of the party-group "power relationship" and that of their "competitive"-complementary connection with the elements of their cooperation moves us some way to a fuller understanding.

In many ways the peculiarities of the American party-group connection are clear evidence that the crucial importance of individual circumstances in a country is the major determinant of these relations. Because of the nature of American political development, the party-group relationship may, paradoxically, be more important in shaping politics and policy in the United States than in many countries generally considered to have a long tradition of close party-group ties.

Part 2

The Post–World War II Democracies

6

Germany: The Continuing Dominance of Neocorporatism

Winand Gellner and John D. Robertson

Although descriptions of political party–interest group relations may be difficult to apply to some political systems, a decade after unification Germany clearly remains a "classic" neocorporatist political economy. Thus, structural and functional relations between the major political parties and "big player" interest groups are still solid, institutionalized, and largely governed by peak associations that continue to serve their traditional roles of stabilizing and strengthening the postwar German democracy. With a highly skilled workforce, an export-based economy built on sophisticated manufactured goods and services, a divided nation (until 1990) in the center of Europe, and the legacy of a failed Weimar Republic serving as the backdrop, the regulated and highly coordinated nature of a neocorporatist society was much more than a merely temporary experiment on the road to ordinary pluralist democracy. This neocorporatist political economy is built around institutionalized bargaining between government and peak associations of labor, business, and agriculture. Although this system of concerted action weakened during the 1990s, it remains the defining aspect of German party-group relations and shapes both the content of major policies and the strategy for securing them within the German Federal Republic (FRG) (Hollingsworth 1997; Streek 1992).

Since the 1970s the dominance of neocorporatist arrangements linking parties, through government, to the peak associations within Germany has also spawned a vibrant array of social movements (Koopman 1995). This is evidenced most by the success of ecological and antinuclear groups, with formal representation in the Green Party. However, social movements remain clearly secondary in measured impact, largely because of their peripheral role in traditional neocorporatist structures (Halfmann 1989; Koopman 1995).

With these fundamental factors in mind, in this chapter we explore four questions: (1) What is the nature of the relationship between parties and groups in historical perspective; (2) What shapes the party-group relationship today, and what factors are working to modify it; (3) What are the general patterns to the relationship between parties and groups; and (4) What are some specific arenas of party-group relations in the FRG today—including within parliament, the executive, and other areas of contact—and how does the relationship play out in those arenas?

The essence of the argument we present is as follows. Although in the twentieth century Germany was a major player in international politics—including defeat in two world wars, occupation by the Allies, and as a prominent member of the European Union—and thus external forces have played a part in shaping the party-group connection and will be increasingly important in the future, the major explanation for past, present, and likely future party-group relations is to be found in factors internal to the German political economy.

THE PARTY-GROUP RELATIONSHIP IN RECENT GERMAN HISTORY

In this section we provide an overview of how political parties and interest groups have interacted in the policy process since the late nineteenth century. This review supports our thesis that in the main, internal factors of German politics have shaped party–interest group interactions.

In general, interest groups dominated party factions at the end of the nineteenth century and into the early twentieth century, in part because the character of the authoritarian state allowed no room for political parties, which were supposedly harmful to the common good, whereas interest groups developed as the result of the social and economic emancipation process. This process laid the foundations for class and representative organizations to flourish throughout Germany. The relationship changed during the Weimar Republic when political parties evolved into more powerful institutional actors, although they remained subject to deep suspicion and contempt by a large section of the German electorate (Hesse and Ellwein 1992). As a result of persistent suspicion and disdain for parties, interest groups were able to sustain their influence during this period of political and economic instability. Thus, a pattern of competition and cooperation, dominated by interest groups, best describes the relationship between political parties and interest groups in the period between 1919 and 1933.

For example, the forerunner of the present Federation of German Industry (BDI), which organizes major industrial groupings, was the Reichsverband der Deutschen Industrie (Reich Association of German Industries), the central organization of German industry at the time. The organization was particularly influential in the executive bureaucracy and virtually ignored parties and parliament. All of its top-level officers had been former bureaucrats in the German Reich under the kaiser. In addition, the Reichsverband was the first organization to use the newly institutionalized *Geschäftsordnung* (rules of procedure established to systematize organization contact with the executive and departments) for lobbying. Another equally successful lobby in the Weimar Republic was farmers' groups. In times of chronic political instability, caused in particular by the parties of the extreme left and right, the bureaucracy was the only lasting and reliable political institution (Ullmann 1988, 138–142, 178–179).

The victory of Nazism and the rise of the Third Reich brought a complete reversal of this pattern, with total domination by a single totalitarian mass political party over society and its various mediating organizations. By the late 1940s, however, this relationship had been totally discarded in the western regions of the old Reich with the emergence of the FRG. Political parties became the primary instruments of democratic consensus and stability within the new democracy. To ensure that parties would be the vehicles through which both interest articulation and aggregation would be assured in the new Germany, parties were constitutionally designed to largely dominate interest groups within the policy process. As we will see in more detail later, the FRG's Basic Law (*Grundgesetz*) guarantees political parties an explicit right to participate in decisions concerning the formulation of public opinion and political demands and objectives (Article 21). This ensures a basic element of parliamentary democracy, which in the German case has been described as a multiparty state or a multi–political party democracy (Haungs 1981; Leibholz 1952; S. Padgett 1993).

The way parties and groups have related to and affected policymaking and democracy in this new German system, given the predominant place reserved for parties and within the context of continuing neocorporatism, is the subject of the rest of this chapter. Although some publications make passing reference to the party-group relationship in Germany (for example, Dalton 1993; Katzenstein 1989) and some deal with it indirectly in investigating topics like social movements and parliamentary behavior (for example, Crouch and Menon 1997; Koopman 1995; Kropp 1997), there is no general work on the subject. Therefore, this chapter synthesizes numerous sources to develop the first specific treatment of the past and particularly the contemporary forms and consequences of this central relationship in German politics.

CONTEMPORARY POLITICAL PARTY AND INTEREST GROUP "BIG PLAYERS"

Political Parties

The big players within the German party system today are the right-center Christian Democratic Union (CDU) and its Bavarian-based sister party, the

Christian Social Union (CSU); the left-center Social Democratic Party (SPD); the Free Democratic Party (FDP); the "postmaterialist" Alliance '90/Greens; and the leftist Party of Democratic Socialism (PDS). The CDU currently claims 636,000 members (just over 1 percent of the 60.5 million eligible German voters), and the CSU has another 180,000 members. The two parties together control 35 percent of the 676-member Bundestag, the lower chamber of Germany's Federal Parliament. The CDU-CSU was the plurality party *fraktion* (the caucuses of each political party) within the Bundestag from 1983 through the September 1998 general elections. CDU leader Helmut Kohl served as chancellor from October 1982 until his resignation in the fall of 1998.

The SPD has around 774,000 members and, following the 1998 general elections, controls 41 percent of the seats in the Bundestag, making it the largest party (in terms of seats) in the Federal Republic's 14th Bundestag session. The party is currently led by centrist Gerhard Schröder, who replaced the more leftist Oskar Lafontaine in April 1999. Schröder was elected German federal chancellor following the September 1998 general elections (*Deutschland*, No. 3, January 1998).

The Free Democrats claim 69,000 members and control 6 percent of the seats in the Bundestag as of 1999. The Alliance '90/Greens claim 50,000 members and control just under 7 percent of the seats in the 14th Federal Bundestag. The party developed from the merger of the Green Party (Die Grünen), originally founded in 1980 around ecological and antinuclear issues, and a number of opposition groups from eastern Germany. In 1998 the Alliance '90/Greens joined the SPD to form a coalition government for Germany. The PDS, a leftist rump of the former East German Communist party (Socialist Unity Party—SED), has 96,000 members, mostly from the Länder of the former German Democratic Republic (GDR). Following the September 1998 election, the PDS controlled 5 percent of the seats in the German Federal Parliament (*Deutschland*, No. 4, April 1998).

Interest Groups

Although there are currently thousands of interest groups in Germany, the big players are organized around occupational groupings, as one would expect given the economic priorities of the postwar German Federal Republic. These big players are professionally staffed, hierarchically organized within the German federal system, and devoted to a broad range of social, political, and economic issues of crucial importance to their broad-ranging membership and affiliates. They not only pressure members of the German Federal Parliament and their Länder counterparts throughout the republic, but they have been at the forefront of strong lobbying efforts in the European Union (EU), in both Brussels and Strasbourg, since the 1992 Maastricht Treaty.

German labor and its various unions are represented by the German Trade Union Federation (DGB), which claims to represent 85 percent of the approximately 10 million unionized workers in the German workforce (31 percent of German workers were unionized as of 1995). Because of the FRG's codetermination laws (*Mitbestimmung*—worker representation on company boards), the DGB has maintained close working relations with both the CDU and the CSU, as well as with its natural ally, the SPD. Approximately half of the board members of the 482 largest firms in Germany are elected union members, the vast majority associated with the DGB. The neocorporatist logic of Germany requires that the DGB be an active player in negotiations among government, business, and labor regarding wage levels and pension schemes, as well as actively participating in the shaping of federal policy in both the bureaucracy and the various Bundestag committees (Thelen 1991).

The two peak associations representing employers' interests are the BDI, organizing thirty-nine separate major industrial groups, and the Federation of German Employers' Associations (BDA), consisting of sixty-four employer associations that represent nearly all large and medium-sized businesses within the Federal Republic. The BDI is the more political of the two. It represents employers' interests with government, within the Bundestag, and on various social and economic planning committees at the federal level. The BDA works more closely with unions, negotiating wage levels, pensions, social security, health benefits, and other matters concerning working conditions in Germany (Edinger 1986, 184–186; Essen 1986; Dalton 1993, 238–253).

In addition to the BDI and the BDA, the German Industrial and Trade Conference (DIHT) represents the venerable German *Mittelstand,* or small and medium-sized businesses. Although not as publicly visible as the BDI or the BDA, the DIHT is a powerful force within the German political economy and is a major player in structuring policy and coordinating interests among government, business, and labor. The *Mittelstand* is defined specifically as employers within industry, commerce, skilled trades, and service sectors who employ fewer than 500 persons and have a gross sales turnover of less than 100 million marks annually. As of 1996 it consisted of approximately 3 million small and medium-sized firms. In the new federal states of the former GDR, the *Mittelstand* alone accounts for 500,000 small and medium-sized enterprises that provide more than 3 million skilled jobs for German workers. Across the republic as a whole, the *Mittelstand* represents 99.6 percent of all enterprises subject to German VAT (value added tax) laws, accounts for over half of all sales in Germany, employs over two-thirds of the German workforce, trains nearly 80 percent of apprentices and trainees, and accounts for 44 percent of the gross value added to the German gross domestic product. Germany's federal and state governments maintain approximately 600 different programs designed to assist the *Mittelstand* (*Deutschland,* No. 3, June 1996).

Although naturally closer to the center-right CDU-CSU, these three employer associations have also maintained close working relationships with the SPD. Indeed, with the election of Schröder as chancellor (and especially following the resignation of the more left-wing Lafontaine as SPD chair in April 1999), these three associations have found a more sympathetic ally than they likely imagined.

The German agricultural sector is represented by the German Farmers Association (DBV). Much smaller in size than the major employer and union peak associations, the DBV nonetheless has fervently and tenaciously defended the interests of German farmers. This role has become increasingly important as German farmers have fought to stave off assaults on the European Union's Common Agriculture Policy farm subsidies and threats posed by the expansion of the EU, particularly threats to farm support within the union.

Dalton (1993, 266–267) reported that German citizens clearly perceive partisan preferences among the various peak associations. Seventy-four percent of German citizens (within the western Länder) see unions as pro-SPD, 65 percent see business peak associations as pro-CDU-CSU, and 57 percent see farmers as pro-CDU-CSU.

INTERNAL FACTORS IN CONTEMPORARY GERMAN PARTY-GROUP RELATIONS

The diverse but often separate literature on political parties and interest groups draws attention to a number of crucial factors shaping the complex relationship between political institutions and agents of interest aggregation and articulation. Central to this relationship are the lessons of the past that pervade a nation's broader political culture and the constitutional rules that have evolved over time in response to these cultural influences. No country more clearly illustrates these factors at work than the German Federal Republic's liberal democracy. In less than a century the German public has been governed by an imperial monarchy, a semipresidential system, a totalitarian dictatorship in both fascist and communist manifestations, and a parliamentary federal democracy. More recently, the FRG has absorbed the former GDR, ushering in yet another chapter in the complex saga of German politics. Today Germany stands as a model of both political and economic consistency, tempered by a distinct blend of statist authority and balanced with a healthy commitment to political decentralization, mobilized civic participation, and centralized economic coordination that has earned the German Federal Republic a reputation as a stable but flexible democracy.

As explained earlier, the contemporary German democracy is best described as a neocorporatist liberal democracy (Crouch and Menon 1997, 152–154). This classification requires that party-group relations be placed within the context of the unique structural perspective of the German democracy as of the 1990s, in part because this party-group relationship is very much affected by the two critical issues confronting the contemporary German neocorporatist political economy. First, the new Germany must successfully manage its precarious balance between a historical and a cultural commitment to state welfare in the face of an aging population and an increasingly competitive world trade system. Second, in seeking to protect and extend the export-based German political economy, the big players must not only manage the historically complex flow of critical pressures at work in the relationship between political parties and interest groups but must also face up to the difficult tasks of long overdue institutional reform such as improving labor relations and banking laws, structural transformation such as fully integrating eastern Länder, and managing the federal system within a broadened European Union.

In line with the basic argument of this chapter, in analyzing the party-group relationship in Germany it is useful to distinguish between internal factors shaping the relationship and the most important external factors affecting it. As we argue that internal factors are more important, particularly in past and contemporary Germany, in this section we focus on those factors and leave external factors to a later section.

The first important internal factor affecting this relationship in Germany is the nature and structure of the federal system (Reuter 1991). German federalism segments the political economy and determines the strategy of party-group interaction within the Federal Republic. The pattern of interaction among government ministries, unions, employer associations, and interest groups is sectionalized and decentralized in accordance with the federal constitutional design of the German democracy (S. Padgett 1993, 12; Klatt 1993; Leonardy 1993).

Second, the modern German democracy is designed to maximize two central components of the contemporary German political culture: the priority of a welfare state system and the demands of economic efficiency. This combination is usually associated with small European liberal democracies such as the Netherlands, Belgium, and Austria, but it is also true of Germany. In combination with the history preceding the current constitutional democracy of Germany, this balance imposes strict discipline on the major institutional actors within that democracy. This discipline is designed to coordinate interests and priorities through a neocorporatist strategy to ensure a degree of political-economic stability and certitude consistent with the expectations of welfare priorities and economic competitiveness and success (Katzenstein 1989). To illustrate this we can use the example of *Konzertierte Aktion* (concentrated action). Initiated between 1966 and 1969 by then secretary for the economy Karl Schiller, the process successfully brought together representatives from, among others, the DGB, DIHT, BDI, and the large metalworkers' trade union, IG-Metall, to achieve a compromise over economic policy rather than increased competition among the major groups involved (Von Beyme 1969, 123–133). Almost thirty years later the new Social Democratic government sought to emulate that successful role model by creating a Bündnis für Arbeit (Alliance for Jobs). This time, however, business groups have been reluctant to join, although they still cooperate (*Die Welt,* 7 July 1999).

Third, a clear appreciation of the party-group relationship must take into account the unique legal provision stipulated in the German constitution regarding the formal role of political parities. This constitutional provision, Article 21 of the *Grundgesetz,* stipulates that parties are to play the leading role not only in formulating and articulating interests but also in aggregating those interests within the FRG's policymaking arena (S. Padgett 1993). On the one hand, this implies that unlike the U.S. political system, political parties are not just another extragovernmental actor fashioning public policy. Rather, parties in Germany enjoy a legal priority over interest groups and any other quasi-public organizations acting to shape the policy process. Equally significant, Article 21 has the secondary effect of casting parties as the embodiment of the political establishment. As such, they become an instrument of governmental policy stability—a clear intention of the architects of the 1948 German constitution (Basic Law).

This has the effect, however, of exposing a gap between the state and its instruments of support and execution—political parties—on the one hand and society on the other. In time, this has loosened the bonds between the electorate and political parties in Germany. Seen less and less as vehicles for change and reform in a era of turbulence and threat wrought by the complexities of the post–Cold War world and global financial and commercial competition, parties have had to adjust to the public's perception of them as part of the often unspecified "problem" rather than as legitimate instruments for rectification (S. Padgett 1993). This gap has been filled since around 1980 by a wide array of social movements with the aim of influencing established interest groups and other quasi-public institutions by shaping public opinion in various ways (Halfmann 1989).

Thus, to understand the role of interest groups in Germany one must extend the scope beyond the traditional groups widely represented within the German corporatist political economy (mainly trade unions and employer organizations). On the one hand, account must be taken of the relationship between parties and traditional interest groups and, on the other, of the role of social movements and their influence on the dense network of interactions between the more traditional public and quasi-public groups shaping the German political economy and contemporary democracy (Katzenstein 1989; Halfmann 1989). In this regard, Halfmann (1989) identified various voluntary organizations and the equality-feminism, environmental, peace, antinuclear, and various alternative movements as the main social movements coloring the German political landscape from the 1970s until the late 1980s.

These three crucial characteristics of German liberal democracy have come under pressure from three external sources of influence: European integration, especially its broader and recent political and economic union; the financial and social implications of globalized capital markets; and the social and political transformation of Eastern and Central Europe coupled with the lingering effects of the unification of the two German states. However, we argue here that the influence of these external factors on the party-group connection will likely be more significant in the future than it is at present. We will discuss those factors later after characterizing the past and present array of party-group relations in Germany and examining some of their contemporary interrelations.

CHARACTERIZING PARTY-GROUP RELATIONS IN GERMANY

As indicated in Chapter 1, only a few attempts have been made to classify the relationship of political parties and interest groups—for example, Sternberger (1952/1953), who classified systems in general—and two attempts to classify liberal democracies, Yishai (1995) and Thomas and Hrebenar (1995). All three classifications can throw light on the party-group connection in Germany. Here, however, we focus on the Sternberger and Thomas and Hrebenar models as the most useful in understanding the German experience.

Sternberger (1952/1953) used five classifications in his model. First is the extreme case of direct control of a party by an interest group, usually resulting from the development of a party from an interest group. There are many examples of this type in Germany such as the Christian movement, which between 1870 and 1933 organized itself in the Center Party (Zentrum); the Association of the Homeland Expelled and Deprived Germans, which existed between 1950 and 1957; and, more recently, the development of the Greens out of the environmental protection and peace movements.

The second type of relationship is cooperative, characterized by strong, reciprocating dependencies between parties and interest groups. Examples include the relationship between Social Democrats and the unions and between agrarian associations and the conservative parties.

The third patterned relationship is that of the traditional pluralistic model. This is characterized by strong independence of parties and interest groups, a condition that cannot be seen as typical for the big players in the FRG today. The neocorporatist political economy of Germany complements a production base within which pluralism cannot flourish; nor can it be tolerated within the structural confines of a national consensus model of politics dictated by a statist corporatist political culture. However, the pluralist model does apply to the numerous groups—likely the vast majority of interests in Germany in terms of numbers—that have few, if any, contacts with parties, such as the thousands of citizen lobbies and many new, locally based and organized citizens' initiative groups (the Bürgerinitiativen), especially those interested in environmental matters, generally represented by the Federal Association of Citizen-Action Groups for Environmental Protection—BBU (Dalton 1993, 194; Koopman 1995).

Sternberger's fourth category is the party-system domination model, which describes a situation characterized by the clear control of an interest group by a political party. The first two decades following the establishment of West Germany in 1949 were characteristic of this relationship. His fifth pattern is the dominant party model. This depicts a situation where interest groups are completely controlled by a central political party, specifically a totalitarian party, as was the case in the Third Reich and in the GDR.

Whereas the Sternberger model attempts to classify party-group relations at the system level, the Thomas and Hrebenar (1995) model focuses on the relationships between individual parties and groups. Like the Sternberger model, it also offers a five-part typology: the Partisan Model, the Ideological Model, the One Party Leaning/Neutral Involvement Model, the Pragmatic Model, and a Noninvolvement Model.

The Partisan Model depicts a situation where an interest group is attracted to, and dominated in the policy process by, a party that articulates a strong partisan ideological message, usually the result of close organizational ties and long historical association. This was essentially the relationship between the SPD and the unions for many years, but it has weakened somewhat in recent years. The Ideological Model differs from the Partisan Model in that both parties and interest groups have ideological positions derived independent of each other. Their alliance is a direct product of the match between these ideological proclivities. This has been and largely remains the relationship among the CDU-CSU, the FDP, and the business and farmer group.

The One Party Leaning/Neutral Involvement Model depicts a slightly less congruent relationship between a party and an interest group than in either the Partisan or the Ideological Model. The interest group–party relationship remains ambivalent, leaving open the opportunity for the interest group to find another, more profitable opportunity with another political party, and vice versa. An example was the members of the BDA in Germany during 1998–1999, many of whom favored the new chancellor, Gerhard Schröder, despite the fact that he was a member of the leftist Social Democratic Party. These groups soon discovered that Schröder's "pro-business" mantra did not preclude his willingness to move against employers' interests in the fall of 1999 when he proposed a wealth tax in Germany. And when the SPD's electoral fortunes began to fade in the face of open resentment toward Schröder's austerity package, the opportunity costs of remaining committed to the employers' interests became too costly for the pragmatic Schröder and he tempered the policy.

The Pragmatic Model is one in which an interest group is free of any formal or informal attachment to a party on a long-term basis but may want to temporarily align with a party depending on the electoral and policy circumstances affecting an issue central to the group. This model is evidenced in Germany today in the form of professional interest groups, such as the German Civil Servants' Federation, as well as various leisure groups, such as the German Sports Federation.

Finally, the Noninvolvement Model describes the lack of any relationship between a party and an interest group. In other words, an interest group chooses to remain completely free of any party. This is similar to Sternberger's third category, the pluralistic model. Today it is true of the vast majority of groups in Germany, and in the past it was the case, for instance, with the Reich Association of German Industries during the Weimar Republic.

At any one time, the simultaneous existence of several of these models will be in evidence across the spectrum of party-group relations in Germany. However, at least since 1949 and with respect to the big players—the four major parties and the major peak associations—the party-group relationship in Germany is best described as interdependent, characterized by a partisan/ideological priority.

PARLIAMENTARY AND GOVERNMENTAL DIMENSIONS OF GERMAN POLITICAL PARTY–INTEREST GROUP RELATIONS

Parliament and the executive are the major political institutions for interest group activity at the federal level. In parliament the main targets of groups are *fraktions* and committees. Over 1,000 registered interest groups lobby the Bundestag (Dalton 1993, 267; Ronit and Schneider 1998). The main entry points for groups are committees within the Bundestag. The key specialty committees that directly serve the specialized needs of the various peak associations and their affiliated members are the Labor and Social Relations Committee, for union and employers' groups; the Nutrition, Farming, and Forestry Committee, for agricultural groups; and the Youth, Family, and Health Committee, again important for unions (Dalton 1993, 267–268).

A high percentage of parliamentarians, particularly those in the Bundestag, have some form of affiliation with an interest group. Over the years the association affiliation in the CDU-CSU has been higher than that in the SPD. Von Beyme (1969) goes so far as to describe the CDU *fraktion* as a loose coupling of different interest grouplike subdivisions of that party. This is much the same in the SPD *fraktion,* although subdivisions are traditionally more limited. Almost three-fourths of SPD representatives are members of the DGB. In contrast, the FDP has a high percentage of members of business interest groups and employers' associations. Kropp (1997, 550, 551) has identified these group affiliations for the Tenth, Eleventh, and Twelfth Bundestags, 1983–1994. Her data document that the close relationships between groups and members of the German Bundestag become visible for a wider public during hearings, when the allied interest groups testify before the committees. These affiliations become even more obvious during election campaigns, when trade unions openly support the SPD, usually under heavy criticism from the CDU-CSU (*Frankfurter Allgemeine Zeitung,* 18 February, 5 May, and 12 June 1998), and with equal condemnation from the SPD when business groups support the CDU-CSU (*Frankfurter Allgemeine Zeitung,* 11 March 1998).

Indirectly related to this parliamentary tie are the formal connections big player groups have with federal ministries. For instance, in the 1980s the Interior Ministry had sixty formal standing advisory committees whose function was specifically to serve as a vehicle for recognized interest groups to inform the ministry of their preferences with respect to policy, as well as to allow the ministry an open channel to groups critical of its policy implementation. The Ministry for Food, Agriculture, and Forestry had fifty-six such standing advisory committees; the Ministry of Labor and Social Affairs had seventy-five; and the Ministry for Youth, Family, and Health had eighty-four. The extent to which peak associations gain entry and have a significant impact on policy vis-à-vis parliament and government is illustrated by the representation given the German Trade Union Federation. In the late 1980s the DGB was represented on forty-six committees across a wide range of ministries (Dalton 1993, 271).

In addition to access to formal committees in the Bundestag and to formal advisory committees in the federal bureaucracy, peak associations gain important access to policymaking and power circles through the formal public administrative board structure within the German state. These boards help supervise the agencies of government created by the Bundestag. For instance, when the Bundestag passed the law creating the Second Television Network (ZDF), three seats were allocated to unions, two seats to the BDA, two seats to the DBV, and so on. In the early 1990s the DGB was represented on twelve administrative boards (Dalton 1993, 271).

On the government side it is important to distinguish among the ministerial bureaucracy, the cabinet, and the chancellor. Whereas it is relatively easy for interest groups to exert strong influence on departments through membership in advisory committees, by exploiting the political party membership of civil servants, or through the institutionalized hearing process, it is less easy in the case of the cabinet. It is even more difficult to gain access to the chancellor. Here the Federal Republic resembles the institutional setting of the Weimar Republic, where lobbying had been rationalized by introducing the formal *Geschäftsordnung*.

Today, in Article 23 of the FRG's *Geschäftsordnung*, interest groups are guaranteed a formal right to present their opinion on draft legislation. This privilege has led to the establishment of *Verbandsherzogtümer* (interest group empires), meaning they virtually govern the law-making process in its first, often most important stages. An empirical study early in the FRG's existence reported that more than 80 percent of initiatives of the leading German business group, the BDI, were directed to the ministerial bureaucracy, and less than 10 percent went to parliament (Hennis 1961, 27–33). This situation appears much the same today.

OTHER FORMS OF PARTY-GROUP RELATIONS

Another important dimension of the party-group relationship in Germany is that of the relationship to the media, perhaps the most important quasi-public institution in a democracy. In this regard parties have the upper hand. They have a privileged position within the German public broadcasting system that enables them to determine interest group representation on media matters and ultimately to influence the content of broadcasting. Parties have the sole right to propose members of broadcasting advisory committees, which are supposed to be composed of so-called society-relevant groups. Representatives of these advisory groups are organized in formal networks that are run by the parties.

Through the different Länder broadcast laws, parties actually define which interest groups best represent a given interest, which in effect means those that best represent a particular party's interests. For instance, SPD-run Länder governments prefer Social Democratic trade unions over those sympathetic to Christian Democratic parties and favor leftish teacher organizations over conservative or traditional ones. In contrast, CDU-CSU governments prefer agrarian interest groups over environmental groups and religious interest groups over cultural groups. For instance, if the SPD appoints to a broadcasting advisory committee representatives of the Arbeiter-Samariterbund (a self-help organization created by trade unions and the SPD in the 1920s to help those wounded in street fighting in the Weimar Republic), which is considered left wing, they are often removed by the CDU when it wins power and are replaced by representatives of the German Red Cross, which is considered more conservative.

Although parties have the upper hand in parliament, the executive branch, and the media, there are other interactions between parties and interest groups in which a more equal relationship exists and even some cases in which parties are dependent on groups. These fall into a category of relationships we can call procedural or organizational cooperation. Four important examples illustrate this form.

First, party financing in general and campaign financing in particular provide interesting insight into the party-group relationship as exemplified by the *Staatsbürgerliche Vereinigungen,* institutionalized de facto auxiliary organizations of employer peak associations designed to channel funds to parties at the Länder level (Lösche 1993, 222). Second, interest groups heavily influence the formation of the state electoral lists, which are decisive in the FRG's electoral system of proportional representation. State lists are used by parties to incorporate the representation of interest groups that are particularly close to the party. Third, interest groups attempt to influence election outcomes directly through voting recommendations to their members. These recommendations are a direct reflection of the specific party–interest group relationship.

Finally, parties sometimes depend on interest groups for their electoral and, ultimately, policy success. Indeed, in certain circumstances they serve the interests of interest groups rather than vice versa. This sometimes occurs at the Länder level where the tactics of parties may seem contrary to their traditional, or national, ideological orientation. For instance, the struggle for control of the Bavarian senate in 1998 found the SPD being pressured by various new social movements in Bavaria to push for a referendum that would dissolve the Bavarian *Land* Senate. In the eyes of these movements and the SPD, the senate had become the exclusive vehicle for the CSU and its policies. Indeed, the CSU even found support for its control of the senate from moderately left-oriented trade union groups, which understood the advantage of cooperating with the CSU on various issues coming before the senate. Under pressure from a coalition of new social movements and acting against the general interests of its moderate-left trade union supporters, the SPD successfully orchestrated a *Land* referendum that dissolved the senate.

EXTERNAL FACTORS LIKELY TO AFFECT FUTURE PARTY-GROUP RELATIONSHIPS

As Germany enters the new century, the most important external factors likely to influence traditional interdependent and partisan relationships between parties and interest groups are the emerging European Union and the political-economic consequences associated with a single currency throughout most of Western Europe. Related to this are the ramifications of a growing world capital market. Finally, there is the continued political and economic transformation of East-Central and Eastern Europe.

These external factors—especially the European Union and the single currency market—present a scale of change unlike anything Germany has experienced during the last half century, including reunification and the end of the Cold War. The immediate effect of the EU on the relationship between parties and interest groups is an extended geographical reach of resources available to groups, thereby reducing the importance of domestic parties. This reach is most likely to enhance the political position of business vis-à-vis the German corporatist state. The EU also requires that groups be actively involved in regional issues beyond the traditional democratic confines of Germany. This places even greater pressure on parties to reevaluate their traditional partisan and ideological preferences, or they risk further erosion of their electoral base in the face of a new political environment that views traditional parties as inadequate for the new realities of Europe.

The growing importance of regional issues as a function of a broad European political-economic market, as well as the new realities of a global capital system, suggests that the traditional patterns of interaction of interest groups and parties will be confronted by a growing presence of new social movements throughout Germany and the European Union. Immigration and unemployment are just two of the most obvious threats to the social welfare and economic security of workers in Germany. The traditional German corporatist structures are not likely to effectively manage the pressures of employment uncertainty, the vulnerability of pensions and earnings to the vagaries of global capital markets, and the pressures of legal or illegal immigration as a function of both political and economic dislocation experienced (at least initially) by the new pan-European markets. Following the logic of Halfmann (1989), we expect that the most likely social movements to expand in the next decade throughout Germany (and Europe) will be self-help movements. These movements are a direct response to the dislocations of technological innovation, the massive pressure on traditional industrial and manufacturing production markets, and the rising uncertainty confronting workers and citizens throughout Europe as the continent and its major economies enter a new transnational system of political and economic organization.

CONCLUSION

The future of the party-group relationship in Germany, inextricably bound as it is to the FRG's neocorporatist political economy, stands at the crossroads. The immediate future of Germany's complex matrix of peak associations and social consensus within this neocorporatist environment confronts the realities of a new European political economy and the attendant demands of a European single currency. As the chief defenders of that single currency, German markets may find a social consensus logic whose most visible manifestation is a rich social welfare system and an implicit veto authority extended to labor. To the extent that peak associations in Germany are a deep-rooted cultural reality within the political system, any speculation over their demise would be hasty. As we argued in this chapter, they are both a powerful symbolic reflection and a real political force within the German political economy for the near future.

On the other hand, to the extent that the neocorporatist logic of party–interest group relations is the result of a unique conjunction of circumstances that may be impossible to sustain, their survival is in doubt as new market realities ripple through the trade and commercial relations of industrialized democracies. These forces may permanently shift the priorities within Europe's broader political economy and the global economy upon which Germany depends. At present, it seems logical for trade and professional unions to look aghast at the Social Democrats' willingness to tie their policy agenda to the Clinton-Blair logic of the "third way"—a middle course between the old social democracy and the traditional conservatism. There is no room in this model for social consensus or for peak associations that demand equal choice and equal reward through joint planning and coordination.

If the peak associations for labor and eventually agriculture cannot protect their clientele, it stands to reason that the clientele will seek refuge elsewhere, in similar organizations that either extend beyond the borders of Germany or, logically, find their strongest and most effective support within localized regions of Germany. The immediate ramifications are twofold.

First, the nature of the social contract in Germany will be significantly modified. This will entail a redefinition and reevaluation of strategy for the peak associations representing key interests within the German Federal Republic. Second, the structural foundations of the German party system, as well as the complex and successful federal system, will be impacted. At present the pressures of the new Europe and the German role within that Europe are bearing hard on the internal consensus of the Social Democrats, as well as their coalition Green Party. These same pressures have already forced the CDU-CSU and their former ally, the Free Democrats, to reevaluate their ideological foundations. Relations between the Länder and the German federal government, especially with respect to financial and social policies, will be subject to shifts in the neocorporatist structure in Germany brought on by a broadening base of interests defined by a constitutional European Union.

Whatever the immediate future holds for the German neocorporatist system, the parties and big player interest groups (in the form of their key peak associations) will likely remain the instruments through which any change within the complex German political economy will be negotiated. The internal factors outlined in this chapter may not preclude the changes that will be borne by the new European Union and its single currency. Nor will they insulate the German political system and its public from the strategic realities of an Eastern Europe still on the precarious path of democratic transition and nationalist aspirations. Parties and groups will, however, serve as the forces that regulate and buffer the German political economy from these shocks. They are the locks along the rivers of change that will ensure, in all probability, a stable transition to the new Europe and will be indispensable in establishing the legitimacy of a refined and modified social consensus within the German Federal Republic of the twenty-first century.

7

Italy: The Erosion and Demise of Party Dominance

John Constantelos

As scholars have long observed, what has characterized Italian politics during most of the period since World War II is not the superficial political instability often highlighted in the foreign media but rather the entrenched and pathologic stability of Christian Democratic Party dominance. Christian Democrat–dominated governments ruled Italy from 1945 until the early 1990s. What ended the party's dominance and produced a metamorphosis in Italian politics was the so-called Tangentopoli corruption scandal (roughly translated as Bribesville or Kickback City) that erupted in 1992–1993. The scandal involved the investigation or arrest of over 1,500 politicians—including cabinet members and former prime ministers—as well as bureaucrats and businesspeople, on charges of corruption in awarding government contracts (Zariski 1998, 344).

Because of the pioneering work of LaPalombara (1964) and later work by others (for example, Lange and Regini 1989; Martinelli and Lanzalaco 1994; Morlino 1991), the party-group relationship in Italy has received more attention from scholars than has been the case with this relationship in most other Western democracies. This attention results largely from two aspects of party-group relations these and other scholars have identified as central to Italian politics and policymaking: the practices of *clientela* and *parentela*.

The practice of *clientela*, referred to here as clientelism, is a close quid pro quo relationship between government and certain key groups. The government (that is, the governing party) recognizes a specific group as representing the collective interests of a particular sector such as business or agriculture. In return, the group helps that party obtain and maintain power through financial, electoral, and other support. In general, however, clientele groups are subservient to parties. The practice of *parentela* involves "a relatively close and integral relationship between certain associational interest groups, on the one hand, and the politically dominant [party], on the other" (LaPalombara 1964, 306). State agencies intervene on behalf of the interest groups because of the latter's close ties to the dominant party. *Parentela* groups attempt to get their members, particularly group officials, elected on a party's list. These groups usually have very close official ties with the party on whose list they run and once elected may openly operate as separate factions of that party in parliament (Zariski 1998, 404). The Christian Democrats have been particularly rife with such factions.

In this chapter we argue that clientelism and *parentela* were important elements of a broader phenomenon that fundamentally shaped Italian party-group relations: party dominance of the party-group connection. The chapter examines the fundamental factors that have shaped this crucial relationship in post–World War II Italian politics. Within this general theme the chapter analyzes the rise, erosion, and demise of party dominance in party–interest group relations in Italy and its implications, focusing on the pre-Tangentopoli period. The conclusion offers thoughts on how this relationship is developing in the post-Tangentopoli era.

BACKGROUND ON PARTY-GROUP RELATIONS IN POST–WORLD WAR II ITALY

Benito Mussolini's regime (1922–1943) banned most of Italy's interest groups. Therefore, only a few contemporary groups trace their origins to the liberal state that preceded the fascist regime. Two notable exceptions are the lay religious association Catholic Action, and Confindustria, the confederation of industrialists. Interest group–political party relations were recast after World War II. As politics in Italy began to polarize, many new interest groups were formed by, or affiliated in some fashion to, political parties representing Italy's three broad political subcultures: Catholic, left, and laical (LaPalombara 1964, 131–153; 1987, 35).

In understanding party-group relations, six parties were particularly important between World War II and the early 1990s. The Christian Democratic Party (Democrazia Cristiana—DC; renamed the Popular Party in 1994) represented the Catholic subculture and was Italy's largest party. The far left was represented by the Communist Party (Partito Comunista Italiana, PCI, which in 1991 was renamed the Democratic Party of the Left—PDS—and is now known as the Democrats of the Left, DS); the center and moderate left were represented by the Socialist Party (Partito Socialista Italiano—PSI) and the Social Democratic Party (Partito Socialista Democratico Italiano—PSDI). The major laical parties have been the centrist Republican Party (Partito Repubblicano Italiano—PRI) and the moderate conservative Liberal Party (Partito Liberale Italiana—PLI). In the

1990s several other parties became important, especially the far-right neofascist party, the Italian Social Movement (Movimento Sociale Italiano—MSI; renamed the National Alliance in 1992), the regional separatist Northern League (Lega Nord), and media magnate Silvio Berlusconi's conservative populist Go, Italy! Party (Forza Italia!).

Shortly after World War II, Italy's broad coalition government crumbled amid heightening East-West tensions. Under U.S. pressure, communists and socialists were expelled from government, and nearly fifty years of Christian Democratic political dominance began. The DC led all but three of Italy's governments between 1945 and 1992. The majority of these governments were coalitions that included the regular participation of liberals, Republicans, Social Democrats, and, after 1963, socialists. The exclusion from government of Western Europe's largest communist party for most of this period eliminated the possibility of a meaningful alternation of power.

Most key policy decisions were taken not in Italy's weak formal institutions but in deals made between key DC factions, their coalition partners, and, at times, the political opposition in a manner reminiscent of the nineteenth-century tradition of transformism (*trasformismo*). This was the practice of transforming political opponents into coalition partners through pragmatic ideological and material accommodation (D. Smith 1959, 110–112). Parties engaged in a "sharing out" (*lottizzazione*) of the spoils of office, from policymaking positions to financial and other resources, and extended their control over key sectors of the economy. Governing parties dominated public and private institutions to a degree unmatched in the rest of Europe, a model that came to be called partyocracy (*partitocrazia*) and that had great consequences for economic and other interest groups.

In certain respects Italian party-group relations are not out of the ordinary. Groups and parties in Italy are tied through the traditional bonds of ideology, electoral agreements, overlapping memberships, formal institutional affiliations, and money. However, the factors outlined earlier that shaped Italian political development and policymaking, particularly after World War II, gave two important characteristics to the Italian party-group relationship down to the early 1990s.

First, both interest representation and political representation were and still are highly fragmented. Political, ideological, economic, and geographic cleavages have divided both the labor movement and business interests. Political representation has also been highly fragmented, both across and within political parties. The result has been a system of interest intermediation characterized by a high degree of pluralism, despite the periodic successes of peak-level tripartite negotiations (Golden 1986; Regini and Regalia 1997). The extreme fragmentation of groups and parties in Italy has led to a multiplicity of political party–interest group relations.

The second trait that differentiates the Italian case from most others is that in general, and stemming from party control of public and private institutions, political parties have dominated party-group relationships, and interest groups have been incapable of autonomously articulating interests or placing their preferences directly on the decisionmaking agenda (Pasquino 1989, 32). Until Tangentopoli, Christian Democratic dominance was an important factor shaping relationships between interest groups and political parties in Italy. In fact, not only the DC but other parties often dominated the relationships with organized groups. In the case of both the DC and other parties, however, this dominance eroded gradually as the post–World War II period progressed until it came to an abrupt end in 1992–1993.

The Tangentopoli scandal plus factors such as the end of the Cold War and the increasing importance of the European Union in policymaking have profoundly affected the party-group connection in Italy since the early 1990s, including the apparent end to party dominance. At the end of the 1990s, Italy's political landscape had not yet stabilized, and the realignment of party-group relations remained incomplete. Some patterns that may indicate future party-groups connections were evident, but much of the future of those relations were in the domain of speculation.

THE PATTERN OF PARTY-GROUP RELATIONS FROM WORLD WAR II TO TANGENTOPOLI

In this section we examine party-group relations in Italy from 1947 to 1992 across five categories of interest groups: party-affiliated groups, sometimes referred to as auxiliary or flanking organizations; trade unions; business groups; agricultural groups; and postmaterialist groups. As we shall see, particularly significant was the fragmentation of these sectors in regard to the association of groups with parties plus the existence of clientelistic and *parentela* relationships as aspects of party dominance of the party-group connection.

Party Auxiliary Organizations

The groups with the closest relations to Italy's political parties have been the various auxiliary associations, often created or sponsored by the parties themselves and sharing their ideological objectives. For example, the DC was closely connected to a youth group, a women's group (Italian Women's Center—CIF), and various religious groups—most important, Catholic Action. The PCI's auxiliary organizations included a veterans' association (National Association of Italian Partisans—ANPI), a women's group

(Italian Union of Women—UDI), and a strong youth group (Federation of Young Italian Communists—FGCI) (LaPalombara 1964, 137–139).

As set out in Box 1.2, at their inception these ties most closely approximated the Integration/Strong Partisan Model, but over time some of these ties weakened, and the Cooperation/Ideological Model became a more accurate description. The Catholic and Communist associations were critically important sources of support for their parties from the end of World War II through the 1960s, but their influence has waned considerably since then. A particularly important Communist support organization was FGCI, whose membership dropped from 500,000 in the 1960s to less than 50,000 in the 1980s (LaPalombara 1987, 35). The UDI, seeking greater autonomy, distanced itself from the PCI at its 1982 congress when it decided to reorganize, integrate with other women's groups at the local level, and self-finance instead of receive party financing (Confalonieri 1995, 145).

Catholic Action was for many years one of the most important groups in Italy. Founded in 1867, it was the leading association for the promotion of Catholicism among the laity. Growing rapidly during the early twentieth century, it was one of the few organizations permitted by the fascist government. Membership rose to more than 3 million by the 1960s. In general, Catholic Action heeded the official line of the church, and until the mid-1960s it was also a powerful and generally uncritical source of support for the DC (LaPalombara 1964, 331–338; Leonardi and Wertman 1989, 209–212). Catholic Action's electoral clout was crucial for the DC, but its control of the nominating process at the provincial level concerned certain party leaders including Amintore Fanfani, who made great efforts to reduce the DC's dependence on the association (LaPalombara 1964, 337). The relationship between Catholic Action and the DC changed fundamentally during the second half of the 1960s with the rise of the student and labor movements. Membership declined precipitously, falling below 900,000 in the mid-1970s to about 550,000 by the mid-1980s. The association began refocusing its attention on religious rather than overtly political issues, began to distance itself from the DC, and ultimately lost its considerable influence with the party (Leonardi and Wertman 1989, 210, 212).

New, youth-led Catholic groups were formed in the 1970s that filled the void left by Catholic Action and sought to renew Catholic activism in social and political life. Two of these, Communion and Liberation, and the latter's close, more political affiliate, Popular Movement, were more independent of the DC in terms of organization, but they were more ardent than Catholic Action in supporting the DC as the only defender of Catholic values in public life. The Popular Movement leadership tended to support the party faction led by Giulio Andreotti (Leonardi and Wertman 1989, 218–221).

The Italian Association of Christian Workers (ACLI) was another important auxiliary association in the DC network. Founded at the end of World War II as a social movement (not a trade union) to promote Catholic values among workers, it was regarded as an essential counterweight to the Communist-dominated unitary trade union (explained later). Membership was approximately 1 million during the 1950s, and it served as an important source of electoral support for the DC. In 1961, 12 of the 144 members of the DC National Council came from ACLI (LaPalombara 1964, 226). In *parentela* fashion, ACLI leaders were elected to parliament on the DC ticket, and relations were generally strong through the 1960s. As with the Catholic Action–DC relationship, the rise of labor activism at the end of the 1960s had important consequences for ACLI-DC relations. Support for the left had increased at this time, and ACLI leaders began to distance themselves from the DC, declaring at their 1969 National Congress the end to the preferential relationship with the DC and support for the principle of the "free vote" for the membership. Although ACLI-DC relations improved again after the mid-1970s, the Christian Workers could no longer be considered an automatic and reliable source of political support for the Christian Democrats (Leonardi and Wertman 1989, 212–214).

Trade Unions

The trade union movement also came to be divided across partisan lines. The Italian General Confederation of Labor (CGIL) was founded in 1944 by the antifascist resistance forces—mainly communists and some socialists—as a general labor organization. Shortly after, however, the exclusion of communists and socialists from government caused the labor movement to break up into three main branches. Each trade union became closely affiliated to one or more political parties. The CGIL was dominated by communists but had a sizable socialist minority. Anticommunist Catholic forces broke away from CGIL to form the Italian Confederation of Workers' Unions (CISL) in 1948, which had links with the Christian Democrats. The smaller Italian Union of Labor (UIL), founded in 1950, had good relations with the small lay parties of the center, the PSDI and PRI, and, later on, the PSI. On the far right was the Italian National Confederation of Workers' Unions (CISNAL), tied to the neofascist MSI.

Early studies of Italian political behavior found strong relationships between union membership and party preference, especially among CGIL members (Galli and Prandi 1970, 68). Barnes's (1977, 54) survey found that 90 percent of CGIL members supported left parties (mainly the PCI, PSI, and PSDI), whereas 70 percent of CISL members were DC supporters. A 1980 survey indicated that 56 percent of CGIL officials were PCI members, 25 percent were members of the PSI, 3 percent belonged to small left parties, and 15 percent were not party members (ETUI 1985, 30).

The political divisions of the Italian trade union movement have had a decisive effect on the relationship between organized labor and political parties. Above all, the political divisions undermined the ability of labor to act in a unified manner in its relations with industry and made it difficult for labor interests to be represented effectively in the political process. Until the Hot Autumn of 1969, Italian trade unions could be described as weak and highly dependent on political parties.

CGIL served the traditional role of the "transmission belt" for the Italian Communist Party until the mid-1950s; that is, it acted as a vehicle for promoting the PCI's political ideology and agenda. However, Joseph Stalin's death and the decline in international and domestic polarization decreased the value of identity incentives for members, and a declining membership called for a new strategy. CGIL and the PCI agreed jointly to abandon the transmission belt relationship. The union retained its revolutionary rhetoric but moved in a direction favoring incremental material gains and social reform. CGIL was also responding to the Catholic confederation, CISL, which had already moved to a strategy emphasizing material gains through collective bargaining. A second major change in CGIL's focus was brought about by strong economic growth and high employment in the early 1960s, which led the union to adopt a moderate posture toward the center-left government's Keynesian economic policies. The CGIL's new position here was in part the result of strategic considerations regarding CISL. A radical posture would have made it more difficult for CGIL to respond to an increasingly active and independent CISL (Lange, Ross, and Vannicelli 1982, 110–124).

During the years of labor mobilization (late 1960s through the mid-1970s), CGIL's relationship with the main political parties changed again. A tight labor market strengthened labor's position, and a new generation of workers called for greater autonomy from political parties and closer cooperation with the other unions. This led to the creation of the landmark CGIL-CISL-UIL unitary federation in July 1972 (Lange, Ross, and Vannicelli 1982, 125–141). The firm grip of parties on the unions was relaxed (Bardi and Ignazi 1998, 99).

Cooperation among unions and between the unitary federation and the governing parties was threatened by the recession of the mid-1970s. The federation's position was conditioned by the July 1976 Historic Compromise between the governing parties and the PCI. Initially, the PCI abstained rather than opposed the government, and in 1978 it began casting votes in support of the government's policies. To some union members, the PCI appeared to be demanding labor moderation to gain formal participation in the government. In 1978 the confederation formally embraced moderation in wage and benefit demands in exchange for government promises of structural reforms. As it became clear that fundamental changes were not forthcoming, in early 1979 the PCI withdrew its support of the government and returned to opposition (Bedani 1995, 231–242; Lange, Ross, and Vannicelli 1982, 142–184).

The unions found themselves on the defensive in the 1980s as large firms such as FIAT attempted to cut operating costs and reassert employer authority. Political alliances often undermined labor solidarity. CISL and the UIL remained relatively close to the governing parties, but the PCI's political isolation placed strains on its relations with CGIL. The unitary federation broke apart in 1984 over differences over the reform of wage indexation (Bedani 1995, 251–262).

The end of the Cold War contributed to the dealignment of labor-party ties. Under the leadership of party secretary Achille Occhetto, the PCI abandoned communism and recast itself as the PDS. In October 1991 Occhetto addressed the CGIL congress and called for a more autonomous union, declaring the end of the automatic "special relationship" between the party and the union (Bedani 1995, 271). Ties between CISL, the UIL, and their party allies ended more abruptly as Italy's long-standing governing parties collapsed amid the Tangentopoli crisis.

Business Groups

The representation of business in Italy is even more fragmented than that of organized labor. The multiplicity of groups reflects sectoral, size, functional, political, and legal divisions (Lanzalaco 1990b, 104). Peak associations in the service industries include Confcommercio, which had ties to the DC, and Confesercenti, which was close to the PCI. In Italy's important handicrafts sector, Confartigianato provided representation for Catholics, and the Confederazione nazionale dell'artigianato (CNA) represented the left (Lanzalaco 1990a, 59–60). In the industrial sector associations of private firms include Confapi, representing small and medium-sized firms, and Confindustria, which includes most of Italy's large private firms but also thousands of smaller ones. Intersind (recently abolished) represented most state-owned industries, except for those in the energy sector, which belong to the Association of Petrochemical Firms (ASAP). The leading financial group is the Italian Banking Association (ABI). Confindustria has been the most politically influential of the business associations, and therefore it will be the focus of this discussion.

Confindustria, founded in 1919, "became one of the major instruments through which organized Italian industry achieved functional representation in the Corporative State" (LaPalombara 1964, 133). The confederation had close ties to the PLI. In *parentela* fashion, prominent members of the association often appeared on PLI electoral lists (LaPalombara 1964, 75, 85; Mattina 1993). But the PLI was always of marginal political importance, winning only 1 to 7 percent of the lower house vote in most postwar elections. The PLI participated in four of Italy's coalition governments in the 1950s but not again until the five-party (*pentapartito*) coalitions of the 1980s. More consequential was the connection between Confindustria and the dominant Christian Democratic Party. Relations between Confindustria and the DC were generally harmonious from about 1947 through the mid-1950s (Mattina 1993, 163; Morlino 1998, 216). Economic growth was strong, and the DC granted Confindustria considerable authority in economic policy formulation, relying to a great extent on the technical expertise provided by the business association. Confindustria developed a strong clientelistic relationship with key bureaucratic institutions, especially in the Ministry of Industry and Commerce (LaPalombara 1964, 267). The DC-Confindustria relationship has been described as a

> relationship between two homogeneous political organisations with separate areas of influence: the ruling party, together with its allies, was in charge of organisation of consensus, the maintenance of law and order and foreign policy matters; *Confindustria* was in charge of the governance of the economy, either directly, through its own staff, or, more often, indirectly, through political leaders and government officials who were very responsive to its views (with the notable exception of some leftist Catholics). (Martinelli 1980, 72)

Relations began to sour in 1954 when Fanfani became the DC's new leader. Fanfani attempted to strengthen the DC's political dominance by expanding state control of banking and key industrial sectors, especially energy. The new public enterprises were required to withdraw from Confindustria by legislation passed in 1956. As a result, ASAP was founded to represent public firms in the energy sector, while Intersind would provide employer representation for state-owned firms in all other sectors.

This strategy enabled the DC to reduce its financial dependence on organized business, and consequently the mediating role and political clout of Confindustria diminished. Large firms such as FIAT increasingly took independent political action, strengthening their ties with party and faction leaders who had direct control over key state resources. The large private firms and state enterprises were successful in obtaining state-controlled finance, but the small and medium-sized firms were left in a relatively disadvantaged position. The superficial compact between the DC and Confindustria broke apart amid factional conflict within the governing party and the increasingly irreconcilable differences among large, small, and state enterprises within the association (Martinelli 1980, 74–77).

The DC-Confindustria relationship worsened further with the Opening to the Left—the inclusion of the Socialist Party in the governing coalition in 1963 (Martinelli 1980, 74, 76). These developments fundamentally changed the relationship between the DC and Confindustria. As Martinelli (1980, 73) put it, "The link between a unified party and a rather homogeneous business class became a fragmented network of influences in which different party factions were related to different centres of economic power." This situation would prevail through most of the 1980s.

The weakness of organized business and relative strength of labor became plainly apparent during the Hot Autumn of 1969, as Italy entered a period of labor activism. Labor won a number of important concessions between 1969 and 1973, including substantial wage increases, new pension laws, and the passage of the Workers' Statute. The real turning point came in 1973 while Gianni Agnelli was president of Confindustria. Agnelli and his successor, Guido Carli, articulated a new strategy for Confindustria that called for a more assertive political posture, emphasis on the centrality and political independence of private capital, and a direct dialogue with the trade unions. The economic recession of the 1970s gave business the upper hand in industrial relations, and Confindustria once again became a central player. For lack of a credible alternative, however, Confindustria continued to depend on the DC for political representation through the 1970s and 1980s.

Confindustria held largely defensive postures in industrial relations and in public policy in general. Relations with the DC- and PSI-led governments were generally harmonious, and lobbying by the association was typically aimed at securing particularistic interests (Mattina 1993). Even though Christian Democratic ideology and objectives were rather different from those of the industrialists, the DC was seen as the only party capable of maintaining a governing coalition that could defend business interests (Mattina 1993). Thus, Confindustria's relationship with the Liberal Party resembles the Cooperation/Ideological Model, and its relationship with the DC more closely approximates the Separation/Pragmatic Involvement Model (see Box 1.2).

Economic and political circumstances, both domestic and international, played an important role in changing Confindustria's relations with the parties in the late 1980s. Increased international economic integration and heightened competition, especially in the context of the emerging single European market, caused industrial leaders to consider more seriously Italy's unimpressive productivity levels. Internally, a moribund bureaucracy and an entrenched political class came to be seen as obstacles to economic growth. And the fall of communism and rebirth of the PCI as the PDS caused traditional party alignments to begin to fade.

Between 1988 and 1992, during the time Sergio Pininfarina was president of Confindustria, the association shifted its strategy. FIAT and many other large industrial firms pushed Confindustria to move beyond the largely defensive strategies of the past to stabilize industrial relations and respond to global competition (Lanzalaco 1990b). The dominant parties—the DC and PSI—were seen increasingly as the causes of economic stagnation and as the obstacles to fundamental political and economic reforms. Relations with the governing parties became more conflictual, and Confindustria sought out new, reform-minded allies. Relations between Confindustria and the PLI were generally harmonious, but the association started moving closer to the relatively independent PRI. This was evidenced in the 1992 elections, in which an increased number of industrialists ran on the PRI lists. The DC-Confindustria alliance was effectively over, and the association took on an explicitly multiparty strategy as the 1992 political crisis began to develop (Mattina 1993).

Agricultural Groups

The agricultural sector was also divided in terms of party relations, and it remains so, although it has been less fragmented than labor or business. Three interest groups have dominated the agricultural sector in Italy. Coldiretti, the association representing smaller farmers, was tied closely to the DC. Confagricoltura, representing larger landowners, was also tied to the DC, but more for instrumental than ideological reasons (Morlino 1991, 467). Confcoltivatori was associated with the PCI. Agriculture provides a classic example of both clientelistic and *parentela* relationships with parties in postwar Italy. This is one of the reasons agricultural groups, particularly those tied to the DC, have been among the most powerful Italian interest groups since 1945.

The Christian Democrats relied heavily on agricultural groups for resources and electoral support. In return, in this clientelistic relationship the DC offered monopolization of the Ministry of Agriculture, which it controlled in thirty-one of thirty-two coalition governments between 1945 and 1988 (Leonardi and Wertman 1989, 230). As a staunch supporter of the DC (especially the Dorotei faction), Coldiretti particularly benefited from this and as a result had the greatest political clout of any agricultural group. Founded in 1944, it grew rapidly after the war, attaining a membership of nearly 2 million families by the 1960s. Coldiretti members were beneficiaries of a variety of state interventions in the agricultural sector, particularly in the south. The group's clout was derived in part from its control of farmers' social welfare and medical insurance programs and the Federconsorzi, the quasi-public extension and agricultural finance agencies (LaPalombara 1964, 235–246; Leonardi and Wertman 1989, 216–217).

Thus, Coldiretti support of and participation in the party, and DC control of the Ministry of Agriculture, provided the foundation for the mutually beneficial exchange of electoral support for material resources of the state. The DC-Coldiretti relationship epitomized the pervasive clientelistic system of the pre-Tangentopoli period. The *parentela* relationship between the two organizations is evidenced by the fact that Coldiretti members often ran on DC electoral lists. In 1953 Coldiretti obtained thirty-three seats in the Chamber of Deputies, and in 1958 it obtained thirty-five—almost 6 percent of the seats (Lanza 1991, 90).

The influence of agricultural groups has decreased as employment in agriculture has fallen from 45 to 7 percent of the workforce since 1950. Yet these groups, especially Coldiretti, continue to be disproportionately important for their size. Agricultural groups continue to have considerable influence in the south, where 12–15 percent of the workforce remains directly involved in agriculture.

Postmaterialist Groups

Like other advanced industrial countries, Italy witnessed the development of various anti–nuclear weapons, environmental, women's, and other postmaterialist groups in the 1960s and 1970s. Most of these groups arose in the wake of the student, worker, and New Left movements. The new social movements and postmaterialist groups had complex relationships with the traditional parties of the left. At times the PCI was the object of their harshest criticism, but on many other occasions they would enter into short-term alliances with the Communist Party (Della Porta 1996, 39–44, 91–127; Tarrow 1989, 143–336). Most of the anti–nuclear missile groups eventually disbanded.

Other new social movements—neofeminism, for example—endured, but they never became powerful and independent groups. The women's movement was divided by numerous political, ideological, and cultural differences. Neofeminist groups challenged the class-based conceptions of feminism espoused by the Communist Party's flank organization, the UDI. The new feminism, which emphasized gender identity and difference, became influential and ultimately transformed the UDI and brought substantial change to the new PDS platform (Confalonieri 1995). However, the feminist movement's loose networks of women's cooperatives and coordinating committees were unable to unify and never posed a serious political challenge to the established parties (Beccalli 1994; Ergas 1982).

The environmental movement became the most institutionalized of the new social movements. Several Italian conservation associations were formed in the nineteenth century, as in other Western countries. Environmental groups did not become politically important, however, until the 1980s. Their weakness has been attributed to Italy's late economic development and to dominance of the political parties. The new "political ecology" groups like the World Wildlife Fund were far more politically active than the older conservation groups, and they developed ties to traditional left and New Left parties (Diani 1995, 68, 135, 155). At the national level the environmental movement received the support of left-libertarian opposition parties such as the Radicals and Workers' Democracy (Diani 1995, 31, 38), but they remained largely outside national party politics until the 1980s.

The League for the Environment (Lega per l'Ambiente), an umbrella group formed in 1980, was initially set up as a formal branch of the Italian Association of Culture and Recreation (ARCI), which had strong ties to the Socialist and Communist parties (Diani 1995, 34–35). The Greens, benefiting from the strongly proportional electoral system, finally attained political representation in parliament when they won fifteen seats in 1987. The Greens have brought environmental issues to parliament, but the electoral successes also produced new divisions within the environmental movement. For many activists, political participation entailed too many compromises and distractions. Ideological divisions, particularly between moderate conservation and more activist and left-leaning political ecology groups, and an absence of strong leadership have made relations between the environmental groups and Green politicians difficult at times (Diani 1995, 40–41). An important cleavage in the environmental movement was eliminated in 1990 when the two major Green parties unified to form the Green Federation (Federazione dei Verdi).

Summary: Pervasiveness of Fragmentation and Party Dominance

The review of party-group relations in postwar Italy shows some aspects of the connection that are common in other Western democracies. Groups like ACLI and Coldiretti provided essential electoral support for the Christian Democrats, while CGIL turned out voters for the left parties. Ideological ties between the liberals and Confindustria were strong, while key industrial interests provided critical financing for the Christian Democrats.

In particular, however, the review shows the pervasiveness of fragmentation and party dominance in the party-group connection. In particular, the extreme degree of party control of the government and the public agencies (*sottogoverno*) profoundly distorts the Italian version of pluralism (Martinelli and Lanzalaco 1994, 329–330). Organized interests certainly focused on traditional targets such as legislators and bureaucrats (LaPalombara 1964, 194); however, although they did not readily admit it, the primary targets of interest groups were the parties. The groups were critically important clients for the parties at large and for individual party factions. But the parties—particularly the DC—typically had the upper hand because of their control of state resources (Morlino 1991, 464–477). Control of resources through an expansion of the state (for example, in the agricultural sector and the giant holding companies IRI and ENI) was the key that enabled the DC to attain greater autonomy from the Catholic

Church and the industrialists and later to exert considerable leverage over all segments of society. Clientelism was the cement of party-group relations, and *parentela* groups were a key component of the party-group connection. Party dominance did not characterize all party-group ties, but it was the case in many of the crucial relationships.

THE PATHOLOGY OF PARTY DOMINANCE

Criticisms of Italy's party-dominated clientelistic system are long-standing and plentiful. Beyond the immediate ethical concerns about systemic corruption, questions were also raised about the health of Italian democracy. Critics charged that party collusion and consociational practices (Ferrante 1998, 88; Martinelli and Lanzalaco 1994, 329–330)—involving even the Communist opposition—degraded democratic values such as choice and accountability. When combined with clientelism and corruption, political equality is diminished, and the political system loses its legitimacy (Della Porta and Vannucci 1997). The Italian system has been described as "paralyzed pluralism" (Pizzorno 1993, 291) and "oligopolistic pluralism" (Lanzalaco 1993, 127–130).

Clientelism has had a negative impact on public policy. Many policy areas have lacked coherent policy, and Italian policy outputs have been characterized by large numbers of *legine*—"small laws" satisfying the particularistic objectives of key social interests (Martinelli and Lanzalaco 1994, 332). Clientelism also contributed to the poor performance of the bureaucracy in social welfare functions. State expansion and political control of the economy led to comparatively poor economic performance in key sectors. The most dynamic segments of the Italian economy were in the medium and small-scale manufacturing districts outside the oversight of the state.

Party control and patronage were not news to either citizens or students of Italian politics (LaPalombara 1964, 322–327; Spotts and Wieser 1986, 14–16, 140–149). The Clean Hands investigation of the Tangentopoli affair revealed the remarkable depth and pervasiveness of corruption in Italian politics, as well as the extent of the clientelistic structures established first by the Christian Democrats and then extended and institutionalized to include all of Italy's governing parties. The DC-led coalition had extended state control over large segments of the Italian economy, and firms would routinely pay *tangenti* (bribes and kickbacks) to party officials in exchange for state contracts. The case of the chemical firm Enimont showed just how institutionalized the system had become. The affair involved Raul Gardini, the chairman of the Ferruzi group that owned the chemical giant

Montedison. Gardini paid around $100 million in bribes when he resold shares of Enimont's stock to the state for a handsome profit. Not only did he make large payments to the Socialist and Christian Democratic Parties, but he also made payments to each of the smaller governing parties and to the leaders of each important DC faction in shares reflecting their political importance (Frei 1995, 20–21).

According to some reports, the large business associations were the normal conduit for business financing of political parties until the mid-1970s, when industrialists began negotiating payments directly with the parties (Ball 1997, 55; Rhodes 1997, 68). The involvement of business associations in illegal party financing since then is unclear. Nevertheless, individuals in leadership positions of many important interest groups (for example, Carlo De Benedetti, who served on Confindustria's executive committee) were implicated in their personal business dealings with state agencies.

The Tangentopoli crisis brought an end to the system of bribes and kickbacks.

PARTY DOMINANCE AND ITS EROSION

What, then, explains why Italian political parties were so dominant in their relationships with interest groups? And what explains the erosion and ultimate demise of that dominance? Several important international and domestic variables must be examined to answer these questions. The relevant factors are historical, political, economic, and social.

Certainly, some of the patterns are the result of national historical circumstances, particularly Italy's experience with fascism and the subsequent process of political and economic development. Particularly important were the events that led to the quick consolidation of Christian Democratic dominance in the early post–World War II years (Morlino 1991, 448). The choice of relatively weak political institutions for Italy's postwar constitution reflected the precautions taken to prevent the return of dictatorship. Civil society was also weak after twenty years of fascism and then war. In Italy, more than in the other southern European states, we have the experience of party dominance over organized social interests (Morlino 1995), and this is a crucial—if not the crucial—element in the party-group relationship. Some scholars have pointed to Italy's weak institutional framework as the reason for the Italian parties' ability to embed themselves throughout public and private life (Martinelli and Lanzalaco 1994, 333–334; Pasquino 1988, 126–152; 1989, 34, 47; Zariski 1993). Certain political institutional peculiarities have also had an impact. For example, the absence of an electoral threshold for representation in parliament led to a proliferation of parties and the necessity to form broad coalitions, which in turn led to a sharing out of the state and the need to solidify clientelistic ties for political gain.

However, we must also look beyond national factors. The Italian case reveals the profound impact of international politics. The key factor was the development of the Cold War and the rapid polarization of "white" and "red" political subcultures that accompanied it. The Cold War structured partisan and party-group alignments in the late 1940s, and the end of the Cold War underlay their dismantling (Martinelli and Lanzalaco 1994, 330). Party dominance of many groups occurred simply because the groups were created by the parties themselves. The Christian Democrats benefited from U.S. support and from the extensive network of church institutions, and they won a decisive victory in 1948. The isolation of the main opposition party, the PCI, combined with the division of the labor movement, of agricultural interests, and of artisan and business interests, led to a demobilization and weakening of organized economic interests relative to the government parties. The DC strengthened its domination through an expansion of the state (Morlino 1998, 215–219). Once "domination and control over groups and sectors of civil society were established and at the same time the propertied associations no longer felt a serious danger from the left, they became less relevant" (Morlino 1998, 221).

A variety of economic and political factors led to the gradual erosion of party dominance. Short-term economic fluctuations had a significant impact on the relationships between trade unions and the parties. The trade unions were also able to gain some autonomy during the height of labor militancy with the tight labor market of the early 1970s. More important are the longer-term economic structural changes that led, for example, to the relative decline in the political importance of agricultural groups. Confindustria distanced itself from the Christian Democrats when it became clear that the party was incapable of responding to heightened international economic pressures. The rise of postmaterialist movements, the end of the Cold War and the reform of the Communist Party, and the general secularization of political life led to a decline in both traditional incentives for identification and memberships of the parties' main auxiliary organizations. The Communist women's group, the UDI, broke away when it found the party unresponsive to nonclass-based feminist ideas. Other groups, however, like the small farmers' association Coldiretti, maintained close, although more balanced, ties with the parties throughout this period. In Italy we also see the important impact of international economic change on party-group relations. Economic integration and liberalization in Europe, for example, led Confindustria to distance itself from its close ties to the governing parties.

AFTER TANGENTOPOLI

Before 1992 political party–interest group relations in Italy manifested certain general patterns, prominent among which were a relatively high (although diminishing) degree of partisanship and the pervasiveness of clientelistic and *parentela* connections within an overarching context of party dominance. But within the general patterns a multiplicity of specific party-group relations existed and continues to exist. For instance, we find traditional ties between business associations and conservative parties and between labor unions and parties of the left. But we also find more complex relationships between interest groups and various factions of catchall parties. The Christian Democrats, for example, found themselves having to appease and mediate between traditional labor and business constituencies. And although the period until 1992 can be characterized as one of relative stability, party-group relations were far from static. Thus, an analysis of party-group relations must consider the underlying factors that account for the general patterns but also those that explain their short-term variability.

Although the breakdown of traditional party-group relations was already well under way by the early 1990s, Tangentopoli ultimately brought about the demise of party dominance and an abrupt break with long-standing party-group ties. The Italian party system is still in flux, and only recently have scholars begun to examine the consequences of the upheavals on party-group relations. A number of profound changes are restructuring the party-group connection in Italy. The most fundamental difference is the change in the political actors. The old governing parties (DC, PSI, PSDI, PRI, PLI) were all brought down by the Tangentopoli crisis and no longer exist. The main opposition parties—the PCI on the left and the MSI on the right—have adopted new, moderate identities. The old party groups splintered, then formed and reformed a variety of new parties and electoral alliances. New parties like the regional separatist Northern League and Berlusconi's Go, Italy! Party have quickly become important political forces (Newell and Bull 1997).

Changes have also occurred on the interest group side, although they have not been nearly as profound. In this highly fluid and uncertain political environment, groups—especially those in the old Catholic subculture—have had to reexamine their identities and organizational structures. Old political strategies have to be discarded or adapted to a new institutional environment that features fundamental reforms of electoral and campaign finance laws. Traditional interest group activities, such as the provision of technical information, take on new importance in Italy. And with a few exceptions, groups have sought to maintain public postures of partisan impartiality (Ferrante 1998, 97). Confindustria, for example, took an explicitly neutral position in the 1994 elections (Regini and Regalia 1997,

222). Associations that traditionally were less politically important, such as those representing small firms, and the service and crafts sectors, have been accorded a more prominent role during the Ciampi, Dini, Berlusconi, and Prodi governments (Ferrante 1998).

The political void left by the discredited parties could in theory be filled by interest groups, but interest fragmentation makes this highly unlikely. The breakdown of ideological ties between parties and groups has produced heightened competition for members among groups in the same economic sectors. Business groups in several provinces have responded to these changes by merging, and there are also discussions of mergers at the national level (Ferrante 1998, 101). The major trade union federations, facing declining memberships, have also discussed creating a single union organization (Regini and Regalia 1997, 220).

The weak position of parties and groups in Italy, along with the fiscal pressures emanating from European economic and monetary union, has led to a greater willingness of unions, employers, and governments to enter into peak-level negotiations on jobs, wages, and pensions (Regini and Regalia 1997, 213–229). Concertation, however, has limits. Neither employers nor unions felt obliged to restrain themselves from engaging in intense public relations campaigns, demonstrations, and strikes when it came time to respond to the taxes and expenditure cuts passed by the Romano Prodi government in 1997 and 1998 to meet the criteria set out in the 1992 Maastricht Treaty for membership in the European Monetary Union.

CONCLUSION

Tangentopoli and European integration have profoundly weakened the dominant role and gate-keeping function of Italian parties. Nevertheless, there are some indications that the political party–interest group connection remains important. A survey of business associations in Liguria indicated that political parties remain one of the most frequently used lobbying targets of regional interest groups, exceeded in frequency only by indirect lobbying through the national associations (Constantelos 1999). Thus, the interest group–political party connection persists, standing alongside other traditional influence-seeking strategies, just as LaPalombara observed back in 1964.

Continuity, however, has been overshadowed by change. And with the massive disruption of long-standing political relationships have come new and more sophisticated efforts to adjust to domestic, European, and international change. No longer is the political party channel paramount for interest groups. Italian interest groups are using a variety of new and old, direct and indirect, multilevel lobbying strategies that target legislators, administrators, and other decisionmakers from the local to the supranational levels (Constantelos 1996). Neither classic pluralist nor neocorporatist models accurately depict the new and still evolving political environment. Rather, we see a fluid and highly complex situation where traditional pluralist patterns are found alongside evolving sectoral policy networks and various macro and micro neocorporatist initiatives (Lange and Regini 1989, 249–272; Martinelli and Lanzalaco 1994, 333; Regini and Regalia 1997, 213–229).

8

Israel:
The End of Integration

Yael Yishai

As Israel celebrated its fiftieth anniversary in 1998, interest groups were becoming increasingly detached from political parties. They have become more autonomous organizationally and more challenging to parties ideologically. Old-style parties have lost their power, as well as their attraction to interest groups. Parties and groups exist in separate spheres; at the same time, the line distinguishing between them is blurred in many unexpected ways. First, many parties are interest groups in disguise; second, parties often establish groups as part of an electoral campaign; and third, a party-group alliance may confront a ruling party or promote a common cause. Part of these patterns is "new politics"; part is well embedded in the Israeli heritage. Given that Israel has been termed a "land of paradoxes" (Yishai 1991) where old and new, modern and traditional are complementary, the complexity of the relationship between groups and parties is hardly surprising.

On a more specific level, this chapter demonstrates the end of integration between parties and groups and identifies the new forms of linkage taking place between the two kinds of organizations, reflecting patterns of adjustment to changing circumstances. Two parallel processes can be identified. First, from intimate members of the same political family, members of parties and groups have turned into bitter rivals, if not enemies. Simultaneously, changes are noticeable in almost every aspect of Israeli life. Which process came first is a question of the chicken and the egg. Developments are so rapid that one can hardly stop and contemplate what will come next. Will groups win the game? Will parties regain their former power? Will society continue to change? The processes are in the making. This chapter attempts to take a bird's-eye view of the current situation, bearing in mind the dynamics of transition, as well as the power of tradition so pervasive in the Israel of the past.

POLITICAL BACKGROUND

The State of Israel formally came into existence on May 15, 1948, following a half-century struggle for political sovereignty and culminating as part of the aftermath of World War II. In the first three decades of independence Israel was characterized as a party state, a centralized state, an ideological state, and a compliant democracy.

The major players on the political scene were political parties, particularly the Mapai/Labor Party and the conservative Herut/Likud Party. Even in the years before statehood, parties and their subsidiary institutions had been growing powerful and centralized, playing a decisive role in the struggle for national independence—in part because of their functional contribution to the process of nation building. By providing social services, including welfare and health, parties played a vital role in enabling the new immigrants to cope with hardships involved in adjusting to the new land (Elazar 1986). Consequently, party machines became extremely strong, as their control of the political arena was virtually unlimited. Within their respective spheres parties remained the prime (often the sole) decisionmakers, and decisionmaking was concentrated increasingly in the hands of party leaders (Galnoor 1982; Medding 1972; Yanai 1981). Parties also controlled nominations to political offices. They colonized the state by succeeding in acquiring stipulated proportions of patronage positions in the bureaucracy and in the major public and quasi-public corporations. In short, they established a network of relationships based on the allocation of benefits and state assistance in exchange for votes and political activism.

To perform these functions, Israeli parties established a highly disciplined organizational structure and a dense network of interest groups. In a party state such as Israel, political parties fulfilled an essential role in the policy process; their influence was decisive in determining the course of the nation. These attributes had a profound effect on the relationships between parties and groups, the latter subservient to the enormous powers of the former. Parties began to lose their potency as they lost responsibility for functions, and their ideological appeal waned. Many parties became vote seekers, searching for electoral support among all social sectors and disregarding their traditional constituencies.

Israel was also characterized by a strong statist orientation. The state was viewed as a major instrument for social change and, accordingly, was expected to be comprehensive in its approach to its citizens and prepared to intervene in every aspect of life (Elazar 1986, 186). It was further expected that the state would be centralized, since it required centralization of power to achieve its comprehensive economic, social, and political goals—particularly the overriding goal of national survival in a region of hostile neighbors.

Centralization has had clear economic and legal manifestations. A few examples will suffice. In the past Israel was first among Western democracies in government expenditure, which amounted to 70 percent of gross domestic product (GDP). Government budget outlays ranked between 80 and 85 percent of GDP in some fiscal years. Government control of the national budget allowed wide political manipulation, including financing of political affiliates. The relatively high share of defense expenditure in the national income was another, perhaps a major, source of state centralization and was also a reason for the state's excessive involvement in economic life.

Another manifestation of centralization was seen in the pattern of employment, as a disproportionately high share of employment in Israel is in public service. Today the state still determines welfare payments, salaries, and the degree to which wages and other items are linked to the cost-of-living index. As a welfare state, Israel expends large sums on subsidies and transfer payments, which account for over 20 percent of the national budget. The high rate of state involvement in the economy has produced a heavy tax burden that is both direct and indirect. Economists have noted that despite the strong socialist orientation in the past, the share of indirect taxes is much greater in Israel than in other developed countries.

Finally, the state controls the supply of money through the Bank of Israel, which is responsible for the country's monetary policy. Although privatization of the economy took place in the 1990s, the State of Israel is still very powerful by Western standards. Statism affirmed the importance of state interests and the centralization of power at the expense of nongovernmental organizations and institutions and gave rise to values and symbols that recognized the state as an ultimate entity, legitimized its power, and mobilized the population to serve its goals.

Israel was a typical ideological society (Arian 1989). As may be the case in other new societies, the organizing principle in the foundation of the state was ideological. In this context ideology refers to a coherent body of ideas designed to shape the thinking of large publics by providing them with explicit guidelines (Elazar 1986, 13). The fundamentals of Zionism were established at the founding of the state and remained embedded in it, shaping its subsequent development. Israel was not considered another state, a member of the family of nations, but a state with a mission: to provide a safe homeland for Jews persecuted for generations and uprooted from their ancient land. Consequently, there was little tolerance for deviation from mainstream ideology, and narrow-minded sectarianism was branded as dissent. The term *interest* had a pejorative meaning because it signified partial sentiment not harnessed to the national effort.

Israel was a compliant democracy because of the high extent to which its citizens were mobilized to support the national cause. It was also termed a nonliberal democracy (Ben Eliezer 1993) because participation in politics was determined not by the motives and preferences of individual actors or by elite manipulation but by the institutional environment that defines social and political reality. Studies have shown that Israelis did not tend to translate their political involvement into activities such as communal work, political meetings, and contact with public officials. A practice of "critical compliance" became a habit, which has persisted until recently. Not even the 1977 electoral victory in which Likud replaced Labor, which had ruled (first as Mapai) for a generation, produced any substantial change in the norm of compliance. In Israel participation meant adhering to the unwritten rules of the game rather than influencing or severely challenging the authorities. In fact, few Israelis believed in their ability to change the system.

These characteristics—partyism, centralization, ideology, and compliance—affected party-group relationships in ways to be discussed later.

POLITICAL PARTIES, INTEREST GROUPS, AND THEIR RELATIONS

Relationships between political parties and interest groups in Israel have barely been studied. There are various accounts relating to the partisan arena (e.g., Medding 1972; Yanai 1981). Other studies have been devoted to political participation (Wolfsfeld 1988), particularly to political protest (Lehman-Wilzig 1992). Accounts of interest politics placed within the general description of Israeli politics (Arian 1989, 1993, 1998) have paid only marginal attention to the interaction of parties and groups. Exceptions are a chapter in a book devoted to interest politics in Israel (Yishai 1991) and a study delineating the relationship between interest groups and members of the Knesset (MKs) acting as party representatives (Yishai 1997).

Who are the major actors on the political scene? A review of the partisan and interest groups map presents the mélange of the Israeli scene. Worth noting is that both parties and groups are mandated to register in order to qualify for any legal action. An Association Law (Yishai 1998) and a Party Law specify the conditions for registration. Currently, four major blocs of parties are represented in the legislature: left-wing, right-center-wing, religious, and Arab parties. In Israel the distinction between left and right is based on a single indicator—attitude toward the peace process. Economic positions or attitudes toward the environment, for example, have nothing to do with the partisan division.

Political Parties

The left-wing bloc is dominated by the Labor Party, which recently amalgamated with two small factions, appearing in the 1999 elections as Yisrael

Ahat (One Israel). The Labor Party is the successor of Mapai, which for three decades was the unrivaled dominant party. Mapai was the largest vote getter and the major player in all government coalitions, as well as the standard-bearer of society's goals and the articulator of its aspirations (Arian 1998). Mapai, which enjoyed a broad-based, well-functioning, and flexible political organization, controlled the country's major economic and human resources. The Labor Party, formed in 1968, espouses moderate to dovish stands on security issues and advocates peace. Yitzhak Rabin, a Laborite, initiated the Oslo accords that led the way for peace with the Palestinians. The party is supported in the government by Meretz, a party situated further to the left in terms of its security orientations and social policy. The Labor Party endorses a moderate version of social democracy, leaning toward a policy of free markets. It enjoys the support of the upper classes, including well-to-do Jews of European descent and dwellers in old, established cities.

The right-wing bloc is headed by Likud, the successor of Herut, an arch-nationalist party. Herut was the direct ideological descendant of the Revisionists, a party opposing any conciliation with the Arabs. During the first two decades of independence Herut was "opposition in principle," lacking legitimacy and recognition. Since the mid-1960s, however, it has allied with other parties and gained access into mainstream Israeli politics. In 1977 Likud won the election and for the first time in Israeli history formed the governing coalition. Since then, Likud and Labor have alternated in controlling the government. In recent years Likud was an avowed supporter of Greater Israel, advocating uncompromising attitudes toward the Arabs. However, Likud leader Menachem Begin was the first prime minister to sign a peace treaty with an Arab state (Egypt). Binyamin Netanyahu, also a Likud leader, carried conciliation through by signing the Wye agreements. These changes reduced the ideological distance between left-wing and right-wing parties.

Rapprochement is also evident in regard to economic policy. The parties in the two major blocs repeatedly declare their commitment to aid the poor, yet neither converts its statements into actual policy. Likud attracts the support of the underprivileged in Israel who reside in development towns and distressed urban neighborhoods. Most Jews from Arabic-speaking countries and their descendants vote for Likud. To the right of Likud there is only a splinter party with four MKs. The right-wing position appears to be losing ground in Israel, whose people are yearning for peace.

The religious bloc comprises three main parties: Agudat Israel, the National Religious Party (NRP), and Shas. Three major elements differentiate the religious parties: their degree of religiosity, their militancy regarding the territories, and ethnic origin of party supporters (Arian 1998, 127). Agudat Israel is the most extreme in its orthodox stand. Although it supports the current coalition composed mainly of secular parties, it refused to accept a ministerial portfolio and is content to offer passive support from the outside. Its adherents often stage demonstrations against the desecration of the Sabbath. The NRP is the most militant of the three religious parties regarding the territories. Its major base of support consists of the settlers in the West Bank. Shas was established in 1984 as a reaction against discrimination toward Jews from Asia and Africa in Agudat Israel. It is the only "social" party in the country and genuinely represents the interests of the underprivileged. Agudat Israel and Shas have their own educational systems, which insulates the younger generation from society at large. Worth noting is an ardent antireligious party, Shinui (Change), which joined the electoral race in 1999 and won six seats. This amazing success, in Israeli terms, reveals a deep antireligious sentiment among the public.

The Arab parties constitute the last bloc. Presently there are three Arab parties: Hadash, previously the communist party; Ra'am, an Islamist-oriented party; and Balad, an arch-nationalist party. Around 70 percent of Arabs residing in Israel vote for Arab parties, with the rest dividing their support among the numerous Jewish parties. In the past the Arabs were considered outsiders and lacked access to the locus of authority. They are still not members of any governing coalition, but they have come much closer to the inner circles of power. For example, in July 1999 for the first time in Israeli history a member of an Arab nationalist party was granted a seat on the Knesset Committee on Foreign and Security Affairs, a prestigious position reserved for "insiders."

As noted, in the past almost all parties were closely linked to all types of interest groups including women's associations, settlement movements, educational enterprises, and economic groups, to name just a few. With the growing distance between state and society, parties have become detached from the interest arena, focusing mainly on obtaining votes. The process had been accompanied by the cartelization of political parties (Katz and Mair 1995)—namely, relying on state resources for organizational purposes, penetrating the bureaucracy, and developing professional machinery to handle party affairs. Parties, however, were injected with new energy with the adoption in 1994 of a new electoral system establishing direct election of the prime minister simultaneously with voting for the party of one's preference. The double ballot enabled voters to pronounce their broad disposition on the one hand and assert their particular interest on the other. This caused a proliferation of parties, fifteen of which were represented in the Knesset after the 1999 election. Many of these parties advocate particular interests.

Interest Groups

The universe of interest groups is ever changing and growing. Its origins lie in the prestate era, when the entire structure of the community was based on voluntary arrangements. The largest economic associations are the Histadrut (the Israel Labor Federation) and the Manufacturers' Association. In the past, the Histadrut hardly fit the simple category of a trade union. Although it represented the interests of salaried workers, it undertook wider tasks of nation building. It was engaged in training workers in its economic enterprises, providing them with social and health services, offering cultural and recreational activities, and educating their children. Today the Histadrut resembles trade unions in other Western societies. Deprived of most of its economic assets (including the sick fund, whose relations with the Histadrut were severed by law) and far less engaged in social activities, the organization focuses on winning economic benefits for salaried workers.

The Manufacturers' Association (MA), organized along functional lines (such as chemicals or electronics), leads the business groups. The MA exerts considerable influence on economic policymaking, with its leaders well integrated into the centers of power. The MA also heads the Coordinating Office of the Economic Associations, an umbrella organization representing the business community, in tripartite wage negotiations. Other important associations are the Chamber of Commerce and the Associations of Contractors and Builders, all with deep roots in Israel's economic history. Other interest groups important in shaping policy are professional associations such as the Israel Medical Association, the Teachers' Federation, and the Bar Association (the only association granted legal recognition; each practicing lawyer is required to register).

Most economic interest groups enjoy a high density of membership, particularly groups whose members are wage earners. Density results from a tradition of organizational affiliation derived from norms prevalent in the prestate era but is also sustained by legal regulations. The Extension Law stipulates that only one group is eligible to represent its sector. Consequently, interest groups are not legally barred from splitting, but the splinter group will be deprived of the status of a "recognized" group. Most interest groups not only have dense memberships but actually monopolize their area of interest. There is, for example, only one manufacturers' association, one medical association, and one bureau of engineers.

Public interest groups have not been very active throughout Israel's history. Israel is a collective-oriented society whose citizens have been mobilized to support the national cause, so challenging authorities has not been a daily practice. Environmental and consumer groups are still rudimentary, lagging far behind their counterparts in Western societies. Social protest movements have appeared rarely; women's associations have traditionally branched off from political parties.

The one area in which groups have been extremely active is in promoting peace and security. The future fate of the territories occupied during the

Six Day War (1967) and the relationship with the Palestinian population occupy a prime position on the political and public agenda. Parties are founded and movements are formed to promote a position at either end of the political spectrum: either advocating retaining the territories and opposing far-reaching concessions to the Palestinians or supporting territorial retreat and compromising attitudes in line with the Oslo agreements. The territorial issue has become a major problem in electoral campaigns and a major focus for collective action. The most noted of the groups preoccupied with the issue of peace and security are Gush Emunim, made up mainly of settlers of the territories, and Peace Now, advocating retreat from certain lands. There are a few dozen splinter groups from these parent associations, including subgroups organized on the basis of demography (Women for Peace, Professors for Security) or degree of militancy. Public interest groups are also active in regard to the basic cleavage in Israeli society—that between religious and secular groups. The orthodox and those opposing what they regard as religious coercion have staged the most vociferous protests.

The voluntary sector grew enormously in the 1990s. In the past the highly bureaucratized and centralized state, dominated by political parties, cared for the weak and vulnerable (Kramer 1981). Its control of welfare was sustained by the widespread belief that the state was responsible for solving almost any personal problem. Today welfare associations are proliferating. Many have strong ties with government agencies, which support them financially and functionally.

Finally, some interest groups are unique to Israel's short history. There are the settlement movements, comprising cooperative farming groups (kibbutz and moshav), whose past contribution to the process of nation building has been invaluable. There are immigrant associations that mirror the kaleidoscope of Israel's demographics. For example, there are around forty associations of immigrants from the former Soviet Union and twenty-five organizations of Ethiopian Jews, to name just two examples.

Political Party–Interest Group Relations

This analysis of party-group relations in Israel follows my classification (Yishai 1995) identifying five possible forms across a "positive-negative" spectrum—integration, cooperation, separation, rivalry, and confrontation (see Box 1.2 for a modification).

In the past the relationship between political parties and interest groups tended to be highly integrative, to the extent that the former absorbed the latter. This is particularly true for trade unions and settlement movements, but other organizations—such as the Teachers Federation, unions of immigrants, and even economic groups such as the Association of Artisans and

Small Industrialists—were also integrated with political parties. Integration Israeli style matched what Joseph LaPalombara (1964) called *"parentela* relationships"—denoting consanguinity, lineage, or kinship independent of immediate benefits or instrumental considerations. A parent is a member of one's family and is thus entitled to special privileges. Today, however, integration is the exception rather than the rule. It exists primarily in the ultra-religious parties, whose educational enterprises are organized as groups but for all practical purposes are part of the party milieu.

Relations between settlement movements and parties vividly illustrate the pattern of past integration. The kibbutz embodied the most cherished ideals of Zionism. Although most newcomers preferred urban life to rural communal settlements, farming epitomized the fundamental tenets of the return to the ancient homeland. The persuasiveness of the settlement idea cut across the political spectrum; almost all political parties had their own affiliated settlement movement. Even Herut, an urban-centered right-wing party, and non-Zionist parties, such as the ultraorthodox Agudat Israel, were patrons of settlement movements. The unique affinity between politics and land persisted long after the establishment of the state. Relations between parties and their respective settlement movements were founded not on rewards but on overarching solidarity. Farming in Israel embodied the very essence of politics.

The Histadrut was also integrated with political parties. The integrative relationship between Histadrut and the parties was manifested in three domains: internal elections, selection of leadership, and funding. Histadrut internal elections served as an arena for party control, and competition for party control was a microcosm of national politics. Political parties not only determined the composition of Histadrut governing bodies but also took measures to safeguard and consolidate their power by establishing a bureaucracy on whose loyalty they could count. The Histadrut thus became a stronghold of political parties, particularly of the Labor Party, an integrated partner that controlled its apparatus and governing institutions. Here, too, ideology served as a cohesive element. The pioneer spirit in Israel was embodied in the Labor Federation whose declared task was to found a state for, rather than represent the interests of, the fledgling working class.

The relationship between political parties and interest groups is no longer integrative. The links with settlement movements were attenuated as a result of political and economic changes, discussed later. Instead, settlement movements became "clients" seeking support on the basis of material claims. The kibbutz movement, for example, competes with other sectors for state resources, deriving its bargaining power not from its past role in Israel's history but from its contribution to the contemporary economy. The relationship between the Labor Party and the Histadrut has also lost much of the radiance it enjoyed in the past. The party can no longer rely on the

Histadrut as a source of either human or financial support. Relations, in fact, have become competitive. In 1999 the Histadrut presented its own list for the Knesset elections, actually diverting votes from the establishment parties. The Histadrut list, comprising two MKs, was not even invited to join the coalition headed by its former "parent party," the Labor Party.

Integration seems dead, but in some areas it has apparently survived the changes occurring on the political scene. The security domain—the major policy arena in Israeli politics—provides a good example. Right-wing parties (in December 2000 members of the opposition) are integrated with nationalist movements, the most prominent of which are the settlers of the Occupied Territories. Likewise, the left-wing parties, headed by the Labor Party, are coalescing with peace movements that endorse conciliatory attitudes toward the Arabs. Integration, however, is assuming new forms, as no one group is attached to a particular party and no structured organizational relationship is evident. Parties and groups employ joint strategies and act in concert to promote their cause. Rather than being chained to each other, they associate to the extent of amalgamation. Top leaders may be active in both party and group, and the door revolves for activists in both organizations. Integration is apparent particularly during an election campaign when groups spring up to act on behalf of a national leader aspiring for the premiership. These associations are defined as interest groups, but for all practical purposes they are part and parcel of the partisan milieu. After elections the groups dissipate, lying low until the next election. Thus, this form of integration is ephemeral.

Economic groups continue to maintain cooperative relationships with political parties. As in other Western countries, they have become part of the ruling class, which, however, is accessible to newcomers. The dramatic upsurge of the high-tech industry has brought to the fore of the policy arena a technological sector of engineers and experts. The newcomers have no party affiliation, maintaining a close relationship mainly with the state bureaucracy. Bearing in mind the ongoing party penetration into the civil service, it can be claimed that economic groups enter into cooperation not with the state machinery but with tacit agents of parties. Obviously, these relations have nothing to do with ideology or with traditional patterns of party-group linkage.

Professionals are at present, as in the past, detached from political parties. Their power vis-à-vis political authorities has somewhat weakened. Privatization of government-owned companies, which is under way, has made them vulnerable partners at the wage negotiating table. Doctors' threat to strike and close down public medical facilities is much less effective when private medicine is readily available. Charity associations, on the other hand, are becoming more robust. This so-called third sector is rapidly expanding in Israel, occupying its own milieu without partisan interference. Growth is evident in both volume and function as welfare organizations increasingly cover more areas of social activity. For example, groups dealing with domestic violence obtain state resources without allowing the government to interfere with their strategies or goals.

Rivalry is evident on the electoral scene. Groups fostering identity (such as Jews of Moroccan origin) or specific interests (such as immigrants from the former Soviet Union) have established parties in the local and national arenas. As noted, the power of the two major parties, Labor and Likud, has substantially declined because, among other things, of the mounting attraction of "interest parties" concentrating on one particular interest. In 1999 forty-seven MKs (39.2 percent of the total) represented such groups in the legislature, including Arabs, religious constituencies, and past or recent immigrants. According to these criteria, rivalry between parties and groups is lively and intense.

Finally, the politics of confrontation is rampant, particularly among public interest groups that have become much more vocal in their opposition to authoritative decisions. This is true for women's groups, disgruntled workers (only some of whom are unionized), and environmental groups, which often merge to prevent what they deem to constitute an ecological disaster. The tune of these groups has changed radically. Even a formerly compliant group such as the Nature Society (Hahevra Lahagant Hateva) is now applying militant strategies to counter political decisions.

To sum up, Israeli interest groups exhibit all types of relationships with political parties. Changes over time are evident: integration is far less prevalent today, with many groups moving toward cooperation. Separation is increasing, and competition is reshaping the partisan map. Challenge is a daily phenomenon, although it is exercised mostly within the context of the overarching consensus characterizing a compliant democracy. Changes are also manifested in the four dimensions of linkage between parties and groups: the organizational, economic, ideological, and personal. The legal requirement to register and the scrutiny of groups' organizational activities virtually ended direct organizational links between parties and groups. The banning of contributions to party activities severed the economic ties between parties and groups. The ideological ties have loosened but are not yet undone. Parties and groups still share worldviews and interests, mutually sustaining each other. This may be the case regarding the personal aspects of their relations as well. More often than not, group activists are renowned party members, and vice versa. Integration is no longer the name of the game; it is only one game among others.

DETERMINANTS OF THE PARTY-GROUP RELATIONSHIP

Relationships between political parties and interest groups in Israel have been affected by economic, cultural, political, and legal changes. Economic changes have turned Israel into an affluent society, with average annual growth of nearly 6 percent throughout its existence. Average per capita annual income in Israel was approximately $17,000 in 1998, not far behind the Western European level. The standard of living, as measured by the diffusion of durable goods, has risen dramatically. Around 60 percent of Israelis own their own homes; nearly half of the population possesses a car. Airline tickets must be reserved months ahead because of the massive exodus of Israeli travelers during summer vacation. A letter in a daily paper was headed: "We are tired of raising the banner. We want to enjoy life" (*Haaretz,* 22 June 1996). In contemporary Israel consumerism is the epitome of the good life, not draining the swamps or making the desert bloom as it was in the early days of the nation. This striking rise in the standard of living has increased the inclination toward group politics and decreased party identification.

The most important cultural factor contributing to the changing relationship between parties and groups has been the shift from collectivism to individualism. Emphasis on the private realm is evident in art, music, poetry, and literature. Israel's intellectual and cultural elite has warded off the collectivist mores of young Israel, mores that sustain mobilization to the national cause. Young Israelis, like their Western counterparts, are turning into a "me generation" centered on the self rather than on the future fate of the Jewish people. These changes have evolved gradually. Amos Elon, who has pinpointed the generation gap in Israeli society, perceived them in the early 1970s: "The old pioneers pursued essence; the younger generation's approach is existential. . . . The former were oriented to a future perfect; the latter are living intensely in the here and now" (Elon 1971, 260). Surveys comparing needs in 1970 and 1990 reveal a decline in all collective-oriented spheres. Fewer people are "proud we have a state"; fewer are interested in "what the world thinks of us." A striking decline of 13 percent from 1970 to 1990 is evident in feeling a need to trust our leaders. At the same time individual-oriented items, such as "having a good time," "relaxing," or "getting to know myself," rose substantially in importance (E. Katz et al. 1992).

Political changes have both resulted from and precipitated the alterations in the economy and in society that led to a shift in the relationship between political parties and interest groups. There are macrolevel changes triggered by the inception of the peace process. Peaceful societies are more inclined to adopt postmaterialist attitudes and shy away from traditional party politics. More relevant to the subject under discussion are the microlevel changes, particularly the expansion of the bodies selecting candidates to national elections, the electoral reform referred to earlier, and the changing modes of electoral competition. Public relations agencies have assumed a major role in election campaigns, with their professional staff replacing grassroots volunteers. The political implications of these practices for the polity at large are beyond the scope of this chapter. Here suffice it to note their impact on relations between parties and groups. One obvious manifestation is the weakening of parties on the one hand and the growing salience of groups, movements, and grassroots associations on the other.

Finally, legal changes have also affected party-group relations. In the mid-1990s a Party Finance Law was introduced that strictly limited financial contributions by individuals to small sums. Groups and corporations were barred from donating money. A statutory committee was formed, authorized to determine the amount of money available for party use. Parties thus could not solicit more state funding, but they were also prohibited from mustering substantial contributions. These legal arrangements contributed to a rapprochement between parties and groups. Interest groups were prohibited from donating money but were allowed to aid parties by roundabout means, as, for example, the Women's Network did for all women candidates by coaching them and providing them with professional advice. Netanyahu's victory in 1996 was attributed, among other things, to the mass support mustered by Habad, a religious group. Associations could also act on behalf of candidates by disseminating their message. Free of the financial shackles imposed on parties, interest groups could innocently advocate a cause that happened to coincide with that of the party.

To sum up, all changes enumerated here—economic, cultural, political, and legal—influenced the relationship between parties and groups. Growing prosperity turned Israel into an affluent society whose members are profit seekers. This trend was nurtured by an individualistic ideology that prepared the ground for privatization. In many cases ideology no longer glued parties and groups together. The political context, centered on the decentralization of the political process, precipitated the change of relations. The fading of compliance, coupled with the decline of establishment parties, further contributed to the detachment. Legal arrangements regarding party financing, however, drew parties and groups closer.

CONSEQUENCES FOR DEMOCRACY

In the previous section the relation between parties and groups was analyzed as a dependent variable, a result of economic, ideological, political, and legal changes. In this section this relationship serves as an independent variable, explaining changes in the political system. Briefly stated, these changes are manifested in the power structure, in the policymaking process, and in forms of representation.

First, in the past, parties occupied the center of power, so groups used them to get issues onto the political agenda. However, empirical data from a study conducted by the author in 1990 on the interaction of groups with parties reveal the dearth of appeals by groups to parties. Groups were also asked whether their relationship with parties had weakened, strengthened, or remained the same in the decade preceding the study (the 1980s). The proportion of groups that claimed to have had "no relationship with parties" was strikingly high. The most common answer revealed a tendency of weakening ties with parties, even among groups identified in the study as party affiliated (such as the Histadrut and settlement movements). Only 20 percent of the group activists participating in the study (n=162) reported having contacted parties in their attempts to influence policy decisions (Yishai 1991). This finding reflects (rather than explains) the shifts in power structure, removing parties from their preponderant position.

Second, consequences are evident in the policymaking arena. The severance of integrative links with political parties has enabled interest groups to gain direct access to decisionmakers. In fact, more than in the past, representatives of interest groups themselves are part of the policy process. The Knesset's popularity among interest groups is steadily growing. The practice of lobbying, previously uncommon in the legislature, is gaining momentum. Group representatives roam Knesset corridors, prodding MKs to promote their area of interest or to refrain from supporting a cause they oppose. Attempts by disgruntled legislators to qualify lobbyists' access and to impose restrictions on their activity have failed. The "privatization" of politics has made the relationship with interest groups important for MKs seeking reelection. It remains unclear, however, if interest group personnel attempting to influence legislators perceive them as partisan representatives or as members of an important political institution who happen to have previously appeared on a partisan list.

The Knesset lobby for children's welfare provides a good example of group influence on the policy process. For the lobbyists, the need to curb violence against children and to protect their rights is an overriding concern. They exert pressure on legislators without resorting to party mediation. This does not imply that movements are replacing parties but rather that their power has substantially increased. Groups are no longer absorbed by political parties but exercise autonomous influence on the policy process.

Finally, relations between parties and groups carry implications for the representation system. As noted previously, interest groups have gained direct access to the legislature by presenting lists for national elections. The parties of new immigrants and veteran Moroccan Jews have been mentioned. To these we can add the settlers of the Golan, members of the kibbutz movements, members of trade unions, members of women's associations, the representative of the Teachers' Federation, and settlers in the

Occupied Territories. This is not a conclusive list of legislators recruited by political parties to represent groups and movements. Admittedly, group representation was also evident during the integration era, but group representatives then were loyal proponents of their respective parties' ends and barely spoke up on behalf of their associational interests. This is no longer true in contemporary Israel.

To sum up, the underlying question is whether civil society in Israel has matured to the extent that it is replacing the model of the party state that typified Israel in its first three decades of existence. The answer is equivocal. There is little doubt that interest groups, growing in both numbers and power, cannot be ignored as an influence on the policy process. This is evident in the local and national arenas of power. Citizens organize to block the construction of skyscrapers in urban neighborhoods; students strike for lower tuition and to improve the quality of higher education. At the same time, parties and groups still merge in many respects, leaving Israel outside the family of pluralist societies.

CONCLUSION

The foregoing has set out the changes taking place both in Israel's political arena and in the particular sphere of party-group relations. The discussion has demonstrated the attenuation of the *parentela* relationship and its replacement with a more down-to-earth, instrumental, cooperative one. Modifications in party-group relations are not confined to cooperation, however. Some groups still pursue party support if not patronage, some are turning into parties themselves, and others seek means other than partisanship to enter the core of power. For them the Knesset is not the political home of parties but the source of policies, the overwhelming majority of which were not previously debated in partisan forums. Traditional partyism, centralization, ideological affinity, and compliance are perishing, clearing the way to different types of party-group relations.

What does the future hold for party-group relations in Israel? Speculations depend on the likelihood that socioeconomic and political changes will persist. Interest groups will probably grow more salient as individuals become increasingly aware of their own needs, shying away from the collective mood that used to be pervasive. The question remains open, however, as to the direction relations between groups and parties will take: toward the positive or the negative end of the scale. Integration is unlikely to return in its past form. The easing of rules governing party financing is likely to weaken the present forms of quasi-integration. Cooperation is likely to increase if the standard of living continues to rise, if the peace process culminates in the termination of belligerence, and if society's demographic composition stabilizes. Separation will be more common with further modernization of society, the expansion of high-tech industry, and the ascent to power of experts and professionals. Rivalry is likely to decline if the blocking percentage is increased (the minimum percentage of votes needed for a party to secure a seat in parliament, presently 1.5 percent of the valid vote) or the direct election of the prime minister is eliminated, which has recently been under discussion. Challenge is expected to increase if the cleavages ripping Israel apart endure; these include rifts within the Jewish community based on country of origin, religiosity, and gender and on the national division between Jews and Arabs. Confrontation is likely to challenge the existing rifts and to intensify the demands groups make on parties and their governing representatives.

The Israeli case, unique as it may seem, can provide clues to a broader understanding of the party-group relationship. Three conclusions emerge.

First, in line with findings in other societies, especially those characterized by a strong party system (e.g., Selle 1997), it is evident that integrative relationships between parties and groups are declining. Groups are becoming less dependent on parties and are functioning on their own merits. This does not imply the total shattering of traditional structures but a more balanced political system where power is divided among various actors and not monopolized by one.

Second, changes in the relationship between parties and groups are evidently structured not only by internal processes occurring within these two types of organizations or by the expanding political market (J. Richardson 1995) but by macro processes as well. In this regard, the relationship between the two important mediating organizations may serve as a yardstick for examining broader political processes.

Third, relationships between parties and groups, although an important indicator of broader changes, may in themselves trigger further modifications in the policy process. These are evident on the two levels of the political system: on the input level, where demands are shaped and articulated, and on the output level, where demands are processed into policy outputs. Relations between parties and groups thus not only mirror the input-output balance but can modify it in a way that tilts the balance of power from state (party) to society, or vice versa.

9

Japan: Strong State, Spectator Democracy, and Modified Corporatism

Ronald J. Hrebenar

It is appropriate for Japan to be the sole Asian nation in this comparative study of interest groups and their relationship with political parties in liberal democracies for several reasons. Japan was the first Asian nation to modernize following the Meiji Revolution in the 1860s, which destroyed the feudal regime of the Tokugawa Shogunate, the rulers of Japan since the early 1600s. Japan had never been colonized by Western powers, thus maintaining a distinctly Japanese political system and political culture whereas all other Asian nations (except Thailand) were ruled by foreigners.

Even more important than these historical developments is that Japan has not only become the richest and most modern economic system in Asia, it was also the first democracy in Asia and is the most developed and firmly established democracy in the region. Partly as a consequence of these characteristics of its political economy, Japan has the most developed interest group system in Asia, in many ways comparable to systems in countries like Britain, France, Germany, and even the United States. Furthermore, it can be argued that the Japanese system exhibits a form of corporatism that appears to place it within the tradition of many liberal democracies, particularly those of continental Europe.

Given all these factors, particularly the corporatist element, what has influenced the party-group relationship in Japan and continues to do so is a triangular relationship among the state, parties, and interests. In this regard the shaping of the party-group connection in Japan has parallels to France, where the state plays a major role. At the same time, elements of the Italian clientelistic relationship of parties and groups are also evident. Yet in the end the Japanese version of the triangular relationship shaping party-group relations is peculiarly Japanese. The melding of Western-style parties and interests with the particulars of Japanese development and political culture has produced a situation in which the state, especially the bureaucracy, plays the major role in affecting party-group relations. The peculiarities of the Japanese case also mean the typology developed in Box 1.2 regarding classifying party-group relations has some relevance to Japan but needs some modification and qualification within the nation's Confucian traditions.

A body of literature exists on parties, interest groups, and the bureaucracy in Japan and on the role of all three in policymaking. However, no treatment specifically focuses on the party-group relationship in a comprehensive way to provide an overall picture of these relations and to assess their importance for democracy and policymaking in Japan. Largely through a synthesis of the existing literature, this chapter provides a big picture of the party-group connection in Japan and the nuances of its significance, past and present. What we will see, and what forms the central theme of this chapter, is the important cementing role the Japanese bureaucracy has played in this connection, mainly in conjunction with the Liberal Democratic Party and the Japanese business community, with the qualification that recent developments have changed the situation somewhat.

BACKGROUND

The Tokugawa Shogunate set the tone for interest group development in Japan's premodern era (1600–1865). The samurai, or warrior class, dominated Japan as military rulers, as well as staffing the Tokugawa bureaucracy. Businessmen were formally on the bottom of the Japanese Confucian hierarchy (from top to bottom: samurais, peasants, artisans, and merchants). However, after hundreds of years of peace the samurai lost much of their fighting skill and became bureaucrats more than warriors. Many fell into serious debt to the prosperous merchant class.

Later, when the Tokugawas had been defeated and Japan decided to open itself to the world and modernize as quickly as possible to avoid the colonial fates of other Asian nations, the important new industries were managed by either prominent merchants or former samurai. The new economic interests of the Meiji era (1865–1912) were government financed and "controlled" even though they were in the private sector. The two most powerful economic conglomerates that emerged from these government-supported industrialization plans were the Mitsubishi and Mitsui *zaibatsu*. A *zaibatsu* was a multicompany conglomerate with very close ties to government, organized around a holding company with control of the associated companies. Japan set up a series of trading companies to control most imports and exports; these companies were usually part of the powerful *zaibatsu* systems.

Perhaps the most important characteristic of the political party system in pre–World War II Japan was that the two major parties were controlled by Mitsui and Mitsubishi, respectively. Another Meiji-era decision was to exploit the agricultural sector to pay for industrialization. The Japanese government would tolerate nothing that might destabilize the farming communities and their essential role as the foundation of the economic and political system.

Consequently, the Meiji government held a tight rein over the industrial sector and its labor force, as well as the agricultural sector. No real interest groups were allowed to operate unless they agreed to become part of the ruling system. Groups that threatened the system were outlawed, persecuted, and destroyed by the government. Political parties and elections were also tightly controlled by the government. Thus, while Japan adopted political parties and democracy from Western Europe when it modernized in the late nineteenth century, as it did with every Western institution it imported, it grafted these very foreign concepts onto a Japanese political foundation.

During the Tokugawa era a centralized government bureaucracy began to emerge, and that tradition was picked up by the Meiji reformers. Powerful ministries developed in Tokyo that channeled participation of the nation's now modernized interests into the political decisionmaking process. When the militarist government surrendered to U.S. forces in 1945, one of the most significant decisions by Gen. Douglas MacArthur as he administered the occupation reforms was to utilize the Japanese national bureaucracy as the tool for administering the "democratization." Subsequently, a substantial part of interest group access to the political system has continued to be channeled through the appropriate national-level government ministries.

The postwar party systems also provide a channel of communication and access for the interest group system. In 1993 the First Postwar Party System died and the Second Postwar Party System began to emerge. This second party system has provided new opportunities for interest representation in Japan.

MAJOR PARTIES, GROUPS, AND SOCIAL MOVEMENTS

Political Parties

The Liberal Democratic Party (LDP) ruled Japan without the need for coalition from its formation in 1955 until a split in the party in 1993—one of the longest ruling periods in any democracy in the world. Every prime minister during those thirty-eight years came from the LDP. The LDP led Japan from just after the end of the occupation to a point in the late 1980s when Japan was, by one account, the richest nation in the world (Boyle 1993, 354).

The LDP is a pragmatic party that is basically conservative in upholding traditional Japanese values, coupled with a strong probusiness orientation and a pro-U.S. military and foreign policy. The LDP members are divided into five major factions that provide support groups for selecting party and government leadership posts such as the party president or prime minister and cabinet members, raise funds for election campaigns, and provide support groups for those campaigns. The factions are not distinguished by issue or ideological differences, merely by their desire to access power for its own rewards.

The LDP lost power in 1993 when one of its five major internal factions left the party, and the dissidents joined with other existing parties to form a government. Non-LDP governments were formed under former LDP members Morihiko Hosokawa and Tsutomu Hata before the LDP joined with the Socialists and an LDP splinter group to form successive governments between 1994 and 1996.

From 1955 to 1993 Japan's main opposition party was the Japan Socialist Party (JSP), which was highly ideological. In many ways it was much more left than the Japanese Communist Party (JCP), which has functioned as the nation's main protest party since just after World War II. These two parties never came close to winning national-level political power on their own. The Socialists were part of several coalition governments in the mid-1990s after the LDP fell from power. However, following the 1996 elections to the House of Representatives (the lower chamber of the Japanese Diet), the Socialists fell from their position as the party with the second-highest number of seats, gained in 1993, to just a handful of seats, which they retained in the 2000 elections.

Japan had essentially a two-party system immediately after the formation of the LDP and JSP in 1955. There was a very small Communist Party, but it was insignificant. In 1960 a splinter group from the JSP formed the moderate Democratic Socialist Party (DSP). One other party emerged in 1964, the Clean Government Party (CGP), based on the huge Buddhist lay sect, the Soka Gakkai. The CGP generally wins about 10 percent of the seats in the House of Representatives.

After the LDP split in 1993, a number of new parties were formed, mainly by former LDP members. These new parties merged in 1996 to form the New Frontier Party (NFP), led by several former LDP leaders and their followers plus members of the JSP, DSP, and CGP. With the establishment of the New Frontier Party a two-party system emerged in Japan, as was the situation between 1955 and 1960. However, the NFP broke up within two years—in January 1998—and after a period of small splinter parties that formed from the NFP's wreckage, two new parties emerged, the

Liberal Party (LP) and the Democratic Party (DP; not to be confused with the Liberal Democratic Party).

The new Japanese party system, Japan's Second Postwar Party System, is composed as follows. Once again the dominant party is the ruling LDP. The Democratic Party has emerged as the main opposition party. Two parties have joined the LDP in coalition governments—the Liberal Party, led by former LDP and NFP leader Ozawa Ichiro, and the CGP, which reemerged in the late 1990s. Finally, there are the remnants of the old left, the JCP and JSP, or Social Democratic Party of Japan as it now calls itself (Hrebenar 2000).

Interest Groups and Social Movements

The most powerful private-sector political interests in Japan are in the business world, whose political elite is relatively easy to identify (Yanaga 1968; Curtis 1975). In a society based on hierarchical rankings, the apex of business's lobbying pyramid is occupied by one umbrella organization, the all-powerful Keidanren (Japan Federation of Economic Organizations). Founded just after World War II, Keidanren represents the elite of the Japanese business world. Its regular dues-paying members include over 100 industrial associations and nearly a thousand major corporations. Although its membership accounts for only 1 percent of Japanese companies and 10 percent of Japanese employees, the organization represents 40 percent of Japan's sales and half of the nation's capital (Allinson 1987; Woronoff 1986; Pemple 1977). Keidanren's chairman is considered by most Japanese to be the spokesman for the Japanese business world and is treated like an ambassador by politicians and bureaucrats.

On the second tier of corporate political power are three specialized umbrella organizations: Nikkeiren (Federation of Japanese Employers), the Renmei (the Japan Chamber of Commerce and Industry), and the Keizai Doyukai (the Japan Committee on Economic Development). Nikkeiren handles labor relations for corporate Japan and deals with wage demands during the unions' spring and fall labor offensives. Renmei represents the tens of thousands of companies on the local level of Japanese business. These companies are organized into local chambers of commerce, as in many other nations. The Keizai Doyukai originally represented middle-level management in midsized, more progressive Japanese companies and functioned somewhat as a think tank for producing new ideas and solutions to the business world's problems. In recent years, however, the group has stagnated; it now has an older, more conservative membership and has lost its progressive image.

These three umbrella organizations together with Keidanren have significant membership overlap, but that does not always produce a single voice representing the business world. Intraindustry and interindustry conflicts occur, and conflicts between major umbrella organizations such as Keidanren and Renmei develop on occasion. When such conflicts occur, business lobbying is often handled by the giant industrial families, the appropriate trade associations, or even individual corporations. Conflict can occur within many business sectors as noted by Horne (1988), who studied conflicts in the financial community among major securities companies and banks.

Also located on this second tier of business organizations are the major industrial groups. Called *kigyo shudan* (enterprise groups), *keiretsu,* or just *gurupu,* these are the various postwar manifestations of the prewar *zaibatsu* such as Mitsubishi, Mitsui, and Sumitomo. Other groups have formed around major banks such as Dai-Ichi Kangyo or vertically integrated entrepreneurial groups such as Toyota.

The third rank of business lobbies is composed of the hundreds of trade and industrial associations. With the Japanese tendency to organize and develop groups and associations, many industries in Japan may be better organized than those in Western industrial nations—for example, the Japan Eraser Manufacturers Association, the Japan Gas Lighter Association, and the All Japan Curry Manufacturers Association.

Development of a Japanese labor movement was encouraged in the early years of the occupation (1945–1948), but the Americans allowed the Japanese government and the business world to crush the movement under an anticommunist crusade. Unions became company unions, and Japanese labor became the most docile labor force in any major industrial nation. The Japanese labor movement has been dominated by large labor federations. One, the Sohyo, was leftist and was constituted largely of public employee unions; the other, the Domei, was moderate and was made up largely of private-sector unions, especially those in the automobile industry. A new combined labor federation emerged in 1989 when Rengo (full name Zen Nihon Rodo Kumiai Rengo Kai) was formed under Domei leadership to combine the moderate private-sector unions that had been divided between Sohyo and Domei since 1960.

Perhaps the most powerful specialized interest in Japan is the agriculture lobby as represented by its two peak associations, Zenno (National Federation of Agricultural Cooperative Associations) and Zenchu (Central Union of Agricultural Cooperatives). These two organizations draw support from the more than 6 million members of farmers' cooperatives (Nogyo Kyodo Kumiai, or nokyo) that represent Japan's 21 million people with an interest in agriculture, which includes around 4.1 million households and approximately 2 million part-time farmers.

Among the other groups that have a strong impact on Japan's politics in a specialized sector is the medical profession, which is well represented by the Japan Medical and Japan Dental Associations and their political activities committees such as the Political Alliance of Japanese Doctors.

Generally, religious associations have very little political impact in largely secular Japan. The only strongly politicized religious group is the new Buddhist religion Soka Gakkai, which started its own relatively conservative political party in 1964. This is the Clean Government Party (Komeito), referred to earlier, a coalition partner in the LDP-led government.

Despite some determined efforts, the consumer and environmentalist movements have never developed in Japan as they have in other Western industrial nations. Almost all environmentalist groups that do exist are oriented toward a particular pollution problem in a particular locale (McKean 1977; Reed 1981; Krauss and Simcock 1989). Japan has many small consumer organizations, many locally based, but none have become a major national organization. The consumer group that perhaps comes closest is Shufuren (Japan Housewives Association), which played a major role in electing many female candidates to the Diet's upper house, the House of Councilors, in 1989. Women's liberation movements as such do not exist as effective organizations in Japan. Most women's groups that do operate concentrate on such topics as food cost reductions and local issues (Woronoff 1986, 202). The Japanese Women's Voters League represents a broad range of women's issues including calls for more reform in Japanese politics. In the 1989 House of Councilors elections, the president of the organization, Teiko Kihara, won a seat and thus was able to carry her group's agenda into the Diet.

Although not on the same level of importance as big business, right-wing and left-wing interest groups are heard loudly in Japanese politics. The right-wing uyoku is unique among conservative political groups around the world in that it combines traditional conservative opposition to communism, Communist countries, and leftist labor unions with an element of emperor worship and imperial absolutism. In 1988 the National Police Agency estimated that there were 840 "right-wing" groups with over 125,000 members. Many of these have ties with Japan's organized crime groups, the yakuza.

On the left wing a range of interest groups revolves around two large sponsoring party organizations, the Communists and the Socialists. One of the major leftist organizations is the Japan Teachers Union (JTU) (Nihon Kyoshokuin Kumiai, or Nikkyoso), with close ties to both parties. The JTU engages in a running political battle with the Ministry of Education over the rules and regulations of the nation's education system.

On the anniversaries of the atomic bombing of Hiroshima and Nagasaki, various antiwar and antinuclear groups hold public ceremonies, meetings, and demonstrations to highlight their opposition to nuclear weapons and the use of nuclear power in general. Both movements have had an impact on policy, as Japan has not developed nuclear weapons and occasionally limits the development of nuclear power plants.

The relatively small number of left-wing organizations in Japan reflects the basic conservative political values of much of Japanese society and the hostility of the police and government to left-wing organizations in the postwar era. Clearly, the right wing has access to the government and the ruling LDP, although the left wing occasionally wins a political battle if public opinion can be rallied behind its cause.

Finally, government is frequently a lobbyist and an interest group in Japan. Local government officials, because of the unitary system of government, must extensively lobby the bureaucracy and the LDP to obtain the authority and funding they need to carry out their programs. Interministerial conflict is also common on the national level, as ministries defend their programs and clienteles against the program demands and clienteles of other ministries.

THE CRUCIAL ROLE OF THE BUREAUCRACY

The key to understanding the relationship between Japanese political parties and interest groups during most of the post–World War II period is through an appreciation of the role the Japanese central bureaucracy has played in dealing with interests. Japan's bureaucracy is a mandarin elite recruited from the best colleges and universities in the nation. Bureaucrats are among the most respected groups in a neo-Confucian society, in part because of the accumulated expertise they have acquired over the years. A short explanation of three elements of the political economy of Japan will help to explain the crucial role played by the bureaucracy in shaping party-group relations since World War II. These three are the Gyo-Ho, or industrial law system; the Japanese version of corporatism; and the central role the bureaucracy plays in policymaking.

Gyo-Ho

A major link in the interest group–political party (mainly LDP) connection was shaped by the state bureaucracy's development and administration of the Gyo-Ho, or industry laws, which provide government protection of key Japanese industries from foreign competitors. To accomplish this the Diet passed separate laws to administer each industry. Thus, there is a Banking Law, an Automobile Industry Law, and so on, for various industries. This government protection was called the "convoy system," with the government the flagship in the center of the formation and the other ships (banks, automakers, and other groups) following its orders and sailing safely together.

Under the Gyo-Ho, various industries have been well protected and have developed into prosperous sectors of the Japanese economy. In the automobile industry, government protection secured a near monopoly for Japanese automakers in the large domestic market. In the banking and finance sector, protection was so effective that it allowed the industry to survive and prosper even as it pursued counterproductive and inefficient policies. The banking industry failed to develop new innovative policies and services or the research capabilities needed in world markets, and it failed to allow new enterprises into its business; thus, it stagnated.

The Gyo-Ho system has also been prominent in the health and welfare sector. An example is the creation of a public organization to test syringes supplied to hospitals in Japan, created by the companies whose products must pass the test. Testing requirements are specified in such a way as to keep possible competitors from marketing their products in Japan. The same procedures operate in the publishing sector to keep "nonapproved" books and publishers out of the market.

For Gyo-Ho to be effective and to successfully protect the various industries, those industries had to submit to nearly complete government regulation. In exchange for government protection from all competitors, both domestic and foreign, the industries responded with the political funding the ruling Liberal Democratic Party needed to maintain its hold on the central government and its ministries. This cooperative arrangement among the three entities (the government ministries, the LDP, and various key interest sectors in the economy) operated more or less smoothly until the Japanese economic miracle turned into an economic nightmare in the late 1980s. At the same time, foreign pressures (*gaietsu*) to open up the Japanese economy became particularly strong, and by 1993 the LDP had lost control of the Diet.

Corporatism Without Labor

Zeigler (1988) wrote of the special category of Confucian tradition nations that exhibit two fundamental principles: groups are more important than individuals, and society is organized on a hierarchical basis. These nations also have traditions of elite bureaucracies that tend to dominate the development and administration of public policies. Asian Confucian nations also share a preference for single ruling party governments. These nations have developed a form of corporatism—societal corporatism—a system with interest groups sanctioned by government and with all but a few peak associations effectively excluded from the decisionmaking process.

According to Zeigler, how labor is handled—whether co-opted, neutralized, or excluded—is the key element in the success of a corporatist system. In Western Europe labor is made docile by involving it in the policymaking process. In quasi-authoritarian Asian nations such as Taiwan, South Korea, and Japan, a "corporatism without labor" has emerged in which organized labor has been repressed and is not directly involved in government decisionmaking. In Japan labor unions are legal, but the more radical private-sector unions were crushed early in the postwar era. Docile company unions became the norm, and labor is largely excluded from the policymaking process.

Despite the weakness of labor, among the Asian nations Zeigler (1988, 164) studied, only Japan had developed the formal institutions common to the European style of corporatism. And as categorized by Schmidt (1979), Japan has one of the world's highest levels of corporatism, is dominated by business interests, and is one of the world's most conservative democratic nations—similar in the latter characteristic to Switzerland and the United States.

Pemple and Tsunekawa (1979) also concluded that Japan is a corporatist nation with the distinguishing feature that labor is excluded. They saw key elements of corporatism in both prewar and postwar Japan. The prewar version is that of state corporatism, with almost all peak interests represented in the Imperial Rule Assistance Association formed in 1940. In the postwar era Japan's version of liberal corporatism has almost all major interests organized into powerful trade or peak associations. However, the authors correctly note that labor has not been represented by such an organization or been included in the regular policymaking processes of Japan.

Central Role of the Bureaucracy in Policymaking

When Japan experienced political instability in the summer of 1989, as it went through three LDP prime ministers in a few weeks, many were surprised that the Tokyo stock market continued its seemingly relentless rise in spite of the problems in the political world. Some suggested the stock market rise merely reflected how little impact the ruling LDP really had on the policymaking process. Some have argued that the LDP rules the nation but the bureaucracy runs it on a day-to-day basis.

C. Johnson (1982, 309–312) has argued that there are three basic components of business-bureaucratic encounters: self-control, state control, and public-private cooperation. In contemporary Japan all three can be and are used simultaneously. Self-control is practiced by the private sector when it receives authority to regulate itself with government approval, in state control the bureaucracy regulates the private sector, and cooperation is a combination of the two. All three forms are consistent with a corporatist style of interest group politics.

The bureaucracy is often the site of lobbying interaction between political parties and interest groups (Woodall and Hiwatari 1988). The windows of vulnerability used by interests groups include establishing relations with career bureaucrats, Diet members, and especially those in the ruling LDP and making personal contacts with government through retired bureaucrats.

Almost all important interest group–political party–bureaucrat interaction takes place behind closed doors. As C. Johnson (1982, 91–92) succinctly expressed it, "The invisible political process . . . is much more important for actual decision-making, and it takes place in 'private' if nonetheless institutionalized meetings among bureaucrats, Liberal Democratic Party members, and the *zaikai* [the large post–World War II private-sector industrial conglomerates] leaders." These meetings, which reconcile conflict between bureaucrats and interest group leaders, are important to the smooth operation of the policymaking process. Additional government-sponsored advisory committees (*shingikai*) have been established to review and modify the recommendations of the bureaucracy's own policy review committees (Harari 1980). These advisory committees give the various interests associated with a particular ministry a chance for direct input into the policymaking process.

POLITICAL PARTY–INTEREST GROUP CONNECTIONS IN JAPAN

The LDP's Policy Research Affairs Committee and Policy Tribes

Besides the bureaucracy, the only other major alternative source of expert information and frequent party-group interaction is the Policy Affairs Research Committee (PARC) of the most powerful party in modern Japanese history—the Liberal Democratic Party. PARC is the forum in which interest groups and public officials debate fashioning future laws and amending existing ones. All policy issues must be studied in the PARC prior to becoming LDP policy and appearing in the Diet on the government's agenda. Consequently, the central bargaining site of Japanese politics is not on the Diet floor or in the Diet's committees but in the seventeen ministry divisions (*bukai*) paralleling the LDP's PARC. Normally, bureaucrats will bring issues and proposed legislation to PARC, but on occasion interest groups also perform that task. The various divisions have produced over 100 subcommittees, which have become the spokespersons of various interests such as the Japan Medical Association.

The *zoku* are found in PARC. *Zoku,* or policy tribes, are made up of LDP Diet members who have specialized in a particular interest area such as agriculture, construction, or education (Inoguchi and Iwai 1987). They are the inside lobbyists within the LDP. Once LDP Diet members join a division, they tend to remain with that division as long as they retain their Diet seats. Consequently, over the years these politicians will build a very close relationship with an interest and accumulate a great amount of information about an interest area. In the 1980s the media called these relationships "*zoku* politics"—LDP subject-area specialists working for the best interests of their clientele groups, which included both interest groups and bureaucrats. Famous LDP leaders are often closely identified with their *zoku*. Former prime minister Toshiki Kaifu, for example, has long been a member of the education *zoku* and twice served as Japan's education minister. The rise of the *zoku* and the increased power of PARC in an era of stagnating or even declining budgets combine to increase the power of the LDP and its key politicians in Japan's policymaking process. The PARC-*zoku* connection is similar to the clientelism in Italy before the early 1990s (see Chapter 7).

The Electoral Connection

Perhaps the major avenue of access to the Diet in Japan is through the support of candidates seeking Diet seats, either by supporting official candidates of major parties or by a group running its own candidates for public office. Many interest groups are asked to support a party's slate of candidates or a particular candidate in a constituency. Private-sector labor unions helped establish, and until 1993 supported, the DSP and the new labor slates of Rengo. Public-sector unions supported the JSP as well as the JCP in some cases. Support often meant providing candidates with the money, staff, and workers needed to run the campaign. Consequently, the distinction between interest groups and political parties blurs to the point that they are nearly the same organization. To use the terminology of Box 1.2, close cooperation bordering on integration between party and interest occurs. An extreme example occurred in the 1974 House of Councilors elections when the LDP asked particular corporations to sponsor specific candidates and to use corporate factories, distributors, and other units to campaign for those candidates.

Many interest groups regularly have their leaders run as Diet candidates so they can secure an inside lobby in the Diet. Those groups directly represented in the Diet by officials or members of their groups, as counted by George (1988), included labor unions, agricultural groups, health groups, corporations, cultural/religious/political groups, sports groups, professional groups, youth groups, forest/fishery groups, transport groups, local government groups, insurance/pension groups, consumer and women's groups, and postal/banking groups. Again, there is a similarity with an element of party-group relations in Italy before the Tangentopoli scandal in the early 1990s. In this case the Japanese practice resembles the *parentela* relationship of groups and factions working closely with parties—mainly the LDP—to get their members elected and to exert influence on their behalf once in office.

The Party-Funding Connection

Political financing of parties, major factions, and individual candidates has long been a major access-creating tactic for big business, labor unions, and some single-issue groups. Japanese Diet election campaigns are very expensive, especially those of the LDP, which has no single large sponsoring group as do most opposition parties. The amount of political funds officially reported to the government is usually well over $1 billion a year. Of the major parties, the LDP usually receives 50 percent of its funds from corporate sources. The list of the top corporate contributors to the LDP is a list of Japan's top corporations, banks, and manufacturers. One way the LDP "extorts" funds from corporations and interest groups is by holding fund-raising events for individual candidates that attract up to 10,000 supporters who purchase up to 30,000 tickets at ¥30,000 (about $300) each. Such an event can raise up to ¥1 billion (close to $10 million) in a single evening for an especially powerful LDP faction leader. Large corporations such as Toyota have been known to purchase 500 to 1,000 tickets for a single event (Hrebenar 2000).

The large trade associations, such as the Tokyo Bankers Association and the Japan Steel Association, have annually contributed funds to the LDP based on a formula related to the fiscal size of their members. The interests that have prospered under LDP rule are the largest political fund contributors. Although big business made some small contributions to the more moderate opposition parties to keep access open if they should ever come to power, over 90 percent of business's political contributions were made to the LDP during the First Party System.

When Toshiki Kaifu was selected LDP president and Japan's prime minister in August 1989, Keidanren's chairman, Eishiro Saito, announced that the business community was ready to give Kaifu its full support. Keidanren's aggregate financial power forms the "bank" of contributions that have kept the LDP in political power nearly continuously since 1955. The powerful organization does not hide its desire to have significant input into contemporary Japanese decisionmaking. It is an automatic member of every commission or committee of significance; in fact, many committees were suggested by Keidanren, such as the powerful committee on administrative reform headed by a former Keidanren chairman.

The *gurupu*, discussed earlier, also provide LDP politicians with huge amounts of funds for campaigns. They also exert their political influence in policymaking in two other major ways: influencing the bureaucracy by providing jobs for retiring bureaucrats in their satellite companies and thus gaining access for themselves and supplying *gurupu* leaders and staff to chair key *zaikai* policy study committees.

The pattern of corporate giving has changed somewhat during the Second Party System and the emergence of new conservative parties such as the Liberals and Democrats. Now, although it still gives large amounts of money to the LDP, corporate Japan also gives to the conservative parties, which pose a reasonable alternative to LDP rule. In 2000, corporate contributions to individual politicians were made illegal. Since most interest groups connect with Japanese political parties as supporter groups, as financial "godfathers," or through ties forged in the government bureaucracy, indirect strategies and tactics—such as demonstrations and media advertising—used to connect interests to government decisionmakers in nations such as the United States are used infrequently in Japan.

CONSEQUENCES FOR POLICYMAKING AND DEMOCRACY IN JAPAN

The debate over who has power and who runs Japan's policymaking process is about whether the bureaucracy dominates the LDP or vice versa, and whether the number of interests that effectively participate is represented by a small number of peak or umbrella associations or by a much larger range of interest groups. Stockwin (1988, 4) has argued that the LDP and its one-party rule has been the central political reality in Japan since 1955. The party does not rule Japan by itself, for it is seriously checked by major interest groups, its own factional rivalries, bureaucrats representing key government ministries, major corporations, and even foreign governments and interests. Some have even argued that the LDP is composed of a collection of conservative interest groups. The bureaucracy, although not all-powerful, plays "a pivotal role" by setting objectives and designing and carrying out policies (Rix 1988, 54–76).

Although the range of interests represented in Japanese policymaking is far wider than in 1940, 1950, or 1960, the fact that a few interests enjoy almost unimpeded access and almost all others have limited or little access undermines the validity of describing Japan as a pluralist interest group system. However, support for the elite theory has diminished because the range of interests that have moved to create access to the bureaucracy or to the LDP is much wider than just the Keidanren and other peak associations.

There is also no doubt that the bureaucracy in Japan is very powerful, that it has established effective linkages with the party that has ruled Japan since 1955 and with the major interests of the business world, and that

Japanese politics has, as Stockwin (1988) has persuasively concluded, become bureaucratized and immobilist. The relative power of the bureaucracy, the LDP, and major interests tends to ebb and flow as a result of short-term circumstances. During the 1950s and 1960s the bureaucracy was the dominant partner in the decisionmaking process. As the oil shock of the 1970s unfolded, the LDP seemed to rise to the top of the political decisionmaking process because tough decisions concerning limited resources had to be made by politicians. In the affluent 1980s bureaucratic controls over the business world lessened significantly, giving the *gurupu* and major corporations greater independence from bureaucratic suggestions and guidance if they wanted it. As the 1980s closed, the instability of LDP leadership and public reaction to LDP scandals reduced its power without effectively increasing the power of either the bureaucracy or interest groups.

There has been a long-standing discussion in Japan about what many have called Japan's "spectator democracy," which refers to the fact that the average Japanese citizen participates very little in the political process beyond casting an occasional vote. This seems especially true in terms of political party participation and interest group lobbying. Clearly, there is a lack of citizen participation in the policymaking process. Even with the recent rise of citizen movements on the local government level, there is still almost no such participation at the national level. In short, spectator democracy seems to be a good description of the role of Japanese citizens in both party and interest group politics. Policymaking is still conducted largely by an iron triangle of government bureaucrats, leaders of important business groups, and senior LDP politicians. A lively debate may occur as to which of these three groups is most powerful at any given moment, but no one seriously suggests a significantly different summary of the political process.

CHANGES IN THE PARTY-GROUP CONNECTION DURING THE 1990s

In summary, until very recently the Japanese system was characterized by an overall corporatist style with a respected and confident Confucian bureaucracy and a powerful and aggressive interest group world dominated by its business sector, which has enjoyed unparalleled access to all important sites of policymaking. The system also included a largely excluded labor movement and a ruling political party that has single-handedly run a major democratic industrialized nation longer than any other ruling party in the postwar era (Richardson and Flanagan 1984, 325–328; George 1988, 126–128).

Japan had a political realignment in early summer 1993 when the

LDP's thirty-eight years of ruling Japan crashed at the national level. The crash was a direct result of a split in the LDP when a major faction led by two LDP politicians (Ichiro Ozawa and Tsutomu Hata) voted against the LDP cabinet of Prime Minister Kiichi Miyazawa and facilitated a Diet vote of nonconfidence that toppled the LDP government. After the subsequent elections, three non-LDP prime ministers in succession governed Japan until the October 1996 House of Representatives elections brought the LDP back to power with a minority government. As noted earlier, a number of new parties have come and gone since 1993. By 1998 the New Frontier Party had collapsed, and the Democratic Party had emerged as the major opposition party to LDP rule.

Several developments of importance to the party-group connection in Japan have resulted from these party system changes. First, there are several conservative parties—the LDP, the Democratic Party, and the Liberal Party. No significant left-wing parties remain at the national level. Voters have a choice of various conservative parties differentiated largely by the personalities of their leaders. These parties offer the nation multiple access for interest group representation and subsequent access to the Diet, even for labor, which has more access than ever before. Japanese big business, which used to support the Socialist parties in case they accidentally gained real political power, are the financial godfathers of these new alternative conservative parties. Japanese politics and interest group politics have abandoned the right-left division of the 1955 system. The new division line is right-right.

At roughly the same time these changes were occurring in the party system, bureaucratic political power declined and with it the relative advantage for Japanese interest groups to build solid and expensive ties to national ministries. Admittedly, the national-level bureaucrats had enjoyed quite a run. From 1945 to the late 1980s, almost every decision seemed to lead to a success. With the crash of the Japanese economy in 1989–1990, however, the bureaucracy seemed to pursue a series of policies with little apparent success. This, combined with bureaucratic corruption and other scandals, led bureaucratic leadership to retreat to a posture of protecting the status quo and its policies.

One could summarize current Japanese political party–interest group relationships as the end of normal politics. National-level policymaking seems to have come to a halt. It is truly a politics of inaction, of stagnation, of preserving the status quo advantages of various interests in society and dealing with the demands of other interests seeking to enter into the policymaking process. As the rest of the world—particularly Asia—waits for Japan to lead Asia back to higher levels of economic growth and stability, Japan seems to have produced a type of politics and party–interest group relationships seemingly incapable of responding to the challenges facing the nation: the politics of the Japanese bureaucracy, the Second Postwar Party System, and its interest group satellites.

CONCLUSION

We return to a point made in the introduction regarding attempts to classify Japanese party-group relations along the lines suggested in Box 1.2 on a continuum from integration at one end to rivalry at the other. In some ways the typology is applicable, but in other ways it does not fit the Japanese case, past or present. This divergence tells us much about the peculiarities of the party-group relationship in Japan, shaped as it has been by the Confucian tradition and Japanese political culture.

During the thirty-eight years of LDP rule ending in the early 1990s, on the surface the relationship was one of close cooperation, in some cases bordering on integration, based on strong ideological ties among the left-wing parties, the JSP, the JCP, even the DSP, and the unions and between the LDP and many prominent business interests. Furthermore, LDP–business group relations resembled the clientelistic and *parentela* relations in Italy. The elitist, exclusionary nature of party-group-bureaucratic relations meant that separation or noninvolvement was the norm for most interest groups in Japan. And the nature of Japanese culture meant that the confrontational/conflict relationship between parties and groups was rare—in fact, virtually nonexistent.

However, a closer look at the relationship of the LDP with interest groups, the only party-group relationship that really counted during those years as far as policymaking was concerned, reveals that the categorization needs modification. Although a great deal of cooperation and a degree of integration did occur between the LDP and business groups, made possible in part by the conservative and pragmatic nature of the LDP, this was facilitated largely by a bureaucracy that provided the cement for the relationship. This situation gives a particular twist to the clientelistic and *parentela* analogies with pre-Tangentopoli Italy. The LDP did not dominate both relationships as the Christian Democrats did in Italy. Rather, the LDP and interests were more or less on a par, with the bureaucracy as the facilitator. Is the Japanese case, then, similar to France where the state has played a decisive role in shaping party-group relations? Again, there are similarities and differences. The main difference is that the Japanese system—led by the bureaucracy—has been much more exclusionary in its access but at the same time much more accommodating of the few interests it did sanction by granting them not only legitimacy but major benefits.

In sum, the relationship between the LDP and interests was both greater and lesser than the combined categories of integration and cooperation as set out in Box 1.2. It was lesser because it excluded many groups, particularly of the left and center, and was less flexible and lacked the variation than usually is the case within these two forms of relationship. It was greater in that it was not just a party-group relationship but involved a third, indispensable partner—the bureaucracy. In fact, to talk simply of party-group relations in Japan is, as we have seen, to tell only two-thirds or less of the story. The relationship was best described as symbiotic and triangular with the power of party, interests, and bureaucracy in relation to each other waxing and waning over time but with no one of the three able to dominate or function without the other two.

As to the future, the situation is still fluid. Since the advent of the Second Party System in 1993 and the end of the Cold War, the ideological basis of Japanese group-party relationships has largely eroded. The corporate world is still found in the LDP camp but now also supports the other two conservative parties (the DP and LP). The very close relationship between the socialist parties and large labor confederations has ended, and labor is now closer to the LDP, the DP, and the LP. Furthermore, the position of the bureaucracy has gone through significant changes in recent years. The Japanese pattern may be in transition to the Separation/Pragmatic Involvement Model (Box 1.2), but it is too early to be sure. Whatever happens, as in the past, the future party-group relationship in Japan is likely to be more a product of factors particularly Japanese—the Confucian tradition, political culture, the political economy, and so on—than of external influences.

Part 3

The Transitional Democracies

10

Spain: Changing Party-Group Relations in a New Democracy

Kerstin Hamann

Compared with other advanced industrialized countries, Spain's associational life has traditionally been poorly developed. However, given the country's relatively short history of liberal democracy and free organization of political parties and interest groups, the development of parties and the emergence of a large variety of associations are remarkable. In response to the policymaking environment evolving during the new democracy, linkages between political parties and interest groups have been dynamic and subject to change. Although labor unions presented the best-organized interests during the transition to democracy and were closely tied to leftist political parties, by the mid-1990s a multitude of interest groups were operating. These groups are generally autonomous of, and pragmatic in their relationship with, political parties.

The most visible and politically important interest groups are the major labor union confederations, the General Workers' Union (Unión General de Trabajadores—UGT) and Workers' Commissions (Comisiones Obreras—CCOO), and the employers' umbrella organization, the Spanish Confederation of Employers' Organizations (Confederación Española de Organizaciones Empresariales—CEOE). Until the late 1980s the UGT had strong ties to the Spanish Socialist Workers' Party (Partido Socialista de Obreros Españoles—PSOE). Workers' Commissions, established in the 1960s during the Francisco Franco regime, were linked to the underground Spanish Communist Party (Partido Comunista Española—PCE) and eventually became an antiregime force. The CEOE was not founded until 1977 and has remained independent of any political party.

Even though associational life in Spain has been traditionally weak, interest groups played an important role in stabilizing the nascent Spanish democracy after Franco's death in 1975. Workers' and employers' organizations were strong supporters of the democratic transition and participated in a series of social and economic pacts (Hamann 1998a). After democracy was consolidated, unions became more independent from leftist political parties and have since followed a more pragmatic relationship with parties, with less importance attached to ideological ties. Today the influence of interest groups on democracy and policymaking is less direct and less obvious than in the early phase of Spanish democracy, but interest groups increasingly represent the specialized interests of Spanish citizens not adequately captured by political parties.

SPANISH PARTIES, GROUPS, AND THEIR RELATIONSHIPS

The study of interest groups is relatively new in Spain, and very few analyses deal explicitly with the relationship between parties and organized interests. This in part reflects the fact that interest organization is still a relatively young phenomenon in Spain—after the end of the Civil War in 1939, political parties and interest groups were not legalized again until the late 1970s—but it also reflects the fact that interest groups play a less pivotal role in democratic Spanish politics than they may in other industrialized democracies. The number of associations surged in the late 1970s, underwent a steep downward trend in the 1980s, and increased again in the 1990s. To illustrate these changes, a Eurobarometer survey conducted in 1987 found that only 25 percent of Spaniards participated in any association, which placed Spain second-to-last above Italy among member countries of the European Union (then the European Community). By the mid-1990s, however, about 40 percent of Spaniards participated in some kind of organization, which placed Spain in the middle in a European comparison. At the same time, the number of associations had practically doubled (Iniciativa Social y Estado de Bienestar n.d.a, 1–2).

Although some studies of the democratic transition period (1975–1982) have analyzed the linkages between trade unions and leftist political parties (for example, Sagardoy Bengoechea and León Blanco 1982), most other analyses have focused on either political parties—often in conjunction with electoral outcomes—or interest groups (for example, Fishman 1990; Pérez-Díaz 1993; Martínez 1993b; McDonough, Barnes, and López Pina 1984; Morlino 1998). A few studies have concentrated on the ties between parliament and interest groups, often in cross-national comparison (Liebert 1995a, chapter 3; 1995b), or on overall strategies of sector-specific interests (for example, de la Fuente Blanco 1991; Rodríguez 1992). Gillespie (1990) and Wozniak (1992) provide empirical accounts of the changing relationship between the PSOE and the UGT.

Studies have pointed to the relatively high proportion of deputies who have represented economic interest groups during their concurrent memberships in producer or labor organizations and in political parties during the early years of Spanish democracy. Employers tended to be elected on Union of the Democratic Center (Unión Centro Democrático—UCD) and Popular Alliance (Alianza Popular—AP) lists, UGT members held PSOE seats, and CCOO affiliates were generally deputies for the PCE (Liebert 1995a, 284–288, 307). These patterns, however, became less relevant after the mid-1980s. Although a small number of studies have analyzed interest group politics, very few focus specifically on the linkages between interest groups and political parties. Even a study focusing specifically on parties and groups in southern Europe in recent years, which includes Spain (Morlino 1998), pays scant attention to party-group linkages and their consequences in the Spanish case. Given this relative dearth of literature, a review of the development of the party-group connection in Spain is useful for understanding the current form of the relationship and its effects on policymaking and democracy.

POLITICAL PARTY–INTEREST GROUP RELATIONS BEFORE 1982

The Period Preceding Franco's Death in 1975

Historically, trade unions were among the first interest organizations to form and have been the most prominent and politically important type of interest association in Spain.[1] Links between trade unions and political parties have generally been close, especially between the PSOE and the UGT. The PSOE was founded in May 1879 and established the UGT nine years later. Until the beginning of Franco's rule (1939), these two organizations had tight links in terms of organization—including personnel, leadership, and ideology (see Lieberman 1986, chapter 1)—despite occasional ideological and strategic differences. For example, the UGT's 1928 congress "elected to its Executive Committee practically all of the same men who served on the Executive Committee of the Socialist party" (Lieberman 1986, 67). The other main union at the turn of the twentieth century, the anarcho-syndicalist National Labor Confederation (Confederación Nacional de Trabajo—CNT), remained unaffiliated with any major political party.

During the Franco dictatorship the lack of other organized interests, such as business or agriculture, paralleled the absence of freely organized trade unions. Agricultural interests were part of the corporatist state structure and were not allowed to form independent organizations. The same was true for labor and employers. Following the logic of corporatism, both business and workers formed part of the same state-controlled *sindicato*, the Syndical Organization (Organización Sindical—OS), a vertical organization with compulsory membership. Business, however, enjoyed privileged access—often informal—to Franco's political elites and was well represented in decisionmaking bodies and the bureaucracy, especially toward the end of the regime (see Gunther 1980; Martínez 1993b, 174).

When political parties and interest groups were officially outlawed during the authoritarian regime, many continued to operate by organizing partly underground, partly in exile, and partly by taking advantage of existing state structures. Thus, workers presented one of the most formidable opposition groups to Franco's regime (Maravall 1978). Most active were the Workers' Commissions that developed after the government passed the Law of Collective Bargaining in 1958.

The commissions were created as companywide bargaining units during the economic boom in the 1960s but were banned in 1976 (Amsden 1972). The commissions continued to exist semiclandestinely and simultaneously used the official structures of the *sindicato* to represent workers' interests. The CCOO portrayed itself as a nonpartisan organization representing the interests of all workers and housed a wide variety of ideologies among its members including "Communists, members of various Catholic organizations, independents, leftist Falangists, Christian Democrats, and others" (Lieberman 1986, 90). Despite this diversity, many leadership positions were filled by remnants of the likewise outlawed but secretly organized Communist Party.

The socialist union UGT refused to follow the strategy set out by the CCOO—namely, to use existing official structures in an attempt to infiltrate the *sindicato*. The UGT was active in only a few regions, with the leadership mostly in exile or under cover. Union leaders involved in the resistance against Franco had close contacts with the underground segment of the PSOE. Numerous leaders of the Socialist Party also worked from exile. Other underground unions, especially the Workers' Syndical Union (Unión Sindical Obrera—USO), remained independent of political parties.

Limited pluralism was possible, especially after the 1964 Law of Associations was passed, but the only groups allowed to form were groups such as the Catholic charity organization Caritas, the Red Cross, or groups that provided support for the disabled (Iniciativa Social y Estado de Bienestar n.d.b, 2). None of these officially condoned groups had close relations with the clandestine political parties. The Franco regime continued to organize most interests under the controlling tutelage of the state. Nonetheless, neighborhood organizations with a social movement character were formed starting in the late 1960s. These associations were generally linked to leftist political parties, in particular the PCE. Despite formal autonomy from the party, neighborhood associations' "leadership, technical assistants, and allies were nearly all Communist militants or leaders" (Hipsher 1996, 288).

The first wave of Spanish women's organizations developed at the beginning of the twentieth century and was split between women working within leftist political parties (the PSOE and, after its founding in 1921, the PCE) and anarchist feminist movements. However, as a rule the larger organizations—both political parties and movements—tended to absorb women's issues as a smaller item on their agenda of promoting general political, social, and economic change, such as a classless or anarchist society (Valiente 1997, 26–27). Other noneconomic interests did not develop a national profile.

Women also organized during the years of authoritarian rule, but mainly in state-controlled associations, in church groups, or clandestinely. Parts of the women's movement remained close to the PCE, but the relationship can be characterized as one of women working within the PCE rather than of any ties linking women's groups and underground political parties. During a period of limited liberalization of the regime, a few equal rights organizations were founded, mostly involving professional women (Valiente 1997, 6).

The Democratic Transition and Consolidation Period

The democratic transition and consolidation period lasted roughly from Franco's death in November 1975 until about 1982. By then a democratic constitution had been ratified, the new democracy had survived a coup attempt, and Spain had experienced a peaceful transfer of power from the center-right UCD to the leftist PSOE after the 1982 general elections. At the onset of the transition, both political parties and unions were still illegal. Political parties were not legalized until July 1976 (with the exception of the PCE, which gained legal status in 1977), and unions were free to register in April 1977.

A host of political parties formed in response to the liberalization of the political system and the prospect of democratic elections. In the 1977 elections to a constituent assembly, the major parties included the UCD, which, headed by Adolfo Suárez, won the election with 34 percent of the vote and 166 seats (out of 350). The PSOE emerged as the second-largest party with 29 percent of the vote and 118 seats. Other parties included the PCE, the rightist AP, and some smaller regional parties.

Although political parties quickly became protagonists in Spanish politics, the formation of interest groups lagged considerably behind, and the most significant interest organizations were once again labor unions.[2] With the slow dismantling of the official vertical union structure, unions were crucial in mobilizing the workforce in strikes and demonstrations. At the same time they were also instrumental in actively supporting democracy and moderating the demands of the workforce. In the first round of the so-called union elections (workplace elections for representatives on works committees) in 1978, the CCOO emerged as the largest union, followed by the UGT and smaller unions, including some regional unions. The second round of union elections in 1980 consolidated the union system, and the two largest unions together presented about 60 percent of the representatives on the works committees (see Hamann 1998b, 438).

During the transition, then, party–interest group connections existed primarily between leftist political parties and labor unions, which cooperated briefly in democratic opposition groups during the early transition period. Once democratic rule was reinstalled, the socialist UGT remained closely connected to the PSOE. The relationship between the two was described as "close" and "fraternal," and significant leadership overlap and mutual consultation existed. UGT leaders competed for parliamentary seats on PSOE lists, and by party rules PSOE members were also expected to join the UGT.

Likewise, the PCE and the Workers' Commissions maintained close relations, with significant policy coordination and leadership overlap (see Sagardoy Bengoechea and León Blanco 1982, 87). Nonetheless, despite the obvious ideological and personnel affinity of the two organizations, the Workers' Commissions have never officially taken a partisan stand and have become less closely tied to the PCE. Instead, the commissions emphasize their movement's character and attempt to appeal to all workers regardless of party affiliation. CCOO members are not required to join any political party, and General Secretary Antonio Gutiérrez is not a member of the PCE. Political and strategic differences became visible in the discussion of the 1980 Workers' Statute, for example, which resulted in increased distance between the Workers' Commissions and the Communist Party. The two main unions and leftist parties were thus linked through ideological affinity, organizational overlap and linkage, and similar strategic interests; in addition, their members provided mutual electoral support. During this period, then, their relationship followed the cooperative or ideological connection with a slight tendency toward the Strong Integration/Partisan Model (see Chapter 1). Interestingly, the dominant party during the democratic transition, the UCD, had no electoral or organizational support from a trade union, and a centrist union was never founded.

Other interest groups were less well organized during the transition and were also more distanced from political parties. Business was organized in several smaller confederations, joining in a nationwide confederation, the CEOE, in 1977. Small and medium-sized businesses continue to have their own organization, the Spanish Confederation of Small and Medium-Sized Firms (Confederación Española de Pequeñas y Medianas Empresas—CEPYME), which is affiliated with the CEOE.[3] Although as a rule business was conservative, it nonetheless supported the democratization efforts and remained largely autonomous of political parties. Business confederation leaders were generally in favor of democratic reforms but were more conservative than enterprise chief executives. Association leaders who had been part of Franco's *sindicato* leaned toward the rightist AP, while business leaders overall were more supportive of the center-right UCD (Martínez 1993a, 127).

However, the CEOE did not limit itself to cooperation with only one party. Instead, association efforts to improve the situation for business have been flexible and have included the UCD, despite severe criticism of the party's failure to implement economic reforms during the economic crisis in the late 1970s and early 1980s (Martínez 1993a, 125–126). As a consequence of the government's commitment to a social welfare state and compromises with labor, the CEOE went as far as cutting relations with the UCD government for five months in 1978 (Martinez Lucio 1991, 44). Business thus pursued a strategy approximating the Separation or Pragmatic Involvement Model during the transition, despite ideological affinities with conservative parties.

Besides marking the end of the Franco dictatorship, 1975 was also the UN International Women's Year. Subsequently, numerous women's groups were founded, but no umbrella organization was created. The parties of the left (the PSOE and PCE) established women's sections within their parties, and many politically active women utilized parties to advance their agendas. Most women's organizations, though, remained autonomous and did not develop particular linkages with political parties. In fact, the question of whether membership in a feminist organization was to be feminists' exclusive commitment or whether they should also be allowed to hold membership in other political organizations (such as labor unions or parties) was a major point of contention among Spanish feminists and led to a split in the movement by the end of the 1970s (Valiente 1997, 8–9). Many women's groups followed a model of noninvolvement, while at the same time women's offices in political parties and trade unions attempted to integrate women's interests into the larger goals of their organizations.

PARTY-GROUP RELATIONS SINCE 1982

Relations between political parties and interest groups have changed considerably since the early 1980s. With respect to trade unions (still one of the most prominent types of interest groups), their links to leftist political parties have turned from close and fraternal to distant and at times hostile, approximating the Separation and Pragmatic Involvement Model with occasional short-term episodes of conflict and confrontation (see Chapter 1). This is particularly true for the UGT and the PSOE (see Gillespie 1990; Smith 1998). Shortly after the PSOE won the 1982 elections under Felipe

González with a majority of the seats in parliament, UGT criticism of the government's market-oriented social and economic policies mounted. Arguing that the workers were carrying a disproportionate share of the cost of the government's adjustment policies, after 1984 the UGT withdrew its initial support for the industrial restructuring programs. Animosity between the UGT and the PSOE grew and culminated in the nationwide general strike against the government's social and economic policies, called jointly by the UGT and the CCOO in December 1988. In the 1989 election the UGT refused to support the PSOE; the PSOE, for its part, changed its statutes at the 1990 party congress to abolish the requirement that party members must also join the UGT.

In the 1990s the relationship between leftist political parties and trade unions could be characterized as distant and sometimes conflictual, especially in the case of the PSOE and the UGT. Until the PSOE lost the 1996 election, contacts between the PSOE and the unions were restricted mostly to the government level, and few official connections remained between the party organization and its formerly closely affiliated union. The relationship between the Workers' Commissions and the Communist Party has also grown more distant but generally lacks the open hostility of the socialist bloc. The PCE was incorporated into the leftist electoral coalition the United Left (Izquierda Unida—IU) in 1986, and the commissions have retained their strategy of cooperation while maintaining their formal autonomy from the party.

Business, represented by the umbrella organization CEOE, has continued to pursue a nonpartisan strategy, operating with a mixture of criticism of and collaboration with whatever party is in power. Although ideologically closer to the Popular Party (Partido Popular—PP; formerly the AP and elected into government in 1996 under Prime Minister José María Aznar), business is by no means a partisan organization. Immediately before the 1981 election, business leaders evaluated PSOE Secretary-General Felipe González very favorably, especially compared with the leaders of rightist parties (Martínez 1993a, 134–135). After the PSOE's electoral victory in 1982, the CEOE cooperated—although frequently accompanied by severe criticisms—with the PSOE and was involved in various trilateral social and economic pacts with the government and the trade unions.[4] The business association had also been known to disagree with some AP proposals such as pension policies (Martinez Lucio 1991, 48).

Overall, then, the CEOE has retained a pragmatic attitude toward political parties and, although ideologically closer to the conservative PP, has no formal organizational ties to any party. It thus best fits the Separation/Pragmatic Involvement Model identified in Box 1.2. A further example of the pragmatism of the business community is the existence of close but informal links between banking elites and dominant sectors within the Socialist Party (Pérez 1997; Chari 1999).

Agricultural groups are less important politically in Spain than in most Western democracies. They have maintained strong ties to the administration through agricultural "chambers," carried over from the corporatist-type organizations of agricultural interests set up by the Franco regime, with a limited representational function. Today agricultural interests are fragmented among those holding large estates *(latifundios)*, farmers with smaller landholdings, and agricultural laborers (see de la Fuente Blanco 1991). Although agricultural interests have no close organizational ties to any particular political party, the rural population in general benefited from the politics of the Socialist government (1982–1996) and formed part of the PSOE's electoral coalition (see Boix 1998; Hamann 2000).

One of the best nationally organized interest groups is the National Organization of the Spanish Blind (Organización Nacional de Ciegos Españoles—ONCE), which represents the interests of and provides welfare services for the blind. The organization, originally created during the Civil War and maintained during the Franco dictatorship, has expanded to include the representation of and welfare provision for other disabled Spaniards. To achieve its political goals, ONCE primarily deals directly with the government and state administrative bodies rather than political parties in what has been labeled a corporatist arrangement (Garvía 1995).

Women's groups are manifold, but they continue to operate without an umbrella organization. Women are especially active within the main leftist parties (the PCE and PSOE) and labor unions, which have organized women's sections. Individual women's groups, however, do not foster close relations with political parties. During the PSOE government (1982–1996), the Women's Institute (Instituto de la Mujer—IM) was established as part of the bureaucratic structure of the state. Nongovernmental women's groups are poorly represented, though, and a considerable degree of animosity exists between many women's groups and the IM. These groups complain of being excluded from access to the IM and accuse the IM of playing partisan politics and allocating funds to groups and projects close to PSOE policies, especially during the long period of PSOE rule (Valiente 1997, 24; 1995).

The numerous professional associations are mostly nonpartisan. In fact, in the early 1990s the PSOE government began to criticize the monopoly many of these professional organizations had and proposed a bill that would weaken some of their powers, such as that making health service workers' membership in the corresponding association compulsory (Newton 1997, 257). Interest groups related to the medical field are multiple and fragmented. Although the unions representing employees in the medical profession were close to the PSOE early in that party's period in government, the increasing distance between the Socialist government and the unions over time also affected union representation of medical interests. Different organized medical interests have put varying degrees of emphasis on negotiating with the government, the administration, and parliamentary party groups; and parties differ in the frequency with which they invite medical groups to participate in the policymaking process. However, the medical sector as such operates mostly autonomously from political parties (see Rodríguez 1992).

The 1980s and 1990s also witnessed the formation and growth of many other interest groups and associations, among them professional organizations, environmental groups, associations advocating an increased role of the Spanish state in promoting international development, gay and lesbian groups, youth groups, sports associations, church-related groups, groups advocating or opposing the liberalization of abortion, and neighborhood associations. Nongovernmental organizations (NGOs) are also rapidly growing in number (see Avià and Cruz n.d.).

Many of the new interest groups are locally organized and nonpartisan. They attempt to influence policies through an exchange of information and contacts with the major parliamentary parties in both government and opposition.[5] For example, some studies indicate that the PSOE is generally open to cooperation with new groups or will at least consider their agenda (Craig 1995). Nonetheless, in comparison with other countries in Western Europe, the Spanish parliament stands out for its relatively low level of lobbying activity, including lobbying efforts of major economic interest groups (Liebert 1995b). The relationship between those interest groups and political parties is generally fluid and open (interviews with deputies, June 1998). Liebert (1995b, 424) has labeled the fluid interactions between interest groups and parliamentary parties *cross-partyness*.

Overall, then, two major types of changes in the political party–interest group connection can be observed. First, the host of newly created interest groups is overwhelmingly nonpartisan and follows the Separation/Pragmatic Involvement Model identified in Box 1.2. Second, the close party–interest group connections that existed at the beginning of the transition (particularly between unions and leftist parties) have also been modified to follow the Pragmatic Involvement Model or the one from integration to separation. It seems there has been a process of convergence in the relationship between political parties and interest groups across different sectors. That is, regardless of which sector an interest group belongs to, its relationship to political parties over time tends to follow a pattern resembling that of other groups, best described as one of autonomy from political parties with respect to formal organizational linkages, ideological orientation, and strategies.

EXPLAINING THE RELATIONSHIP
BETWEEN PARTIES AND INTEREST GROUPS

One of the most striking features of the linkages between political parties and interest groups is the weak associational life in Spanish society, which is still present despite the recent growth in the number of organizations (see Gunther 1997, 270; Avià and Cruz n.d.). Both recent history and the institutional design of Spanish democracy help explain this underorganization of Spanish society, the current formation of new groups, and the weak linkages between major interest groups and political parties.

During the almost forty years of authoritarian rule, most voluntary organizations were outlawed. The interest organizations that did exist were state controlled or directed by the Catholic Church. On the one hand, this lack of free interest organizations meant that no culture or tradition of forming interest groups existed at the beginning of the democratic transition. On the other hand, the experience with state-controlled interest groups had made many Spaniards weary of joining organizations. The only interest organizations that enjoyed widespread support and experienced a surge in membership during the transition were labor unions because of their reputation of having fought for democracy during the Franco regime (see Hamann 1998b, 434). In the 1980s the prominence of interest groups declined. Spaniards looked to political parties and the state to solve their problems (Iniciativa Social y Estado de Bienestar n.d.a., 4). In addition, the leaders of political parties rather than interest groups were most visible as protagonists during the Spanish transition (Gunther 1992; Hamann 1998a).

However, as noted earlier, in the 1990s Spain experienced a resurgence in the formation of interest groups, as well as in the number of group members. This increase can be explained in part through citizens' use of "readily available opportunity structures for citizen participation" (J. Richardson 1995, 116) that exist in liberal democratic regimes but were absent during the dictatorship's "limited pluralism" (Linz 1964). Moreover, the rapidly increasing social and political differentiation that followed the transition period has encouraged the formation of special interest groups beyond political parties. Parties, for their part, have become less class-based and oriented instead toward broad electoral coalitions, which gives special interest organizations the opportunity to represent those interests not captured by the parties.

More than the mere existence of interest associations can be explained by historical factors; those factors also explain the relationship between parties and organized interests. Given the traditionally strong and close ties between the PSOE and the UGT, it was not surprising that both organizations remained closely linked once interest politics was again legalized. Likewise, given the fact that the PCE was the most active party in resisting

Franco, it appears logical that the party continued its affinity with the Workers' Commissions, the most active resistance movement in the workplace. This connection also existed with women's groups and neighborhood organizations. All of these groups were striving for an end to the authoritarian state as their overarching strategy to obtain their varied goals. Interestingly, though, these linkages were modified soon after democracy was consolidated. Instead of remaining close and cooperative, the groups became more autonomous and flexible (in the case of the PCE, the CCOO, and other interests) or distant and sometimes even hostile (in the case of the PSOE and the UGT).

These changes can be accounted for in part by the institutional structures guiding Spanish politics, but also relevant were changes in the political and economic environment that led to a redefinition of interests, strategies, and allies by both political parties and unions. As Rodríguez (1992, 127) cogently argued, because of the relatively weak position of parliament and individual deputies, "the political capacity of interest groups remains seriously limited (especially if they oppose governmental projects)."

Both the PSOE and the UGT entered the democratization period with the expectation that once in power, the Socialist Party would pursue an economic policy course modeled on other Western European countries in the postwar period: the development of an extensive welfare state under the guidance of an interventionist and active government, based on a mutually beneficial exchange relationship between the PSOE and its affiliated UGT (see Hamann 2000; Stephens and Wallerstein 1991). The linkage between the party and the union was expected to help the party amass electoral support and the union to successfully defend workers' interests through party policies. Soon after the PSOE's 1982 victory, however, the party strayed from its traditional program and socialist ideology and adopted an economic policy course geared toward increasing economic efficiency.[6] This economic program included an industrial restructuring program and other market-oriented reforms to make Spain more competitive in international markets and facilitate integration into the European Common Market in 1986. As a consequence, unemployment rose to over 20 percent, and real wages were stagnant or increased only slightly, even during the period of rapid economic growth after 1986. As unions saw workers bearing the brunt of these adjustments they became less cooperative with and supportive of the governing party and its policies. Ideological and strategic differences preceded weakening organizational ties.

Nonetheless, the argument has been made that institutions are prone to inertia and reticent toward change (see Meyer and Zucker 1989; Knight 1992; Hall 1992, 90). A broad definition of *institution* includes the relationships between political actors as part of the rules that govern political behavior, and those relationships could thus be expected to be stable and predictable.[7] However, even though the relationship between the PSOE and the UGT dated back to the nineteenth century, the political context of interest representation in a liberal democracy was new, and the party–interest group relationship in a democratic context was only weakly institutionalized when the PSOE came to power. This facilitated the redefinition of divergent interests and strategies of the party and the union, respectively, and allowed for a surprisingly quick breakup of what had appeared to be firmly established linkages (Hamann 1998b).

The establishment of the new interest groups and their pragmatic relationship with political parties is mainly explained by institutional arrangements. Spanish electoral laws are based on a proportional representation (PR) system. A closed-list, multimember district system minimizes ties between party organizations and district representatives (see Martínez 1993a, 132). Spain has a low proportionality index as a consequence of district size (many districts have a small number of seats) and uses the d'Hondt formula for converting votes into seats (see Montero, Llera, and Torcal 1992). Larger parties are thus overrepresented while smaller parties are underrepresented. This electoral system has produced single-party governments (either majority or minority) in democratic Spain, but many specific interests are not well expressed by broad, multiclass parties. Especially in the 1990s, this resulted in a growing number of interest associations adopting a nonpartisan stance as an alternative way of voicing citizens' political concerns.

The specifics of the Spanish policymaking process can further explain the loose and multiple ties between interest associations and parties. The crucial organizational units of the lower house of parliament (Congreso de los Diputados) are the parliamentary party groups.[8] Party votes are determined through internal discussion within the groups, and party discipline is very strong and is broken only in exceptional circumstances.[9] Decision-making within these parliamentary groups is strongly influenced by the groups' leadership. Although individual deputies have the right to propose amendments within their group or to bring issues of potential legislative interest to the group's attention, the final decision about the group's vote is made by the leadership after consultation with the entire group or, more commonly, with committees formed within the group.

Legislative initiatives originating from an individual deputy have to be signed by the leader of the parliamentary party group and must be supported by at least fourteen other deputies. A "lobbying" approach that focuses on interest groups' direct contact with individual deputies is thus of little value. Instead, interest associations pursue as many avenues as possible to voice their concerns and issues in an attempt to get those issues on the legislative agenda. They may have more frequent or closer contacts with parties that overlap with their own ideology, but given the structure of parliament and electoral outcomes, ideological proximity is not an exclusive criterion for contacts between interest groups and political parties. This is especially true during periods of minority rule (1977–1982 and 1993–present) when even smaller parties may have considerable policymaking influence and are thus potentially valuable allies for interest groups.

In addition, the Spanish party system has undergone significant changes since the introduction of democracy, which also illustrates the need for interest groups to be flexible in their choice of party allies as the electoral fortunes of parties may change. From the perspective of political parties, in turn, it makes sense to be engaged in an open and fluid exchange of information with a wide variety of interest organizations. Both major parties, the PP and the PSOE, portray an image of multiclass catchall parties. Thus, from an electoral standpoint, it might be disadvantageous for parties to limit their contacts to strong ties with a few interest organizations that are ideologically close, as that would run the risk of alienating a potentially large number of voters who do not concur with those narrowly defined interests.

CONSEQUENCES FOR SPANISH POLICYMAKING AND DEMOCRACY

The relationship between parties and interest groups has had clearly identifiable effects on the policymaking process. Again, the most important illustration is provided by unions and leftist parties. During the transition, which has been described as the prototype of a consensual democratization process (see Gunther 1992), the close relationships facilitated the formation of a broad social consensus that went beyond anything represented by the political parties. Unions were instrumental in reaching and implementing a series of social pacts designed to counter the severe economic crisis (mid-1970s to the mid-1980s), thereby encouraging social and economic stability and facilitating the transition and consolidation of democracy. Social pacts, then, were a reflection of a broad consensus that built in part on the close linkages between leftist parties and unions (see Hamann 1997a). They were not, however, a mechanism to overcome differences between parties and interest groups. In fact, when the formerly close relationships between leftist parties and interest groups became weaker, the practice of broad social pacts also came to an end.

The links between the unions and leftist parties also influenced legislative politics beyond the social pacts. As union leaders were elected to parliament on the ticket of leftist parties, their issues and interests were frequently given a direct voice in the legislature, although not always successfully. A prime example of the impact of unions in the policymaking process during the transition period was the Workers' Statute, in which both the PSOE and the PCE defended the positions of their respective ideologically close unions. In the end, the UGT was considerably more successful in modifying the bill than the commissions. This difference can be explained by various factors: the legislative importance of the PSOE as the second-largest party in parliament (after the UCD, which formed a minority government), the UGT's strategy of negotiating a previous pact on the statute with the employers' organization, the greater internal consensus and cohesiveness of the PSOE, and tighter links between the socialist organizations than that between the Communist Party and the union (Hamann 1997b).

With the deterioration of the relationship between the PSOE and the UGT, the government's policymaking patterns changed from a consensual model to one clearly dominated by the interests of the governing party. The PSOE's economic policies emphasized structural adjustment—including labor market reforms aimed at reducing labor rigidities—and were frequently passed without the consent, or against the explicit opposition, of the unions. It became increasingly obvious that unions could no longer count on leftist political parties to voice their interests in the legislative process. Consequently, unions have readjusted their strategy, established working relationships with all political parties, and begun to negotiate with the government on specific issues rather than rely on broad social pacts and particularistic relationships with leftist parties. In 1997 unions finally negotiated a labor market reform with the employers that was subsequently passed by the government. Interestingly, this compromise was concluded under Aznar's conservative PP government, whereas a similar reform compromise had failed repeatedly with the previous Socialist government, which illustrates the unions' pragmatic strategy.

Other interest groups also attempt to influence particular issues through contacts with political parties, especially parliamentary parties. Meetings between interest group representatives and deputies mostly serve as forums for exchanging opinions and information and raising issues (interviews with deputies, June 1998). As party discipline in the Spanish legislative system is very strict, direct lobbying of individual deputies is a less promising strategy than laying out viewpoints parliamentary party groups can take up. Some other interest groups, such as the Women's Institute, interact primarily with the state because they have been linked to the state's administrative apparatus. Likewise, ONCE negotiates primarily with the government rather than fostering linkages with specific political parties. The government is also legally obliged to inform professional organizations of proposed legislation that concerns their profession, which means they are consulted on the respective draft legislation (Newton 1997,

257). Even if these groups have some ideological affinity with individual parties, their status or history makes them formally independent of particularistic partisan interests.

Overall, the policymaking influence of interest groups is reactive. That is, interest groups become most active when they respond to existing laws or pending legislation. Interest group representatives can be invited to committee hearings during the legislative path of a bill, and it is also during this stage that they most frequently contact parliamentary party group leaders to ask for a meeting or to send a written position paper (Liebert 1995a, 309).

CONCLUSION

The Spanish example illustrates well that relationships between interest groups and political parties in new democracies have the potential to be very dynamic over time and can also be sector specific. Despite the recent surge in the number and size of interest associations, Spanish interest organization still appears to lag behind other countries, and interest articulation remains fragmented. Although linkages between parties and interest groups were largely defined by Spain's history during the democratic transition and consolidation period, they were soon subject to change. On the one hand, relationships between unions and political parties were rapidly redefined during the 1980s. On the other hand, as democratic rule has become more established, multiple interest groups have been formed to raise issues and channel public opinion without developing formal ties with political parties. The way these interests are expressed and the type of linkages with political parties are influenced largely by the institutional rules guiding the policymaking process. The specifics of the Spanish political process and its outcomes (such as strict party discipline, electoral laws, and single-party governments) have helped define the strategies pursued by interest organizations, of which ties to political parties are only one facet.

A convergence has occurred in the type of political party–interest group connections across sectors, even though the ideological affinity between interest groups and parties may differ. That is, most interest groups follow the Pragmatic Model in their relationships with parties, whereas at the beginning of Spanish democracy some sectors—especially labor—had very close and sometimes formal ties with parties. In addition, profound changes in the party system, as well as ideological shifts of the major parties since around 1980, have alerted interest groups to the fact that party allies may be unexpectedly unreliable and short-lived, which has also encouraged organized interests to pursue pragmatic relationships with parties.

The relationship between parties and interest groups will be further influenced by two parallel processes that have a fundamental impact on the

Spanish policymaking process in general. First, with the growing budgetary and policymaking powers of the seventeen Spanish regions (autonomous communities), interest groups will need to focus on the regional level, and that often includes regional parties (see Hamann 1999). Regional trade unions in the Basque Country and Galicia, for example, are serious competitors to the two major national unions. Second, at the same time Spain is going through a process of "federalization" (Moreno 1997), the country's policymaking powers are increasingly being absorbed by the decisionmaking processes of the European Union (EU). Interest group strategies and policies will thus have to respond to these shifts in decisionmaking away from the level of the state to both the regions and the EU. This is especially true for agricultural associations, which are heavily subject to EU regulations (Liebert 1995a, 337). Together with "declining intensity of ideological and traditional party identifications" (Pallarés, Montero, and Llera 1997, 168), these processes will likely further the creation and growth of interest organizations and encourage their autonomy from national political parties.

11

The Czech Republic: Party Dominance in a Transitional System

Robert K. Evanson and Thomas M. Magstadt

When asked about interest group activity, Czechs often do not understand. Asked about lobbies, on the other hand, they understand instantly, like the private farmer who responded with a laugh and said they were "everywhere" nowadays.[1] Likewise, political parties have proliferated since the end of Communist rule in 1989. The Czech Republic today is a young but stable democracy with many features familiar to citizens in more established pluralist parliamentary systems.

It would be a mistake, however, to try to understand the Czech party-group relationship purely in Western terms. Although similarities are found with the Western European and even the Anglo-American experiences, the Czech pattern has always been distinctive and remains so today. It is no surprise, for example, that in the Nazi and Communist periods, opposition parties were suppressed and group aspirations were channeled through the single ruling party. More striking have been the concentration of power and the collusion among the major parties during the past and present democratic periods, which have served to limit and channel interest group lobbying activities. Despite the inclusion of business and labor in tripartite consultations with government, Czech political parties continue to monopolize a rule-making function that in many democratic systems is more fully shared by interest groups. This party dominance is one of two principal themes of this chapter.

Especially important in encouraging party dominance of contemporary policymaking has been the fact that government leaders share the party-state mentality described earlier and regard most group demands as incompatible with the development of a globally competitive market economy. Other aspects of Czech political culture, including elements of the Communist legacy, have been influential, as have the neoliberal ideology and strong leadership of former prime minister Václav Klaus and the underfinancing and inexperience of the groups themselves. This emergent pattern has given the national government greater freedom to make macroeconomic decisions at odds with the preferences of major economic interests. At the same time, it has probably not been conducive to the development of a vibrant civil society after years of totalitarian rule and may be contributing to the under-the-table payoffs that have too often been the preferred way for some lobbyists and government officials to do business. Meanwhile, the fact that domestic commercial interests are dwarfed by the giant multinational corporations has placed them at a distinct competitive disadvantage with regard to foreign firms (although this development is beyond the scope of this chapter).

We will find that in the contemporary Czech Republic, although some informal party-group links are based on ideology, close historical ties, or policy preferences, they are less important to the political system overall than ad hoc relationships between groups and the party or parties in power. This ad hoc relationship between groups and governing parties is the second of the chapter's themes. Yet the party-group relationship is also evolving as Czech democracy is consolidated. So to what extent can this present and evolving party-group relationship be explained by the transitional nature of the Czech polity and economy? Or are the political behaviors we observe today reminiscent of previous historical periods? If so, an explanation anchored in the preexisting political culture might be in order, one that would suggest a slower process of change or no change at all. Before we undertake the precarious task of prediction, however, we provide an overview of party-group relations in the pre– and post–World War II democracies and the Communist period, followed by a description and analysis of present party-group linkages in the Czech Republic.

POLITICAL BACKGROUND: DEVELOPMENTS BEFORE 1989

During Czechoslovakia's First Republic (1918–1938), policy was shaped by a de facto shadow cabinet popularly known as the Pětka. This group was composed of the heads of the main political parties, which ruled in a coalition virtually without parliamentary opposition. The Pětka's monopolistic role and process of compromise, although producing stability in parliament, limited the utility of lobbying in cabinet and legislature and the ability of the ruling parties to deliver on promises to interest groups and other constituencies (Mamatey 1973, 8–10; Seton-Watson 1965, 328–330; Wallace 1976, 143–148, 150–156, 163–194). Following their country's occupation and dismemberment during World War II, governing elites in the short-lived Third Republic (1945–1948) reverted to the prewar pattern when a coalition of major parties, again without parliamentary opposition, ruled through a National Front until the Communist Party (Kommunistické Strana Československa—KSČ) assumed complete control of the government in February 1948 (Luža 1973).

During the next four decades the communists imposed a dictatorship in which they reserved for themselves leading positions in government and social organizations, which executed the regime's will rather than representing the collective interests of their memberships. The regime, like its Soviet role model, did not recognize the legitimacy of organized interests apart from the general interest of the working class as embodied in the leadership and policies of the Communist Party. Constant vigilance and countermeasures were taken to make sure existing social organizations did not become the basis for political opposition. With very few exceptions, this pattern prevailed in states throughout the Soviet bloc.

Under these circumstances, scholars were reluctant to apply Western concepts of interest groups to Czechoslovakia and other Communist countries. Those interested in studying interest groups in these states regarded them as significant largely within the confines of the party-led bureaucratic apparatus. That is, organized interests were based solely in—to employ David Easton's terminology—the "withinput" sector of the political system, rooted in the major bureaucratic groups that vied for influence over regime policy and for larger pieces of the budgetary pie. Moreover, these groups—or rather their representatives in the innermost policymaking bodies—operated outside the public eye and without any formal claim that they represented organized interests. Their advocacy was thought to be centered around ad hoc alliances of party and government leaders who reflected to some extent the perspectives of the organizations they headed on an issue-by-issue basis. In the post-Stalin period general tendencies rooted in ideological distinctions were also identified, suggesting that there were liberal/reformist and conservative/orthodox orientations under a monolithic facade. However, since political elites were co-opted from on high and not accountable to the memberships of the organizations they headed, their representative role seemed tenuous at best.

The more independent interest group activity, which emerged in the 1960s in Czechoslovakia and other Communist states in response to liberalizing trends in the region, spawned a considerable literature on the subject in the West (Skilling 1966, 1976, 1981, 1983; Skilling and Griffiths 1971; Janos 1970; Solomon 1983; Odom 1976). In Czechoslovakia a variety of stimuli, including pressures for change from Moscow and economic decline at home, fueled a growing challenge to the status quo. In several documented cases institutionally based groups exploited divisions in the political hierarchy to engage in open interest advocacy and succeeded in influencing public policy (Korbonski 1971; A. Brown 1966, 458, 465; Wolchik 1981, 135–139). Party bodies took on a mediating role in response to group pressures, and the normally rubber-stamp National Assembly became an occasional forum for cautious interest representation (Janos 1970, 442–443; A. Brown 1972).

Interest advocacy went much further during the "Prague Spring" of 1968, when organizations inside and outside of government, encouraged by party leaders, openly advocated their members' interests; there was also organizational momentum at the grassroots (Golan 1971, 1973; Kusin 1972; Skilling 1976). Pluralism went beyond the regime's control and helped trigger the Soviet-led occupation in August 1968. During the post-1968 "normalization" the new leadership expelled reformers from public life, reimposed tight controls on society, and imprisoned political dissidents (Kusin 1978, 1979, 44–51; Skilling 1981; Ramet 1991, 387). As a result, there was little scope for independent group activity until the late 1980s when, under the weight of Mikhail Gorbachev's reforms, Communist power collapsed throughout Eastern Europe. In November 1989 a weakened regime gave way to democratic forces in the virtually bloodless Velvet Revolution.

The post-Communist government was led by former dissident Václav Havel, who moved Czechoslovakia out of the Soviet bloc. A parliamentary system was created, but Czech and Slovak leaders were unable to agree on how to share power under a new constitution. In June 1992 it was announced that on the first of the following year, Czechoslovakia would divide into two separate countries. Thus was the Czech Republic born on January 1, 1993.

POLITICAL PARTIES, INTEREST GROUPS, AND GOVERNMENT IN THE CZECH REPUBLIC

To set the scene for understanding the contemporary relationship between parties and interest groups, in this section we identify the most important political parties, followed by a description of major interests and their informal neocorporatist relations with government.

Political Parties

From 1989 to 1992 Czechoslovakia was led by two broad coalitions, the Civic Forum in the Czech Lands of Bohemia and Moravia, and Public Against Violence in Slovakia, that had been formed in 1989 to coordinate opposition forces and negotiate with the old regime. The two coalitions were umbrellas for various individuals and political factions united solely by a desire to displace the communists. They initially dominated parliamentary elections but, with their revolutionary mission accomplished, gradually broke up into competing political parties and movements (Wolchik 1991, 49, 77–83). The 1992 elections brought to power a neoliberal coalition headed by the Civic Democratic Party (Občanská Demokratická Strana—ODS) and former finance minister and economist Václav Klaus as prime minister. Klaus extolled the virtues of the free market and devoted his energies to bringing capitalism to the Czech Republic while pressing for his country's membership in the North Atlantic Treaty Organization (NATO) and the European Union. For a time his policies were successful, but mounting economic difficulties and scandals in his government led to his resignation as prime minister in November 1997. After a brief period under new leadership, the ODS-led coalition was replaced in the June 1998 national elections by a left-of-center minority government under the Czech Social Democratic Party (Česká strana Sociální Demokratická—ČSSD) and Prime Minister Miloš Zeman.

Zeman's government, which has only 74 of the 200 seats in the Chamber of Deputies, survives by virtue of a power-sharing arrangement with the ODS (63 seats) in the chamber that protects the government from no-confidence votes. Other parties reaching the 5 percent electoral threshold for securing seats in parliament include the Communist Party (Komunistická strana Čech a Moravy—KSČM), with 24 seats; the Christian Democratic Union–Czechoslovak People's Party (Křestanská a Demokratická Unie–Československá strana Lidová—KDU-ČSL), a former coalition partner with the ODS (20 seats); and the Freedom Union (Unie Svobody—US), a neoliberal spin-off from the ODS led by opponents of Klaus's leadership (19 seats). Outside the parliament are two other noteworthy parties, the ultranationalist Republican Party (Republikanská strana Československá—RSČ-SPR) and the upstart Pensioners' for Secure Living (Důchodci ža životná jistota—DŽJ). Discussions about displacing the current government with an ODS-KDU-US coalition have gone nowhere as of this writing.

The Three Major Interest Groups and Their Relations with Government

There has been a proliferation of special interest groups, as well as various public interest organizations, in the Czech Republic.[2] As is true in many countries, Czech interest groups include economic peak associations representing management, labor, and agriculture. The largest of these is the Czech-Moravian Chamber of Trade Unions (Českomoravská komora odborových svazu—ČMKOS), with a membership of 1.3 million (down from 4.4 million in 1991) from thirty-five affiliated unions representing the vast majority of unionized workers. Prominent among its target groups are retired workers, youth, women, and the unemployed, as well as all categories of Czech wage earners.[3] The largest business lobby is the Union of Industry and Transport (Svaz průmyslu a dopravy České republiky—SPD), which represents large and midsize enterprises that, combined, employ over 20 percent of the Czech workforce. The principal agricultural umbrella organization is the Czech Agriculture Chamber (Agrární komora—AK).

Major government economic and social legislation and collective bargaining issues are discussed in the tripartite Council for Economic and Social Agreement (Rada hospodářské a sociální dohody—RHSD), a voluntary arrangement that includes representatives of business and labor—mostly from the SPD and ČMKOS—and the government. The council was created in 1990 as a neocorporatist arrangement designed to keep social peace during the economic transition. An integrated union structure already existed. The government created a business umbrella to match it and perhaps to preempt independent activity. Evidence suggests that the government tended to dominate the proceedings and was successful for a time in using the umbrella to hold down wages and unemployment. For its part, labor has felt relatively powerless in the forum (Orenstein and Desai 1997, 48; Leff 1998, 197) and has used strikes and protests more frequently.

In late 1994, in retaliation for a warning strike against proposed pension reform, the government insisted on redefining the council's role as purely consultative rather than one of negotiating binding agreements. The council met less regularly, and substantive agreements became impossible. In 1997, however, Prime Minister Klaus, facing mounting economic difficulties, felt constrained to attend a tripartite meeting for the first time, and serious discussions resumed.[4] As for business, one study concluded that large corporations wield influence directly on the Ministry of Industry and Trade and do not need the council, while other enterprises focus their efforts on the council at the expense of grassroots organization with little to show for it (Orenstein and Desai 1997, 45). The following sections expand on the power relationship among governing parties, major peak associations, and other interest groups.

DYNAMICS OF PARTY-GROUP RELATIONS

Although there is a great deal of anecdotal information about the activities of both parties and interest groups in the Czech Republic and some recent valuable discussions of business associations, parties, and social cleavages (Orenstein and Desai 1997; Blahož, Brokl, and Mansfeldová 1999; Brokl 1999), little of a systematic nature has been written about the party-group relationship in the post-Communist era. Thus, it is useful to provide an overview of this contemporary relationship. The overview illustrates our dual theme that this connection is dominated by parties and that the ad hoc relations between groups and parties in power are the most important element of party-group relations in the contemporary Czech Republic.

Organized Labor

The Czech Republic has no parallel to the long-standing ties between a giant labor peak association like the Trade Union Congress (TUC) and the Labour Party in the United Kingdom or the even closer ties between the General Confederation of Labor (CGT) and the Communist Party in France. There is, however, a small union federation tied closely to the Communist Party and another to the KDU-ČSL, based on their respective leftist and Christian values. More consequential in Czech politics is the informal cooperation, rooted in shared ideology, that has emerged between the ČMKOS and the ČSSD. Union leaders have worked on behalf of the ČSSD in election campaigns and have run on its parliamentary list, including the chairman of the ČMKOS, Richard Falbr, who is a member of the upper house. At a labor rally in Prague in 1997, Miloš Zeman stood at Falbr's side and spoke to the crowd (*Carolina*, No. 251, 14 November 1997). In September 1999, however, Falbr dramatized the limits to the cooperation when he announced his opposition to ČSSD and ODS joint overtures to change the national election law in a way that would favor large parties (ČTK News 1999). We have already noted that ČMKOS's relations with the ODS have been largely conflictual.

Business Interest Groups

As in the United States, the business sector leans right of center, which suggests a primary affinity toward the ODS or US. This affinity has not been expressed in formal terms, however, and with the exception of the Association of Entrepreneurs (Szdružení podnikatelu), which launched its own small party, there does not seem to be a high level of cooperation between the business sector and a single political party such as exists in the United States between, say, the National Association of Manufacturers and the Republican Party. The business-party relationship overall can best be described as a pragmatic one carried out on an ad hoc basis. Informal cooperative ties between individual companies and the ODS do exist, as dramatized by the scandals involving high-rolling entrepreneurs and key figures within the ODS in which private money was given for public favors—events that were instrumental in bringing down the ODS-led coalition in 1997. These incidents, however, are by nature ad hoc, informal, personalistic, and secretive—not the kind of routinized and permanent relationships that exist between interest groups and political parties that share ideologies, aims, and constituencies in many other parliamentary democracies.

Agricultural Groups

As a large umbrella organization, the AK is limited in its ability to represent the demands of any specific category of farmers, much as the Farm Bureau Federation in the United States cannot replace more highly focused commodity-based organizations. Czech farmers, however, are poorly organized and funded at all levels compared with their U.S. counterparts. This is true of both the large cooperative sector, a holdover from the Communist era, and private farmers, who are poorer and even less influential than the cooperatives. Further, as we show later, farmers have not been especially effective at influencing public policy through boycotts or other disruptive actions, as farmers have been in France. One problem for farm interests has been weak representation in the government. No formal links are found between farm lobbies and existing political parties. The KDU-ČSL, which has a strong rural base and is the closest any Czech party comes to being an agrarian party, held the agriculture portfolio in the ODS-led cabinets but had little success in shaping policy.

Health Care Professionals

The deteriorating state of health care is a major issue in the Czech Republic, as few Czechs want to give up the comprehensive national health system that is the most popular legacy of the Communist period. One of the most common fears associated with the "transition" to a market economy—a fear freely expressed by Czech adults of all ages—is that doctors will transform the system to the everlasting detriment of patients. Tensions between doctors and patients and between doctors and insurance companies have led to numerous strike threats and actions by doctors and other health care workers.

The Czech Chamber of Doctors (Česká lékařská komora—ČLK) is the physicians' umbrella organization, and the Patients' Association (Sdružení na ochranu pacientu—SOP) represents consumers' interests. Several other sizable interest groups represent various combinations of health care workers including the Union of Health and Social Workers (Odborový svaz zdravotnictví a sociální péče České republiky—OSZSP), which boasts 90,000 members, including doctors, making it the largest union of health care workers in the country (Fronk 1999b). The Health Ministry is the other key player in the politics of health care.

There are apparently no formal links between any of these groups and existing political parties. The various health care unions had an adversarial relationship with the Klaus government, which tried to hold down costs in the still large public health care sector. The current Social Democratic government has also opposed union demands and has sided with the large health consumer movement.

Interest Parties

Several parties, all failures at the polls, are direct creations of interest movements and groups. The Party of Entrepreneurs, Tradesmen and Farmers (Strany podnikatelu, živnostníku, a rolníku—SPŽR) is a creature of the Association of Entrepreneurs; the Green Party (Strany zelených—SZ) emerged from several environmental organizations; the Movement for Moravian and Silesian Self-Rule (Hnutí samosprávné moravy a slezska—HSMS) is a regionalist party; and the DŽJ, the largest of the four, grew out of the pensioners' movement and claims to represent it. The DŽJ has twice failed to reach the 5 percent threshold to obtain seats in parliament despite preelection polls in 1998 showing it winning 10 percent of the vote. Part of the DŽJ's problem is that the Communist Party claims the loyalty of many retirees, who comprise more than half its vote. The pensioners' movement also lacks resources for lobbying and campaigning and is divided across the ideological spectrum.

PUBLIC POLICYMAKING IN THE PRESENCE OF DOMINANT PARTIES AND THE ABSENCE OF CLOSE PARTY-GROUP RELATIONS

In the absence of strong links between political parties and interest groups and against the backdrop of dominant parties, how, and how well, has the contemporary political system brought group interests into focus and converted their articulated goals into public policy?

Mixed Success of Organized Labor

What role has organized labor played in influencing economic and social policy? One model posits an embryonic corporatism in which trade unions remain compliant in return for a hands-off government approach to trade union properties and operations (Rutland 1993, 121). Rather than accept large numbers of layoffs, the Klaus government in effect gave labor an exemption from the pains of adjustment—continuing subsidies to industries, putting off bankruptcy laws, and pointing with pride to a low unemployment rate (around 3 percent officially in the mid-1990s) as a sign of economic health. Actually, high employment went hand in hand with low labor productivity; management, unable to shed old habits, resisted firing workers.

At the same time, the Klaus government sought to hold down wages and benefits despite strong objections from labor. Although its motives were mainly economic, its determination was strengthened by apparent doubts about the legitimacy of strikes, demonstrations, and even open policy advocacy by unions. In 1994, after parliament amended labor laws, Economics Minister Karel Dyba publicly dismissed union complaints with a contemptuous, "Trade unions? What is that?" (Leff 1998, 197). The following year, when teachers struck for better pay and working conditions, Klaus responded with stinging criticism, in effect lecturing the lecturers. The Ministry of Education refused to talk with teachers' union representatives, and the protest fizzled out.[5] That same year members of the ODS parliamentary fraction remarked that protesting unions should confine their entreaties to "parliamentary soil" and stay out of issues like health care policy that are "not really their business" (Živnustková 1995). In April 1998 the post-Klaus ODS government rejected talks with civil servants after they engaged in protest demonstrations (ČMKOS 1999).

Government-labor relations, therefore, are not truly corporatist. The tripartite council seldom produces binding agreements, the ČMKOS represents only a small minority of employees, and unions have become less compliant with each passing year. The government's original full-employment strategy may have been designed to avoid labor unrest, suggesting to one writer a proletarian legacy of the Communist era (Orenstein 1996); it also suggested implicit union influence. As time went on, relations between unions and government grew more openly contentious, as in 1994–1995, when a wave of strikes nearly scuttled the tripartite forum. For a time strikers seldom realized their demands, with notable exceptions such as in February 1997, when railway workers shut down the railroads (still largely public) for five days and won government concessions. Increasingly, however, union actions have succeeded in forcing the government to place employees' issues on the political agenda. Labor's leverage had been limited by public perceptions that the unions are a Communist holdover (Tucker et al. 1997, 407) and that strikes are contrary to the public interest (*Lidové noviny* 1995), but popular sentiment has shifted toward labor in recent years. A declining economy and ever weaker governments have also aided labor's cause.

The Social Democrats gained power in 1998 with support from the trade unions. Once in power they increased public-sector wages and moved to renationalize some parts of Czech industry in an effort to placate their labor base (*The Economist* 1999). The Zeman government needs labor cooperation as it tackles a faltering economy. However, the union movement is still relying more on the strike, and the Zeman government is in no better position to reward labor's demands than was its predecessor.

Business Groups' Insider Status Despite Antipathy Toward Lobbying

Center-right governments are typically sympathetic and accessible to business. In the Czech Republic, however, the business community's task of influencing high-level decisionmaking was complicated by former prime minister Klaus's view that pressure groups in general are obstacles to rational policymaking and to weaning society from state subsidies: "In the economic sphere, termination of the existing economic paternalism . . . is crucial. Swift elimination of subsidies of all kinds, which brings about a dramatic upward shift in prices, must be undertaken without hesitation. Later on it becomes difficult or impossible to do that because newly formed pressure groups successfully block it" (Klaus 1997, 20). Similarly, commenting on the anticipated public reaction to liberalization and deregulation, Klaus wrote:

> New [pressure] groups are formed, and they begin to misuse the existing institutional vacuum, the weak markets as well as various gaps and holes in rapidly changing legislation and in the initiated privatization process (especially during the "spontaneous" privatization process). Disparities in wealth and income grow, markets remain imperfect, and privatization revolutionizes the whole social structure. . . . [A] "turning point" [occurs at this stage] . . . either the original transformation strategy is adhered to with consequent positive results, or chaos and a vicious circle of half measures and concessions to [pressure] groups is initiated, with the inevitable loss of "the whole." (Klaus 1997, 21–22)

In 1996 Klaus called the "problem of special interests" his "topic No. 1" (Klačová and Příkryl 1996).

Despite Klaus's open antipathy toward pressure groups, the public came to believe ongoing government-business collusion and widespread corruption existed under ODS rule. The absence of conflict-of-interest laws, weak campaign finance laws, and a lack of transparency in corporate contributions added to the problem. As late as 1995 many members of parliament sat on corporate boards, and it was legal for state-owned or state-subsidized enterprises to donate money to the parties—an open invitation to corruption. Legislative remedy came only after a public outcry following revelations of blatant influence peddling.

The privatization process has been plagued by corruption and mismanagement. New banks were chartered in a helter-skelter fashion after 1989 without benefit of good laws and close regulation. They lent money indiscriminately, and only in 1995 were laws passed to counter the use of banks for money laundering. Bank funds were also frequently embezzled ("tunneled" in Czech parlance) by crooks masquerading as managers (*The Economist* 1997). State-owned banks are often in collusion with "privatized" industry and in some cases control mutual funds, which in turn are the largest shareholders of big enterprises. In one case a bank allowed the managers of an investment fund to rob shareholders, with the money then transferred out of the country with the approval of the Ministry of Finance.

Another investment fund was robbed of $9 million while being run by government-appointed administrators (Magstadt 1998, 17).

Both Klaus and his Social Democratic successor have done little to remedy the situation. It seems paradoxical that collusive practices were so common when the head of the government (Klaus) disapproved of private lobbies. One study of Klaus argued that his insensitivity to corruption stemmed from his assumption that financial markets would regulate themselves and not require government-imposed transparency (Saxonberg 1999, 414). Klaus's antipathy to interest groups may also have encouraged under-the-table and illegal dealings by shutting off conventional routes of influence.

The Modest Success of Farm Lobbies

Czech idealization of rural life and sympathy for the plight of farmers have not translated readily into policies farmers favor. The Klaus government was philosophically ill disposed to high subsidies for agriculture, and transnational pressures have made matters even more difficult. The Zeman government, however, appears a little more responsive. In October 1998 pork prices on the Czech market plummeted 25 percent, leaving pig farmers unable to compete with inexpensive imports from the European Union (EU). In November frustrated farmers staged a protest against EU dumping of cheap pork products on local markets. The threat was in effect to imitate the militancy of, say, French farmers—blocking traffic by herding hundreds of pigs onto the highway from Brno to Prague. The actual "protest," however, was a feeble effort: "At 7 A.M. in a parking lot off the D-1 highway 4 kilometers outside of Brno, farmers unloaded five pigs in a pen, while about 80 protesters with signs listened to speeches for two hours" (Oldweiler 1998, A1).

Despite the comic futility of this effort, farmers did receive some relief when AK and the Agriculture Ministry agreed on remedial counterprotectionist measures including import tariffs, surcharges, and minimum prices. In return AK distanced itself from the threat of protests, saying it opposed putting animals on the road. On 25 November the Zeman government abolished preferential tariffs on EU pork imports, thus making good on its promise to the farmers. About two weeks later the EU relented, cutting subsidies on pork exports to associate members (including the Czech Republic) by half (Moran 1998b).

The pork skirmish, despite its happy outcome for Czech farmers, is a rather misleading measure of agricultural influence over economic policy. Czech agriculture has suffered mightily since the Velvet Revolution, in part as a result of deliberate public policy. According to the Vienna Institute for International Economic Studies, Czech agriculture receives the lowest subsidies in Europe as measured by the producer subsidy equivalent (PSE)—basically state subsidies as a percentage of gross farm income. The Czech PSE was about 11 percent in 1997 compared with 16 percent in Hungary, an average of 42 percent in EU countries, and 30 percent in the United States. This low level of state support for Czech farmers represented a decline from almost 70 percent in 1986. Not surprisingly, the number of people employed in farming and forestry dropped from 630,000 in 1990 (12 percent of the total labor force) to 275,000 (5 percent) in 1997 (Moran 1998b, A5–6).

Clearly, the agricultural sector has had only modest success in influencing policy. The action taken by the Social Democratic government in the pork-dumping case, however, suggests that it has fewer philosophical compunctions about intervening in the market and may be more open to influence from the agricultural lobby, provided it does not exact a high economic cost. The fact that the ČSSD was walking a thin line in this regard was apparent in June 1999 when unhappy farm unions demonstrated against agricultural policy despite an increase in wheat and sugar subsidies (*Carolina*, No. 335, 4 June 1999).

Weakness of Green Lobbies

Despite public concern about pollution, the environmental movement has had little success in the policy arena. The Klaus government saw extensive environmental protection as unaffordable during the transition; Klaus himself also thought free market solutions were the best approach to environmental problems and called environmentalism "an ideology, not a science." The ODS is unique in excluding environmental issues from its platform (Bisschop 1996). The Social Democratic cabinet has been divided on Green issues, such as in its May 1999 decision to go ahead with completion of the controversial Temelín nuclear power plant in southern Bohemia. The cabinet split eleven to eight, with the minister of the environment opposing the project and the minister of industry and trade leading the fight on its behalf (*Carolina*, No. 333, 5 May 1999). On pollution matters the ČSSD supports tax incentives and higher energy prices rather than government regulation.

The Temelín defeat was a blow to environmentalists. Some progress has been made in environmental protection, such as improved air quality; still, nearly one-quarter of Czechs breathe "heavily polluted" air that falls short of international standards, according to the Organization for Economic Cooperation and Development (OECD) (Fronk 1999a). Moreover, despite the Greens' success in gaining media attention on environmental issues, the public has not been particularly generous in donating time and money to Green groups or in voting for the Green Party, which has yet to gain a seat in parliament.

Health Care Lobbies: Providers Versus Patients

Physicians, overworked and underpaid, have been protesting and engaging in sick-outs for years. The government initially ignored their efforts, but by the fall of 1995 their constant pressure began to elicit concessions on privatization, hospital closings, and wage formulas. Nonetheless, wage gains have been modest, as health care employees continue to be weakened by internal divisions, an unsympathetic government, organized consumers, and macroeconomic constraints. This was apparent in September 1999 when the Doctors' Club (Lekařský odborový klub—LOK) announced a day of protest followed by a strike to support a demand to the Health Ministry for a 63 percent pay hike. Although LOK promised to maintain emergency care and basic services and won the support of the ČLK, the mere hint of a strike brought threats of countermeasures from the Patients' Association and opposition from the largest health union (the OSZSP). Also, the Health Ministry weighed in on the side of patients, insisting that the government could not meet the doctors' demands and warning the doctors not to endanger the health care system (Fronk 1999b).

Summary: The Practical Reality

Party dominance has limited the importance of the party-group relationship in the policymaking process. Efforts by leaders of the governing party to monopolize policy and maintain institutional separation have encouraged informal collusion and even corruption between business and government and increasingly strident open-air challenges from labor and agriculture; these have had some impact on isolated policy decisions, but overall policymaking has been relatively insulated from private pressures. To the extent that cooperation has occurred, organizational links have been a weak factor in forging it. Ideology has counted for more, as has electoral strategizing between labor and the ČSSD, but neither factor has balanced the impact of transitional economic imperatives.

THE PECULIARITIES OF PARTY-GROUP RELATIONS

The major political parties have sought to monopolize the policy process and limit the participation and impact of interest groups on that process. A major reason has been the government's effort to hold down wages and prices to attract foreign investment and maximize global competitiveness. Adding to the pressure has been the European Union: although the government has been willing to confront the EU on selected issues, it has had to reduce protectionism to qualify the country for membership.

Under the ODS government, macroeconomic concerns were reinforced by ideological opposition to government interventionism, for example, in environmental matters. Sometimes, though, economic and ideological considerations conflicted, as in Klaus's misgivings about government interference in labor-management relations while he was using tripartite discussions to hold down wages and prices. The ČSSD leadership is more disposed ideologically to respond favorably to the labor and agrarian lobbies but is constrained by budgetary considerations and its working arrangement with the ODS.

Cutting across ideological boundaries is the influence of political culture, or relatively persistent patterns of beliefs and attitudes about public affairs. One element of Czech political culture is a preference for centralized control of policymaking, which has meant control by party leaders who in all previous Czech(oslovak) systems negotiated policy outside normal parliamentary structures. The current Czech system fits a regional pattern where, according to Attila Agh, post-Communist elites have adopted a "hegemonistic party system" in which a small number of "cartel" parties prefer to share resources and power at the expense of smaller parties, interest groups, and other social formations (Agh 1998, 12, 109). Czech parties receive the largest portion of their financing from state subsidies allocated according to the percentage of the vote each party received in the last parliamentary election. This practice heavily favors the ČSSD and ODS, which have a government-opposition power-sharing arrangement and in 1999 and 2000 were discussing electoral reforms to further strengthen the larger parties at the expense of the smaller ones.

It is also clear that the leaders of the two major parties are uncomfortable with an open style of governance. In addition to opposing pressure groups, Klaus is said to believe "citizens should be politically passive and leave daily politics to professional politicians in professional parties" (Saxonberg 1999, 402). Like politicians from the rival ODS, Prime Minister Zeman has told labor and business leaders to confine their opinions on policy to the tripartite council (*Radio Free Europe* 1999); both he and Klaus have responded to media criticism with sarcasm and insults.

The impact of political culture has also weakened groups in their relations with parties. The Czech tradition of economic and social egalitarianism is expressed today in suspicion toward special interests—intensified by the media's preoccupation with scandals—and opposition to group demands that threaten welfare benefits such as health care. The political cultural impact of geography is also apparent. The Czech Republic is a small country in which most public and private elites know each other and converge on Prague. Direct lobbying by the heads of organizations is encouraged by this fact and by the inability of most groups to pay expensive lobbyists. Both the personalism of Czech pressure tactics and the corruption sometimes attending it may also be partly compensatory. That is, it is a way to leap across the barriers put up by the elitist exclusivity of the government and the high spending (and occasional well-publicized bribes) of foreign competition. Corruption is also a consequence of the get-rich-quick mentality in a society in which money is still scarce.

The Communist experience has also left its mark. Czech elites have retained both the party-state mentality of the previous era and an emphasis on personal ties, the latter reinforced by the sluggish restoration of formal rules. Among the masses, harsh repression and widespread collaboration decimated civil society and led most Czechs not to trust people outside their closest circles. Out of habitual passivity or distrust, many remain reluctant to join or support organized groups or to engage in political advocacy. Some observers note the absence of support for public interest groups (Moran 1998a) and a preoccupation with material benefits, which they attribute to the moral legacy of totalitarianism under which an atomized society abandoned social concerns (Čulík 1996). Today most people will organize only to defend the benefits of the welfare state.

The effectiveness of independent interests is also limited by inadequate financial resources and inexperience with pressure techniques. A middle-level manager at Aerovodochody, an aircraft designer and manufacturer, commented that "we are learning to play the media game and our American friends are teaching us."[6] Aerovodochody's new U.S. partner is Boeing, which will have to provide the cash because few Czech businesses can afford Western-style media campaigns. Money also puts Czech businesses at a disadvantage against multinational firms, which also gain from government efforts to attract foreign investment.

In sum, group relations with the parliamentary parties and particularly with the party or parties in government are unequal, unstructured, and informal. Using the categorization set out in Box 1.2, some are characterized by separation/pragmatic involvement (professional groups, agriculture, perhaps parts of the Green movement). Others are marked by a fluctuation between separation/pragmatism and loose and ad hoc cooperation, such as business's relations with the ODS and labor's with the ČSSD. It also matters which party is in power: labor-ČSSD relations appear more separated since the ČSSD assumed responsibility for the economy. The ODS's public interactions with organized labor, on the other hand, have been conflictual, sometimes even bitter. Business relations with the ČSSD outside the tripartite council are informal and separated but not nearly as conflict ridden as labor relations with the ODS. By the same token, business-government relations under Klaus underline the greater degree to which the political environment in the Czech Republic is configured for collusion than is the case in established Western democracies. There is a thin line between "pressure" and corrupt practices.

The general characteristics of separation in party-group relations and party dominance have probably retarded the development of civil society. Certainly, the implications that people should leave government to the "bosses" and that payoffs from the privileged are the way to do business in Prague are unfortunate messages to a posttotalitarian society. It would be ironic if all of this leads to increasingly anomic behavior by unions and the consequent paralysis of the economy that party-state elitism is intended to serve.

CONCLUSION

Party dominance in the Czech Republic has been consciously encouraged by post-Communist elites who have been especially influenced by the tasks of economic reconstruction and an inherited elitism and party-state mentality. Czech personalism, egalitarianism, and wariness of special interests, as well as the neoliberal ideology of some political leaders, have also shaped the party-group relationship, as have the relative impoverishment and inexperience of interest groups themselves. The upshot is that informal party-group links based on ideology, close historical ties, or policy preference are less important than ad hoc relationships between groups and the party or coalition in power. Although democracy has been restored to the Czech people, party-group relations have not been helpful to the restoration of civil society.

At the same time, party dominance is in part a result of the transitional nature of the country's political and economic systems. This fact suggests some potential for change. The breakdown of the ODS-led coalition and emergence of strong competition from the left may force the major parties to compete for group support and forge stronger party-group links. Memories of communism will fade, and civil society will grow stronger. Czech society will become more acculturated to interest group politics, and corruption will decline as legitimate pressure tactics become more affordable and the legal system more effective. As the Czech economy grows, labor costs may seem less onerous, and political leaders may decide that cooperation with unions serves their policy goals better than confrontation. Increasing standards of living may, as they have in Western democracies in general, increase support for public interest groups like environmentalists and force parties to embrace these and other public interest concerns more fully. All of this will occur in the context of growing Czech integration into the European Union and the persistence of those cultural values—such as personalism, egalitarianism, and elitism—that predate the trauma of Communist rule.

12

Poland: Parties, Movements, Groups, and Ambiguity

David Ost

Western experience is a poor guide for understanding party-group–social movement relations in post-Communist Poland. Most scholarly literature, including the chapters in this volume, assumes meaningful differences among these three forms of collective political action. But in a country where party competition was long forbidden, interests could not be articulated outside of the ruling party, and a social movement—Solidarity—ultimately took over the political realm, positing that firm distinctions between apparently diffuse political forms hamper rather than help our understanding. The defining characteristic in Poland has been the inability and unwillingness of political actors to take on roles that can be categorized precisely by the traditional party-group–social movement triad. Instead we have a blurring of realms, a political ambiguity that over a decade after 1989 seems to have become institutionalized.

Yet, although commentators on Poland agree on the imprecise nature of Solidarity and on the difficulties it has posed for democratic transformation (for example, Staniszkis 1991; Grabowska and Krzeminski 1991), no one has examined the issue in terms of party-group relations compared with relations in other liberal democracies. The general purpose of this chapter is to help fill this gap in the literature by explaining the role of Solidarity, parties, and interest groups and their relationship in contemporary Poland.

POLITICAL PARTIES, INTEREST GROUPS, AND SOCIAL MOVEMENTS: TRADITIONAL DISTINCTIONS VERSUS THE POLISH CASE

Burstein (1998) has challenged the usual consensus about discrete political forms. Groups, movements, and parties, he argues, ought to be considered part of a single overarching political phenomenon rather than separate spheres of organization and action. There are "no meaningful differences" between groups and movements, Burstein argues, and "few" differences between them and parties. Groups and movements seek to bring into the center of political consideration the views of those ("outsiders") not already in it or to sustain a political presence once obtained. Scholars used to contend key differences existed between structure and tactics, with the tighter control and more formalized tactics of groups contrasted with the loose discipline and confrontational style of movements. But recent studies have shown that social movements are structured in precise ways, their tactics fitting into well-honed "repertoires" (Tarrow 1998, 30). Political parties seem to be different in that they nominate candidates and compete for public office and are thus directly involved in the governing process groups and movements seek to influence. Yet like groups and movements, parties can also be seen as organizations of collective action that arose to influence government policy, and as has been seen in U.S. politics since 1968, even putative outsiders can play a decisive role.

For those studying the polities of Western liberal democracies, Burstein's argument appears to have several holes. Even if the Republican Party in the United States seemed to behave like a fundamentalist Christian social movement in its vendetta against and impeachment of Bill Clinton, its official and governmental functions remain sufficiently different from those of the Christian Coalition to mar any unified theory seeking to embrace them both. It is also difficult to see Amnesty International and the British Labour Party as the same type of organization, even if both supported the indictment and extradition to Spain of former Chilean strongman Gen. Ugarte Pinochet to be tried on human rights charges.

If he had studied Poland, Burstein would have had a much stronger case. Since 1989 the premier political organization in the country has been Solidarity, which has operated as a convincing organizational incarnation of all three types of political phenomena. Having begun as a social movement seeking to open the boundaries of civic participation—although in factories it was simultaneously an interest group, a trade union representing the interests of workers—by 1988 it had reinvented itself as a unified political organization negotiating systemic transformation with the ruling Communist party, the Polish United Workers' Party (Polska Zjednoczona Partia Robotnicza—PZPR) and running parliamentary candidates in the first elections in 1989.

Refusing to become a full-fledged political party but nevertheless installed in power, Solidarity stifled its social movement identity, trying to be a simple trade union in public and a political king maker behind the scenes. But it could not sustain this gambit, particularly as signs of social movement protest arose outside its ranks. To deal with this challenge

Solidarity the trade union began openly embracing politics. In 1991 and 1993 the union ran a limited slate of candidates in parliamentary elections, and in 1996 it formed a political coalition, Solidarity Electoral Action (Akcja Wyborcza Solidarnosc—AWS) that performed like a party and rode into state power as a parliamentary victor a year later. The president of Solidarity, Marian Krzaklewski, kept his seat as trade union leader while making himself head of the political coalition. He refrained from taking the post of prime minister, thus making sure the organizational ambiguity would continue as it had since 1989.

The theoretical goal of this chapter is to rescue the concept of ambiguity. Although Burstein's claim about the ontological permeability of these three forms of collective action is correct if applied to Poland, I disagree with his insistence that we should therefore seek to find a single conceptual framework that can embrace parties, groups, and movements. The truth, it seems to me, is located not in what unites them but in the necessary ambiguity of their indispensably separate individual identities. Holding ambiguity fast tells us much more about the nature of politics in general, and of Polish politics in particular, than attempting to resolve that ambiguity into something more manageable. The gain in conceptual clarity by attempting to develop a single conceptual framework as Burstein suggests is only apparent. The cost of that clarity is the loss of the particularities that give context and meaning to political actions.

In demonstrating and defending the need for ambiguity, I will examine the specific organizational features of post-Communist Polish politics to assess the relationship among groups, movements, and parties. Box 12.1 outlines what can be a confusing array of players in Polish politics in recent years, particularly political parties.

THE CHANGING NATURE OF SOLIDARITY

An understanding of Polish politics since 1989 hinges on an understanding of Solidarity, which is like the molecule on which Heisenberg shined the light: as soon as you see it, it moves. You finally think you understand it and then see that from a different perspective it is clearly also something else. This fundamental fact about Solidarity stems from its very foundations and from its dual role as institution and symbol. Its name, which is unlike any trade union organization in the Western world, originated to describe the nature of the strike in Gdansk in 1980 and came to denote both a specific trade union organization and the general, largely uncoordinated and autonomous movement (or movements) for social, political, and frequently moral change the trade union inspired.

Ambiguity was built into the union from the start, largely because of

Box 12.1 Polish Political Parties and Politicians

Center Alliance: Formed in 1990 as a secular right-wing party within the still-partyless Solidarity movement. It was particularly concerned with the continuing power of the former Communists and the need to continue the fight against them. It is a member of Solidarity Electoral Action, or AWS (explained later).

Christian National Union: Formed in the early 1990s as a right-wing Catholic party from within the broad Solidarity camp, emphasizing religious values and anticommunism. It is a member of Solidarity Electoral Action, or AWS (explained later).

Freedom Union—UW (Unia Wolnosci): A political party led by liberal intellectuals close to the Solidarity movement, founded in 1993 as the successor to Democratic Union, which arose in 1990 when the Solidarity parliamentary contingent began to break apart.

General Accord of Trade Unions—OPZZ (Ogolne Porozumienie Zwiazkow Zawodowych): Trade union movement close to the former Communist Party, founded in 1984 after the delegalization of Solidarity.

Krzaklewski, Marian: Born 1951, Solidarity leader after Lech Walesa, first elected in 1991.

Kwasniewski, Aleksander: Born 1955, leader of Social Democracy of the Polish Republic, SDRP (explained later), from 1990 until 1995; elected president of Poland in 1995 and reelected in October 2000.

Movement for the Republic (Ruch dla Rzeczypospolitej): Formed in 1992 by right-wing former Solidarity political activists with the almost sole plank of "decommunization," understood as taking power and property away from former Communists.

Party X: Party formed in 1990 by businessman Stan Tyminski, returned émigré from Canada and Peru, to support his presidential campaign; the party did not survive long after his failed bid.

Polish Peasant Party (Polskie Stronnictwo Ludowe): Successor to a pro-regime party allowed during the Communist years, trying to represent farmers' interests.

Polish Socialist Party—PPS (Polska Partia Socjalistyczna): A small democratic left-wing party made up of former Solidarity activists, opposed to Social Democracy of the Polish Republic, or SDRP (explained later), from the left, although it agreed to run parliamentary candidates in 1993 from within the SLD (explained later). The PPS's name was taken from a pre–World War II party (1898–1939) that led Poland to independence.

(continues)

> **Box 12.1 Continued**
>
> *Polish United Workers' Party—PZPR (Polska Zjednoczona Partia Robotnicza):* The ruling Communist party in Poland from 1948 to 1989, dissolved in February 1990.
>
> *Social Democracy of the Polish Republic—SDRP (Socjaldemokracja Rzeczpospolitej Polskiej):* Founded in 1990 as the successor party to the Polish United Workers' Party, or PZPR, with a moderate pro-market and pro-reform platform; in power 1993–1997. It usually contested elections under the name Union of the Democratic Left. The party changed its name to SLD in 1999.
>
> *Social Movement (Ruch Spoleczny):* The name of the new political party formed in 1998 by Solidarity activists within AWS (explained above). Until that time Solidarity had been the leading force within the AWS coalition, but the only one not to formally have its own political party.
>
> *Solidarity Electoral Action—AWS (Akcja Wyborcza Solidarnosc):* The self-proclaimed right-wing political coalition formed by Solidarity in 1996. It won the 1997 parliamentary elections and formed a coalition government with the Freedom Union, or UW (explained above).
>
> *Solidarity of Labor (Solidarnosc Pracy):* A social democratic party formed by Solidarity activists; refused to give the mantle of social democracy to former communists. Formed in 1990, it changed its name in 1992 to Union of Labor (Unia Pracy).
>
> *Union of the Democratic Left—SLD (Sojusz Lewicy Demokratycznej):* The name of the left-wing electoral coalition led by Social Democracy of the Polish Republic, or SDRP (explained above); since mid-1999 the new name of the SDRP itself.
>
> *Walesa, Lech:* Born 1943, electrician in Gdansk who led strikes in 1980 and became head of Solidarity trade union. Elected president of Poland in 1990; served until 1995.
>
> Source: Compiled by the author.

the nature of the enemy it confronted—the PZPR. To fight a centralized party-state, Solidarity needed a central organization of its own. It had to be able to call people out on a general strike or to prevent workers from striking, and it needed to do so on a nationwide basis to keep the party from chipping away at the union piece by piece. At the same time it had to maintain a radically decentralized structure to prevent the PZPR from crushing the movement by arresting its leaders. This precarious balancing act, which I have elsewhere called its "indispensable ambiguity," influenced the organization's political nature as well (Ost 1988). As is well-known, Solidarity could not be an explicitly political organization. The concept of politics had been coercively monopolized by the party, which together with its Soviet protectors had made it clear since crushing the Hungarian uprising in 1956 that any attempted entry onto this turf would be met by force. Solidarity thus turned famously to "antipolitics," attempting to shape political outcomes by transforming civil society instead of the state, thus denying that the formal political sphere was the only one that counted.[1] The essential ambiguity was rooted here, as antipolitical politics was not a hoax but a conscious attempt to affect politics by what was considered nonpolitical means. Thus, an attempt to fit Solidarity into one box—as political or nonpolitical, as an institution or a movement—robs it of its true identity.[2]

SOLIDARITY DURING THE COMMUNIST ERA—1980-1989

Solidarity began in 1980 as a movement of workers in Gdansk trying to form trade unions independent of the PZPR. Since a ban on independent organizations was at the heart of the Communist system, the call to abolish that ban meant Solidarity could not just become a group to represent workers' interests. The system hinged on the party's monopolization of public life and on the inability of social groups—workers in particular, this being a "workers' state"—to represent themselves. The appearance of Solidarity thus threw the entire political system into crisis. Solidarity, it seemed, would have to become a political movement. But it could not and would not do so—could not because the terms under which the PZPR legalized Solidarity explicitly ruled that out, and would not because union leaders were aware that previous attempts at explicit political challenges in Eastern Europe had led to Soviet intervention. Solidarity thus had no choice but to present itself legally as an interest group—in this case, a trade union.

The problem was that Solidarity was systemically unable to be only a trade union because its very existence as an independent organization, in a society where everything depended on coordination among organizations subservient to the party, necessarily threw the economy and polity into disarray. It could not be just a trade union and could not constitute itself as a political organization, so it became a social movement instead. "We are a trade union and a social movement," its spokespersons kept repeating—the trade union articulating interests of workers on the job and the social movement fighting for guarantees of societal autonomy.

By any standard definition of a social movement, Solidarity seemed to fit. It represented people outside established political institutions and engaged in "noninstitutional forms of political participation" such as sit-ins, strikes, quasi-legal publications, public lectures, and "happenings"

(McCarthy and Zald 1977). It sought to "chang[e] elements of the social structure" and made "publicly visible demands for changes in the distribution or exercise of power" (Tilly 1984, 304). In line with antipolitics, Solidarity did not commit itself to try to enter government per se, but, as noted before, its antipolitics was itself a form of politics, with power understood as located not in the state but in civil society (Soviet-style communism, of course, located power in the state, civil society, and the economy, which is why it insisted on controlling all three). The result was a social movement disguised as an interest group and occupied with political matters pretending to be social ones. Attempts to distinguish carefully among group, movement, and party in Poland during this period can thus be a challenge.

After the imposition of martial law in December 1981, the chameleon character of Solidarity became even more vivid. Most of its leaders had now been imprisoned or gone underground, so it ceased being any type of organized political association. Martial law meant the derecognition of Solidarity as a trade union, the impossibility of organizing a coherent movement strategy, and the inability to force a political discussion with those who had the guns.

But if an interest group cannot exist when its activities are banned, a social movement can; it just becomes a very different kind of movement. So Solidarity moved from being a movement taking advantage of legal rights to organize (conditions normally treated as a given by social movement theorists) and became an underground movement instead. With its leadership unable to lead, underground Solidarity was made up of anyone who distributed a leaflet, participated in a protest, or just considered themselves members. Over time, the two most prominent union activists to escape arrest, Zbigniew Bujak of Warsaw and Wladyslaw Frasyniuk of Wroclaw, tried to consolidate an underground Solidarity leadership, but it lacked the clear structure typical of established political associations. For the first five years after the imposition of martial law, Solidarity was an inchoate, leaderless social movement.

The situation did not change until 1986, when the PZPR declared a general amnesty and political opportunities again opened up. Some workers wanted to use Solidarity to push trade union activity. But Lech Walesa and his associates (chosen chiefly from the more liberal underground circles grouped around Bujak and Frasyniuk) chose a narrower, more specifically political strategy: to develop an elite Solidarity leadership that could force broad-based political reforms through negotiations with the PZPR. Mass activism was shunned in favor of pressuring the elite. As it turned out, however, this plan could make no headway without workers' activism backing it up. In August 1988 workers declaring their allegiance to Solidarity went on strike to demand the union's relegalization. Even though many "official"

Solidarity leaders did not even know the strikers, they quickly took advantage of the movement from below to push their own movement from above.

Successfully parlaying this social pressure into political pressure, Walesa's political team secured PZPR acceptance for a renewal of political contacts, which soon led to the roundtable negotiations of February–April 1989. Pushing the political agenda further, Walesa created a Civic Committee of leading pro-Solidarity intellectuals to help prepare for the negotiations and for political reconstruction afterward. Only at this point did he finally set about revitalizing the trade union that still constituted Solidarity's official identity. The union (interest group) and movement were subordinated to the political organization (nascent party), but the latter still needed the former to convince the authorities to make major concessions. When the roundtable talks ended in April, Solidarity was relegalized as a trade union and suddenly found itself turned into a political party as well. The final accord stipulated that parliamentary elections were to be held within two months, and "Solidarity"—which at this point was a political leadership more than anything else—became a party for the purpose of contesting the elections. No major internal discussion preceded this transformation.

Solidarity in Power

When Solidarity decisively won the June 1989 elections and went on to form a government three months later, the group was partly a union and partly a party. Ironically, the only thing Solidarity was not at that time was a social movement. As its activists advanced into parliamentary and then government positions, they explicitly sought to restrain the growth of a movement. Aware of the difficult economic times ahead and under the influence of a neoliberal revival that swept across opposition circles in the late 1980s, Solidarity's leaders distrusted any activism that might jeopardize the policies the new government was trying to push through.

At the same time, Solidarity was reluctant to push too far toward becoming a powerful interest group or political party. Suspicions of popular activism led to suspicion of trade union activity, and so it tried to keep unionism within tight limits. Walesa opposed a strong union, even though he ostensibly headed one, because he believed such a union would "decisively oppose" the reforms he believed were necessary. "We will not catch up to Europe if we build a strong union," he said in fall 1989.[3] Emergence as a single political party, meanwhile, was blocked by rivalry within the elite, for as the Communist opposition disappeared, internal unity began to shatter. As a result, Solidarity's parliamentary representatives split into several political parties, each claiming to represent the "real" legacy of the union.

Thus, at the very moment they came to power, Solidarity authorities did not know what to be. They feared movements, distrusted strong unions, and could not agree to become a single party. On the verge of disintegrating, Solidarity revived its union identity—although as a weak one, providing social cover for the economic reforms of Solidarity-affiliated politicians. This ostensible return to interest group status was dictated by the group's resources. Solidarity leaders in 1989 may not have been enthusiastic about trade unions, but a trade union proved their only solid institutional base with its hundreds of thousands of dues-paying members (though not the millions of 1981). In 1990 Solidarity had no choice but to become a union again, a necessity accelerated by Walesa's election as president of Poland in 1990 and his subsequent resignation as president of Solidarity. The union elected Silesian activist Marian Krzaklewski, who promised to concentrate on union affairs, as his successor.

Continuing Ambiguity

Solidarity said it wanted to become a "real union," but its activities suggested otherwise. The key problem was that like its former leaders, most of Solidarity's new leaders did not want to be mere unionists. Some sought to use the union as a vehicle to promote privatization and marketization; others hoped to use it as a moral weapon against secular liberalism. Even Krzaklewski, contrary to his protestations, was unsatisfied being a unionist alone. It is hard to avoid the conclusion that this second tier of Solidarity leaders—after the first tier had gone off to politics—got involved in trade union activities because the union provided stable resources for their broader political activity and ambitions. Their predecessors had ridden the union to political power, and they wanted to do the same.

And so, the erosion of roles began again. The union's desire to play a political role was accompanied by the declining legitimacy of the post-Solidarity parties (arising from Solidarity's motley parliamentary contingent) and an acceleration of the economic crisis that drove increasing numbers of workers to look for new leaders. In 1992 thousands of workers went on strike against the Solidarity-supported government, and when the union refused to go along it became a strike against Solidarity as well. Fearful of marginalization, in 1993 the union broke with the government, forcing its ouster. For the first time since 1989, Solidarity was not explicitly represented by any political movement.

The 1993 parliamentary elections changed things once again. Anger over the economic situation and divisions within the former Solidarity camp led to a decisive victory by the former Communist parties, over the Social Democrats (SDRP/SLD—see Box 12.1) and the Peasant Party (see Box 12.1). Most of the post-Solidarity parties did not break the 5 percent threshold for gaining representation in parliament. Yet the defeat meant new opportunities for union activists tired of being union activists as it created a giant hole on the political right into which the union now stepped. Other right-wing organizations (referring more to ideological and religious cleavages than to economic ones) initially sought to block the union's new claim to political preeminence. But that attempt changed after the 1995 presidential election in which young SLD leader Aleksander Kwasniewski spectacularly defeated Lech Walesa.

In 1996 the Solidarity union brought together more than two dozen self-proclaimed right-wing political organizations and created the AWS coalition. As the most prominent organization within the coalition, Solidarity demanded—and received—50 percent of the key leadership positions, all the while insisting that it was not a party. The formula proved successful. In the 1997 parliamentary elections AWS won over 30 percent of the vote and went on to form a government. The connection between union and party became an issue once again. The new government appointed union activists to many senior administrative positions, leading to charges of a "unionocracy" (Janicki 1998). These union activists, however, acted merely as government officials, just as the 1989 union activists had done.

This Solidarity government proved no more interested in helping workers per se than any previous government had been. Instead of the union taking over politics, politics had again taken over the union. The only thing missing was a formal Solidarity political party, which became even more important as the small Christian parties within the AWS tried to assert themselves. And so, the union finally decided to call forth its own party. Further complicating the picture is the name it chose for its new party: the Social Movement (Ruch Spoleczny). In January 1999, when the first formal conference of the AWS Social Movement took place, Solidarity was mired in the same institutional ambiguity that had been its chief characteristic since 1980.

Could the group, movement, and party aspects of Solidarity come unstuck in the future? Politicians have tried to force that solution, but its realization seems unlikely. In an effort to force unions to be unions, the 1997 constitution explicitly forbids trade unions from running candidates for national elections. But the creation of the Social Movement bypasses this rule, as does Solidarity's 1998 decision to forbid individuals from simultaneously holding leadership posts in the union and the Social Movement, although that does not include the union and AWS. The results could be seen at the Social Movement's first national congress. Although he announced that he would remain union president and not seek leadership of the Social Movement, Krzaklewski completely stage-managed the congress and personally appointed all of the group's new political leaders. This is the path not to organizational differentiation but to a perpetuation of institutionalized ambiguity. The announced separation of group and party appears dead on arrival. Poland's institutions continue to diverge from models based on Western experiences.

Consequences of Ambiguity for Politics and Policymaking

The lack of differentiation between movement, group, and party has had one major consequence for policy outcomes: it has dramatically impeded the establishment of a new and secure system of industrial relations. With Solidarity clinging simultaneously to group, movement, and political identities, the different sides necessary for fashioning a stabilizing neocorporatist deal were not in place. In 1989–1990 the union acted as point man for the government, trying to win workers over to neoliberal shock therapy without offering them anything in return. Ten years later union leaders took control of the government, and again government lacked a separate, differentiated labor interest in the traditional neocorporatist fashion with which it could strike a deal. The result has been consistent small-scale industrial unrest and a large number of illegal (though unpunished) local strikes, most of which have ended inconclusively. Stable industrial relations require rivalries and deals among unions, employers, and governments. By blurring the boundaries among these groups, Poland's institutionalized ambiguity keeps industrial relations unsettled and unstable (see Pankow 1993; Morawski 1994; Gardawski 1999).

Another consequence of ambiguity has been to push political discourse to the right, away from interest-based conflicts into identity ones. Groups representing workers are unwilling to forcefully defend labor's economic interests, so they have tried to maintain labor support by focusing on substitute targets instead, such as aliens, atheists, and former Communists. For a time in 1996, blocking a liberal abortion law was the number one issue for the ostensibly trade union Solidarity.

THE PARADOX OF RELATIONS BETWEEN MOVEMENTS AND PARTIES IN CONTEMPORARY POLAND

After 1989, Solidarity's first parliamentarians tried to build their own political parties out of the grand movement the union had spawned. However, the various attempts to do so—such as those by the Center Alliance, the Christian National Union, and the Movement for the Republic (see Box 12.1)—have come to naught. The parties seemed to founder because they had no movement on which to build. The paradox is that the Solidarity movement collapsed at the very moment it succeeded. When power was won and the new sphere of power sucked in the movement's representatives, few leaders saw any reason to maintain a movement. But without a movement, how could the new parties build themselves? To succeed, Solidarity's would-be party builders needed to represent a movement, but in 1989 all that remained of Solidarity were its parliamentary contingent and the trade union. Only the liberal intelligentsia wing of Solidarity was able to create a political party, the Freedom Union (Unia Wolnosci—UW), because it had a base of prominent leaders and underground activists on which to build and was content with under 15 percent of the vote.

The other groups within Solidarity that wanted to form a party found their paths blocked by an unimpressed public. To win public support some—notably the Movement for the Republic led by former prime minister Jan Olszewski—tried to become social movements, but after 1989 few people were interested in movements fighting for general political causes. And so Solidarity was caught in a paradox: you cannot build a new political party without having a movement on which to build it, but there was no space to build a broad movement when the doors to parliament were open and beckoning.

The former ruling Communist Party has had an easier time, but even here the boundaries are not clear. Having negotiated the Roundtable accord with Solidarity in 1989, the PZPR went down to a humiliating electoral defeat later that year and disbanded itself in February 1990. A successor party, the Social Democracy of the Polish Republic (Socjaldemokracja Rzeczpospolitz Polskiej—SDRP), was created immediately, but it was by no means clear that this new party would become the dominant player it has in Polish politics. Hard-line apparatchiks and radical reformers each formed their own would-be successor parties. Two other left parties—the Polish Socialist Party (Polksa Partia Socjalistyezna) and the Solidarity of Labor Party (Solidarnosc Pracy)—were formed by groups that had opposed the PZPR all along. Solidarity of Labor (renamed the Union of Labor) had been particularly close to Solidarity but now feared the union was moving too far to the right, yet it refused to align with the SDRP because of the latter's past.

Besides the socialist parties, women's contingents and environmental groups also felt left out of the new political scene and were thinking about forming their own parties in the aftermath of the "extinction" of the old regime (Jowitt 1991). To complicate the picture further, émigré businessman Stan Tyminski, who had made his fortune in Canada and Peru, returned to Poland in 1990 and made a startling, nearly successful run for the presidency. He won votes former Communists had hoped would be theirs and formed the enigmatic Party X to try to maintain that support in the future.

The leaders of the SDRP understood that they could not sit back and count on the support of the entire left and, unlike Solidarity's leaders, that they would be unable to keep their camp together easily. They had the advantage of inheriting organizational structures, cadre, and resources from the old PZPR; but the elimination of political parties from the workplace, where the PZPR had been based, meant the new party would have to proceed very differently to keep its supporters. The SDRP did what it took Solidarity six more years to do—formed an electoral coalition. Taking advantage of its financial resources and name recognition, the SDRP offered places on its electoral lists to left parties, to women's and environmental groups, and, most important, to the strong General Accord of Trade Unions (Ogolne Porozumienie Zwiazkow Zawodowych—OPZZ)—the once official union confederation and now Solidarity's main rival. The OPZZ was offered about a quarter of the spots on the lists. By 1991 the SLD coalition was firmly established.

The coalition tendency in Polish politics has had two important consequences: social movements have tended to decline as their representatives were bought off by offers to sit in parliament, and parties as such have been unable to consolidate. In other words, both movements and parties in Poland remain weak. Before 1989 movements, not parties, were strong. When a new party system had to be created, after 1989 it could come only from the strong amorphous social movements sponsored by Solidarity. But creating parties depleted movements of their activists, and creating coalitions depleted them further.

Given this situation, I disagree with the claim in Chapter 1 of this volume that group-party relations are often "determined by the organizational capacity and the ability and willingness of political parties to perform political functions." The problem with this approach from the perspective of some post-Communist societies is its *assumption* of party primacy. In Poland parties emerged after 1989 almost as an afterthought from the enormous group-movement known as Solidarity. Most parties were able to perform political functions only insofar as Solidarity allowed them to do so. Furthermore, Solidarity could not decide whether to sanction parties emerging from its midst or to become a party itself. Thus, the ambiguity became institutionalized and endured well into the period in which the AWS governed the country.

OTHER MOVEMENTS

Although by far the most dominant, Solidarity is not the only movement to have emerged in Poland in recent years. Others have had an equally difficult time maintaining an identity separate from that of the party coalitions. Here we examine three: the peace movement, the women's movement, and the Catholic nationalist movement.

The Peace Movement

A peace movement arose in Poland in 1983, about the time the large peace movements arose in Western Europe. This movement was called forth not to champion the aims of the Western movements but to use the same form to undermine the Eastern governments that ostensibly supported those movements in the West. Far from opposing the North Atlantic Treaty Organization (NATO) military buildup that inspired the Western movements, the Polish Freedom and Peace movement directed its wrath almost solely at Eastern European militarism, with occasional remarks about the need for peace in general to refute charges of being simply an anti-Communist organization.

In Poland youth activists saw a peace movement as a possible way to revive opposition political activity despite the strict government ban in the repressive period after Solidarity was banned in 1981. Freedom and Peace did carve out some public space for itself but never sought to use that space as anything other than a proxy for Solidarity. When Solidarity activity was tolerated again in the late 1980s, peace activists immediately quit their "own" movement and actively joined in, just as environmental activists in the USSR had deserted the cause when the Soviet Union finally collapsed (Dawson 1997). Freedom and Peace leaders became Solidarity political activists and were never again associated with peace issues.

The Women's Movement

The women's movement is more complex. Before 1989, unlike the peace movement, it could not stand as a proxy for Solidarity, if only because so many Solidarity activists and not just militant Catholics disliked its implications.[4] A women's movement could only be organized by women who believed in it, and as it happened, few did. The Communists had proclaimed women's emancipation for too long and too cynically for women to take the concept seriously. Some saw emancipation as a way to get mothers out of the home so an atheistic government could turn children against Catholicism. Others identified feminism as antimale and saw it as silly and superficial. But even women favorably inclined toward feminist ideas and gender equality usually opposed building a women's movement while Solidarity was still outlawed. They supported Solidarity, and even though to their chagrin (though not their surprise) Solidarity did not support them, they did not want to raise gender as an important cleavage while the state-versus-society paradigm proposed by Solidarity prevailed.[5]

So a women's movement began to develop only after 1989. Along with the overall issue of gender equality, the movement was inspired by three factors: (1) increased labor market discrimination, in which women were frequently the first fired from manufacturing enterprises and were hired in the service industry on the basis of their looks; (2) the successful efforts of the Catholic Church and its parliamentary supporters to ban abortion; and (3) the considerable interest among Western women's movements and non-governmental organizations (NGOs) to fund such movements in the East. By the mid-1990s a women's movement had been formed. Although it was decentralized it was able to mobilize demonstrations at parliament, build a network of crisis centers, and chip away at the negative opinion surrounding the idea of gender movements.

Unlike the peace movement, therefore, the women's movement has not withered away. As communism has faded, feminism has increasingly been seen as part of the modern West rather than the cynical window dressing of hypocritical ruling parties. Activists organize campaigns against domestic violence, writers and critics talk of the emergence of a "feminist literature," and in general gender consciousness has become vastly more commonsensical than it was in 1990.

The movement has enjoyed this success, however, only by underplaying its movement aspects and turning increasingly to political parties. With Solidarity spearheading a right-wing Christian coalition, one of whose main aims has been to completely ban abortion rights, women's groups found themselves wooed by the SLD, which publicized their cause and invited them to run candidates on its electoral list. Many feminist activists found it difficult to take this step since, as democratic oppositionists, they had opposed the Communists in the past. But others thought they had to accept, given political realities. Those realities consisted of a strong parliamentary contingent (AWS) that put a premium on an antifeminist agenda, a liberal party (UW) so obsessively intent on economic liberalism that it regularly sold out choice on abortion rights in exchange for AWS support on market reform, and a party system based on coalitions that gave women's movements the power to affect policy only if they accepted the SLD's offer to sign on. By 1997 some of Poland's leading women's activists had begun to work closely with the SLD. For example, prominent Wroclaw underground Solidarity activist Barbara Labuda quit the liberal Freedom Union (which had demoted her because of her increasingly strident pro-choice rhetoric) and became a key adviser to President Kwasniewski, former head of the SLD. Other prominent activists in the campaign to legalize choice accepted spots on the SLD electoral list and subsequently won parliamentary seats.

Catholic Nationalist Movements

On the right of the political spectrum, radical Catholic and nationalist movements have also moved closer to political parties. An extremist right-wing movement has consolidated around the Catholic radio station Radio

Maria, which regularly denounces liberals as traitors, considers democrats more of a threat than Communists, and has been a major instigator in the anti-Semitic affair of placing crosses at Auschwitz. This group first showed its strength by organizing, together with Solidarity, petition campaigns urging that Kwasniewski's election in 1995 be invalidated and that the 1997 constitution be rejected. Both campaigns failed, but they won for the movement the respect of right-wing political organizers. Politicians in the Christian National Union soon offered to be spokespersons for Radio Maria in exchange for support in the 1997 elections. As a result, approximately forty members of the AWS parliamentary contingent were allied with Radio Maria. Coalition practices here, too, have blurred the boundaries between movement and party.[6]

CONCLUSION

Clearly, the specter of Solidarity hovers above all attempts to institutionalize the relationship between parties and groups in Poland today. In the end, then, how should we characterize Solidarity's relationship to political parties? In his introduction to this volume, Thomas, drawing in part on the work of Yishai (1995), offers five models: integration, cooperation, separation, conflict, and confrontation/rivalry. The first two seem closest to characterizing the Polish situation. Cooperation is marked by a "loose partnership" and the "informal understanding that the party is favorable to the group's objectives," while integration refers to a close, symbiotic relationship of "joint ideology, organizational linkage, and consensual strategy" in which the group acts like a faction within the party (Yishai 1995, 2–8). Neither fits exactly, however.

Solidarity's 1989 leaders, who wanted only political and economic reform, hoped the relationship would be one of cooperation. That is, they hoped the union, once it re-created itself, would feel represented by the party they were trying to build. But by 1992 the union had rejected this, both because Solidarity's political representation had fractured and because the dominant political fractions were favorable to Solidarity's objectives only when the defense of workers' interests was not one of Solidarity's main aims. Integration seems more applicable for the current relationship since the union and the AWS do have a joint ideology and strong organizational linkages, particularly with Marian Krzaklewski as chairman of both. But integration refers to organized cooperation between two distinct groups, and in Poland these two groups do not have separate identities, as Krzaklewski's dual role underlines. When I asked Warsaw union officials in January 1999 exactly what their relationship was to the Social Movement of the AWS, they laughed and said, "Good question!"

In some ways Solidarity resembles what Yishai calls an "interest party," a group that joins the electoral arena and runs candidates to advance the interests of a particular group. On closer analysis, however, this does not work either since Solidarity's political representatives have never fought merely, or even mainly, for members' interests. Interest parties are the defining feature of Yishai's rivalry model, with groups setting up only quasi-parties. In Poland, however, AWS was set up to create a real and lasting political party—an ongoing ambition of Solidarity's that continually throws into crisis its existence as a viable interest group or union. The rivalry model, therefore, does not work here. As for the typology's other models, separation assumes that the group does not seek to influence party decisions, something Solidarity has always tried to do; conflict refers to groups that see themselves as opposed to all parties, whereas Solidarity has always looked for a party to represent it.

In fact, the closer one looks at the nature of Solidarity and its curious triple role as interest group for workers, social movement for political change, and fledgling political party, the less appropriate any model seems. Each model assumes a clear distinction between party and group (or movement), and in Poland that distinctiveness has not been achieved.

The challenge, therefore, is to find one model that best explains the relationship. Following Burstein and declaring that no difference exists among groups, movements, and parties goes too far the other way. The point about the union-movement-party relationship in Poland is that the roles are distinct, as we see in Solidarity's attempts to perform all three. But to say that the roles are distinct is not to say that the organizations are distinct, as is assumed by those who try to characterize the relationship with scientific definitiveness. The only way to capture this subtle combination of sameness and distinctiveness is to embrace the idea of institutionalized ambiguity. Groups try to defend interests of their constituents, movements try to champion grand visions of social change, and parties seek to direct the energies of groups and movements into electoral outcomes. These are different roles, but with Solidarity one organization performs them all. Existing theories on the relationship between groups and parties do not capture this dynamic. Solidarity has to act like a group when it collects dues and fights over wages, like a movement when it tries to articulate general concerns, and like a party when it seeks to realize its group-based and movement-based goals in the context of the post-Communist political tabula rasa. Collapsing all three activities into one does injustice to the breadth of Solidarity, but separating them into three distinct realms does injustice to the depth of its activities. Solidarity's relationship to the political arena and its role in that arena are indispensably ambiguous, a dynamic likely peculiar to some post-Communist societies. Thus, without beginning from ambiguity we have no way to understand the group-movement-party nexus in contemporary Poland.

13

Argentina: Parties and Interests Operating Separately by Design and in Practice

Diane E. Johnson

Argentina has long been home to two parties that have dominated electoral politics at the national level, the Radical Civic Union (Unión Civica Radical—UCR) and the Justicialist Party (Partido Justicialista—PJ).[1] It has also long been home to large and powerful organized interests. These interests, however, have not generally presented their demands through a system of competing political parties. Instead, for the most part, parties and interests emerged independent of each other, with distinct purposes, and have continued to operate separately to achieve their goals.

Given the peculiarities of Argentine political development, this chapter argues that interests have generally appealed to the strong national executive instead of working through relatively weak intermediaries such as parties. If the appeal failed, one option was to turn to the military or at least to cooperate with the installation of a "temporary" authoritarian government. Meanwhile, parties viewed themselves rather grandly as movements embodying the nation instead of as broad-based coalitions seeking to win government control through elections, and opposition parties often supported the removal of a regime as their best hope for regaining power. The party-group disconnect was reinforced by recurring authoritarian regimes that routinely repressed or even dissolved groups and some or all parties. As this cycle continued, Argentina developed a political culture "unfavorable for democracy" (Catterberg 1994, 330).

This party-group separation has been a key characteristic of Argentine politics. However, only a scant literature deals with it specifically and thus addresses explanations for weak party-group connections. Much of the valuable information on the subject is a by-product of other studies, such as Cavarozzi's (1986) work on political cycles. Of the sources that focus more directly on this relationship, those by Manzetti (1993) and McGuire (1997) are exceptionally helpful. There is also scholarship on both parties, especially since the return to democracy in 1983, and organized interests, particularly labor (for example, Collier and Collier 1991). Literature on the political system confirms the historical weakness of parties and the party system (Mainwaring 1994; McGuire 1995, 1997; Snow and Manzetti 1993) and the relative strength of the presidency (O'Donnell 1996; Snow 1996). Other scholars demonstrate the movementlike nature of parties, notably Rock (1987) and McGuire (1995, 1997). Recent work suggests changes in the party system (Adrogué 1995; Catterberg 1994; Cavarozzi and Landi 1992; Emmerich 1994; Gibson 1996; Levitsky 1998; Mainwaring and Scully 1995) and in interest-state relations (Acuña 1995; Erro 1993; Feijoó and Nari 1994; W. C. Smith 1990), although scholars disagree on the implications of these changes.

As part of the process of synthesizing this literature to lay the groundwork for a fuller understanding of party-group relations (or lack of them) and their ramifications in Argentina today, it is helpful to first provide some historical background. Accordingly, the first two sections of the chapter outline the development of parties and groups, divided at the watershed year 1983 when Argentina's present democratic system originated. In section three we explain the reason for this ongoing separation between parties and groups—namely, the strength of the executive branch, particularly the presidency, relative to other political institutions. The fourth section focuses on the implications of party-group relations for policymaking, which predictably has been largely ad hoc and president centered. The final section offers observations on the relevance of the typology of party-group relations set out in Box 1.2 to the Argentine case. Although this chapter characterizes parties and interests as functioning independent of each other most of the time, it also contends that Argentina does not fit neatly into any of the proposed party-group models. Rather, there is evidence of at least four models—Integration, Cooperation, Separation, and Noninvolvement—as well as fluctuation of some relationships between models over time.

POLITICAL PARTIES AND INTEREST GROUPS BEFORE 1983

This section argues that whereas the strongest party to emerge in the late 1800s in Argentina was virtually identical with one powerful interest, the development of major parties and interests in the twentieth century (especially after 1930), perhaps excepting student groups, reveals an ongoing pattern of separation.

Development of Political Parties

The National Autonomist Party (Partido Autonomista Nacional—PAN) grew out of a number of smaller conservative parties in the 1870s. PAN primarily represented the major agricultural groups—as Manzetti (1993, 247) put it, the party was "nothing more than the political expression of the pampas landowning interests." From the 1880s until 1916, PAN retained control of the government through rigged elections and limited suffrage. The UCR, established in 1890 by PAN's middle- and upper-class opponents, refused to participate in national elections until the Sáenz Peña Law of 1912 eliminated most electoral fraud and vastly increased the number of voters. PAN dissolved, and the UCR became the country's first mass-based party, although it was typical of the political movements discussed in the fourth section of this chapter.

In the 1920s the conservative pampean elite—in opposition but now essentially partyless at the national level—grew increasingly worried about its loss of political space. And the radicals in the UCR were divided over economic policy and leadership style between the "personalists" or "Yrigoyenists" who supported President Hipólito Yrigoyen and the "antipersonalists" who opposed him. In 1930, with the political schism exacerbated by economic crisis, a military coup launched a period of conservative restoration. After 1930 Argentina lurched back and forth between authoritarianism (usually military led and conservative) and democracy with distressing regularity. Each transition was supported by at least one major party or group acting to pursue its own special interests.

The second major political party is the PJ, originally founded as the Partido Peronista (Peronist Party) by President Juan Domingo Perón (1946–1955, 1973–1974). Although formally a mass party with millions of members, it was actually a movement closely controlled by Perón. The party had close ties to the big labor unions, from whence Perón derived much of his support; in fact, he relied more on the unions than on the party to mobilize the vote. After Perón's ouster in 1955, Peronist parties could not legally participate in national elections for nearly two decades. Collier and Collier (1991, 735) have argued that this proscription of Peronist parties prevented the Peronists from taking advantage of their "potential majority status" on their own or as part of a coalition and thus "helped to block the construction of an integrative party system." The Peronists have also been fractious and have continued to bicker over various political and organizational issues.

Although the UCR and PJ are often linked to the middle classes and working classes, respectively, their constituencies include members of all social classes. In traditional left-right terms, political ideology in the two parties has not been very significant, although it becomes critical if we expand our definition to include the fundamental divide between Peronists and everyone else (Coppedge 1998, 552).

Development, Nature, and Strategy of Interests and Interest Groups

Most frequently the major interests have sought formal representation at the national level vis-à-vis peak associations, struggling with the government and each other mainly for a favorable distribution of resources and increased political privileges. Manzetti (1993), following the work of Olson (1971, 1982), aptly refers to these entities as "distributional coalitions." Of these organizations, four are especially noteworthy. Together they represent the major economic forces in Argentina, and each serves as the most important voice of its sector (Erro 1993).

The first is the Argentine Rural Society (Sociedad Rural Argentina—SRA). Founded in 1866, the SRA represents a relatively small but powerful group of wealthy landowners, led by the ranchers, that has retained its prominence in the agricultural sector for more than a century. As noted previously, the SRA and PAN were practically synonymous, and even until 1943 a significant share of political and military leaders were SRA members. With the growth of industry and particularly with the rise of Perón, however, the SRA's political fortunes changed. Since then, neither major party has seriously sought to represent these economically and socially influential elites. The SRA's inability to build ties with a party that could win fairly in national elections and its ability to deal directly with the executive branch led to its indifference or even hostility toward the party system.

The two major associations representing industry and business have been the Argentine Industrial Union (Unión Industrial Argentina—UIA) and the General Economic Confederation (Confederación General Económica—CGE). The UIA dates from 1887 and has traditionally spoken for larger industries in and near Buenos Aires. The CGE, created by Perón in the early 1950s, has generally represented smaller industry in both Buenos Aires and the interior provinces. Its close association with Perón led successor military governments to ban the CGE, although it subsequently reappeared.

The fourth group is the General Confederation of Labor (Confederación General de Trabajo—CGT), the major voice of the large and politicized labor movement that emerged independently from the parties in 1930. Its size and wealth exploded in 1943 when Perón became minister of labor, and CGT leaders created the Labor Party (Partido Laborista), which helped to elect their champion in 1946. But President Perón soon dissolved the party, replacing it with the Partido Peronista (later renamed the Partido Justicialista). Perón transformed the CGT into his main means of political support, although it remained officially separate from the government. The proscription of most Peronist parties after his fall in 1955 only strengthened the CGT vis-à-vis the parties since the unions were "the only avenues of political action open to the Peronists" (Manzetti 1993, 7). In 1957 Peronist labor leaders in the CGT created the "62 Organizations," informally the PJ's labor representation. Another informal institution, the tercio, granted the "62" the right to appoint a third of the PJ's leaders and candidates (Levitsky 1998, 456). However, the CGT has been divided, and despite its close ties to Perón, more moderate factions have long advocated Peronism without Perón.

In addition to these peak associations, several other, often overlapping groups also merit mention. Any discussion of interests in Argentina would be remiss in excluding the armed forces, namely the officer corps, which has so often figured politically both as a collaborator with various groups and parties and as an entity seeking to advance its own interests. Broadly speaking, the armed forces have been politically conservative but fractious and view themselves as above the parties in their ongoing efforts to defend the nation from its (mainly internal) enemies.

Like the military in Argentina, the Catholic Church is highly politicized, although it is generally less significant politically than elsewhere in Latin America. Nonetheless, a number of informal and formal interests or movements with strong ties to the church have appeared over the years. These include the disparate Catholic nationalists who oppose political parties (and other liberal democratic institutions) as anticlerical and anti-Argentine, the often militant university group Catholic Action (Acción Católica), and the leftist Movement of Third World Priests.[2] Numerous Catholic parties have also emerged, usually small and short-lived with the exception of the Christian Democratic Party (Partido Democráta Cristiano), founded in the mid-1950s.[3]

A final group of historically significant organizations are those representing university students. Argentine universities are much more politicized than their U.S. counterparts, and key student groups have close party ties, such as the Purple Band (Franja Morada) to the UCR and the Peronist University Youth (Juventud Universitaria Peronista) to the PJ. Since the University Reform movement in 1918, elected councils have governed the public universities, and many in Argentina—including the national media—regard the frequent university elections "as a barometer of national politics" (Snow and Manzetti 1993, 168). Governments starting with Perón's have routinely interfered in university affairs, and following the students' trend toward radicalism in the 1960s and 1970s they became a particular target of repression by the military government of 1976 to 1983.

PARTY-GROUP RELATIONS SINCE 1983

Argentina has experienced significant political developments in recent years, but despite changes among the parties and the interests themselves, this section suggests that the relationship between them has not experienced any fundamental alteration. Moreover, the executive branch has continued to exercise a relatively dominant role in Argentine politics.

Presidential Policies and Changing Party Fortunes

After a brutal seven-year military dictatorship called the Process of National Reorganization (Proceso de Reorganización Nacional), Argentina returned to democracy in 1983 with its economy in a tailspin and its national pride wounded by a humiliating loss to Britain over the Falkland Islands (Islas Malvinas). The military regime had banned all parties, jailed many politicians, purged the universities, and commandeered major organizations including the CGT, the UIA, and the CGE. When they reemerged in the early 1980s, the two major parties were polarized, fractious, and loosely organized at the national level. The PJ was closely associated with groups such as the CGT and the CGE (although each performed separate functions); a plethora of small conservative parties represented narrow (usually regional) interests; and the UCR, as Snow and Manzetti (1993, 40) put it, "refused to be compromised with specific interest groups whose demands it viewed as being selfish." The parties enjoyed a dramatic if short-lived burst of popularity, but elements in both the PJ and the UCR determined a need for reform. Perhaps the main point about the parties during this period, however, is that they finally appear to have accepted each other as legitimate contenders for power.

The UCR's charismatic Raúl Alfonsín became president in 1983. During the campaign Alfonsín dismissed the idea of a pact with opposition parties or major interests (including the military), which was consistent with the UCR's traditional representation of itself as the voice of the "common citizen" and its perception of the interests as "selfish and unreliable" (Manzetti 1993, 57). Once in office, however, Alfonsín adopted a proindustry stand that reversed the military regime's bias toward agricultural-exporting and financial groups (Gibson 1996, 162), and he tried with limited success to develop relations with business elites. Groups left out of government negotiations and those that objected to the administration's policies made their positions clear. The SRA declared its opposition to Alfonsín's economic policies in mid-1985, and the CGT, refusing to negotiate with the administration, called thirteen general strikes "in an effort to bring the government to its knees" (Snow 1996, 97). Both the SRA and the CGT also worked to torpedo the Spring Plan (Plan Primavera), an austerity package implemented in August 1988 with the initial backing of the UIA, the Argentine Chamber of Commerce (Cámara Argentina de Comercio), and the so-called captains of industry.

The UCR fared poorly in the 1987 midterm elections, dashing the hopes of those who had begun to refer to Alfonsinismo as the Third Historical Movement (following Yrigoyenismo and Peronismo). A major cause was the administration's inability to resolve urgent economic problems, including a spiraling foreign debt and almost unparalleled rates of inflation. In the 1989 presidential election disparate factions of the PJ united behind Carlos Saúl Menem, who easily won the presidency. Menem ran as a populist in the tradition of Perón, but once in office he abandoned the old Peronist agenda of massive state spending on the poor and working classes. Instead, he implemented stringent neoliberal economic measures, including the suspension of industrial subsidies and privatization of state enterprises. Menem also worked closely with major business organizations, the Peronists' traditional enemies, and with leading corporations. The result was an unprecedented coalition between a populist movement and the most influential economic groups (Manzetti 1993, 67; Cavarozzi and Landi 1992, 216), although some business interests—even those advocating economic reforms—complained bitterly about the loss of long-standing government subsidies.

Menem's policies alienated many traditional Peronists, to some degree splitting the labor movement and his party. The link between labor and the PJ had begun to erode in the late 1980s when party reformers including Menem successfully deinstitutionalized the "62" by ending its role as the labor branch within the PJ and eliminating the tercio system. As president, Menem quickly countered the CGT's threat of a general strike with an executive decree limiting strikes by workers in essential public services, and he utilized a divide-and-conquer strategy with union leaders. Despite this, Menem managed to maintain the support of most labor leaders, along with most PJ leaders and rank-and-file members (Levitsky 1998, 449). Meanwhile, in 1994 many who could not stomach Menem's break from traditional Peronist policies joined dissident groups from the UCR and other smaller groups from the left and center-left (including the Christian Democrats) to form the Front for a Country in Solidarity (Frente del País Solidario—FREPASO). In the 1995 presidential elections the FREPASO candidate lost to Menem but fared significantly better than the UCR candidate, who ran third.

Changes in the Orientation of Major Interests

In addition to the developments associated specifically with Menemismo, we can discern some general trends among the major interests in recent years. Erro (1993) contends that the large peak associations, with the possible exception of the SRA, have become decidedly weaker and more factionalized since the late 1960s when the fundamentally corporatist structure of interest representation began to break down. Moreover, the state's declining ability to redistribute resources in light of economic woes has reduced the influence of peak organizations, making it more difficult for them to mobilize support and lessening the potential returns from protest activity. Erro contends that between 1966 and 1989, these large associations declined from what he calls "corporatist entities" to mere interest groups.

Other major interests have also experienced changes, particularly since the return to democracy in 1983. The armed forces still wield considerable clout but figure less prominently as a political force. Alfonsín sought to reduce the military's influence by retiring generals, reducing the military budget, installing a civilian over the armed forces, and initiating trials for human rights violations during the Proceso. In response, the military launched a prolonged opposition including several armed uprisings. By the early 1990s, however, the commitment to democracy was probably strong enough and the armed forces weakened enough to deter yet another coup. Further, Menem privatized the General Directorate of Military Manufactures (Directorio General de Manufacturas Militares), lessening the armed forces' long-held economic influence, and he acted decisively to crush another brief but bloody revolt in December 1990 by a group of nationalist military leaders called the "painted faces" (*carapintadas*). One sign of change—bearing in mind the military leaders' traditional disdain for political parties—was the subsequent creation of the Dignity and Independence Party (Partido por la Dignidad y Independencia—MODIN) by former *carapintada* leader Aldo Rico. MODIN won three seats in Congress in 1991, where it sought to advance its nationalist, promilitary platform through democratic channels.

The Catholic Church remained fairly neutral during the 1983 elections, perhaps in light of its controversial ties to the harsh (and recently disbanded) military regime, which had provoked criticism by human rights groups and others (Snow 1996, 98). In 1986, however, the church joined other conservatives to lobby forcefully against a bill that would have legalized divorce, and by the early 1990s Catholic leaders were denouncing Menem's capital accumulation model because of its exclusion of numerous formerly integrated social groups (Manzetti 1993, 75).

University student groups reemerged in the early 1980s, resuming their role in democratic national politics after 1983. The flavor of university politics had changed since the 1970s, however, as indicated by the appearance of strong center-right groups and new organizations independent of the national parties (Snow and Manzetti 1993, 182–183). The most important new group was the Union for University Opening (Unión para la Apertura Universitaria—UPAU). The group has links to the small conservative parties but has sought to depoliticize the student movement by emphasizing pragmatic issues such as university curricula. Student leaders of all political affiliations have shown a deep concern for issues linked to democratic consolidation and have attempted to convince the parties to include in their platforms issues raised by human rights groups and other grassroots movements (Snow and Manzetti 1993, 182).

Other Key Developments in Party and Interest Group Activity

Three other recent developments warrant attention. The first was the birth of the Democratic Center Union (Unión del Centro Democrático—UCD), a new regional conservative party based in Buenos Aires. The UCD's organizing principle was neoliberal economic reform, making it more ideologically oriented than most Argentine parties. During the 1980s the relatively small conservative parties led by the UCD tried to create a nationwide bloc and court their natural allies, the business associations. This failed for the most part, largely because Alfonsín was willing to lend his ear to organizations such as the UIA and eventually the SRA, although UCR ties to big business remained weak. Still, Gibson (1996, 134) has claimed that party politics in the 1980s was more hospitable to activists, professionals, and business elites than in the past.

The second development was the increased prominence of interests such as human rights groups and feminist groups. Of the former, the best known is the Mothers of the Plaza de Mayo (Madres de la Plaza de Mayo), created in 1977 during the Proceso. These groups became a "focal point of the democratic opposition to the military" (Feijoó and Nari 1994, 125), but their relationship to political parties remains somewhat ambivalent—the groups cooperate with parties on some common issues but not on any permanent basis. Feminist groups began to appear in the 1970s, including the Front for Women's Rights (Movimiento para Liberación Feminina—MLF), an umbrella organization for feminist groups and women from the political parties. Banned by the Proceso, several of these groups survived and others have emerged since. In 1981 a reorganized MLF became the Argentine Feminist Organization (Organización Feminista Argentina). The UCR and PJ courted female voters in 1983, in particular through the creation of women's fronts. Despite their critical role in the return to democracy, however, women have since been relegated to traditional roles and limited political participation. Feijoó and Nari's work suggests that feminists and political party women have recently developed some sense of unity, although little research exists on this topic (Feijoó and Nari 1994, 109).

The third and most recent development was the 1997 formation of an electoral coalition between the UCR and the young FREPASO, the Alliance for Jobs, Justice, and Education (Alianza para el Trabajo, la Justicia y la Educación). The Alianza emerged with 111 of the 257 seats in the lower house, the Chamber of Deputies, in the 1997 midterm elections (compared with the PJ's 119) and captured the presidency in the December 1999 election with Fernando de la Rúa of the UCR, who ran as an Alianza candidate. It is too early to gauge the effects of his election on party-group relations.

CURRENT PARTY-GROUP RELATIONS

Cavarozzi (1986) has discussed the evolution of a "dual political system" in Argentina as a specific result of the proscription of the Peronist parties after 1955. This system featured the non-Peronist parties and Congress working through existing institutional mechanisms on one side and the "popular sector" (particularly the working class) using extraparty and extracongressional means to influence the government on the other (mainly through the large labor unions). This dualism meant that from the mid-1950s until the mid-1960s, the legal parties had little capacity to mediate conflicts among the organized sectors of society (Cavarozzi 1986; Collier and Collier 1991, 723). Here we contend that a similar duality is a much more widespread characteristic of Argentine politics. For instance, the SRA has presented its demands at the national level through extraparty means since the early 1900s—not because the government proscribed its party (or parties) but because the SRA did not (or could not) channel its demands through the parties. The same could be said of other major interests. Cavarozzi's analysis, however, does not tell us why parties and groups have so consistently functioned separately. Here we argue that the answer is tied closely to the strength of the executive branch relative to other political institutions.

Since the late nineteenth century, the major interests have preferred to go straight to the primary source of power—the national executive—rather than advance their interests through relatively weak intermediaries including the parties and Congress. In light of the conflicting and urgent nature of many of the interests' demands, many groups did not secure their goals and became frustrated. These groups, along with the opposition party (or parties) that held little hope of regaining the presidency through fair elections, frequently abandoned the pretense of abiding by democratic rules and turned to the military for help. This situation contributed to the chronic political instability that bedeviled Argentina for most of the twentieth century.

Relations between parties and interests have been complicated by their varying and sometimes conflictual formal and informal arrangements. From the 1930s until the 1980s, a distinct lack of consensus can be detected among the major political actors regarding the rules of the game—combining to form a political stew of limited democracy, competitive pluralism, authoritarianism, and corporatism (Manzetti 1993, 134). Consequently, different structures of popular representation emerged, as they did elsewhere in Latin America in a similar period. In sum, parties were only one of several ways to gain political representation along with populism, corporatism, and clientelism. Moreover, Latin American parties tended to be more personalistic, pragmatic, and opportunistic than their North American and Western European counterparts (Chalmers, Martin, and Piester 1997, 548).

Much of the scholarship on Argentine parties tends to focus on where they have failed. We argue here, for example, that the parties do not aggregate and act as mediators; nor do they serve as umbrella interest organizations. So what do they do? We adopt the position of numerous scholars that we may best characterize the UCR and PJ historically (and probably currently) as political movements (Rock 1987; McGuire 1995, 1997). In contrast to a standard definition of parties as broad-based coalitions of individuals and groups seeking to win formal control of the government through competitive elections, McGuire (1997, 7) defines political movements as "a set of people who share a common political identity and whose leaders aspire to full and permanent control of the state through the most readily available means, electoral or not." Latin Americanists typically refer to this phenomenon as *movimientismo*.

One characteristic of *movimientismo* is the tendency to rely on nondemocratic, plebiscitary means of governing. For much of their long histories, the UCR and PJ have functioned mainly as the electoral vehicle of a strong individual, such as Yrigoyen and Alfonsín (UCR) or Perón and Menem (PJ). As a result, scholars have traditionally depicted party politics as weakly institutionalized or noninstitutionalized, although some recent work suggests that this may be changing (see, for example, Mainwaring and Scully 1995). Moreover, *movimientismo* contributes to parties' inability to provide institutionalized channels through which interests articulate their demands (Snow and Manzetti 1993, 83). Rather, as Rock (1987, 6) tells us, movements "confer leadership on individuals, whose ideas and personalities are believed to embody a set of general interests or goals." Within parties and between parties and other groups, interest mediation has generally fallen to the initiative of the charismatic leader. Hence the party organizations have not played a significant role in such mediation (Snow and Manzetti 1993, 84–86).

The traditional role of parties relates closely to the centralization of the Argentine state. Technically, the political system is federal, but formal and informal practices have led to a heavy concentration of power in the executive branch. For example, the 1853 constitution (reformed in 1994) allows the president to intervene in a province to ensure a republican form of government, which he has done regularly. Further, the twenty-three provinces are financially dependent on central government assistance; and according to a "coparticipation" law, all revenues collected by the central government must be split roughly equally with the provinces. The federal legislature and judiciary, along with the parties, are weak relative to the presidency.

This centralization of power in the presidency and the relative weakness of other democratic institutions have directed the large organized interests to seek national political influence outside the parties. The interests know the president has the power to issue executive decrees, pressure bureaucrats, and push laws through Congress to meet their demands. The interests also realize, however, that the executive must choose among competing demands. For this reason they typically add "incentives" in the form of threats. For example, the CGT may dangle a general strike, or the SRA may promise to withhold produce or to slaughter breeding stock. As Snow (1996, 104) concluded, then, the president is "powerful only in comparison with other individuals and institutions within the government."

One outcome of *movimientismo* was that the relatively small but powerful conservative groups usually felt estranged from the major parties and hence from the government. For example, Perón's populism benefited previously marginalized groups, namely labor, at the expense of the formerly dominant socioeconomic groups. As Manzetti (1993, 84) wrote,

> After 1946 many agricultural, industrial, financial, and commercial interest groups that did not share the goals of either the Radicals or the Peronists did not have a strong conservative party to represent their interests. As a result, they began to look to the military to end their exclusion from power and thus became known as the military party. The failure of the Argentine party system [in the twentieth century] has indeed been this lack of linkage between conservative economic interests and mass-based electoral movements.

Other scholars concur. For instance, Gibson (1996, 160) has stressed that business interests have traditionally eschewed party commitments, preferring "corporatist organization and direct firm-state contacts . . . [to] the more uncertain long-term option of party building in pursuit of business objectives."

If major interests like the UIA, CGE, and CGT have become weaker in recent years, as Erro (1993) has suggested, it may portend change for party-group relations. That is, a substantial decline in the size or influence (perceived or real) of these organizations may reduce their ability to gain the executive's ear and compel them to seek political access elsewhere—perhaps through the parties. Despite the many recent changes discussed in this chapter (particularly since 1983), however, party-group relations do not appear to be developing along the lines of most North American and Western European countries. There is little indication that interests are actively working to achieve their demands through the major parties, and although reformers in both parties have sought greater openness and more routinization in the rules structuring intraparty behavior, the UCR and PJ—as well as the newly formed Alliance—retain important features of *movimientismo*. As Manzetti (1993, 87) wrote, "Both Alfonsín and Menem, at the peak of their success, downplayed the role of their parties while revitalizing the *movimientista* tradition" because it gave them more room for maneuver and helped them keep "internal enemies at bay." Both continued the tradition of conceding to the demands of major interests but remained unwilling to use their parties to channel citizens' claims, and Congress has been unable to cast itself as a crucial mediator. Erro (1993, 206) has contended that Menem sought to concentrate power in the executive branch still further "to ensure greater insulation from lobbying activities from various interest groups and from factions of his own party," and in turn societal support for Menem's restructuring of the economy in the early 1990s represented a mandate not for the PJ or Peronism but for Menem himself.

The upshot of all this is that important developments since 1980 and evidence suggesting the consolidation of democracy would lead us to expect significant change in the nature of party-group relations. For example, the emergence of the center-left FREPASO in opposition to Menem's policies, with its impressive second-place finish in the 1995 presidential election, could indicate an important change. Some observers characterize FREPASO as more of a front than a party. However, although the electoral coalition it formed with the UCR in 1997 (the Alianza) has so far not seriously challenged the tenets of Menem's economic policies, the election of Alianza candidate Fernando de la Rúa to the presidency in December 1999 may change this. But it is too early to assess the effect of these recent developments on long-standing relations between parties and interests in Argentina.

CONSEQUENCES FOR
POLICYMAKING AND DEMOCRACY IN ARGENTINA

The previous section pointed to the significance of the centralized state for party-group relations. The governing party's lack of independence from the president and the absence of loyal opposition parties (at least until recently) created a system in which parties were an important tool for attaining the presidency but rarely played an important role in formulating policy. This is true for members of Congress and provincial legislators as well. Those who represented the party in power found themselves mainly "reduced to the position of enacting into law bills that originated in the executive branch" (Snow and Manzetti 1993, 80). Hence policymaking has largely been the realm of the president.

As we might guess, policymaking during the twentieth century was rather inconsistent. In Snow's (1996, 104) words, policies mainly "seem to have been ad hoc reactions to events rather than part of an overall framework." The dominant role of the executive branch and the incessant and often conflicting series of demands brought before it directly by the major interests have contributed greatly to this inconsistency. History has shown that presidents who ignore these demands or fail to reconcile them adequately do so at their peril. Hence, policy has often vacillated during a single administration, not to mention the more radical fluctuations between different regimes (including those led by the military).

Both Alfonsín and Menem continued to rely on president-centered, exclusionary modes of policymaking. Smith (1990, 34), lamenting Alfonsín's failure to implement rational economic policy during the 1980s, pointed out that the transition from a military government to a civilian one does not necessarily change the way leaders make policy, claiming that the basic process has "demonstrated significant continuities." Further, as suggested in the final section of this chapter, no real evidence indicates that Menem fundamentally altered the way presidents make policy, even if his policies departed significantly from traditional Peronist programs.

The fact that Menem continued to enjoy the support of the traditional constituencies within the Peronist movement, including most powerful labor leaders, was critical to his ability to implement painful economic reforms and prevent mass social protests. The Peronist majority in Congress remained behind him, and the PJ maintained most of its support in the working and lower classes (Adrogué 1995; Levitsky 1998). But we must consider other factors as well. First, many of the interests that might have joined forces against the president, including the armed forces, are arguably weaker politically than in the past. Second, the UCR "fell into disarray" after the 1989 presidential elections and entered a "deep crisis of both ideas and leadership" that continued into the 1990s and was reflected in the radicals' poor performance in national elections between 1987 and 1999 (Snow and Manzetti 1993, 61–62). Third, the general political climate seems far more favorable to resolving policy differences through elections than it has in the past, particularly after the brutality of the last military regime.

Finally, the economic climate has also changed. Argentina continues to face serious problems, including sluggish industrial output and sizable budget deficits, but most Argentines—including the leaders of important economic groups—seemed to concur by the late 1980s that the government needed to substantially alter the way it did business. Furthermore, the Menem administration's economic policies benefited many powerful interests. For instance, the so-called convertibility plan—a cornerstone of Menem's economic policy that pegged the peso to the U.S. dollar at a 1-to-1 ratio to control inflation—was popular with groups such as the importers and large corporations that invest abroad. By the early 1990s some scholars seemed cautiously optimistic that policy goals among the major parties were becoming more rational and ideologically coherent, thanks largely to the internal reforms initiated in the 1980s (see, for example, Erro 1993).

Perhaps this is true, but here is an important caveat: as long as strong presidents can (and are even expected to) largely dictate government policy, it is not clear that any rationalization of policy goals within parties will fundamentally change the existing situation. Menem, as previously noted, campaigned on a platform that resounded with traditional Peronistas. Once in office, however, he did a complete about-face and presided over a very different set of policies. Further, the major interests continue to plea their case directly to the executive, even if many of their threats today carry relatively less weight and he has found ways to effectively circumvent others.

O'Donnell's concept of a "delegative democracy" is instructive here. He includes Argentina among a "new species" of democracies that may be enduring but should not be mistaken for consolidated (that is, institutionalized) democracies. He wrote, "Delegative democracies rest on the premise that whoever wins election to the presidency is thereby entitled to govern as he or she sees fit, constrained only by the hard facts of existing power relations and by a constitutionally limited term of office" (O'Donnell 1996, 98). This has clear and profound implications for policymaking: although "delegative democracy" appears to have the "advantage of allowing swift policy making," it comes "at the expense of a higher likelihood of gross mistakes, of hazardous implementation, and of concentrating responsibility for the outcomes on the president" (O'Donnell 1996, 101). Further, the exclusion of Congress and the parties from important decisions leads to a resentful legislature that senses no responsibility for government policy and to a decline in the prestige of all parties and politicians (O'Donnell 1996, 105).

Of the five general approaches discussed in Chapter 1—the pluralist, neocorporatist, partisan, responsible party, and party-group political system determinant models—the interpretation of party-group relations that most resembles the situation in Argentina is the neocorporatist perspective, with one critical caveat. Unlike neocorporatists who suggest that parties are insignificant as political actors, the two major political parties in Argentina are very important. At the national level they have traditionally served primarily as electoral vehicles for charismatic leaders such as Yrigoyen, Perón, Alfonsín, and, most recently, Menem. But given the importance of the executive in all areas of national policymaking and the fact that a candidate from outside the PJ or UCR stands virtually no chance of becoming president, the role of the parties is vital. At the local level, which is not discussed here, parties perform other important roles. For instance, Levitsky (1998, 458) has explained that the PJ's loosely tied local branches, the "basic units" (*unidades basicas*—UBs), "function as part of informal, patronage-based networks." The UBs supply candidates and votes but also provide services such as legal assistance, administer social programs, and act as cultural centers. But despite these genuinely significant roles, the parties have not typically served as the means by which national-level interests channel their demands; nor have they functioned as mediators among these interests, as pluralists might predict.

CATEGORIZING PARTY-GROUP RELATIONS IN ARGENTINA

At the beginning of this chapter we stated that there are examples of at least four of the models advanced in Box 1.2 regarding historical and current party-group relations in Argentina: Integration, Cooperation, Separation, and Noninvolvement. A summary of the rationale underlying this contention follows.

Back at the turn of the twentieth century, we can best describe the relationship between PAN and the agricultural interests represented by the SRA through the Integration Model, in which the party and the group are nearly identical. This has also characterized many of the regional conservative parties and the SRA. One may be tempted to include in this group the relations between labor and what Erro has called the "national bourgeoisie" (represented by the CGT and the CGE, respectively) and the Peronist parties, but as we look closely these relations become more complicated.

The CGT is an example. The labor unions formed the Labor Party (Partido Laborista), but Perón dissolved the party and assimilated its membership into the Partido Peronista (later the PJ). For several decades the CGT continued to dominate the labor branch of the party, which would suggest cooperation or even integration. This assessment has at least two weaknesses, however. First, the proscription of Peronist parties at the national level for nearly two decades and then again during the Proceso means that for much of its history the CGT represented the unions in the absence of a party that could legally participate in national elections. Second, the extent to which a single person (Perón) controlled both the unions and the Peronist parties adds a variable that confuses the idea of ideological affinity and common strategies (unless one counts loyalty to Perón as ideology)—especially given the Peronist Menem's abandonment of the policies traditionally favored by the CGT and its continued support for his presidency. Hence relations between the CGT and the PJ have vacillated between models, with roots in the Integration Model but more frequently in following decades fitting into the Cooperation Model (and perhaps the Noninvolvement Model during the PJ's long proscription from national politics).

Relations between the UCR and the interests (or the lack thereof) seem slightly clearer, although it is somewhat difficult to choose between the Separation and Noninvolvement Models. Historically, the UCR has refused to associate itself with any of the major groups—which suggests the latter—but to the extent that we are willing to define the major parties by their leadership, one can conceivably argue the former. That is, groups such as the UIA and SRA (or even the church) were willing to "work with any party in or out of power to promote its goals" (Chapter 1), with the important caveat that working with the party "out of power" generally indicated a willingness to replace the party "in power" through means other than regularly scheduled elections.

Finally, we can best describe many party-group relations using the Noninvolvement Model. We have argued in this chapter that major groups often worked around the parties by going directly to the national executive. Recognizing that the president was the primary source of political power, groups regularly decided that their goals were best achieved outside the party system; the more conservative groups in particular, since the demise of PAN, felt their goals and philosophy rendered it virtually impossible to gain access to a national party. The most recent example of this is the unwillingness of business groups to coalesce with the UCD.

CONCLUSION

In sum, Argentina represents a case of major parties and interests that have usually operated separately both by design and in practice. The major parties have functioned largely as movements led by men who sought full control of the government through whatever means necessary or available, and the powerful major interests have sought political access primarily by appealing to the strong national executive—with the relative weakness of other democratic institutions dampening any incentive to work through political parties.

14

Mexico: The End of Party Corporatism?

Jonathan Rosenberg

The story of seventy years of dominance by the Institutional Revolutionary Party (Partido Revolucionario Institucional—PRI), as well as the growing possibility of its demise, is also the story of political party–interest group relations in postrevolutionary Mexico. The PRI embraces a vast network of political, social, and economic institutions with deep historical roots and powerful centralized leaderships. These incorporated groups span sectoral and class interests, as well as a range of ideologies.

The party-group relationship in Mexico is explicitly dealt with in most major studies of Mexican government, but it is rarely treated comparatively, either explicitly or implicitly. Virtually every major work on Mexico discusses the PRI's corporatist structures, but none considers Mexican corporatism in comparison to pluralism or other party-group models as is typical of the literature on Europe. This lack of comparative analysis of the party-group relationship is typical of Latin American studies, which until recently have been more concerned with authoritarianism (and overcoming it) than with interest group activity per se (Rosenberg forthcoming). Mexico, however, is treated as unique among Latin American cases precisely because of party corporatism.

Although this party-group relationship is unique, it defies neither classification nor comparison. In this regard the subtitle of the chapter (The End of Party Corporatism?) is intended to raise three questions. First, What is party corporatism, and how closely does Mexico's party–interest group relationship resemble corporatist and neocorporatist models derived from European studies? Second, How did party corporatism develop in Mexico, and what have been its consequences for the party-group relationship? And third, What is the relationship between recent, arguably democratizing changes in Mexican politics and changes in the established structures of party-group relations?

In answer to the first question we argue that the party-group relationship in Mexico can be considered a form of neocorporatism but of a distinct type labeled *party corporatism*. The answer to the second question forms the bulk of the chapter and is best understood from the perspective of historical political economy. The answer to the third question is less definite. Important changes have taken place in Mexico's political economy since 1980. Increased inter- and intraparty competition since 1988, the steady pursuit of neoliberal economic policies since 1982, and the defeat of the PRI presidential candidate in 2000 have placed significant strains on longstanding links between major interest groups and the dominant party. We can hypothesize with confidence that changes in the Mexican political economy and turmoil within the PRI's corporatist structure are more than coincidental, and we can identify factors common to both. But it is too early to accurately assess the magnitude of the change in party-group relations or to argue convincingly that the system is moving toward pluralism.

PARTY CORPORATISM

As pointed out in Chapter 1 of this volume, the scholarly literature on neocorporatism largely ignores the role of parties, and for good reason. Neocorporatist relationships typically take place between interest groups and governments. Government officials mediate within organized or informal settings and bring their own interests to the table as they help group leaders hammer out sector-specific policies. Participants in neocorporatist arrangements are typically linked to political parties, but party organizations are rarely included. And when partisanship does become a factor in bargaining with government over policy, the effect can sometimes be destabilizing (Lehmbruch 1982, 16–19). By contrast, party corporatism presupposes links between groups and government that run directly through a political party organization. When these corporatist arrangements are working according to design, these links are stabilizing even when group leaders and government officials clash over specific policies.

In party corporatism the party is actually constructed of interest group confederations. The confederations, in turn, are bulwarks of electoral support for the party's politicians and partners in policy implementation with governments dominated by their own party. In Mexico the largest labor confederations, led by the Confederation of Mexican Workers (Confederación de Trabajadores de México—CTM), make up one of the PRI's three constituent branches or "corporations." The largest national peasant confederation, the National Peasant Confederation (Confederación Nacional Campesina—CNC), makes up another. The third branch, the so-called organized popular sector, includes unions of government workers and teachers, independent farmers, professional associations, student organizations, and unaffiliated individual members. It is dominated by the omnibus National Confederation of Popular Organizations (Confederación Nacional de Organizaciones Populares—CNOP). The group includes members of the military who lost their separate corporate identity as a fourth branch of the party in 1946. Each branch is organized hierarchically at the municipal, state, and national levels. The national directorate of the party includes the leadership of each branch.

The controlled mediation of class conflict that characterizes neocorporatism begins within the PRI itself. Party officials are the putative representatives of interest groups in their dealings with the bureaucracy and the president. PRI congressional candidates are selected so that the three corporations will be represented in the legislative branch more or less in proportion to their share of party membership (Hernández Rodríguez 1998, 74–77).

But the Mexican president's six-year term and the constitutional proscription against reelection have provided him substantial autonomy from the party's sectoral organizations, its rank and file, and even its leadership (Centeno 1994, 45–47). Thus, party corporatism has had a limiting effect on democracy in Mexico. Although the party's sectoral leaders control interest group participation, the president of the republic has, until recently, controlled the party's nominating process, effectively selecting his own successor. Until the accession of Vicente Fox to the presidency in January 2001 (see below), the president was always a member of the PRI, but party corporatism actually insulated presidential decisionmaking from the demands of the party's popular-class organizations. Party discipline ensured a compliant congressional delegation and freed the government to act independent of its organized popular base as long as its policies did not undermine the ability of party leaders to keep the rank and file loyal and to get out the vote in elections.

The outcomes of Mexican party corporatism are similar to those attributed to neocorporatism: political stability and social peace achieved through elite accommodation and government mediation of class conflict (Schmitter 1979, 24–25). Government policy struck a lopsided balance that favored dominant class interests over those of the rank and file of the formally incorporated popular-class organizations. This skewed policy orientation is facilitated by a more typically neocorporatist feature of party corporatism. Popular-class interest groups are incorporated within the party, but business and industrial groups belong to mandatory peak organizations that are excluded by law from forming or joining political parties (Luna 1995, 78–79). Since business groups are unfettered by the strictures of party corporatism, this arrangement allowed them unmediated formal and informal contacts with government, including consultation on policies that affect their interests (González Casanova 1970, 48–55). In this regard Kaufman has observed:

> The stability of the Mexican political system has rested on a synthesis of two seemingly contradictory historical legacies . . . the capacity of the Partido Revolucionario Institucional (PRI) and allied sectoral organizations to dominate the electoral arena and mediate class relations [and] attempts by successive presidential administrations to curb reformist impulses, establish collaborative ties with the emerging private sector, and build a cooperative relationship with the United States. (Kaufman 1989, 109)

Party corporatism meant that for most of the history of the PRI, presidential responsiveness to popular-class interest groups was largely discretionary, varying with the requirements of political stability and economic development (Cothran 1994, 71–82). At times Mexican party corporatism resulted in substantive bargaining and compromise over policy among the leaders of party corporations and the president. But increasingly the interests of workers and peasants have suffered at the hands of neoliberal technocrats who have been ascendant within government since the 1970s (Centeno 1994, 213–219). The neoliberal policies of the last three presidencies tipped the balance even further in favor of the private sector, emphasizing economic efficiency and creditworthiness (a critical national issue following the foreign debt crisis of the 1980s) over the populist goals that originally motivated party corporatism in the 1930s. Government and party leaders avoided some of the destabilizing effects of breaking the populist "bargain" with labor and peasants by giving more attention to the interests of the organized popular sector. But at the same time, private-sector groups became increasingly open in their political activities, forming a voluntary national association in 1975 and actively supporting neoliberal tendencies within the PRI since 1982 (Luna 1995, 80–84).

Party corporatism includes elements of the Integration/Strong Partisanship Model and the Cooperation/Ideological Model presented in Box 1.2. But it is more than either model alone and less than the two models combined. Consistent with the first model, the PRI includes several groups whose memberships and programs have become component parts of the party apparatus. But many of these groups can leave the PRI, and have done so, without losing their structural integrity or substantially changing the party. The second model explains the separate leaderships and organizational structures maintained by the PRI's labor and peasant corporations, originally brought into the party by political leaders espousing progressive populist ideologies. But the model does not explain why the corporations have remained largely intact even as the government's ideology shifted away from the active pursuit of popular-class interests.

Corporations, the Party, and the President

The Mexican constitution sets out a presidential system with separation of powers, a bicameral legislature, and a federal structure. The constitution can be amended by a two-thirds majority of the federal Congress. But separation of powers and federalism have been undermined by presidential supremacy and a single-party dominant system, thanks in no small part to party corporatism.

The core structure of party-group relations in Mexico has remained consistent since the early 1940s, despite organizational changes and considerable fluidity at the margins. The hierarchically structured CTM dominates the labor movement, and its leadership provides the leadership of the labor branch of the party. The CNC's membership base is found in rural cooperatives and small farms. Like the CTM, its national organization is hierarchical, and its top leadership represents the agrarian sector in the national party leadership councils. The popular sector, which contains both group and individual members, owes much of its strength to the unions of government employees, thus limiting its autonomy. The party is governed by a National Executive Committee that until 1990 was composed of the top leaders of the three corporations. A 1990 reform aimed at reducing the influence of sectoral bosses gave the president of the PRI (not to be confused with the president of the republic) power to appoint committee members. The reform was effectively reversed in 1993 when the original Executive Committee membership was reconstituted as a consultative body (Hernández Rodríguez 1998, 81–82).

Significantly, although candidates for legislative seats and local offices are often PRI regulars, neither party leadership nor the rank and file has much input into the selection of Mexican presidential candidates. Until 2000 when party primaries were introduced, sitting presidents usually chose their own successors from their cabinets. Since the 1940s Mexican presidents have rarely had prior experience with elected office or party politics (Camp 1996, chapter 5).

In sum, the structure of the PRI can be likened to three institutional pyramids—the labor sector, dominated by the CTM; the peasant sector, dominated by the CNC; and the popular sector, dominated by the CNOP—linked at the top by a national executive. The party was formed to organize and represent group interests in policy decisions made by a strong president in a highly centralized regime. Early in its history the party frequently fulfilled that role. By 1946, however, the control functions of party corporatism overshadowed its representative functions (Centeno 1994, 54).

Although party corporatism is more deeply institutionalized than modern neocorporatism, it is not monolithic. Not all popular-class interest groups are formally incorporated by the PRI. Independent labor unions and confederations occasionally defy the government and the party. Other unions have left, been expelled from, joined, or rejoined the party at various times. Alternative confederations within the party may challenge the CTM for dominance, and the CTM has made alliances with non-PRI unions to assert its positions within the party or vis-à-vis the government (Durand Ponte 1991, 86–102; Samstad and Collier 1995, 10–27). In short, change is possible.

Furthermore, interest groups outside of the labor and peasant sectors, as well as new social movements, have recently asserted themselves on the Mexican political scene—sometimes with direct implications for party politics and democratization. New political parties have attracted the support of unions, middle-sector groups, and intellectuals formerly attached to the PRI (Hernández Rodríguez 1998, 80). New social movements have made their presence felt by electoral and extralegal means. For instance, groups composed of dissident intellectuals began organizing for democratization, social and economic justice, and environmental responsibility in the 1980s. The Mexican Greens (Partido Verde Ecologista de México—PVEM), which grew out of the environmental movement, won representation in the Chamber of Deputies for the first time in 1997 thanks to an electoral reform that awarded additional seats through proportional representation. The Zapatista Army of National Liberation (Ejército Zapatista de la Liberación Nacional, named after the revolutionary Emiliano Zapata) organized the mainly indigenous poor of the southern state of Chiapas in protest against social, economic, and political injustice and came to national and international attention as a result of its rebellion on New Year's Day 1994.

Corporatism, Policy, and the State in Mexico

In existing literature we find variations on corporatist themes developed to describe and explain the PRI. Most authors give considerable attention to the taming of social movements through organization and incorporation within the party. Historical studies also emphasize the processes of elite accommodation and conflict that went into the formation of the party's corporatist structure.[1]

Classic studies of the roles and functions of the PRI focus on the party's unique corporatist structure and the way that structure allows the state to accommodate conflicting societal interests. Such studies make the PRI a central feature of a Janus-faced state, alternating between two distinct approaches to economic policy—one populist, the other capitalist or developmentalist. The best-known studies liken the changing policy orientations of succeeding presidential administrations to the swings of a pendulum—left, center, and right—alternately serving the needs of the popular classes, the state sector, and the private sector (for example, Needler 1971,

47; Story 1986, 27–44). A related thesis sees the government alternating applications of coercion and co-optation to control potentially destabilizing opposition from below, originating either from inside the party or from unincorporated groups and movements (Hellman 1983, 125–172). Both approaches emphasize the importance of the incorporation of organized interests to the state's ability to shift policy orientations, reward supporters, and punish defectors. As the dominant power in government, the president of the republic may reward or ignore party loyalists. Dissidents from the party's lower echelons may be sanctioned or promoted. Protestors from outside the party may be brought in and granted concessions available only to affiliated groups, or be suppressed.

Other treatments of the party-group relationship emphasize the structural properties of state-society relations. For example, Purcell (1975, 5–8) draws on O'Donnell's (1973) models of inclusionary and exclusionary authoritarian regimes, classifying Mexico as "inclusionary" because of the sectoral structure of the PRI. Inclusionary authoritarian systems offer some benefits to popular-class groups in exchange for their subordination to government control. Marxian analyses assume that corporatism in capitalist societies is always an instrument of bourgeois hegemony and emphasize the PRI's special organizational properties for maintaining control over workers and peasants (for example, Hellman 1983; Hamilton 1982; Leal 1986).

All of these types of state-society approaches are valuable, but each has its shortcomings. For instance, conventional notions of corporatism and neocorporatism lead various analysts to conclude that Mexican corporatism is inclusionary or exclusionary depending on the historical periods and issue areas they consider. A short history of the development of the party, applying the concept of party corporatism, will clear up some of the confusion.

DEVELOPMENT OF PARTY-GROUP RELATIONS IN POSTREVOLUTIONARY MEXICO

Emergence of a Dominant Party and Its Associated Organizations

The Mexican Revolution in 1910 unleashed a complex tide of political, economic, and social aspirations from Marxist to Social Democrat to liberal to conservative developmentalist to fascist and agrarian reactionary. In 1917 the surviving revolutionary leaders met to draft a new constitution. The document they created contained ambitious and specific promises of electoral democracy, national economic development, and a major redistribution of wealth through agrarian reform and progressive labor and social policies. But the political decompression caused by the defeat of the old regime also piqued the ambitions of various regional strongmen (caudillos) and agrarian radicals, leading to over a decade of bloody conflict. Finally, in 1920, nine years after the fall of the old regime, the new central government established military control. The next task was to build national political institutions that could accommodate the ambitions of the surviving elites and provide arenas of controlled participation for the organized workers and peasants (Córdova 1976).

Political stability became an end in itself and was eventually achieved by a group of moderate to conservative leaders from the north known as the Sonora Dynasty. The Sonorans' approach to economic development was considerably less progressive and nationalistic than the one suggested by the new constitution. Since they sought the loyalty and cooperation of foreign and domestic capital, they had to avoid fulfilling the constitutional promises of agrarian reform and progressive labor policies while maintaining a popular base broad enough to win elections (Huizer 1970, 446–450). The Sonorans achieved this in part by establishing the first semblance of what was to become the PRI.

By 1924 the president of Mexico and leader of the Sonoran Dynasty, Plutarco Elías Calles (1924–1928), had given up on forming a stable relationship with the peasant organizations and cultivated a base of popular support among the most conservative and corrupt elements of organized labor. He halted agrarian reform (especially land redistribution) and kept labor subservient to private and state capital by playing his co-opted labor leaders against their more militant colleagues. He kept his union leaders loyal by supporting the growth of a labor confederation through which they could enrich themselves and gain occasional wage concessions for their members. Whenever co-optation failed or was not possible, the government applied coercion with the complicity of confederation leaders (Aguilar Camín and Meyer 1993; Ashby 1963).

Calles institutionalized this arrangement in 1929 with the creation of the National Revolutionary Party (Partido Nacional Revolucionario—PNR), which gave him control over presidential succession. His labor cronies ensured support for PNR candidates and allowed the PNR to function as the party of government (Huizer 1970, 459). Elites with a desire for high political office needed to join and support the PNR.

But Calles's policies left many revolutionary elites (both inside and outside the PNR) uneasy and frustrated much of the working class and peasantry. By the 1930s tensions were building. Rather than splinter or destroy the party, dissident elites embarked on a strategy to expand the party's membership and refocus its policy orientations. They eventually invented party corporatism.

The present party-corporatist structures were created during the presidential administration of Lázaro Cárdenas (1934–1940). Cárdenas, although a PNR member, was widely known to champion progressive labor policies and agrarian reform. Therefore, when Calles selected him to run for president in 1934, he proved popular with workers and peasants and was elected easily (Huizer 1970, 462–463). In office he moved rapidly to increase the representation of his supporters within the party. He expelled Calles's labor allies, replaced them with more radical and less corrupt labor leaders, and won over regional peasant leagues by dramatically accelerating agrarian reform (Dulles 1961; Córdova 1976; Michaels 1967; Ashby 1963; L. Brown 1979).

Cárdenas undermined the power of conservative labor leaders and industrialists by encouraging strikes and using the power of the presidency to force settlements that favored workers (Dulles 1961, 629–631). In early 1936 he declared the government arbiter and regulator of social problems, empowered to deal directly and exclusively with an overarching organization of workers. He followed that announcement with the introduction of a new confederation, the CTM, whose leadership pledged its support for PNR control of the state; in exchange, member unions received favorable treatment in contract negotiations and government protection from their rivals. Cárdenas intended that the CTM's primary loyalty would be not to Calles, particular union bosses, or even to himself but to the government (Ashby 1963, 34–35, 50).

Party Dominance in the Party-Group Relationship—the PRM

Both before and after the revolution, Mexico's substantial mineral and petroleum reserves were in foreign hands, especially those of U.S. and British oil and mining companies. The 1917 constitution declared exclusive state control over all subsoil rights, a promise that was ignored by Cárdenas's Sonoran predecessors. On 18 March 1938 Cárdenas announced the expropriation of foreign oil holdings, to popular acclaim. Twelve days later he unveiled the next version of the party, the Party of the Mexican Revolution (Partido de la Revolución Mexicana—PRM).

The new party expanded the reach of party corporatism with four component sectors: the CTM (workers), the CNC (peasant), the military, and the popular sector. Officially, personalistic bases of power were replaced by organized sectors. Internal party politics were no longer carried out among the allies and followers of rival leaders but among the representatives of labor, peasants, the military, government bureaucracies, and state and private capital sectors (Córdova 1976, 211).

But democracy was neither the goal nor the outcome of the transformed party. Instead, Cárdenas achieved a dynamic balance among the groups he brought in to support his policy goals. He frequently secured popular-class support with material concessions, and his objective was popular-class *support*, not hegemony (Wilkie 1967, 75). The mass bases that had been so important in Cárdenas's rise to power were now organized under party control. As long as the party held together, succeeding presidents could move away from Cárdenas's ideal of progressive economic nationalism and still count on the cooperation and electoral support of massive confederations of workers and peasants.

Transition to the PRI and the Restructuring of Party Corporatism

Under Cárdenas the corporatist structure of the PRM facilitated populist programs; with a few adjustments it would support state-led capitalist development and authoritarianism equally well. As some have argued, however, the results of the adjustments were not an unqualified victory for Mexican and foreign capitalists (Hamilton 1982) or for the middle sectors (J. Johnson 1958, 128). The victory fell to the state bureaucracy, the presidency, and the cause of political stability.

In January 1946 the party took its present name, the Institutional Revolutionary Party. The transition from PRM to PRI included the movement of important organizations among sectors. For instance, independent farmers were moved from the peasant to the popular sector. In addition, the military sector was eliminated. The transition supported the policy orientations of Cárdenas's more conservative successors and a general drift toward industrial strategies that linked the interests of the state and private sectors (Story 1986, 30–41; Huizer 1970, 482). As a result, the party's internal balance shifted further in the direction of labor and the popular sector and away from the peasantry (Leal 1986, 35). For example, when President Miguel Alemán (1946–1952) revised the constitution to make it easier for large private landowners to fight state-mandated expropriations by peasant cooperatives, CNC leadership acceded to the changes and agreed not to raise the issue with the peasantry for fear of inciting unrest. The effect on poor peasants was devastating (Huizer 1970, 483–486, 488).

By the 1940s the control features of party corporatism were apparent. Government officials controlled elections for the CNC national executive and virtually appointed state and local officers (Purcell 1975, 18–19). In the 1940s and 1950s frustrated peasants seized land and attempted to establish autonomous organizations and parties. The government responded by distributing patronage through the CNC to lure dissidents back and dispatched troops when all else failed (L. Padgett 1966, 93–94; Huizer 1970, 493–495).

Labor leaders retained more influence than peasant leaders within the party but only because of the increased importance of industrial workers to economic development. In 1941 the original CTM president was replaced by Fidel Velásquez, a conservative political opportunist who worked closely with succeeding presidents to ensure labor cooperation. In Velásquez the

CTM provided the government and private sector with a strong ally in the fight against labor militancy (Durand Ponte 1991, 85). In return, Velásquez gained power for himself, patronage for his allies and members, and government support for continued CTM dominance of the union movement. CTM leaders received government posts, seats in Congress, positions in the party hierarchy, and the perquisites of high office (Purcell 1975, 22–23; Huizer 1970, 481). Labor cooperation with state-led industrialization was assured through a series of prototypically corporatist agreements called Labor Industrial Pacts (Pactos Obrero-Industriales) signed by the CTM, the government, and peak industrial organizations (Huizer 1970, 482; Story 1986, 30). Party corporatism, which under Cárdenas had been based on a populist bargain, now supported "a commitment to 'development'" dominated by conservative groups within the PRI, government, and business organizations (Durand Ponte 1991, 85–86).

The bottom-up channels of representation promised by party corporatism became increasingly constricted. Key posts in the official labor and peasant associations were kept in the hands of government loyalists. Proven party loyalists were kept in union posts through the bribery and coercion of those opposed to such action, creating cadres of virtually professional political operatives in control of the putative representative channels of the party (Huizer 1970, 489). Union officials were notoriously inefficient in collecting dues and forwarding them to higher levels of their organizations. Government subsidies became a major source of funding for unions (Purcell 1975, 22). In return for financial support and political advancement, union leaders rallied support for PRI candidates at election time.

Government retained the upper hand because the CTM was never monolithic. Its status was subject to the power of the government to certify and decertify unions and strikes and the president's ability to play rival confederations against each other (Purcell 1975, 20–21). No matter how well Velásquez played his game, unions remained dependent on presidential power and benefited proportionately to the contribution they made to developmental goals and the preservation of order. When labor leaders became too assertive, presidents used the existence of multiple labor confederations to keep the union movement as a whole disunited and dependent, even supporting the formation of a rival confederation (Purcell 1975, 24–25; Durand Ponte 1991, 86–89).

Organized Middle Sectors

Cárdenas first incorporated middle-class groups in the relatively inchoate popular sector of the PRM. But weak organization proved a liability for the sector and the state. Rapid economic development and the growth of government employment in the 1940s, 1950s, and 1960s made the middle sectors a large and increasingly important segment of society. The founding of the conservative probusiness National Action Party (Partido de Acción Nacional—PAN) in 1940 demonstrated the dangers of inadequate representation of the middle class in the party.

To better organize the popular sector, Cárdenas's successor, Manuel Ávila Camacho (1940–1946), created the CNOP in 1942. By 1943 the CNOP was dominating the PRI congressional delegation and therefore the Congress. When the military sector of the party was eliminated in 1946, the many officers already in government simply transferred their membership to the CNOP. In 1947 President Alemán transferred the main union of government workers from the CTM to the CNOP, swelling the numbers of the popular sector while separating the most important middle-class union from the labor sector (L. Padgett 1966, 125).

The Organized Private Sector

The party corporations allowed the state (and especially the presidency) to play the role of an independent third party in the class struggles between workers and peasants on the one hand and capitalists on the other. However, whereas working-class, peasant, and middle-class interests had to filter up through the dominant party, business and financial interests had direct access to policymakers. Business and finance used this to penetrate the state bureaucracy and form lucrative partnerships with government officials (Leal 1986, 37).

Postrevolutionary business associations first formed in response to the progressive and statist provisions of the 1917 constitution. Rather than resist the organization of the private sector, the government encouraged it. Peak business associations allowed the private sector to speak with a unified voice, provided financial support for political careers, and reassured capitalists that government ties to labor and peasant organizations did not threaten their interests.

The first major private-sector peak organizations, the National Association of Chambers of Commerce (Confederación Nacional de Cámaras de Comercio—CONCANACO) and the National Organization of Chambers of Industry (Confederación Nacional de Cámaras Industriales—CONCAMIN), were formed in 1917 and 1918, respectively. They served as the government's partners in promoting economic growth and as advisers on industrial and commercial policy. The government soon made membership in CONCAMIN and CONCANACO mandatory, thus creating the official private-sector signatories for its Labor Industrial Pacts (Delli Santi 1979, 346–348). Bankers followed with their own national organization a decade later, and in 1929 an intersectoral organization was created to advise the government on labor relations (Delli Santi 1979, 343).

The transition from populism to developmentalism in the 1940s increased the influence of private-sector organizations. By the 1950s government, labor, and industry had achieved a firm mutual commitment to economic development based on commercial agriculture, industrialization, and CTM cooperation with state and private capital. The results were strong aggregate growth and relatively low inflation but increasing poverty (Kaufman 1989, 110–111). Another result was political stability, even after the economic growth slowed in the late 1960s and labor and the peasantry bore the brunt of the costs.

PARTY CORPORATISM UNDER STRESS

Party corporatism enabled the state to maintain fundamental political and social stability, not only through the high growth periods of 1940 to 1970, when gross national product grew an average of 6 percent annually, but through periods of political and economic stress (Hansen 1971, 41). For example, in 1968, when students took to the streets in opposition to PRI domination of the political scene and the conservative, probusiness orientation of the administration of President Gustavo Díaz Ordaz (1964–1970), organized labor did not join in the protests. Velásquez kept CTM unions in line, and the government steadily increased industrial wages for member unions. The rest of the popular classes were compensated in part by the next president, Luís Echeverría (1970–1976), who placated the party's left wing with increased spending on social programs, prolabor policies, and revitalized agrarian reform. But resistance from the private sector and conservatives within the CTM and CNC limited the scope and permanence of his reforms (Hellman 1983, 187–215).

Party corporatism proved extraordinarily resilient. Not until the 1980s, when a foreign debt crisis sent shock waves through society, did the PRI start to lose its grip on its popular-class corporations. In 1982 President José López Portillo (1976–1982) declared Mexico's massive foreign debt unpayable. López Portillo had been the party's moderately conservative answer to Echeverría, yet his economic policies and corruption contributed to massive foreign debt. His successors, Miguel de la Madrid (1982–1988) and Carlos Salinas de Gortari (1988–1994), pushed the pendulum further to the right with an orthodox International Monetary Fund–led stabilization program that included privatization of state enterprises and unprecedented inflows of foreign capital. De la Madrid slashed government subsidies for basic needs and allowed real wages to decrease by 30 percent between 1982 and 1984. Nevertheless, in 1987 business, labor (the CTM), and government signed another *pacto* agreeing to wage and price freezes.

As the neoliberalism of López Portillo's successors deepened, the

CTM and CNC rank and file became increasingly alienated. President Salinas repealed the laws prohibiting the sale of land held by peasant cooperatives, giving commercial growers and foreign investors the opportunity to take advantage of freer trade with the United States. Shortly thereafter, in 1993 the government approved the North American Free Trade Agreement (NAFTA) over the objections of many trade unionists inside and outside the party. Nevertheless, CTM leaders maintained their positions within the party. Velásquez was actively consulted on labor policy until his death in June 1997 at age ninety-seven. But as the costs of neoliberalism mounted, CTM unions began to express open opposition. The gap between leaders and the rank and file widened, and the party-corporatist edifice began to show signs of structural decay even as patronage continued to flow to member unions (Alvarez Béjar 1991, 49).

Public opinion surveys and data on strikes from the late 1970s and early 1980s show a restive working class, with CTM leadership a frequent target of protest (Carr 1991, 137–138; de la Garza Toledo 1991, 159–170). As the economic situation became more difficult, government legitimacy waned. Even local PRI offices, which had been instrumental in maintaining popular support in poor neighborhoods by distributing patronage in times of need, were seen to be failing. Autonomous grassroots organizations arose to fill the gaps (Centeno 1994, 10–11).

In the 1988 presidential elections many CTM union members defied their leaders to vote for Cuauhtémoc Cárdenas, who ran under the banner of the Social Democratic National Democratic Front (Frente Democrático Nacional—FDN), a coalition of five small left-wing parties. Cárdenas, the son of Lázaro Cárdenas, had bolted from the PRI to protest the lack of internal democracy and deviation from revolutionary principles.

With the PRI electoral machine weakened, Salinas won the presidency by the smallest margin in the party's history and under extremely suspicious conditions. Irregularities in the counting of votes and delays in reporting results were officially attributed to computer problems, a claim that did not satisfy opposition supporters. But once again the party adjusted. In a characteristic show of flexibility and presidential supremacy, the party took the elections as a kind of storm warning and moved to deemphasize party corporations as sources of popular support. PRI conservatives even began to look to PAN as a future legislative and electoral ally to support the president's policies in the face of declining party discipline and stronger electoral challenges (Centeno 1994, 62, 225–226).

As president, Salinas further weakened the corporations by usurping their traditional role as distributors of patronage. In 1989 the president introduced a new program for distributing social services, the National Solidarity Program (Programa Nacional de Solidaridad—PRONASOL).

But instead of using the CNC and CTM to implement the new programs, Salinas created a new network of dedicated grassroots organizations responsible directly to the government. In subsequent elections the government, the presidency, and PRI candidates benefited from the rejuvenated image created by PRONASOL, while the CNC and CTM were made increasingly irrelevant (Camp 1996, 169).

ELECTIONS SINCE 1991: THE END OF PARTY CORPORATISM?

Developments

In 1989 the government responded to accusations that the PRI stole the presidency from the FDN by passing a series of electoral reforms that increased the number of opposition seats in the Chamber of Deputies (the lower house of Congress) in 1991 and 1992. The reforms also established a new federal electoral code and independent tribunals to evaluate results and consider complaints. The reforms improved the image of the party, helped relegitimize electoral politics, and further weakened the party corporations. New measures to ensure transparency took aim at the campaign practices that made the labor and peasant corporations indispensable to PRI candidates. And greater representation for opposition parties in Congress reduced the weight of PRI members associated with party corporations. In addition, internal PRI reforms have weakened the influence of corporations and their leaders over candidate selection (Domínguez 1999, 5–7; Alcocer V. 1995).

For the PRI, these reforms and the outlawing of coalition candidates seemed to "right the ship" after the close call in 1988, but the effect was temporary. In preparation for the 1994 elections and in light of the failures of 1988, a new generation of party leaders attacked the party corporations as outmoded and as sources of weakness rather than strength. In 1990 a new PRI president, Luís Donaldo Colosio, proposed the first basic structural reforms since 1946. Colosio intended nothing less than the breakup of the old populist, clientelistic, and highly inefficient party structures in favor of a modern Social Democratic party that could aid the Salinas administration in carrying out economic and political modernization. Some reforms, like the dismantling of the CNOP, were mainly cosmetic and easily undone by PRI sectoral leaders (Hernández Rodríguez 1998, 80–81). But Colosio and Salinas did succeed in curbing some of the power of CTM, CNC, and CNOP bosses at the level of national party leadership by replacing the PRI National Council with the National Political Council (Consejo Político Nacional—CPN). Whereas the National Council had been controlled by representatives of the party's principal sectoral organizations, the CPN brought in state and municipal leaders and federal and local legislators, many of whom had little or no association with the party corporations (Hernández Rodríguez 1998, 82).

The first national test of the new party and electoral systems was the 1994 presidential election. The PRI nominated Colosio. When he was assassinated on the campaign trail, he was replaced quickly and quietly by Ernesto Zedillo Ponce de León, a member of the Salinas cabinet from the neoliberal wing of the party. Although Zedillo won, the 1994 elections were something other than business as usual.

The Salinas government continued to deemphasize the electoral role of the CTM and CNC and used PRONASOL to attract the support of the urban and rural poor. The new law against coalition candidacy forced Cárdenas hastily to reconstitute the FDN as the Party of the Democratic Revolution (Partido de la Revolución Democrática—PRD). The new party continued its efforts among the working class and peasantry. But in the run-up to the elections, the government targeted areas of PRD strength for additional PRONASOL spending and boosted overall spending for "promotion of the economy, employment and social development" by more than 10 percent (*La Reforma* [Mexico City] 1 January 1994, 1). This was a clear attempt by the PRI to use its traditional populist appeals without using the party corporations. In his campaign Zedillo picked up Colosio's reformist mantel, making a credible case to the electorate that he could promote change without disruption. PRI voters accepted the possibility that the party could change itself and stayed loyal in sufficient numbers (*New York Times*, 5 September 1994, 14A). Zedillo polled approximately 49 percent of the vote, PAN candidate Diego Fernández de Cevallos approximately 26 percent, and Cárdenas 6 percent.[2] But the PRI lost its two-thirds majority in the Chamber of Deputies. For the first time a new president would be deprived of the ability to alter the constitution unchallenged.

The congressional, state, and local elections in 1997 took the transformation of party corporatism a step further. The PRI lost its majority in the Chamber of Deputies, and opposition parties established their presence in the Senate—both unprecedented developments. In the Chamber of Deputies the PRI won 238 seats, the PRD 125, the PAN 122, the PVEM 8, and the Workers' Party (Partido de Trabajo—PT) 7. PAN also won three gubernatorial elections, and Cuauhtémoc Cárdenas was elected mayor of Mexico City.

Finally in July 2000 something that first seemed possible in 1988 actually happened. In a three-way race for the presidency of the republic the PRI's Francisco Labastida and the PRD's Cuauhtémoc Cárdenas were defeated by the PAN's Vicente Fox Quesada. What the PAN's unprecedented victory will mean for party-group relations is as yet unclear. The PAN does not represent a radical ideological departure from the neoliberal wing of the PRI, and groups that traditionally support the PAN have also been accommodated by recent presidents from the PRI's neoliberal wing. Furthermore, as president, Fox stands to inherit the patronage networks his predecessors developed to attract popular support away from the old PRI corporations. Whether this stunning electoral outcome also brings major structural change depends on two factors: first, the extent to which the populist wing of the PRI and the parties of the left can cultivate popular class groups as a base of opposition; and second, the changing relationship between the president and Congress. About the first factor, we can only speculate. About the second, we already have some early indications.

Consequences for Party-Group Relations

As yet, there is little on which to base an analysis of the long-term effects of these developments on the party-group relationship. As we have seen, party corporatism has traditionally had little to do with legislative politics. In fact, since the separation of powers promised by the constitution never really existed, legislative politics and party competition have received little serious attention from political scientists (Martínez Rodríguez 1998, 58–59).

The existence of avowedly left-of-center (PRD and PT) and conservative (PAN) oppositions brings a conventional ideological spectrum to Mexican legislative politics within which the PRI must position itself for the first time. With the last three presidents coming from the neoliberal wing of the PRI and party sectoral organizations politically downgraded, the formerly populist PRI is now positioned right of center. Therefore, two outcomes seem likely. First, the influence of interest groups outside the party (especially from the private sector) on the government will continue and probably increase; and second, the neoliberal wing of the PRI and the PAN will depend more and more on each other as closest ideological cohorts, to support the legislative agenda of the new president.

In addition, interest groups now have representation in Congress outside the PRI. At least two opposition parties (the PT and PRD) have links to dissident unions, grassroots organizations, small producers' organizations, ethnic groups, and feminist organizations (Bruhn 1998, 118); and the PVEM is the first successful party to develop directly from a new social movement. A strong coalition of left-wing parties might attract partners from within the increasingly disaffected populist wing of the PRI, further eroding the party's corporatist structure. That could lead to a more fluid situation in which labor, peasant, and popular groups loosen organizational ties to the dominant party and bargain with opposition parties for legislative and electoral support.

But these developments are not likely to happen quickly or smoothly.

The combined effects of an assertive, potentially coequal Congress, the erosion of PRI corporatist structures, and factionalization within the party are largely speculative. They may be democratizing, destabilizing, or both. Furthermore, the prospect of a non-PRI president bargaining with and building coalitions in Congress could open new avenues for interest group activity.

CONCLUSION

In 1975 Purcell labeled Mexico an "inclusionary-authoritarian" system (Purcell 1975, 5–8). At the time, this was essentially accurate and consistent with corporatism. But recent events portend an ambiguous and uncertain future for Mexico's dominant party and therefore for the party-group relationship. For most of its history the party set limits on democratization, economic liberalization, and political pluralism. Whether its structures facilitated representation or control depended on the ideology and social bases of support of the president of the republic, as constrained by prevailing domestic and international conditions. Eventually, power within the party's sectoral organizations accrued to elites like Fidel Velásquez, who used patronage and coercion to maintain party structures in the service of political stability.

Recent electoral reforms may give new importance to groups historically linked to the state but not to the party—especially domestic and foreign capital and the politically and socially conservative middle sectors. The reforms may also loosen the connection between the party and its traditional corporations (labor, the peasantry, and the popular sector). Therefore, it is possible but not certain that a new period has begun in which the PRI will become a more conventional electoral and legislative party engaged in rough-and-tumble campaigns, coalition building, log rolling, and constituent service. Certain signs point in that direction: successful electoral opposition, new interest-based parties, the diminishing role of party corporations, the party's ineffectiveness in settling recent outbreaks of class conflict (e.g., Chiapas), more openly competitive policymaking and candidate selection processes within the party, a more substantive role for Congress in governance, and a more fluid party-group relationship.

Originally, the glue of party corporatism was ideological and programmatic. Cárdenas brought and kept the corporations together with credible appeals to a kind of progressive populism that promoted social equity for the lower and middle classes along with economic progress and sovereignty (L. Padgett 1966, 45–46). The government's subsequent policy directions raised serious questions about the viability of populist approaches for Mexico. Nevertheless, until recently, party corporatism provided a highly resilient and adaptable set of structures for maintaining political stability. But as Mexican elections became freer and fairer and succeeding PRI governments pursued neoliberal policies, party corporatism showed some of the same strains as other forms of party-group relations. In fact, recent developments in Mexico lead to Selle's general conclusion about Norway quoted in Chapter 1 of this volume, that the "weakening of ties with 'old organizations' has increased party competition, supporting conclusions emphasizing the decline of integrative and expressive functions of parties" (Selle 1997, 165). It would be premature and imprudent to predict pluralism for Mexico, but it is beginning to look a lot less corporatist.

Part 4

Conclusions

15

Toward a Systematic Understanding of Party-Group Relations in Liberal Democracies

Clive S. Thomas

The purpose of this book has been to provide a general, holistic understanding of the political party–interest group relationship in liberal democracies by seeking answers to four fundamental questions: (1) Why do some groups have relations with parties while others do not; (2) What forms does the party-group relationship take; (3) How do these relations, or lack of them, affect policymaking and representation; and (4) Can we develop a theoretical explanation of the party-group relationship and its consequences. In this concluding chapter we synthesize the findings from the thirteen country chapters to offer answers to these questions. Addressing them will also enable us to assess the accuracy of the six preliminary guidelines set out at the end of Chapter 1, as well as to gauge the overall significance of the party-group relationship to liberal democracies.

MAJOR FINDINGS: AN OVERVIEW

As the findings relating to the four specific questions of the study are in many ways interrelated, it will be useful to first provide an overview of the major conclusions of the study. These can be grouped into six general categories.

Factors Shaping the Relationship

Certain common patterns do exist between countries when it comes to what shapes party-group relations. With some additions and refinements, these are the factors set out in Chapter 1 and encapsulated in Box 1.1 (guidelines 1, 4, and 5). In particular and as surmised as part of guideline 4, a significant common denominator across countries is that strong parties have an important influence on shaping the party-group relationship. Where they have both the capacity and desire to do so, parties can be the dominant force in determining the relationship.

General influences, however, can tell us only so much about the circumstances of a particular country. Even more than anticipated in guideline 4, the thirteen chapters clearly show how much individual country circumstances are central to shaping party-group relations (or lack of them) in that country and often give elements of those relations a unique character. This is evidenced as much in the old democracies, like France and the United States, as in transitional democracies, like Spain and Poland. From this we can conclude, as suggested in guideline 6, that the party-group relationship is a complex one involving many variables that may operate differently in different democracies.

Forms of the Relationship and Pattern of Development of the Party-Group Connection

It is evident from the thirteen case studies that although the five-part classification of forms of the relationship set out in Chapter 1 (guideline 2 and Box 1.2) is useful, the pattern of party-group relations is more complex. Thus, the framework needs modification. Moreover, as surmised in Chapter 1 (guideline 5), attempts to classify entire countries as having a particular type of party-group relationship are possible only in very broad terms that are not very useful analytically. It is much more useful to break down the relationship to the sector and individual party-group level.

From a political development perspective, although some common elements are found in the development of party-group relations in some countries, such as relations between socialist parties and trade unions and between conservative parties and business groups, no single common pattern of progression is seen in the development of party-group relations in Western democracies. Several patterns emerge in the development of the party-group connection, or lack of it, and not all follow the pattern common in northern Europe.

Recent Trends in the Development of the Party-Group Relationship

If we had confined this study to party-group relations in democracies that have had strong left-wing governing parties and historically strong party-group ties, such as those of northern Europe and Israel, we could have been categorical about the fact that party-group ties are loosening, in some cases in a major way. This is particularly the case in the long-standing relationship between socialist parties and trade unions in countries like Britain, Sweden, and Israel and even a newer democracy like Spain. Here guideline 3 in Chapter 1, based on the work of Selle (1997), is representative of these trends.

But the case study net was cast wider to include a more diverse range of democratic traditions, producing a much less distinct pattern of recent developments in the party-group connection. For example, in Argentina no real pattern of change is discernible; in Mexico, Poland, and the Czech Republic, however, it can be argued that party dominance is being replaced by a new symbiotic connection based on a more equal relationship but not on a movement toward increased independence of either organization. Different patterns are evident in France, Japan, and Italy involving a combination of increased separation and interdependence. In the United States the recent trend is toward increasing dependence between parties and groups. These varying patterns further confirm the complexity of the nature of party-group relations and the importance of individual country circumstances.

The Paramount Importance of Interest Group–Governing Party Relations

Guideline 5 in Chapter 1 posited that a clearer understanding of party-group relations can be acquired in part by making a distinction between party-group relations in general and relations of groups with the party in power. It is clear from this study that of all the aspects of party-group relations—membership overlap, financial connections, ideological affinity, and so on—the relationship between various interests and the governing party is the most significant in the party-group relationship from a practical political perspective. In effect, this means relations with the government because in most countries the governing party *is* the government. This has important implications for assessing the extent of the significance of party-group relations for liberal democracies in general, as we will see later.

Effect of the Party-Group Connection on Policymaking and Representation

It comes as no surprise that the relationship of parties and groups (or lack thereof) does affect the form and substance of policymaking and who is and is not represented in government. What was not clear before this study was that this relationship has a wide range of effects on both policymaking and representation, and the same factors can work in different directions in different countries.

It is one thing to explain the effect of the party-group connection; it is quite another to determine its significance—that is, to assess its overall importance in shaping policy and power relationships relative to other elements of democratic political systems. The evidence in this book suggests that the relationship varies widely in its significance across Western democracies.

Implications for Developing a General Theory of Party-Group Relations in Liberal Democracies

Certainly, we can identify some common patterns of the forms of the party-group relationship across countries and some common denominators that shape it. It is not possible to progress far beyond this, however, and develop *one general inclusive theory* of party-group relations that explains specific developments and patterns in individual Western democracies. The variants produced by individual country circumstances inhibit broadly applicable general explanations that facilitate predictions about future developments. This finding in itself is significant, however, and allows us to provide insights into understanding the development, current status, and likely future directions of party-group relations in individual countries.

The significance of these six major findings will become clearer as we delve into the specific questions later.

DETERMINANTS OF THE RELATIONSHIP

As originally set out in Chapter 1, the question relating to this aspect of party-group relations had two components: Why do some interest groups have relations with political parties while others do not, and for those that do, what determines the type and extent of the relationship? Evidence from this study suggests that the answers are fairly involved because a complex set of factors and variables determines the nature of party-group relations. Thus, any comprehensive explanation must provide insights into common factors across liberal democracies; individual country circumstances; an understanding of relations at the system, sector, and one-on-one levels; and differences in long- and short-term relations between parties and groups.

Box 15.1 presents a theoretical framework that provides such a comprehensive explanation. A synthesis of the information in the individual chapters has indicated that Box 1.1 contained the fundamental factors but that five others needed to be added and some of the original factors needed refining and recategorizing, The five factors added to create Box 15.1 were contemporary level of socioeconomic development (factor 3), contemporary level of political development (factor 4), which political party or party coalition is in power (factor 7), type of electoral system (factor 8), and constitutional/legal provisions regarding parties and groups (factor 11). The importance of each of these factors is explained in Box 15.1.

A general understanding of the common factors shaping party-group relations across liberal democracies can be acquired by reviewing all fourteen factors in the framework. As mentioned in the previous section, the strength or weakness of parties is evident as particularly important in explaining differing party-group relations across countries. The specifics of any particular country can be understood by applying the variables and the applicable elements of each factor to that country. For example, to a large extent the details of the French case are explained by elements of all of the factors but particularly by the circumstances of a particular pattern of

Box 15.1 Factors Determining the Relationship Between Political Parties and Interest Groups in Liberal Democracies

I. Socioeconomic and Political Development

1. Patterns of Socioeconomic Development

Explanation: This factor is concerned with such questions as: Did the system develop with deep social cleavages? Did a major gulf exist between capital and labor, and were strong class distinctions present? Was the society characterized by major economic and social upheaval?

Significance: Deep cleavages in a society are likely to cause groups to ally more with certain parties, such as trade unions with socialist parties. Less class rigidity and less conflict between capital and labor lead to less of an "opposing camps" type of producer group configuration.

2. Political Culture and Political Ideology

Explanation: Political culture is a shared set of knowledge, attitudes, and symbols that help to define the procedures and goals of politics. *Conservative/liberal/socialist ideology* denotes specific attitudes toward the role of government.

Significance: The level of pragmatism and ideology in the political culture tends to affect the extent to which certain parties have close ties with certain groups. It also affects the strength of parties. Compare, for example, the highly pragmatic, minimal ideological political culture of the United States with the reverse situation in Sweden. See factor 6 for the effects of strong/weak parties on the party-group connection and the policy process.

3. Contemporary Level of Socioeconomic Development

Explanation: The key questions here are: Where is the society in terms of class divisions, standard of living, level of economic activity, and similar factors? Is it socially homogeneous or heterogeneous? Is it underdeveloped, developed, or in the so-called postindustrial or postmaterialist phase?

Significance: Different stages of development produce different types of groups and often different party-group relations. As a society develops, major parties and groups tend to become more independent of each other. Parties develop into catchall parties, and major groups' party relations become more pragmatic. This occurs in part because the electoral costs of a party being associated with one group may be too high and because groups need to keep their options open to deal with whichever party is in power. However, even in postindustrial societies there is still a discernible left-of-center/right-of-center

(continues)

Box 15.1 Continued

clustering of relationships among major parties, major groups, and some of the more prominent new interests—for example, environmental and human rights groups associating with left-of-center parties and anti-immigrant and antitax groups with right-wing parties.

4. Contemporary Level of Political Development

Explanation: The concerns here include two main sets of questions: Has the country had a long tradition of liberal democracy or a relatively short one, or is it in transition? Is the country involved in supranational organizations that limit its policymaking capacity and that might affect party and interest group activity?

Significance: This will affect the political culture, the level of pluralism, and, in turn, the acceptance or rejection of certain types of political organizations and ultimately the form and legitimacy of certain types of party-group relations. In general, traditional democracies with older institutionalized parties and interest groups tend to have party-group relations that are more stable and less conflict ridden and confrontational. Newer systems have less stability and more conflict, as is the case in the Czech Republic, increasingly in Poland and Mexico, and to some extent in Spain. Membership in supranational organizations like the European Union may reduce the relevance and need for party-group contacts within a country as fewer and fewer policy decisions are made in the country.

II. Contemporary Constitutional, Legal, and Political Structures

5. Centralization/Decentralization of Government and Policymaking

Explanation: Two factors are of importance: (1) whether the system is parliamentary or based on the separation of power, and (2) whether it is federal or unitary.

Significance: Historically, parliamentary systems, particularly when accompanied by strong parties and major ideological cleavages, tended to encourage certain groups, particularly producer groups, to ally with parties to achieve their goals. At the same time, the categorical nature of government in such systems (government with all the power, the opposition with none) tended to lead other groups to take a neutral or pragmatic stance. In the past, unitary systems tended to close avenues open to groups in regional and local areas, but that is changing in many countries, such as France and Italy. Even so, less variety of patterns of party-group relations is found in unitary systems than is often the case in federal systems. However, the strength of parties can affect this. In federal systems with relatively weak parties, as in the United States and Argentina, a broader range of party-group relations is evident. But

(continues)

Box 15.1 Continued

federal systems with strong parties, particularly when the country exhibits a high degree of corporatism as in Mexico and Germany, can constrain the pluralistic effects of federalism and restrict the variety of party-group relations in the political system.

6. Nature of the Party System

Explanation: If the party system is strong in terms of discipline, it will determine the policy agenda and the enactment and implementation of policy.

Significance: Strong party systems, which also tend to be those with historically sharp ideological cleavages, tend to encourage closer ties of certain groups, particularly producer groups, with certain parties—labor to liberal and left-wing parties, business to conservative parties. The weaker the party system, the more neutral or pragmatic these groups can be in their relations with parties. Because a strong party system, as in Germany and Mexico, gives parties the capacity to control the political process, it enables them to determine their relationship with interest groups. Weaker party systems, like the United States and Argentina, afford parties less control over their relations with groups.

7. The Political Party or Party Coalition in Power

Explanation: This concerns which party or party coalition controls the parliament and cabinet in a parliamentary system, and which parties control the legislative and executive branches in a separation-of-powers system.

Significance: In a parliamentary system groups may have different relations with the same party in and out of power, and the fear of being excluded from policy circles leads many groups to pursue a policy of separation or noninvolvement with parties and to focus their attention on the bureaucracy. Changes in control of particular branches of government can have a similar, although usually less extensive, effect in the U.S. separation-of-powers system.

8. Type of Electoral System

Explanation: Of central importance here is whether the electoral system is a single-member or multimember constituency and if a threshold of a percentage of votes is required before a party can be allocated seats in the legislature, as in many proportional representation systems.

Significance: Multimember constituencies and proportional representation systems tend to increase the number of parties with seats in a national legislature (often including interest parties) and sometimes produce multiparty systems. The result is often a reduced range and type of interests in the society because the smaller parties in the system tend to be less vote maximizers than

(continues)

Box 15.1 Continued

issue maximizers—less concerned with getting votes, as are broad-based catchall parties, and more concerned with promoting an issue. For example, the existence of a strong Green party in a country, as in Germany, may reduce the number of environmental groups. The reverse is often the case in countries with single-member districts and first-past-the-post electoral systems like the United States. In the two-party U.S. system there is no effective national Green party; as a consequence, the country has many national environmental interest groups. Proportional representation systems also tend to produce more competition between parties for group support and sometimes produce coalition governments and the need for parties to court a larger and broader range of groups.

9. Extent of Political Party Dependence on Interest Groups

Explanation: This relates to the extent to which parties are dependent on groups for financing, campaign support, recruiting candidates, technical information, policy enactment and implementation, and similar factors.

Significance: The more dependent particular parties are on groups, the more they will cultivate a relationship with groups. Public funding of elections, for example, tends to reduce parties' need for group contributions, gives parties more independence, and weakens party-group ties. This is the case in Sweden. In contrast, minimal or no public funding is a major force shaping party-group relations in the United States and Japan. Even with public funding, however, other circumstances in a country—such as a high level of corporatism, as in Germany—can override such an influence and keep party-group ties strong.

10. Encompassing Characteristics of the Interest Group System

Explanation: This concerns the percentage of people in the society, particularly in the economic sphere, that belong to groups, and how concentrated or fragmented the group system is in representing the various sectors of society.

Significance: The greater the interest group membership density (the percentage of people belonging to groups), especially producer groups, and the greater the sector concentration (the smaller the number of groups representing business, labor, and other sectors), the greater is the possibility for neo-corporatist intermediation at the national level. Thus, the greater is the likelihood of the existence of peak associations and their ability to engage in policy implementation on behalf of government. Such societies will exhibit close relations between producer groups and parties.

11. Constitutional/Legal Provisions Regarding Parties and Groups

Explanation: Here the central question is: Are there constitutional or legal provisions regarding parties and groups, such as registration requirements for interest groups, limits on the political activities of nonprofit organizations,

(continues)

Box 15.1 Continued

public disclosure/transparency of party-group financial relations, or limits on financial contributions by groups to party candidates or parties?

Significance: Constitutional and legal provisions can shape the relationship between certain groups and parties, as in Germany and France. In countries where financial ties were once permitted (e.g., Sweden and Britain with compulsory union contributions to socialist parties), dependence can result. In situations where there are limits on or prohibitions of contributions by certain groups to parties (as in many U.S. states regarding publicly regulated industries), separation or noninvolvement can occur.

III. Interest Group Development, Goals, Characteristics, and Leadership

12. Interest Group Development

Explanation: This relates to the impetus for group development: Did the group develop under the auspices of a party? Were its origins based on ideology or technical considerations?

Significance: Origin and historical development have an important influence on a group's attitude toward and association with parties. Most labor groups were closely allied with radical movements and, often, socialist parties, and these traditions continue despite differences of outlook. Most professional and many trade associations were founded to improve occupational or commercial conditions and had no ideological origins, and they maintain a neutral or pragmatic approach to party relations.

13. Present Group Goals and Ideology

Explanation: This can be summarized in the following questions: Are the group's current goals political, technical, or a combination of the two? Does the group have a particular ideological stance or none at all? Even so, do its goals place it in a particular ideological category?

Significance: If the group's goals have a strong ideological content, it will likely work with parties of that persuasion; or the perception of the group will force it to do so, and it will be less positively received by parties with other ideological stances. If the group's goals are entirely or largely technical, it will have more options of which parties to work with and may pursue a nonpartisan approach.

14. Group Leadership

Explanation: Leadership is vitally important to the policymaking and day-to-day functioning of a group. Many groups and organizations are viewed through the perspectives of their leadership, and skillful and enterprising leaders can often dominate the operations of a group.

(continues)

> **Box 15.1 Continued**
>
> *Significance:* A particular group's leaders may align themselves with particular parties, even though those parties may not be supported by the majority of the group's members. Another leader of the same group at a different time may take a more neutral stance. Thus, changes in leadership and the perspective of group leaders can determine the extent of short-term interactions, or lack thereof, with political parties. Some group leaders may see a neutral stance toward a party as much more valuable politically, particularly in countries like France, Britain, the United States, and Argentina where dealing with the bureaucracy has proven more fruitful for certain groups than aligning with a particular party.
>
> *Source:* Developed by the author from Thomas and Hrebenar (1995), Yishai (1995), G. Wilson (1990), Berry (1980, 1997), and the thirteen country chapters in this book.

socioeconomic development (factor 1) in regard to a fragmented labor and business lobby, a highly centralized government system dominated by a bureaucracy (factor 5), the regulation of groups (factor 11), and relations between group leaders and government bureaucrats (factor 14).

The explanatory value of Box 15.1 for the system-level, the sector-level, and the one-on-one party-group relationship can be illustrated as follows. For any political system an overview of the characteristics of the relationship between major parties and interests can be gleaned in particular from factor 1 (patterns of socioeconomic development), factor 2 (political culture and ideology), factor 6 (nature of the party system), factor 9 (party dependence on groups), and factor 10 (encompassing characteristics of the interest group system). Party-group relations at the sector level—particularly regarding business, labor, and agriculture—are principally explained by factors 1, 9, and 10 and the three factors in Section III, Interest Group Development, Goals, Characteristics, and Leadership. The one-on-one relationship is also largely explained by the factors in Section III plus factors 2 and 9. Finally, explanations for differences in long- and short-term party-group relations are largely explained by the factors in Section III, the factors in Section I, Socioeconomic and Political Development, and in particular factor 7 (the party in power). Among many additional things, the framework also offers insights into two questions posed in Chapter 1: the extent to which the party-group relationship is a function of the length of the existence of a democratic system, and whether these relations are fundamentally different in two-party and multiparty systems.

Do traditional, new, and transitional democracies have fundamentally different party-group relations? This framework reveals no clear answer. Overall, it appears that the youth or age of a democracy is not a major determinant of party-group relations. In some cases the youth of a democratic system is apparently a factor, such as giving fluidity to those relations in countries like the Czech Republic, Poland, and Spain. In other cases it appears less important—such as in Israel, Germany, and Japan—because of major influences such as strong parties and corporatism. For example, the party-group relations of Sweden and Germany have much more in common than do those of France and Sweden, even though France and Sweden are old established democracies and unitary systems whereas Germany's federal democracy is a post–World War II creation.

This is further evidence that some common denominators between countries shape party-group relations regardless of the age of the democratic system. It is equally important evidence that a country's socioeconomic and political circumstances are fundamental in shaping the relationship no matter when the country adopted democracy. Compare, for example, the integration of one party (the PRI) and groups in Mexico with their almost complete separation in Argentina and the rather different ways party-group relations developed in two former Soviet bloc countries, the Czech Republic and Poland.

The framework also offers insights into the complexity of the issue of two-party versus multiparty states. By itself, a two-party or modified two-party system is not the major determinant of these relations, as the contrasts among Britain, the United States, Germany, and Argentina attest. The existence of a multiparty system—like Israel and, to a lesser extent, France, Italy, and the Czech Republic—is also not the major determinant, as contrasting party-group relations in these countries also reveal. Again, what appears important are local circumstances and particularly the strength or weakness of political parties and their capacity and willingness to shape party-group relations.

FORMS OF THE PARTY-GROUP RELATIONSHIP: A MORE COMPREHENSIVE TYPOLOGY

In reviewing the chapters in this book regarding the relevance of Box 1.2, which set out a preliminary categorization of the forms of the party-group relationship, it is clear that the typology is applicable to most countries to varying degrees but needs refining to provide a more accurate categorization of forms and to take account of recent trends. The expanded typology is presented in Box 15.2. It includes specific examples of each type of relationship and comments on recent developments that have affected the various categories of the typology and their relationships. Of the concerns raised in the individual chapters about the preliminary typology, three are particularly worthy of note and have been instrumental in modifying Box

1.2. All three relate to the fact that the forms and their interrelation are more complex than originally anticipated.

First, it became clear from the country case studies that we cannot categorize entire political systems as having a particular type of party-group relations such as Integration, Separation, and so on. This can be done to a limited extent with major parties and major interests in some countries like Germany and Argentina, but even here a category is too general to be meaningful because a host of party-group relations exist in all democracies. In this regard, the speculation by G. Wilson (1990, 159) that "there is no single pattern of relationships between interest groups and political parties either between or within countries" is borne out by this research. For similar reasons it is also difficult to categorize the sector level, even major sectors like labor and business, as their relations with parties are undergoing major changes. Therefore, the only meaningful categorization is between individual parties and individual groups. This is the level of analysis represented in Box 15.2 and is reflected in its title.

Second, the individual country chapters also indicated that the five original categories in Box 1.2 needed to be expanded to seven because a distinction clearly exists between the Integration form and the Dominant Party form and also between Separation and Noninvolvement. This differentiation and an explanation are presented in Box 15.2.

Third, it became even clearer from the country case studies that the categories are not mutually exclusive. This is apparent in three ways. These relations change over the long term, change in the short term, and can exhibit more than one form at the same time. Box 15.2 more clearly accounts for these three situations than did Box 1.2.

Long-term movement between categories is clearly illustrated by the relocation of the socialist party–labor movement relationship from the Integration to the Cooperation and Separation categories. Short-term relations are very much determined by which party is in power. For example, some groups, like a professional group, that normally follow a policy of separation may become particularly involved with a party (the governing party) when there is a change of government and its area of concern is affected.

Party-group relations can exhibit two or more forms simultaneously for two reasons. First, relations can straddle two adjacent forms during a long-term transition from one form to another, or the relations may permanently exhibit elements of more than one form, as with the PRI in Mexico with regard to the Integration and Dominant forms. Second, although parties and groups can have long-term relations that clearly fit one form, they can simultaneously have short-term relations that fall into another. Again, socialist party–trade union relations provide a good example. Although their long-term relations may fit Cooperation (form 3) or even Integration

Box 15.2   Seven Major Forms of Relationships Between Individual Political Parties and Individual Interest Groups in Liberal Democracies

1. Integration Model

Explanation: Here the political party and the interest group are virtually identical or very close organizationally, perhaps because the interest group was created by the party, or vice versa. The basis of this integration is usually the result of a very close, often identical ideological affinity, and a consequent common strategy exists between the party and its affiliate group or groups.

Examples: One classic example is the relationship between Communist parties and their auxiliary organizations/groups—for example, in Italy and France. Other relationships include the Greens in Germany and several other countries, which developed from the environmental movement; interest parties such as those in Israel, with religious policy goals developed from religious groups, and the Pensioners' Party in the Czech Republic, which grew out of the senior citizens' movement; and ultraconservative parties and certain groups, such as anti-immigrant groups and neofascist parties in France, Germany, and Austria. The relationship of many labor organizations, both individual unions and union peak associations, with socialist and particularly Social Democratic parties was another classic example of this form. Most traditional unions in Britain, Sweden, and Germany and their peak associations developed from or helped establish socialist parties. Mexico also exhibits the Integration Model with the PRI and its affiliate groups; in this case the category fits more for pragmatic than ideological reasons, which means PRI-group relations include elements of both the Integration Model and the Dominant Party Model explained next.

Although the Integration Model has been one of the most stable party-group relationships, it has been on the decline in Western democracies in recent years, particularly in northern Europe and Israel, as well as in Mexico. The trend is for integrative party-group relations to develop into the Cooperation and Separation forms explained later. In regard to a mass party and despite changes since the fall of the Soviet Union in 1989–1990, Communist parties (now often under a different name) in Western democracies and their auxiliary organizations probably still represent the best example of the Integration Model.

2. Dominant Party Model

Explanation: This model has elements of both the Integration and the Cooperation Model (discussed next), but it is fundamentally different from both. It represents a situation where interest groups, particularly major interests, are subordinated to the power of a single dominant party in the country

(continues)

Box 15.2 Continued

to the extent that they cannot achieve access or influence without party sanction. Unlike the Integration and Cooperation Models, the party is so dominant that in effect it controls all avenues of access and influence, including the bureaucracy. In this model the party and groups are separate entities and in most cases had separate origins. Moreover, the model is less the result of ideological affinity or the integration of organizational activity, although these may exist. It is more the result of a pragmatic, symbiotic relationship stemming from historical circumstances and involving an exchange of benefits and resources, particularly groups helping the party get elected and maintain power and the party (which is the government) dispensing financial and other benefits and special privileges to the group.

Examples: For much of the post–World War II period, this was the situation in Italy with the Christian Democrats through the *parentela* and clientelistic relationships the party had with groups. A slight variation has also been the case with the Liberal Democrats in Japan. With some modifications, the model also best fits the situation in the Czech Republic (general party dominance) and appears to be an emerging model in Poland.

3. Cooperation/Proximate Ideology Model

Explanation: In this situation a strong reciprocal connection exists between a political party and an interest group, but it is not a relationship of integration or dominance of one by the other. The connection is likely to be based on ideology, policy orientation, and historical circumstances. Sometimes it is based on political necessity—the result of a group being so weak politically that it has to align itself with a party to achieve its political goals. This model may be the most stable and long lasting of the party-group relationships. A major strategy manifested in this model is that groups attempt to influence a party's program.

Examples: This is often the case with business and many professional groups, conservative parties, farmers' organizations, and rural parties, as well as with the religious right and conservative parties (e.g., Republicans in the United States, the Christian Democrats in Germany). It also fits liberal cause groups (environmentalists, consumer groups, gay rights groups) and liberal or left-wing parties, as well as conservative parties and right-wing groups (such as antiabortion, antitax, and privatization groups)—many of which could not achieve success on their own because of limited political resources.

4. Separation/Pragmatic Involvement Model

Explanation: This model is characterized by the strong independence of parties and interest groups. A group has no particular partisan attachment and perhaps only a weak, if any, ideological attachment to any particular party.

(continues)

Box 15.2 Continued

Consequently, it is willing to work with any party in or out of power to promote its goals. Thus, involvement with a party occurs on an ad hoc basis determined largely by political pragmatism. This form is particularly prevalent in policy areas that have been depoliticized. With the decline of the Integration Model and, to a lesser extent, the Dominant and Cooperation forms of party-group relations, this form is on the increase. It may be the most common form across Western democracies in terms of the number of groups having relations with parties (although Noninvolvement is likely the dominant form in terms of overall group numbers).

Examples: Many professional groups fall under this form—particularly those with technical, nonpolitical goals, such as architects and airline pilots—as do many social issue and public interest groups, such as children's rights, anti-smoking, and anti–drunk driving groups. Many local government and quasi-government groups, both of officials and of jurisdictions, are required to be politically neutral and thus deal with parties on a pragmatic ad hoc basis or in a balanced fashion. In addition, this type of relationship has become increasingly common in recent years among many business groups and new socialist parties in countries like Britain, Germany, and Sweden as the Integration form declines.

5. Noninvolvement Model

Explanation: In this situation a group has no direct relations with political parties. This could occur for one of three reasons. First, a group or organization may feel its goals are best achieved outside the regular party system. Second, its goals and philosophy may be such that it finds it difficult, if not impossible, to gain access to a party or to the bureaucracy. These two categories include many so-called outsider groups in contrast with the insider groups that work hard to cultivate political relationships, including that with political parties. Many nonpartisan activist groups are philosophically opposed to insider politics. Third, parties may not be relevant because of the nonpartisan nature of the issue or issues of concern to the group, or they may be weak or inoperative in a particular jurisdiction like a city. In overall numbers, this form is likely the largest of the seven set out here when we consider the vast number of groups operating in pluralist societies at various levels of government.

Examples: Under the first category in this model fall some protest groups—particularly the more radical antiestablishment groups such as some antiwar and antinuclear groups, which see their success as more likely achieved by gaining public support. Often, these groups seek to draw attention to an issue, raise public concern/consciousness, and influence policy outcomes through high-profile media stunts. The second category includes extremist groups such as Operation Rescue (an extreme U.S. antiabortion group). It is important to point out, however, that not all activist or outsider groups are nonpartisan; in fact, the same group may be nonpartisan at some times and partisan at

(continues)

> **Box 15.2 Continued**
>
> other times. The Conflict/Confrontational Model (form 7 below) embraces circumstances where such groups become partisan in terms of their opposition to parties. The third category includes the vast majority of groups in a society including, among many others, professional, sports/recreational, social issue, voluntary, and community groups and local organizations.
>
> ### 6. Competition/Rivalry Model
>
> *Explanation:* When a party and a group compete with each other as vehicles of representation or in delivering political benefits, competition for members and funds often results. Sometimes the result is intense rivalry between the party and group. Although this form can develop into form 7 (Conflict/Confrontation), it is fundamentally different and manifests itself in different ways. It most often involves parties and groups with a similar ideology or policy goals.
>
> *Examples:* Cases include Green parties and environmentalists, particularly when the party is in power and cannot meet all the demands of the interest group; new socialist parties and labor unions, as in Sweden and Britain; and a women's group within a socialist party running its own parliamentary candidates, as in France in 1978. It is from this type of intraparty competition that interest parties are born.
>
> ### 7. Conflict/Confrontation Model
>
> *Explanation:* In this form open conflict and sometimes confrontation occur between a party and a group. Generally, it involves conflict between a group and the governing party and is less manifest in situations where a party is out of power. The conflict/confrontation most often results from ideological cleavages or major disagreements over policy, often highly value-laden, emotional issues. Most frequently it involves parties and groups at opposite ends of the political spectrum, but it can involve a party and group with close ties that disagree over a policy or its implementation. Conflict and the use of confrontational tactics, such as strikes, boycotts, sit-ins, and street violence, by outsider interests and radical groups are the extreme manifestations of this model.
>
> *Examples:* Instances include the long-standing conflict between many labor organizations, both individual unions and union associations, with conservative parties over issues like public-sector versus private-sector provision of services and, more recently, deregulation; recent conflict between moderate socialist parties and left-wing organizations over privatization; and confrontation between outsider interest and social movements—like extreme animal rights groups, antinuclear groups, and immigrant workers' groups—and the governing party.
>
> *Source:* Developed by the author from Yishai (1995), Thomas and Hrebenar (1995), G. Wilson (1990), Sternberger (1952–1953), Meynaud (1962), and the chapters in this volume.

(form 1), their short-term relations may involve Conflict (form 6) or even Confrontation (form 7). This has become increasingly the case in recent years as socialist parties, both in and out of government, have moved to become catchall parties and appeal to a wider public by abandoning or ignoring many cherished union policies, such as increased government regulation of the economy and increased public ownership. The simultaneous existence of two distinct forms of party-group relations is usually a clear indication of a changing relationship that will likely result in a new form or a much modified version of the existing form of their relations.

EFFECT OF PARTY-GROUP RELATIONS ON POLICYMAKING AND REPRESENTATION AND ITS OVERALL SIGNIFICANCE IN LIBERAL DEMOCRACIES

Ideally, the findings regarding this third area of the project would be of two types. The first would include information on the way various forms of party-group relations affect the patterns of policymaking and representation—how they shape the structures and processes of politics. The second would include assessments of the effect or impact of these various forms in enhancing or stymieing democracy. Although several chapters do refer to the effect of party-group relations on democracy, in general presenting this type of information was beyond the bounds of this project as it involves extensive empirical research. The main findings to be gleaned here relate to the first category of information. Even so, besides some specific observations on how party-group relations affect the structure and processes of politics, the project also enables us to assess the overall significance of party-group relations in Western democracies, which throws some light on the extent to which these relations impact democracy.

Effect on Policymaking and Representational Structures and Processes

The many observations made in the chapters in this regard can be grouped into six general points.

First, in some cases similar party-group relations do have similar effects across and within countries. For example, the close ties of the past between socialist parties and trade unions and conservative parties and business groups, with their overlap of membership and close financial ties, often led to conflicts when these parties were in power and had to be more pragmatic. Another example is dominant party systems, in which the party almost entirely controls the policy process; thus, no effective representation of interests occurs without the dominant party's sanction.

Second, and in contrast, there are examples of similar party-group relations having diverse effects in the same country and in different countries. One example is that the Integration Model can in some ways enhance a group's input into policy and increase its representation, as with the environmental movement and the Green Party, but stifle input in other ways, as it does with auxiliary groups in the Communist Party. Another example is that Separation or Noninvolvement can be advantageous to particular groups in some countries because of the political culture, as in Argentina, but similar groups—as, for example, in Mexico—would have no representation or policy input if they had followed similar modes of relations with the PRI.

Third, with the possible exception of Argentina (with little contact between parties and groups), in terms of an interest group securing benefits and resources, accommodative relations with political parties as in the Integrative, Dominant, and Cooperation Models are clearly more successful than confrontational relations. Although close or cooperative relations of groups with parties do not guarantee success in all instances, they do assure a degree of access to policymakers and in many cases favorable treatment by the bureaucracy. This assures an accepted role in the policy process and in representation that is not ensured and is often inhibited by the Conflict and Confrontational forms. In other words, insider politics, which involves good group-party relations, is more fruitful on average than outsider politics. Furthermore, the more accommodative as opposed to conflict ridden and confrontational party-group relations are in a country, the more stable the policymaking and representational process, although this does not necessarily guarantee it is more democratic.

Interestingly, however, this project reveals that the perceived negative consequences to groups or the irrelevance to their issues of pursuing party relations have the most effect on the structures and forms of policymaking and representation. This leads us to points four and five.

Fourth, the fact that groups and interests must deal with the government to get things done regardless of which party is in power is a major reason the party-group relationship, in terms of groups permanently aligning with one particular party, is important for only a small number of groups—albeit often the most important ones—in their quest to affect policy and representation. Thus, the preferred party-group relationship for most groups is Cooperation, Separation, or Noninvolvement. As we saw in Box 15.2, these modes, particularly the latter two, have increased in recent years. Fifth, and a related point, almost every chapter in this book bears witness to the fact that the major mode of group activity in attempting to affect policy is, in whole or in part, trying to gain access to the bureaucracy. Party connections may facilitate this, but the party connection is the major means to seek to secure access and representation for only a small number of groups. In many countries—France and Japan particularly but also Britain, Sweden, and Argentina—this mode of group operation is further encouraged by the political power and crucial role of the bureaucracy in the policy process.

The sixth and final point is that one major revelation of this project is that it appears that with the possible exception of Italy, party-group relations have more effect on the various aspects of policymaking and representation in the U.S. political system than in almost any other country (see Chapter 5).

Overall Significance of Party-Group Relations

As many of the chapters in this book have shown, the party-group connection has had great importance for certain individual parties and groups, particularly the socialist party–trade union connection and that of conservative parties and business. However, in regard to the overall significance of party-group relations in liberal democracies, points four and five in the previous section place things in perspective and indicate that despite the long-standing, high-profile relations between many parties and groups, the party-group connection across pluralist systems overall is less significant than hitherto assumed when it comes to determining policy, representing interests, and, we can surmise, advancing or stymieing democracy. Thus, although the extent or lack of the connection between parties and groups does give a political system certain identifiable characteristics, this influence may be largely superficial and may not markedly affect what does and does not get done in the society.

Further evidence for this general conclusion is that for many of the countries in this study, including those with long-standing close ties between major parties and groups, little or nothing has been written on the party-group connection at the system level (although several studies exist at the sector and individual party-group levels). Presumably, scholars have not seen the relationship as that important to overall policymaking to warrant investigation. And changes across the Western world since the early 1980s, particularly the weakening of ideology and the increase in political pragmatism with the consequent rise of catchall parties, are making the party-group relationship even less significant.

Yet like most generalizations, this masks the significance of the relationship in particular countries at the system, sectoral, and one-on-one party-group levels. So again, we are back to individual country circumstances when it comes to understanding the specific significance of the relationship. Bearing in mind that Separation and Noninvolvement encompass the vast majority of groups in any society, we can make the following observations on the overall significance of party-group relations in particular countries. The relationship is perhaps most significant in the United States, probably because of the peculiarities of the separation-of-powers system and the particulars of American political culture. Here party-group relations have a major effect—at least at the state level—on party competition, on who does and who does not get elected, on what policies are and are not enacted, and on power relationships between parties and groups. The relationship has had a major effect over the years in Italy and Israel and has been important in Germany, Mexico, Japan, and Sweden. It has had less effect in Britain, Spain, France, the Czech Republic, Poland, and particularly Argentina.

Enhanced Understanding but Inconclusive Evidence

These observations add much to our understanding of how the party-group connection affects political systems. Yet perhaps in part because of the limitations of the investigative range of this project, explained earlier, and also because party-group relations may be less significant than many scholars believe, the answer to the third question of the project, relating to the effect of these relations, is far less definitive than the answers and information on the first two questions detailed earlier in the chapter. This means that beyond the generalizations outlined earlier, the level of knowledge presently available about the effect of party-group relations on political systems does not help much in developing a theory of this impact.

CAN A GENERAL THEORY OF PARTY-GROUP RELATIONS IN WESTERN DEMOCRACIES BE DEVELOPED?

From what has been said in this chapter, it is clear that this project leads to the conclusion that no general integrated theory of party-group relations can be developed that is generally applicable across Western democracies and can be specifically applied to individual countries. This is the case primarily because the individual country circumstances give a particular complexion and often a unique character to party-group relations in that country. Similar general conditions of development across countries, such as the rise of labor unions and employer associations or emergence from a war, produce a different pattern of party-group relations because of these country circumstances. Compare, for example, party group relations in the two post–World War II democracies of Germany and Italy.

Yet, although we cannot produce a general integrated grand theory, as a result of this project we can move toward a much more systematic understanding of party-group relations both across and within democracies. A valuable element in enabling us to do so is knowledge about the importance of individual country circumstances. Of the three main questions we set out to answer in this project, the first two (What shapes party group relations, and what form do they take?) lend themselves more to systematic understanding through the two frameworks developed from the project (Boxes 15.1 and 15.2). As we saw in the last section, the third question (How does the relationship affect policymaking and representation, and what is its overall significance for democratic systems?) does not lend itself to any meaningful general explanations across democracies but can be assessed in part within individual countries.

To be sure, Boxes 15.1 and 15.2 do not answer all questions and can be improved on. But individually and, in particular, in combination they provide the first holistic approach to understanding party-group relations and their various facets. The boxes also help us to understand the dynamic nature of the relationship and to anticipate the likely future development of the party-group connection across and within countries. The specific explanatory value of these theoretical frameworks is clear from the examples given in previous sections. They provide insights into most of the questions raised in Chapter 1, including the importance of the length of the existence of democracy in determining party-group relations, as well as the significance of two- and multiparty systems to the connection. A more in-depth understanding of the party-group connection of each country considered in this book can also be obtained by applying these enhanced frameworks. Most important, the frameworks and general findings of this project provide a hitherto unavailable benchmark for understanding party-group relations in democracies not covered in this book.

IMPLICATIONS FOR ONGOING AND FUTURE RESEARCH

Finally, we offer comments on how the results of this study provide insights into the major ongoing research concern of the competition between parties and groups, and suggest future research topics that will enhance an understanding of some of the important findings here, including pursuing some of the unanswered questions raised by this project.

As to the ongoing debate on party-group competition and its consequences, parties have declined in membership and interest groups have gained (J. Richardson 1995, 123–125; Cigler 1993), and interest groups are more numerous and visible throughout the Western world than ever before (Thomas 1993, chapter 1). However, the evidence from this project suggests that this essentially two-dimensional relationship—either parties or groups—is greatly oversimplified. The chapters in this book point to the fact that party-group competition has no single simple consequence either within or across countries. This confirms the work of Merkl (1988) and Rose and Mackie (1988), who pointed out that the rise of organizations affects different political and party systems in different ways. Adaptation appears to be the major mode of party adjustment in competition with alternative organizations. One form of adaptation, as J. Richardson (1995, 136) pointed out, is that parties and groups may develop differentiated tasks and become more distinct. Rival groups have not carried the day and have only marginally reduced the ability of established parties to secure control of government, and confrontational groups have not seriously hurt institutionalized political parties (Yishai 1995).

This book confirms these developments. Most important, the competitive elements of the party-group relationship need to be placed in the broader context of the overall relationship of parties and groups. Separation and particularly noninvolvement of parties and groups are more major modes of their interaction or lack of interaction than is competition and may have consequences as important, if not more important, for policymaking and democracy.

The evidence presented here strongly suggests that parties, particularly major parties, are not disappearing whether they are challenged by interest groups, social movements, third parties, or interest parties. Parties and groups are not completely interchangeable as political institutions and perform many different as well as overlapping functions. In fact, some places are experiencing a party resurgence, as with the Republican Party in the United States and the redefining of many socialist parties like New Labour in Britain. And parties have been at the forefront of the move to democratization in Eastern Europe. Although they encounter difficulties in maintaining stability, very few political parties and virtually no major parties have crumbled and disintegrated (Mair 1993). Where parties have suffered major losses, like the Progressive Conservatives in Canada, or imploded, like the Christian Democrats in Italy, it was not because of challenges from other political organizations. It appears, however, that Yishai's idea of "interest parties" may be coming more and more into play as political systems become more fluid. This is true as two-party systems loosen, as new democracies do not develop two-party systems, and as the distinction among groups, social movements, and lobbying corporations becomes less clear (Yishai 1995).

Thus, even though major parties are unlikely to disappear, all indications are that the future may be much different from the past, and we may see new elements of the party-group relationship in liberal democracies. The chapters in this book speculate on these developments but raise more questions than they can answer.

In this regard, seven aspects of party-group relations appear fruitful to pursue to throw light on the relationship and its future effects on policymaking, representation, and democracy. One is the extensive issue of the party-group relationship and the extent to which it advances or stymies democracy. Such investigation would prove most useful in regard to the American political system where this relationship appears to have a major influence on democracy. Second, all indications are that although not necessarily the major defining factor in party-group relations, two-party versus multiparty systems do affect the range and types of groups that operate in a country (see factor 8 in Box 15.1), and this would be a fruitful avenue of research. Third is how the devolution of political systems in countries like Britain, France, and Sweden will affect the relationship. Fourth is the effect transnationalism, such at the European Union (EU), will have on the relationship. According to several chapters in this book, the EU in particular is changing the nature of the relationship, and all indications are that it will do so markedly in countries like Germany and Sweden that have strong traditions of corporatism. Fifth is the extent to which the ties between longtime traditional allies, such as left-wing parties and labor and right-wing parties and business, will continue to loosen. Sixth, and a related point, will the development of catchall parties further lessen the significance to the political system of the party-group connection, or will a new set of symbiotic relations replace the old ties? A seventh fruitful area of concern would be to modify the two frameworks presented in this chapter based on the experience of party-group relations in democracies other than the ones considered in this book.

Acronyms

ACLI	Italian Association of Christian Workers
AK	Agrární komora (Czech Republic)
AP	Alianza Popular (Spain)
ASAP	Association of Petrochemical Firms (Italy)
AWS	Akcja Wyborcza Solidarnosc (Poland)
BDA	Federation of German Employers' Associations
BDI	Federation of German Industry
CCOO	Comisiones Obreras (Spain)
CDU	Christian Democratic Union (Germany)
CEOE	Confederación Española de Organaciones Empresariales
CEPYME	Confederación Española de Pequeñas y Medianas Empresas
CFDT	Confédération Française Démocratique du Travail
CFTC	Confédération Française des Travailleurs Chrétiens
CGC	Confédération Générale des Cadres (France)
CGE	Confederación General Económica (Argentina)
CGIL	Italian General Confederation of Labor
CGP	Clean Government Party (Japan)
CGT	Confederación General de Trabajo (Argentina)
CGT	Confédération Générale du Travail (France)
CISL	Italian Confederation of Workers' Unions
ČLK	Česká lékařská komora (Czech Republic)
ČMKOS	Českomoravská komora odborových svazu (Czech Republic)
CNC	Confederación Nacional Campesina (Mexico)
CNOP	Confederación Nacional de Organizaciones Populares (Mexico)
CNPF	Couseil Nationale du Patronnat Français

CONCAMIN	Confederación Nacional de Cámaras Industriales (Mexico)
CONCANACO	Confederación Nacional de Cámaras de Comercio (Mexico)
CPN	Consejo Político Nacional (Mexico)
CSL	Confédération des Syndicats Libres (France)
ČSSD	Česká strana Sociální Demokratická (Czech Republic)
CSU	Christian Social Union (Germany)
CTM	Confederación de Trabajadores de México
DBV	German Farmers Association
DC	Democrazia Cristiana (Italy)
DGB	German Trade Union Federation
DIHT	German Industrial and Trade Conference
DP	Democratic Party (Japan)
DSP	Democratic Socialist Party (Japan)
DŽJ	Důchodci ža životná jistota (Czech Republic)
EU	European Union
FCPE	Fédération des Conseils des Parents d'Elèves (France)
FDN	Frente Democrático Nacional (Mexico)
FDP	Free Democratic Party (Germany)
FGCI	Federation of Young Italian Communists
FN	Front National (France)
FO	Force Ouvrière (France)
FP	Folkpartiet Liberalerna (Sweden)
FREPASO	Frente del País Solidario (Argentina)
FRG	German Federal Republic
GDP	gross domestic product
GDR	German Democratic Republic
IM	Instituto de la Mujer
JCP	Japanese Communist Party
JPC	Joint Policy Committee (Britain)
JSP	Japan Socialist Party
JTU	Japan Teachers Union
KDU-ČSL	Křestankská a Demokratická Unie–Československá strana Lidová (Czech Republic)
KSČ	Kommunistické Strana Československa
LDP	Liberal Democratic Party (Japan)
LO	Landsorganisationen (Swedish Trade Union Confederation)
LOK	Lekařsky odborovy klub (Czech Republic)
LP	Liberal Party (Japan)
LRF	Lantbrukarnas Riksförbund (Sweden)
MA	Manufacturers' Association

MK	member of Knesset
MLF	Movimiento para Liberación Feminina (Argentina)
MODIN	Partido por la Dignidad y Independencia (Argentina)
MP	member of Parliament
MSI	Movimento Sociale Italiano
NEC	National Executive Committee (Britain)
NFP	New Frontier Party (Japan)
NFU	National Farmers Union (Britain)
NRP	National Religious Party (Israel)
ODS	Občanská Demokratická Strana (Czech Republic)
ONCE	Organización Nacional de Ciegos Españoles
OPZZ	Ogolne Porozumienie Zwiazkow Zawodowych (Poland)
OSZSP	Odborový svaz zdravotnictví a sociální péče České republiky (Czech Republic)
PAC	political action committee (United States)
PAN	Partido Autonomista Nacional (Argentina)
PAN	Partido de Acción Nacional (Mexico)
PARC	Policy Affairs Research Committee (Japan)
PCE	Partido Comunista Española
PCF	Parti Communiste Français
PCI	Partito Comunista Italiana
PDS	Democratic Party of the Left (Italy)
PDS	Party of Democratic Socialism (Germany)
PJ	Partido Justicialista (Argentina)
PLI	Partito Liberale Italiana
PNR	Partido Nacional Revolucionario (Mexico)
PP	Partido Popular (Spain)
PRD	Partido de la Revolución Democrática (Mexico)
PRI	Partido Revolucionario Institucional (Mexico)
PRI	Partito Repubblicano Italiano
PRM	Partido de la Revolución Mexicana
PRONASOL	Programa Nacional de Solidaridad (Mexico)
PS	Parti Socialiste (France)
PSDI	Partito Socialista Democratico Italiano
PSE	producter subsidy equivalent
PSI	Partito Socialista Italiano
PSOE	Partido Socialista de Obreros Españoles
PT	Partido de Trabajo (Mexico)
PVEM	Partido Verde Ecologista de México
PZPR	Polska Zjednoczona Partia Robotnicza (Poland)
RPR	Rasemblement pour la République (France)
SACO	Sveriges Akademikers Centralorganisation (Sweden)
SAF	Svenska Arbetsgivareföreningen (Sweden)

SAP	Sveriges Socialdemokratiska Arbetareparti (Sweden)
SDRP	Socjaldemokracja Rzeczpospolitz Polskiej (Poland)
SFIO	Section Française de L'International Ouvriène
SLD	Sojusz Lewicy Demokratycznej (Poland)
SPD	Social Democratic Party (Germany)
SPD	Svaz průmyslu a dopravy České republiky (Czech Republic)
SRA	Sociedad Rural Argentina
TCO	Tjänstemännens Centralorganisation (Sweden)
TUC	Trade Union Congress (Britain)
UB	*unidades basicas* (Argentina)
UCD	Unión Centro Democrático (Spain)
UCD	Unión del Centro Democrático (Argentina)
UCR	Unión Civica Radical (Argentina)
UDI	Italian Union of Women
UFAC	Union Française d'Associations de Combattants et Victimes de Guerre
UGT	Unión General de Trabajadores (Spain)
UIA	Unión Industrial Argentina
UIL	Italian Union of Labor
UNAPEL	Union Nationale des Associations de Parents d'Elèves de l'Enseignement Libre (France)
UNEF	Union Nationale des Etudiants de France
US	Unie Svobody (Czech Republic)
UW	Unia Wolnosci (Poland)

Further Reading

As has been indicated repeatedly throughout this book, there is both a dearth of research on the party-group connection from a comparative perspective—across liberal democracies—and on the interaction of parties and groups in individual countries. Consequently, this list of further reading includes few references on the specifics of the party-group connection. What it does contain are the major works—books, articles, and conference papers—that provide insights on the relationship, past and present. The listing is divided into two parts. The first includes references of use in comparing the party-group relationship across liberal democracies, including works on regions or individual countries with general application beyond their particular focus. The second section contains works on the individual countries covered in this book, listed alphabetically by country.

COMPARATIVE WORKS

Baumgartner, Frank R., and Beth L. Leech. 1998. *Basic Interests: The Importance of Groups in Politics and in Political Science*. Princeton: Princeton University Press.

Berger, Suzanne D., ed. 1981. *Organizing Interests in Western Europe: Pluralism, Corporatism and the Transformation of Politics*. New York: Cambridge University Press.

Burstein, Paul. 1998. "Interest Organizations, Political Parties and the Study of Democratic Politics." In Anne N. Costain and Andrew S. McFarland, eds., *Social Movements and American Political Institutions*. Lanham, MD: Rowman and Littlefield.

Cawson, Alan. 1986. *Corporatism and Political Theory*. Oxford: Basil Blackwell.

Chalmers, Douglas A., Scott B. Martin, and Kerianne Piester. 1997. "Associative Networks: New Structures of Representation for the Popular Sectors?" In Douglas A. Chalmers et al., eds., *The New Politics of Inequality in Latin*

America: Rethinking Participation and Representation. New York: Oxford University Press.
Coppedge, Michael. 1998. "The Dynamic Diversity of Latin American Party Systems." *Party Politics* 4, 4 (October): 547–568.
Dalton, Russell, and Manfred Kuechler, eds. 1990. *Challenging the Political Order.* New York: Oxford University Press.
Duverger, Maurice. 1972. *Party Politics and Pressure Groups: A Comparative Introduction.* New York: Thomas Y. Crowell.
Epstein, Leon D. 1967. *Political Parties in Western Democracies.* London: Pall Mall.
Eyerman, Ron, and Andrew Jamison. 1991. *Social Movements: A Cognitive Approach.* University Park: Pennsylvania State University Press.
Foweraker, Joe. 1994. "Popular Political Organization and Democratization: A Comparison of Spain and Mexico." In Ian Budge and David McKay, eds., *Developing Democracy.* London: Sage.
Ignazi, Piero, and Colette Ysmal, eds. 1998. *The Organization of Political Parties in Southern Europe.* Westport, CT: Praeger.
Jordan, G., and W. A. Maloney. 1992. "What Is Studied When Pressure Groups Are Studied?" British Interest Groups Project, Working Paper Series No. 1. Aberdeen (Scotland), University of Aberdeen.
Katz, Richard S., and Peter Mair. 1995. "Changing Models of Party Organization and Party Democracy." *Party Politics* 1: 5–28.
Lawson, Kay, ed. 1980. *Political Parties and Linkage: A Comparative Perspective.* New Haven: Yale University Press.
———, ed. 1995. *How Political Parties Work.* New York: Praeger, 1995.
Lawson, Kay, and Peter H. Merkl, eds. 1988. *When Parties Fail: Emerging Alternative Organizations.* Princeton: Princeton University Press.
Lehmbruch, Gerhard. 1982. "Introduction: Neo-Corporatism in Comparative Perspective." In Gerhard Lehmbruch and Philippe C. Schmitter, eds., *Patterns of Corporatist Policy-Making.* Beverly Hills: Sage.
Mainwaring, Scott, and Timothy R. Scully, eds. 1995. *Building Democratic Institutions: Party Systems in Latin America.* Stanford: Stanford University Press.
Mair, Peter. 1993. "Myth of Electoral Change and the Myth of Traditional Parties." *European Journal of Political Research* 24: 121–133.
McCarthy, John, and Mayer Zald. 1977. "Resource Mobilization and Social Movements: A Partial Theory." *American Journal of Sociology* 82: 1212–1241.
Merkl, Peter H. 1988. "The Challengers and the Party System." In Kay Lawson and Peter H. Merkl, eds., *When Parties Fail: Emerging Alternative Organizations.* Princeton: Princeton University Press.
Morlino, Leonardo. 1998. *Democracy Between Consolidation and Crisis: Parties, Groups, and Citizens in Southern Europe.* New York: Oxford University Press.
Olson, Mancur. 1982. *The Rise and Decline of Nations: Economic Growth, Stagflation, and Social Rigidities.* New Haven: Yale University Press.
Panebianco, Angelo. 1988. *Political Parties: Organization and Power.* Cambridge: Cambridge University Press.
Richardson, Jeremy, J. 1995. "The Market for Political Activism: Interest Groups as a Challenge to Political Parties." *West European Politics* 18: 116–139.
———, ed. 1993. *Pressure Groups.* Oxford: Oxford University Press.
Ridley, F. F., and Justin Greenwood, eds. 1998. "The Regulation of Lobbying." Special issue of *Parliamentary Affairs* 51, 4 (October).

Rosenberg, Jonathan. Forthcoming. "Latin America." In Clive S. Thomas, ed., *A Handbook of Research and Literature on Interest Groups*. Westport, CT: Greenwood.
Satori, Giovanni. 1976. *Parties and Party Systems*. Cambridge: Cambridge University Press.
Schmitter, Philippe C. 1979. "Still the Century of Corporatism?" In Philippe C. Schmitter and Gerhard Lehmbruch, eds., *Trends Toward Corporatist Intermediation*. Beverly Hills: Sage.
Selle, Per. "Parties and Voluntary Organizations: Strong or Weak Ties?" In Karre Strøm and Lars Svåsand, eds., *Challenges to Political Parties: The Case of Norway*. Ann Arbor: University of Michigan Press.
Skilling, H. Gordon. 1966. "Interest Groups and Communist Politics." *World Politics* 18, 3 (April): 435–451.
Strøm, Karre, and Lars Svåsand, eds. 1997. *Challenges to Political Parties: The Case of Norway*. Ann Arbor: University of Michigan Press.
Tarrow, Sidney. 1998. *Power in Movement: Social Movements and Contentious Politics*. Cambridge: Cambridge University Press.
Thomas, Clive S., ed. 1993. *First World Interest Groups*. Westport, CT: Greenwood.
Thomas, Clive S., and Ronald J. Hrebenar. 1995. "The Interest Group–Political Party Connection: Toward a Systematic Understanding." Paper presented at the annual meeting of the American Political Science Association, Chicago, September.
Tilly, Charles. 1984. "Social Movements and National Politics." In Charles Bright and Susan Harding, eds., *Statemaking and Social Movements*. Ann Arbor: University of Michigan Press.
Ware, Alan J. 1996. *Political Parties and Party Systems*. Oxford: Oxford University Press.
Williamson, Peter J. 1989. *Corporatism in Perspective: An Introductory Guide to Corporatist Theory*. London: Sage.
Wilson, Graham. 1990. *Interest Groups*. Oxford: Blackwell. Especially chapter 6, "Interest Groups and Political Parties."
Yishai, Yael. 1995. "Interest Groups and Political Parties: The Odd Couple." Paper presented at the annual meeting of the American Political Science Association, Chicago, September.
Zeigler, Harmon. 1993. *Political Parties in Industrial Democracies*. Itasca, IL: F. E. Peacock.

INDIVIDUAL COUNTRIES

Argentina

Catterberg, Edgardo. 1994. "Attitudes Towards Democracy in Argentina During the Transition Period." Reprinted in Jorge I. Domínguez, ed., *Parties, Elections, and Political Participation in Latin America*. New York: Garland.
Cavarozzi, Marcelo, and Oscar Landi. 1992. "Political Parties Under Alfonsín and Menem: The Effects of State Shrinking and the Devaluation of Democratic Politics." In Edward C. Epstein, ed., *The New Argentine Democracy: The Search for a Successful Formula*. Westport, CT: Praeger.
Feijoó, María del Carmen, and Marcela María Alejandra Nari. 1994. "Women and Democracy in Argentina." In Jane S. Jaquette, ed., *The Women's Movement in Latin America: Participation and Democracy*, 2d ed. Boulder: Westview.

Manzetti, Luigi. 1993. *Institutions, Parties, and Coalitions in Argentine Politics.* Pittsburgh: Pittsburgh University Press.
McGuire, James. 1995. "Political Parties and Democracy in Argentina." In Scott Mainwaring and Timothy R. Scully, eds., *Building Democratic Institutions: Party Systems in Latin America.* Stanford: Stanford University Press.
———. 1997. *Peronism Without Perón: Unions, Parties, and Democracy in Argentina.* Stanford: Stanford University Press.
Rock, David. 1987. "Political Movements in Argentina: A Sketch from Past and Present." In Monica Peralta-Ramos and Carlos H. Waisman, eds., *From Military Rule to Liberal Democracy in Argentina.* Boulder: Westview.
Snow, Peter G., and Luigi Manzetti. 1993. *Political Forces in Argentina,* 3d ed. Westport, CT: Praeger.

Britain

Baggott, R. 1995. *Pressure Groups Today.* Manchester: Manchester University Press.
Beer, Samuel H. 1980. "British Pressure Groups Revisited: Pluralistic Stagnation from the Fifties to the Seventies." *Public Administration Bulletin,* No. 32 (April): 5–16.
Finer, S. E. 1958. *Anonymous Empire.* London: Pall Mall.
Fisher, J. 1996. *British Political Parties.* London: Prentice-Hall.
Garner, R., and R. Kelly. 1998. *British Political Parties Today.* London: Macmillan.
Grant, Wyn. 1990. *Pressure Groups, Politics and Democracy in Britain.* London: Philip Allan.
Jordan, A. G., and J. J. Richardson. 1987. *Government and Pressure Groups in Britain.* Oxford: Clarendon.
Miller, Charles. 1987. *Lobbying Government: Understanding and Influencing the Corridors of Power.* Oxford: Basil Blackwell.
Ridley, F. F., and G. Jordan. 1998. *Protest Politics: Cause Groups and Campaigns.* Oxford: Oxford University Press.
Rush, M. 1990. "Parliament and Pressure Politics: An Overview." In M. Rush, ed., *Parliament and Pressure Politics.* Oxford: Clarendon.

The Czech Republic

Blahož, Josef, Lubomír Brokl, and Zdĕnka Mansfeldová. 1999. "Czech Political Parties and Cleavages After 1989." In Kay Lawson, Andrea Rommele, and Georgi Karasimeonov, eds., *Cleavages, Parties, and Voters: Studies from Bulgaria, the Czech Republic, Hungary, Poland, and Romania.* Westport, CT: Praeger.
Brokl, Lubomír. 1999. "Cleavages and Parties Prior to 1989 in the Czech Republic." In Kay Lawson, Andrea Rommele, and Georgi Karasimeonov, eds., *Cleavages, Parties, and Voters: Studies from Bulgaria, the Czech Republic, Hungary, Poland, and Romania.* Westport, CT: Praeger.
Čulík, Jan. 1996. "Czech Political Culture in the 1990s." *Britské listy* (Internet edition at www.jcu2@cableol.co.uk).
Orenstein, Mitchell, and Raj M. Desai. 1997. "State Power and Interest Group Formation: The Business Lobby in the Czech Republic." *Problems of Post-Communism* 44, 6 (November-December): 43–52.
Ramet, Sabrina Petra. 1991. "The Catholic Church in Czechoslovakia, 1948–1991." *Studies in Comparative Communism* 24, 4 (December): 377–394.

Wolchik, Sharon L. 1981. "Elite Strategy Toward Women in Czechoslovakia: Liberation or Mobilization?" *Studies in Comparative Communism* 14, 2–3 (summer/autumn): 123–142.

France

Appleton, Andrew, and Amy Mazur. 1991. "Transformation or Modernization: The Rhetoric and Reality of Gender and Party Politics in France." In Joni Lovenduski and Pippa Norris, eds., *Gender and Party Politics*. Thousand Oaks, CA: Sage.
Capdevielle, Jacques, and Rene Moriaux. 1991. "Les rapports partis-syndicats en France: contraints et équivoques." In Yves Meny, ed., *Ideologies, partis politiques, et groupes sociaux*. Paris: Presses de la fondation nationale des sciences politiques.
Daley, Anthony. 1992. "Remembrance of Things Past: The Union-Party Linkage in France." *International Journal of Political Economy* 22 (winter 1992–1993): 53–71.
Duverger, Maurice. 1951. *Les Partis Politiques*. Paris: PUF.
Meynaud, Jean. 1962. *Les Groupes de pression en France*. Paris: Armand Colin.
Wilson, Frank. 1982. *French Political Parties Under the Fifth Republic*. New York: Praeger.
———. 1987. *Interest Group Politics in France*. Cambridge: Cambridge University Press.

Germany

Crouch, Colin, and Anand Menon. 1997. "Organized Interests and the States." In Martin Rhodes, Paul Heywood, and Vincent Wright, eds., *Developments in West European Politics*. New York: St. Martin's.
Essen, Josef. 1986. "State, Business and Trade Unions in West Germany After the 'Political Wende.'" *West European Politics* 9 (April): 198–214.
Halfmann, Jost. 1989. "Social Change and Political Mobilization in West Germany." In Peter J. Katzenstein, ed., *Industry and Politics in West Germany: Toward the Third Republic*. Ithaca, NY: Cornell University Press.
Katzenstein, Peter J. 1989. "Stability and Change in the Emerging Third Republic." In Peter J. Katzenstein, ed., *Industry and Politics in West Germany: Toward the Third Republic*. Ithaca, NY: Cornell University Press.
Koopman, Ruud. 1995. *Democracy from Below: New Social Movements in West Germany*. Boulder: Westview.
Kropp, Sabine. 1997. "Interessenpolitik." In Oscar W. Gabriel and Everhard Holtmann, eds., *Handbuch Politisches System der Bundesrepublik Deutschland*. München: Oldenbourg Verlag.
Padgett, Stephen. 1993. "Party Democracy in the New Germany." In Stephen Padgett, ed., *Parties and Party Systems in the New Germany*. Brookfield, VT: Dartmouth.
Ronit, Karsten, and Volker Schneider. 1998. "The Strange Case of Regulating Lobbying in Germany." *Parliamentary Affairs* 51: 559–567.
Thelen, Kathleen. 1991. *Union in Parts: Labor Politics in Postwar Germany*. Ithaca, NY: Cornell University Press.

Israel

Arian, Asher. 1993. "Israel: Interest Group Pluralism Constrained." In Clive S. Thomas, ed., *First World Interest Groups: A Comparative Perspective.* Westport, CT: Greenwood.

Ben Eliezer, Uri. 1993. "The Meaning of Political Participation in a Nonliberal Democracy." *Comparative Politics* 25: 397–412.

Drezon-Tepler, Marcia. 1990. *Interest Groups and Political Change in Israel.* Albany: State University of New York Press.

Lehman-Wilzig, Sam N. 1992. *Wildfire: Grassroots Revolts in Israel in the Post-Socialist Era.* Albany: State University of New York Press.

Medding, Peter Y. 1972. *Mapai in Israel: Political Organization and Government in a New Society.* Cambridge: Cambridge University Press.

Yanai, Nathan. 1981. *Party Leadership in Israel: Maintenance and Change.* Ramat Gan: Turtledove.

Yishai, Yael. 1991. *Land of Paradoxes: Interest Politics in Israel.* Albany: State University of New York Press.

———. 1995. "Interest Parties: The Thin Line Between Groups and Parties in the Israeli Electoral Process." In Kay Lawson, ed., *How Political Parties Work.* New York: Praeger.

———. 1997. "Legislators and Interest Groups: Some Observations on the Israeli Scene." *Journal of Legislative Studies* 3: 89–111.

Italy

Bardi, Luciano, and Piero Ignazi. 1998. "The Italian Party System: The Effective Magnitude of an Earthquake." In Piero Ignazi and Colette Ysmal, eds., *The Organization of Political Parties in Southern Europe.* Westport, CT: Praeger.

Beccalli, Bianca. 1994. "The Modern Women's Movement in Italy." *New Left Review* 204 (March-April): 86–112.

Bedani, Gino. 1995. *Politics and Ideology in the Italian Workers' Movement: Union Development and the Changing Role of the Catholic and Communist Subcultures in Postwar Italy.* Oxford: Berg.

Diani, Mario. 1995. *Green Networks: A Structural Analysis of the Italian Environmental Movement.* Edinburgh: Edinburgh University Press.

Golden, Miriam. 1986. "Interest Representation, Party Systems, and the State: Italy in Comparative Perspective." *Comparative Politics* 18, 3: 279–301.

Lanzalaco, Luca. 1993. "Interest Groups in Italy: From Pressure Activity to Policy Networks." In Jeremy J. Richardson, ed., *Pressure Groups.* Oxford: Oxford University Press.

LaPalombara, Joseph. 1964. *Interest Groups in Italian Politics.* Princeton: Princeton University Press.

Newell, James J., and Martin Bull. 1997. "Party Organisations and Alliances in Italy in the 1990s: A Revolution of Sorts." *West European Politics* 20, 1: 81–109.

Regini, Marino, and Ida Regalia. 1997. "Employers, Unions and the State: The Resurgence of Concertation in Italy?" In Martin Bull and Martin Rhodes, eds., *Crisis and Transition in Italian Politics.* London: Frank Cass.

Japan

Allinson, Gary D. 1987. "Japan's Keidanren and Its New Leadership." *Pacific Affairs* 60, 3: 385–407.

Curtis, Gerald L. 1975. "Big Business and Political Influence." In Ezra F. Vogel, ed., *Modern Japanese Organization and Decision-Making*. Berkeley: University of California Press.
George, Aurelia. 1981. "The Japanese Farm Lobby and Agricultural Policy Making." *Pacific Affairs* 54, 3: 409–430.
———. 1988. "Japanese Interest Group Behavior: An Institutional Approach." In J. A. A. Stockwin, ed., *Dynamic and Immobilist Politics in Japan*. London: Macmillan.
Hrebenar, Ronald J. 2000. *The New Japanese Party System*. Boulder: Westview.
Ishida, Takeshi. 1974. "Interest Groups Under a Semi-permanent Government Party: The Case of Japan." *Annals of the American Academy of Political and Social Science* 413 (May): 1–9.
Krauss, Ellis, and B. L. Simcock. 1980. "Citizens' Movements: The Growth and Impact of Environmental Protest in Japan." In Kurt Steiner, ed., *Political Opposition and Local Politics in Japan*. Princeton: Princeton University Press.
Pemple, T. J., and Keiichi Tsunekawa. 1979. "Corporatism Without Labor? The Japanese Anomaly." In Philippe C. Schmitter and Gerhard Lehmbruch, eds., *Trends Toward Corporatist Intermediation*. Beverly Hills: Sage.

Mexico

Alcocer V., Jorge. 1995. "Recent Electoral Reforms in Mexico: Prospects for Real Multiparty Democracy." In Riordan Roett, ed., *The Challenge of Institutional Reform in Mexico*. Boulder: Lynne Rienner.
Carr, Barry. 1991. "Labor and the Political Left in Mexico." In Kevin J. Middlebrook, ed., *Unions, Workers, and the State in Mexico*. U.S.-Mexico Contemporary Perspectives Series, 2. San Diego: Center for U.S.-Mexican Studies, University of California San Diego.
Delli Santi, Angela M. 1979. "The Private Sector, Business Organizations, and International Influence: A Case Study of Mexico." In Richard R. Fagen, ed., *Capitalism and the State in U.S.–Latin American Relations*. Stanford: Stanford University Press.
Domínguez, Jorge I. 1999. "The Transformation of Mexico's Electoral and Party Systems, 1988–97: An Introduction." In Domínguez Poiré and Alejandro Poiré, eds., *Toward Mexico's Democratization*. New York: Routledge.
Hernández Rodríguez, Rogelio. 1998. "El Partido Revolucionario Institucional." In Mónica Serrano, ed., *Governing Mexico: Political Parties and Elections*. London: Institute of Latin American Studies, University of London.
Luna, Matilde. 1995. "Entrepreneurial Interests and Political Action in Mexico: Facing the Demands of Economic Modernization." In Riordan Roett, ed., *The Challenge of Institutional Reform in Mexico*. Boulder: Lynne Rienner.
Serrano, Mónica, ed. 1998. *Governing Mexico: Political Parties and Elections*. London: Institute of Latin American Studies, University of London.
Story, Dale. 1986. *The Mexican Ruling Party: Stability and Authority*. New York: Praeger.

Poland

Kenney, Padraic. 1999. "The Gender of Resistance in Communist Poland." *American Historical Review* 104, 2 (April): 399–425.
Morawski, Witold, ed. 1994. *Zmierzch Socjalizmu Panstwowego* [The Dusk of State Socialism]. Warsaw: PWN.

Ost, David. 1988. "Indispensable Ambiguity: Solidarity's Internal Authority Structure." *Studies in Comparative Communism* 21, 2 (summer): 189–201.
———. 1990. *Solidarity and the Politics of Anti-Politics: Reform and Opposition in Poland Since 1968.* Philadelphia: Temple University Press.
Pankow, Wlodzimierz. 1993. *Work Institutions in Transformation.* Warsaw: Friedrich Ebert.
Penn, Shana. 1994. "The National Secret." *Journal of Women's History* 5 (winter): 54–69.

Spain

Fishman, Robert. 1990. *Working-Class Organization and the Return to Democracy in Spain.* Ithaca, NY: Cornell University Press.
Garvía, Roberto. 1995. "Corporatism, Public Policy and Welfare: The Case of the Spanish Blind." *Journal of European Public Policy* 2, 2: 243–259.
Gillespie, Richard. 1990. "The Break-up of the 'Socialist Family': Party-Union Relations in Spain, 1982–89." *West European Politics* 13, 1: 47–62.
Hamann, Kerstin. 1997. "The Legislative Process and Interest Groups in Spain." Paper presented at the Midwest Political Science Association meeting, Chicago, April.
Martínez, Robert E. 1993. *Business and Democracy in Spain.* Westport, CT: Praeger.
Valiente, Celia. 1997. "The Feminist Movement in Post-authoritarian Portugal and Spain (1974–1997)." Paper presented at the American Political Science Association meeting, Washington, D.C., August.
Wozniak, Lynne. 1992. "The Dissolution of Party-Union Relations in Spain." *International Journal of Political Economy* 22, 4: 73–90.

Sweden

Arter, D. 1994. "The War of the Roses: Conflict and Cohesion in the Swedish Social Democratic Party." In D. S. Bell and E. Shaw, eds., *Conflict and Cohesion in Western European Social Democratic Parties.* London: Pinter.
Bäck, M., and T. Möller. 1997. *Partier och organisationer.* Stockholm: Publica.
Hermansson, J. 1993. *Politik som intressekamp: Parlamentariskt beslutsfattande och organiserade intressen i Sverige.* Stockholm: Norstedts Juridik.
http://www.saco.se. SACO [Swedish Confederation of Professional Associations] Internet site.
http://www.tco.se. TCO [Swedish Confederation of Professional Employees] Internet site.
Lewin, L. 1994. "The Rise and Decline of Corporatism: The Case of Sweden." *European Journal of Political Research* 26, 1: 59–79.
Pierre, J., and A. Widfeldt. 1994. "Party Organizations in Sweden: Colossuses with Feet of Clay or Flexible Pillars of Government?" In R. S. Katz and P. Mair, eds., *How Parties Organize: Change and Adaptation in Party Organizations in Western Democracies.* London: Sage.
Rothstein, B. 1996. *The Social Democratic State: The Swedish Model and the Bureaucratic Problem of Social Reforms.* Pittsburgh: Pittsburgh University Press.
Widfeldt, A. 1999. *Linking Parties with People? Party Membership in Sweden 1960–1997.* Aldershot: Ashgate.

United States

Baer, Denise L., and Julie A. Dolan. 1994. "Intimate Connections: Political Interests and Group Activity in State and Local Parties." *American Review of Politics* 15 (summer): 257–289.

Berry, Jeffrey M. 1980. "Public Interest vs. Party System." *Society* 17 (May-June): 42–48.

———. 1997. *The Interest Group Society*, 3d ed. New York: Addison Wesley Longman. Especially chapter 3, "The Party Connection."

Bibby, John F., and Thomas M. Holbrook. 1999. "Parties and Elections." In Virginia Gray, Russell L. Hanson, and Herbert Jacob, eds., *Politics in the American States: A Comparative Analysis*, 7th ed. Washington, DC: CQ.

Cigler, Allan J. 1993. "Political Parties and Interest Groups: Competitors, Collaborators and Uneasy Allies." In Eric M. Uslaner, ed., *American Political Parties: A Reader*. Itasca, IL: F. E. Peacock.

Eldersveld, Samual J. 1982. *Political Parties in American Society*. New York: Basic.

Hrebenar, Ronald J. 1997. *Interest Group Politics in America*, 3d ed. Armonk, NY: M. E. Sharpe.

Hrebenar, Ronald J., Matthew J. Burbank, and Robert C. Benedict. 1999. *Political Parties, Interest Groups and Political Campaigns*. Boulder: Westview. Especially chapter 11, "Parties, Interest Groups and Campaigns: The New Style of American Politics."

Key, V. O., Jr. 1964. *Politics, Parties and Pressure Groups*, 5th ed. New York: Thomas Y. Crowell.

Lowi, Theodore J. 1979. *The End of Liberalism: The Second Republic of the United States*, 2d ed. New York: W. W. Norton.

Maisel, L. Sandy. 1999. *Parties and Elections in America: The Electoral Process*, 3d ed. Lanham, MD: Rowman and Littlefield. Especially chapter 6, "Organized Groups in the Political Process."

Morehouse, Sarah McCally. 1997. "Interest Groups, Parties and Policies in the American States." Paper presented at the annual meeting of the American Political Science Association, Washington, D.C., September.

Paddock, Joel, and Allan J. Cigler. 1997. "The Interest Sources of Political Party Activism." Paper presented at the Western Political Science Association, Los Angeles, March.

Ryden, David K. 1996. *Representation in Crisis: The Constitution, Interest Groups and Political Parties*. Albany: State University of New York Press.

Salisbury, Robert H. 1979. "Why No Corporatism in America?" In Philippe C. Schmitter and Gerhard Lehmbruch. eds., *Trends Toward Corporatist Intermediation*. Beverly Hills: Sage.

Thomas, Clive S., and Ronald J. Hrebenar. 1999. "Interest Groups in the States." In Virginia Gray, Russell L. Hanson, and Herbert Jacob, eds., *Politics in the American States: A Comparative Analysis*, 7th ed. Washington, DC: CQ.

———. 1999. "Toward a Comprehensive Understanding of the Political Party–Interest Group Relationship in the American States." Paper presented at the Western Political Science Association, Seattle, March.

Truman, David B. 1971. *The Governmental Process*, 2d ed. New York: Alfred A. Knopf.

Wiggins, Charles W., Keith E. Hamm, and Charles G. Bell. 1992. "Interest-Group and Party Influence Agents in the Legislative Process: A Comparative State Analysis." *Journal of Politics* 54, 1 (February): 82–100.

Yonish, Steven. 1998. "Impact of Associational Life on Mass Linkages to the American Party System." Paper presented at the American Political Science Association, Boston, August-September.

Notes

CHAPTER 1

I thank Grant Jordan, William Maloney, and Yael Yishai for their comments on drafts of this chapter. Parts of the chapter draw upon their work.

1. This, however, is a perspective of the essential attributes of political parties based on their operation in traditional, mainly U.S. and Western European–style democracies. In contrast to a view of parties as broad-based coalitions of individuals and groups seeking to win formal control of government through competitive elections, McGuire (1997, 7) defined political movements as "a set of people who share a common political identity and whose leaders aspire to full and permanent control of the state through the most readily available means, electoral or not." Latin Americanists refer to this phenomenon as *movimientismo*. See Chapters 11–14 (the Czech Republic, Poland, Argentina, and Mexico) for instances of this contrasting view of party.

2. The time period and geographical location of the scholar have also affected the use of terminology in interest group studies. For example, until the late 1960s in the United States (and in some cases beyond), the term *pressure group* was preferred for what is now termed an *interest group*. Many European scholars (particularly those in Britain) still use the pressure group designation.

3. There is also a literature on the role of interests and their connection with parties in authoritarian regimes, particularly communist systems, a consideration of which is beyond the focus of this book. However, a brief review of this literature is provided in Chapter 11 on the Czech Republic.

4. The explanation of this model and its critique draws on Sousa (forthcoming).

5. It might also be assumed that there would be a Marxist and a neo-Marxist view on party-group relations in Western democracies, but this does not appear to be the case. These perspectives are primarily concerned with the dominance of class and class conflict in the political economy, and they focus on the state apparatus and factors that lead state managers to act in the interests of capital. No coherent perspective of party-group relations arises from this central concern. See, for example, what is generally recognized as the classic work on Marxism and politics by Miliband (1969, 1977).

6. For an excellent encapsulation of the reasons for, and literature on, party decline, see Strøm and Svåsand (1997, chapter 1, 12–20).

7. Some scholars have categorized the forms of party-group relations within particular countries, as did, for example, Sternberger (1952–1953) on Germany and Meynaud (1962) on France. They are detailed in the individual country chapters and will be incorporated into the general synthesis of forms of party-group relations in the concluding chapter. However, in setting out these initial guidelines we confine the synthesis to works concerned with forms of party-group relationships developed for liberal democracies in general.

CHAPTER 2

1. Not all trade unions in Britain are affiliated to the Labour Party. As Fisher (1996, 68) explained it: "Only around 11 percent of the 300 or so trade unions in Britain are affiliated to the Labour Party. Admittedly, this represents around 53 percent of trade union members. . . . Only around two-thirds of trade unions with political funds are affiliated to the Labour Party, and those that are only use on average two-thirds of their political funds for Labour Party purposes."

2. As Panebianco (1988, 263) pointed out, Kirchheimer's catchall thesis was not that a party's "electoral following was so heterogeneous as to represent the whole social spectrum and whose connection with the original class gardée had completely disappeared. . . . The transformation of the mass party into [a] catch-all party was . . . less striking; ties with the old class gardée loosened and weakened; the party opened its doors to different social groups."

3. For a detailed account of the organizational and policy changes implemented under the New Labour project, see Coxall and Robins (1998, 116–121).

4. Bernie Ecclestone donated £1 million to the Labour Party prior to the 1997 general election. Following the election Ecclestone was negotiating with the Labour Party over future donations at the same time the Labour government was considering banning tobacco advertising in sports. The government decided to grant Formula One an exemption, which led to opposition claims that the special exemption was in some way linked to the past and possible future donations from Ecclestone. On advice from Sir Patrick Neill, chair of the Committee on Standards in Public Life, the Labour Party returned the £1 million to Ecclestone.

5. Proposals for reform of party funding include full public disclosure of donations (in cash or in-kind) to political parties of £5,000 or more nationally (£1,000 or more locally); an end to blind trusts; no more foreign donations; anonymous donations of £50 or more to political parties banned; a £20 million national campaign expenditure limit in a general election; auditing and accounting rules for political parties; no new state funding, but tax relief on donations up to £500; scrutiny by an Honours Scrutiny Committee if a connection might exist between the award of an honor (such as a knighthood) and a current or previous political donation to the governing party; increased funding for opposition parties in Parliament; controls on organizations and individuals (other than a political party) spending more than £25,000 nationally on political activity during a general election; continued free access to television and radio for party political broadcasts during an election, but continuation of the ban on political advertising on television and radio at other times; shareholder consent for company donations to parties; and an equal voice for both sides of the argument in a referendum. For fuller information on these proposals, see http://www.open.gov.uk/cspl/reports8.htm.

6. The Oxfam document was not a public or published document but was for internal purposes. Oxfam sent it to the authors of this chapter for review and allowed the essence of it to be used here.

CHAPTER 4

1. Thus, the Liberals had traditional links with two popular movements. The Liberal Party was formed as a coalition between a group of city radicals and a Free-Minded group that had strength in rural areas and was linked to the temperance and Free Church movements. This dualism led to tensions. In 1923 the two factions went their separate ways, and in 1934 the party was reunited under the name Folkpartiet, renamed Folkpartiet Liberalerna (People's Party Liberals) in 1993.
2. In a critical scrutiny of the SAP-LO relationship, Ljungberg (1991, 170ff) estimated that financial donations from the unions to the Social Democrats totaled SEK 23 million (about $2.9 million). If accurate, this would have been 11 percent of total party income, compared with 8.2 percent reported by SAP (SAP annual reports 1990–1992).
3. For the membership strength of Swedish political parties, see Widfeldt (1999).
4. According to Ljungberg (1991, 171), the Municipal Workers Union donated SEK 5 million (about $700,000) to SAP for the 1985 election campaign. Before the 1988 campaign, the union recommended that all local branches assign one staff member to work full-time on the campaign (Ljungberg 1991, 161).
5. These figures are from my analysis of the Swedish election studies. I thank Per Hedberg and Sören Holmberg, Department of Political Science, Göteborg University, for providing these data.

CHAPTER 5

1. Texts on political parties tend to be of two types: those dealing with parties in general and those concerned mainly with parties in the electoral process. General treatments include Beck and Sorauf (1992); Crotty (1984); Eldersveld and Walton (1999); Keefe (1991); Key (1964); Maisel (1990); and Uslaner (1993). Those focusing on elections include Bibby (1987); Hrebenar, Burbank, and Benedict (1999); and Maisel (1999).
2. The major texts on interest groups include Berry (1997); Cigler and Loomis (1998); Hrebenar (1997); Mahood (2000); Nownes (2001); Petracca (1992); Salisbury (1970); Schlozman and Tierney (1986); Truman (1971); Wootton (1985); and Zeigler and Peak (1972).

CHAPTER 10

1. I exclude the Catholic Church from my discussion since the primary purpose of the church is not to "influence public policy" (see definition of interest groups in Chapter 1 of this book). This is not to deny the substantial political influence the church has exerted in Spain. On the conceptualization of the church as part of civil society, especially during the Franco regime, see Pérez-Díaz (1993, chapter 3).

2. It is illustrative that Foweraker's (1994) chapter, "Popular Political Organization and Democratization: A Comparison of Spain and Mexico," focuses exclusively on unions.

3. The CEPYME joined the CEOE in 1980 but maintains organizational independence (see Newton 1997, 258).

4. Liebert (1995a, 313) characterized the relationship between the CEOE and the PSOE as one of "antagonistic cooperation."

5. Results from author's surveys of and interviews with members of parliament, spring 1998.

6. The moderation of the party had already begun in the late 1970s, and socialist rhetoric was virtually eliminated after the extraordinary party congress in 1979. Nonetheless, in 1982 the PSOE campaigned on a program advocating moderate leftist policies, a redistributive economic program, and the creation of new employment (see Boix 1998; Hamann 2000; Share 1989; W. Smith 1998).

7. Hall (1992, 96) has defined institutions as "the formal rules, compliance procedures, and customary practices that structure the relationships between individuals in the polity and economy. Institutions may be more or less formal but invariably serve to regularize the behavior of the individuals who operate within them."

8. The upper house, the Senate, lacks effective influence on the legislative process.

9. A recent example is the debate over liberalization of abortion. Since this issue has a considerable moral dimension, a deputy of the PP who opposed his party's stance was given permission to be absent during the vote to avoid the conflict of having to either break party discipline or vote against his conscience (interview with PP deputy, June 1998). In 1987 some high-ranking UGT leaders (among them Secretary-General Nicolas Redondo), who had been elected to parliament on the PSOE slate, voted against their party on the budget proposal. They subsequently resigned from parliament.

CHAPTER 11

1. Interview with Miroslav Svoboda, a private farmer in western Bohemia, 3 January 1999.

2. There is no Czech term for *interest group,* so Czechs have adopted the English phrase. There is a monthly publication called *Lobby* and a website dedicated to lobbying: www.lobby.cz.

3. See "Czech Moravian Chamber of Trade Unions—ČMKOS" at www.wea.org.ik/eurwea/english/affiliate/czech1.html.

4. Government of the Czech Republic at www.czech.cz; private communications from Andrew T. Green, visiting professor, University of Southern California, and specialist in Czech trade unions, 18 June and 9 December 1999.

5. Interview with Štepanka Korytová-Magstadt, professor at Zapadoćeská univerzita (the University of West Bohemia) in Plzeň, 14 February 1999.

6. Interview with aerospace engineer Jirí Fidranský, 31 December 1998.

CHAPTER 12

1. For an overview of the role of Solidarity as an opposition force and its pursuit of antipolitics, see Ost (1990, esp. chapters 1–3).

2. For one of the best accounts of the changing role of the union in the new political system, see Staniszkis (1991). On how Solidarity's confused identity has affected electoral outcomes, see Grabowska and Krzeminski (1991).

3. These were Walesa's comments at a meeting of Solidarity's National Commission just after the formation of a Solidarity government, cited in "Ile Wytrzymacie?" *Tygodnik Solidarnosc*, No. 18, 29 September 1989: 2.

4. On the difficult clash between Western and Eastern European feminism, see Funk and Mueller (1993) and the special section "Feminisms" in the Hungarian social science quarterly *Replika* (Budapest, special issue, 1996), particularly the articles by Maria Nemenyi ("The Social Construction of Women's Roles"), Jirina Skilova ("Why Feminism Isn't Successful in the Czech Republic"), and Madalina Nicolaescu ("Utopian Desires and Western Representations of Femininity").

5. For these reasons, women's prominent role in underground Solidarity has still not been publicized inside Poland. The activists have been averse to doing so because they saw themselves as Solidarity people above all else. Male Solidarity activists have also refrained from mentioning it—some because they do not recognize gender as important, and others because they do recognize gender as important and consciously seek to revive traditional gender roles, with males dominant in public life. For an account of women in underground Solidarity, see Penn (1994). For a more theoretical account, see Kenney (1999).

6. In some cases the intricacies can be rather bizarre, as with the two retiree parties created in 1997. Since groups are perceived as more legitimate than parties (which are commonly perceived as organizations run by a small coterie of people who talk about universal interests only to take care of their own) but parties need the votes to win, the SLD and AWS created their own retiree interest groups, which then announced they were running candidates themselves. It is difficult to understand the relationship of groups and parties because it is challenging to even begin to draw the lines between the two.

CHAPTER 13

My sincere thanks to Fernando Lopez-Alves, Alistair Hattingh, and Clive Thomas for their kind support and many valuable suggestions during the preparation of this chapter.

1. Numerous smaller parties exist at the national and provincial levels. Based on survey data, Catterberg (1994, 50) estimated that the combined registration of the two major parties constitutes approximately 20 percent of the electorate. No other party can claim 1 percent. Those who sympathize with and vote for these two parties account for the vast majority of citizens. At the provincial level we see a "more varied competitive dynamic" in which smaller conservative parties often "contest the hegemony of Radicalism and Peronism in a multiparty competitive setting" or even dominate electoral politics (Gibson 1996, 222). One standard explanation for the elites' failure to form strong national parties is indeed the long-standing regional cleavages.

2. The Catholic nationalists were most prominent politically during the periods of military rule. For an excellent treatment of this subject, see Rock (1993). The Third World Priests emerged in 1967 but had already begun to decline by the mid-1970s.

3. Snow (1996, 99) noted that the Christian Democratic Party has never achieved 5 percent of the national vote. The party split in the 1970s over Peronism but reunited in 1983, electing only one member to Congress.

CHAPTER 14

1. There are nearly as many critiques of existing models as there are studies of Mexican postrevolutionary politics. Four of the better and more concise discussions are Hansen (1971), Purcell (1975), Hamilton (1982), and Centeno (1994).

2. There are many other reasons for the PRI victory in 1994, such as the fear of chaos engendered by the assassination of Colosio and the Chiapas uprising, but a full discussion of these arguments is beyond the scope of this chapter. For useful analysis see, for example, Domínguez and Poiré (1999, chapter 2).

References

Acuña, Carlos H. 1995. "Intereses empresarios, dictadura y democracia en la Argentina actual (o sobre por qué la burguesia abandona estrategias autoritarias y opta por la estabilidad democratica)." In Carlos H. Acuña, ed., *La nueva matriz politica Argentina*. Buenos Aires: Ediciones Nueva Visión.

Adrogué, Gerardo. 1995. "El nuevo sistema partidario argentino." In Carlos H. Acuña, ed., *La nueva matriz politica Argentina*. Buenos Aires: Ediciones Nueva Visión.

Agh, Atilla. 1998. *The Politics of Central Europe*. London: Sage.

Aguilar Camín, H., and Lorenzo Meyer. 1993. *In the Shadow of the Mexican Revolution: Contemporary Mexican History, 1910–1989*. Trans. by Luis Alberto Fierro. Austin: University of Texas Press.

Albinsson, P. 1986. *Skiftningar i blått. Förändringar i Moderata Samlingspartiets riksorganisation 1960–1985*. Lund: Kommunfakta.

Alcocer V., Jorge. 1995. "Recent Electoral Reforms in Mexico: Prospects for Real Multiparty Democracy." In Riordan Roett, ed., *The Challenge of Institutional Reform in Mexico*. Boulder: Lynne Rienner.

Alderman, Geoffrey. 1984. *Pressure Groups and Government in Great Britain*. London: Longman.

Aldrich, John H., and David W. Rohde. 1997–1998. "The Transition to Republican Rule in the House: Implications for Theories of Congressional Politics." *Political Science Quarterly* 112: 541–567.

Allinson, Gary D. 1987. "Japan's Keidanren and Its New Leadership." *Pacific Affairs* 60, 3: 385–407.

Almond, Gabriel A. 1958. "A Comparative Study of Interest Groups and the Political Process." *American Political Science Review* 52 (March): 270–282.

Almond, Gabriel A., and G. Bingham Powell. 1966. *Comparative Government: A Developmental Approach*. Boston: Little, Brown.

———. 1988. *Comparative Politics Today: A World View*, 4th ed. Glenview, IL: Scott, Foresman and Little, Brown.

Alvarez Béjar, Alejandro. 1991. "Economic Crises and the Labor Movement in Mexico." In Kevin J. Middlebrook, ed., *Unions, Workers, and the State in Mexico*. U.S.-Mexico Contemporary Perspectives Series, 2. San Diego: Center for U.S.-Mexican Studies, University of California San Diego.

Ambler, John. 1996. "Conflict and Consensus in French Education." In John Keeler and Martin Schain, eds., *Chirac's Challenge: Liberalization, Europeanization, and Malaise in France.* New York: St. Martin's.

Amsden, Jon. 1972. *Collective Bargaining and Class Conflict in Spain.* London: Weidenfeld and Nicholson.

Appleton, Andrew, and Amy Mazur. 1991. "Transformation or Modernization: The Rhetoric and Reality of Gender and Party Politics in France." In Joni Lovenduski and Pippa Norris, eds., *Gender and Party Politics.* Thousand Oaks, CA: Sage.

APSA (American Political Science Association Committee on Political Parties). 1950. *Toward a More Responsible Two Party System.* New York: Rinehart.

Arian, Asher. 1989. *Politics in Israel: The Second Generation.* Chatham, NJ: Chatham House.

———. 1993. "Israel: Interest Group Pluralism Constrained." In Clive S. Thomas, ed., *First World Interest Groups: A Comparative Perspective.* Westport, CT: Greenwood.

———. 1998. *The Second Republic: Politics in Israel.* Chatham, NJ: Chatham House.

Arter, D. 1994. "The War of the Roses: Conflict and Cohesion in the Swedish Social Democratic Party." In D. S. Bell and E. Shaw, eds., *Conflict and Cohesion in Western European Social Democratic Parties.* London: Pinter.

———. 1999a. *Scandinavian Politics Today.* Manchester: Manchester University Press.

———. 1999b. "Sweden: A Mild Case of 'Electoral Instability Syndrome'?" In D. Broughton and M. Donovan, eds., *Changing Party Systems in Western Europe.* London: Pinter.

Ashby, Joe C. 1963. *Organized Labor and the Mexican Revolution Under Lázaro Cárdenas.* Chapel Hill: University of North Carolina Press.

Avià, Marc, and Pedro Cruz. n.d. *Guía de ONGs.* Premià de Mar: Ediciones Tikal.

Bäck, M., and T. Möller. 1997. *Partier och organisationer.* Stockholm: Publica.

Baer, Denise L., and Julie A. Dolan. 1994. "Intimate Connections: Political Interests and Group Activity in State and Local Parties." *American Review of Politics* 15 (summer): 257–289.

Baggott, R. 1995. *Pressure Groups Today.* Manchester: Manchester University Press.

Ball, Linda. 1997. "Public Money, Political Parties, and Corruption: The Italian Case." *Italian Politics and Society* 48: 50–60.

Bardi, Luciano, and Piero Ignazi. 1998. "The Italian Party System: The Effective Magnitude of an Earthquake." In Piero Ignazi and Colette Ysmal, eds., *The Organization of Political Parties in Southern Europe.* Westport, CT: Praeger.

Barnes, Samuel H. 1977. *Representation in Italy: Institutionalized Tradition and Electoral Choice.* Chicago: University of Chicago Press.

Baumgartner, Frank R., and Beth L. Leech. 1998. *Basic Interests: The Importance of Groups in Politics and in Political Science.* Princeton: Princeton University Press.

Beccalli, Bianca. 1994. "The Modern Women's Movement in Italy." *New Left Review* 204 (March-April): 86–112.

Beck, Paul Allen, and Frank J. Sorauf. 1992. *Party Politics in America,* 7th ed. New York: HarperCollins.

Bedani, Gino. 1995. *Politics and Ideology in the Italian Workers' Movement: Union Development and the Changing Role of the Catholic and Communist Subcultures in Postwar Italy.* Oxford: Berg.

Beer, Samuel H. 1980. "British Pressure Groups Revisited: Pluralistic Stagnation from the Fifties to the Seventies." *Public Administration Bulletin*, No. 32 (April): 5–16.

Ben Eliezer, Uri. 1993. "The Meaning of Political Participation in a Nonliberal Democracy." *Comparative Politics* 25: 397–412.

Berger, Suzanne D., ed. 1981. *Organizing Interests in Western Europe: Pluralism, Corporatism and the Transformation of Politics*. New York: Cambridge University Press.

Berry, Jeffrey M. 1980. "Public Interest vs. Party System." *Society* 17 (May-June): 42–48.

———. 1997. *The Interest Group Society*, 3d ed. New York: Addison Wesley Longman.

Bibby, John F. 1987. *Politics, Parties, and Elections in America*. Chicago: Nelson-Hall.

Bibby, John F., and Thomas M. Holbrook. 1999. "Parties and Elections." In Virginia Gray, Russell L. Hanson, and Herbert Jacob, eds., *Politics in the American States: A Comparative Analysis*, 7th ed. Washington, DC: CQ.

Bisschop, Gita. 1996. "Reviving the Environment's Political Role." *Transition* 2: 42–43, 64.

Blahož, Josef, Lubomír Brokl, and Zdĕnka Mansfeldová. 1999. "Czech Political Parties and Cleavages After 1989." In Kay Lawson, Andrea Rommele, and Georgi Karasimeonov, eds., *Cleavages, Parties, and Voters: Studies from Bulgaria, the Czech Republic, Hungary, Poland, and Romania*. Westport, CT: Praeger.

Boix, Carles. 1998. *Political Parties, Growth, and Equality*. New York: Cambridge University Press.

Boyle, John H. 1993. *Modern Japan: The American Nexus*. Fort Worth, TX: Harcourt Brace Jovanovich.

Brokl, Lubomír. 1999. "Cleavages and Parties Prior to 1989 in the Czech Republic." In Kay Lawson, Andrea Rommele, and Georgi Karasimeonov, eds., *Cleavages, Parties, and Voters: Studies from Bulgaria, the Czech Republic, Hungary, Poland, and Romania*. Westport, CT: Praeger.

Brown, A. H. 1966. "Pluralistic Trends in Czechoslovakia." *Soviet Studies* 17, 4 (April): 453–472.

———. 1972. "Political Change in Czechoslovakia." In Leonard Schapiro, ed., *Political Opposition in One-Party States*. London: Macmillan.

Brown, Lyle C. 1979. "Cárdenas: Creating a Campesino Power Base for Presidential Policy." In George Wolfskill and Douglas Richmond, eds., *Essays on the Mexican Revolution: Revisionist Views of the Leaders*. Austin: University of Texas Press.

Bruhn, Kathleen. 1998. "The Partido de la Revolución Democrática: Diverging Approaches to Competition." In Mónica Serrano, ed., *Governing Mexico: Political Parties and Elections*. London: Institute of Latin American Studies, University of London.

Burstein, Paul. 1998. "Interest Organizations, Political Parties and the Study of Democratic Politics." In Anne N. Costain and Andrew S. McFarland, eds., *Social Movements and American Political Institutions*. Lanham, MD: Rowman and Littlefield.

Camp, Roderic Ai. 1996. *Politics in Mexico*, 2nd ed. New York: Oxford University Press.

Capdevielle, Jacques, and Rene Moriaux. 1991. "Les rapports partis-syndicats en France: contraints et équivoques." In Yves Mény, ed., *Ideologies, partis poli-*

tiques, et groupes sociaux. Paris: Presses de la fondation nationale des sciences politiques.

Carolina Online. Various dates. Prague: Faculty of Social Sciences of Charles University (Internet edition at www.carolina@cuni.net).

Carr, Barry. 1991. "Labor and the Political Left in Mexico." In Kevin J. Middlebrook, ed., *Unions, Workers, and the State in Mexico.* U.S.-Mexico Contemporary Perspectives Series, 2. San Diego: Center for U.S.-Mexican Studies, University of California San Diego.

Carter, N., H. Evans, K. Alderman, and S. Gorham. 1998. "Europe, Goldsmith and the Referendum Party." In F. F. Ridley and G. Jordan, eds., *Protest Politics: Cause Groups and Campaigns.* Oxford: Oxford University Press.

Catterberg, Edgardo. 1994. "Attitudes Towards Democracy in Argentina During the Transition Period." Reprinted in Jorge I. Domínguez, ed., *Parties, Elections, and Political Participation in Latin America.* New York: Garland.

Cavarozzi, Marcelo. 1986. "Political Cycles in Argentina Since 1955." In Guillermo O'Donnell, Philippe C. Schmitter, and Laurence Whitehead, eds., *Transitions from Authoritarian Rule: Latin America.* Baltimore: Johns Hopkins University Press.

Cavarozzi, Marcelo, and Oscar Landi. 1992. "Political Parties Under Alfonsín and Menem: The Effects of State Shrinking and the Devaluation of Democratic Politics." In Edward C. Epstein, ed., *The New Argentine Democracy: The Search for a Successful Formula.* Westport, CT: Praeger.

Cawson, Alan. 1986. *Corporatism and Political Theory.* Oxford: Basil Blackwell.

Centeno, Miguel Ángel. 1994. *Democracy Within Reason: Technocratic Revolution in Mexico.* University Park: Pennsylvania State University Press.

Chalmers, Douglas A., Scott B. Martin, and Kerianne Piester. 1997. "Associative Networks: New Structures of Representation for the Popular Sectors?" In Douglas A. Chalmers et al., eds., *The New Politics of Inequality in Latin America: Rethinking Participation and Representation.* New York: Oxford University Press.

Chari, Raj. 1999. "Spanish Socialists, Privatising the Right Way?" In Paul Heywood, ed., *Politics and Policy in Democratic Spain.* London: Frank Cass.

Cigler, Allan J. 1993. "Political Parties and Interest Groups: Competitors, Collaborators and Uneasy Allies." In Eric M. Uslaner, ed., *American Political Parties: A Reader.* Itasca, IL: F. E. Peacock.

Cigler, Allan J., and Burdett A. Loomis, eds. 1998. *Interest Group Politics,* 5th ed. Washington, DC: CQ.

ČMKOS (Czech Moravian Chamber of Trade Unions). 1999. At Internet site www.cmkos.cz.

Collier, David, and Ruth Berins Collier. 1991. *Shaping the Political Arena: Critical Junctures, the Labor Movement and Regime Dynamics in Latin America.* Princeton: Princeton University Press.

Confalonieri, Maria Antonietta. 1995. "Parties and Movements in Italy: The Case of Feminism and the PCI." *Il Politico* 60, 1: 127–158.

Constantelos, John. 1996. "Multi-level Lobbying in the European Union: A Paired Sectoral Comparison Across the French-Italian Border." *Regional and Federal Studies* 6, 3: 28–57.

———. 1999. "Local Interests Confront the Euro: Evidence from France and Italy." Paper presented at the Sixth Biennial International Conference of the European Community Studies Association, Pittsburgh, Pennsylvania, 2–5 June.

Coppedge, Michael. 1998. "The Dynamic Diversity of Latin American Party Systems." *Party Politics* 4, 4 (October): 547–568.
Córdova, Arnaldo. 1976. "La transformación del PNR en PRM: el triunfo del corporativismo en México." In Meyer Wilkie and Mouzón de Wilkie, eds., *Contemporary Mexico*. Los Angeles: University of California Press.
Cothran, Dan A. 1994. *Political Stability and Democracy in Mexico: The Perfect Dictatorship*. Westport, CT: Praeger.
Coxall, B., and L. Robins. 1998. *Contemporary British Politics*, 3d ed. London: Macmillan.
Craig, Patricia. 1995. "Political Mediation, Traditional Parties and New Social Movements: Lessons from the Spanish Socialist Worker's Party." Madrid: Estudios/Working Paper, CEACS, Instituto Juan March de Estudios e Investigaciones.
Craine, Susan, Russ Haven, and Blair Horner. 1995. *Taming the Fat Cats: A National Survey of State Lobby Laws*. Endorsed by the League of Women Voters of New York/New York Public Research Interest Group/Common Cause New York. Albany, NY: working paper published by the authors.
Crotty, William. 1984. *American Parties in Decline*. Boston: Little, Brown.
Crouch, Colin, and Anand Menon. 1997. "Organized Interests and the States." In Martin Rhodes, Paul Heywood, and Vincent Wright, eds., *Developments in West European Politics*. New York: St. Martin's.
ČTK (Czech News Agency). 1999. "Senator Falbr Not to Back Election Change Proposed by ČSSD-ODS." Prague: 19 September 1999 (Internet edition at www.ctknews.com).
Čulík, Jan. 1996. "Czech Political Culture in the 1990s." *Britské listy* (Internet edition at www.jcu2@cableol.co.uk).
Curtis, Gerald L. 1975. "Big Business and Political Influence." In Ezra F. Vogel, ed., *Modern Japanese Organization and Decision-Making*. Berkeley: University of California Press.
Daley, Anthony. 1992. "Remembrance of Things Past: The Union-Party Linkage in France." *International Journal of Political Economy* 22 (winter 1992–1993): 53–71.
Dalton, Russell. 1993. *Politics in Germany*, 2d ed. New York: HarperCollins.
Dawson, Jane. 1997. *Eco-Nationalism*. Durham, NC: Duke University Press.
de la Fuente Blanco, Gloria. 1991. *Las organizaciones agrarias españolas*. Madrid: Instituto de Estudios Económicos.
de la Garza Toledo, Enrique. 1991. "Independent Trade Unionism in Mexico: Past Developments and Future Perspectives." In Kevin J. Middlebrook, ed., *Unions, Workers, and the State in Mexico*. U.S.-Mexico Contemporary Perspectives Series, 2. San Diego: Center for U.S.-Mexican Studies, University of California San Diego.
Della Porta, Donatella. 1996. *Movimenti colletivi e sistema politico in Italia, 1960–1995*. Bari: Laterza.
Della Porta, Donatella, and Alberto Vannucci. 1997. "The 'Perverse Effects' of Political Corruption." *Political Studies* 45, 3: 516–538.
Delli Santi, Angela M. 1979. "The Private Sector, Business Organizations, and International Influence: A Case Study of Mexico." In Richard R. Fagen, ed., *Capitalism and the State in U.S.–Latin American Relations*. Stanford: Stanford University Press.
Diani, Mario. 1995. *Green Networks: A Structural Analysis of the Italian Environmental Movement*. Edinburgh: Edinburgh University Press.

Domínguez, Jorge I. 1999. "The Transformation of Mexico's Electoral and Party Systems, 1988–97: An Introduction." In Domínguez Poiré and Alejandro Poiré, eds., *Toward Mexico's Democratization: Parties, Campaigns, and Public Opinion*. New York: Routledge.

Dulles, J. W. F. 1961. *Yesterday in Mexico: A Chronicle of the Revolution, 1919–1936*. Austin: University of Texas Press.

Durand Ponte, Victor Manuel. 1991. "The Confederation of Mexican Workers, the Labor Congress, and the Crisis of Mexico's Social Pact." In Kevin J. Middlebrook, ed., *Unions, Workers, and the State in Mexico*. U.S.-Mexico Contemporary Perspectives Series, 2. San Diego: Center for U.S.-Mexican Studies, University of California San Diego.

Duverger, Maurice. 1951. *Les Partis Politiques*. Paris: PUF.

———. 1972. *Party Politics and Pressure Groups: A Comparative Introduction*. New York: Thomas Y. Crowell.

The Economist. 1997. "Czech Investment Funds: Worrying Trend." 29 March: 82.

———. 1999. "Czech Renationalisation." 6 February: 65–66.

Edinger, Lewis J. 1986. *West German Politics*. New York: Columbia University Press.

Elazar, Daniel J. 1986. *Israel: Building a New Society*. Bloomington: Indiana University Press.

Elder, N., A. H. Thomas, and D. Arter. 1988. *The Consensual Democracies? The Government and Politics of the Scandinavian States*, rev. ed. Oxford: Basil Blackwell.

Eldersveld, Samuel J., and Hanes Walton Jr. 1999. *Political Parties in American Society*. New York: St. Martin's.

Elon, Amos. 1971. *The Israelis: Founders and Sons*. London: Weidenfeld and Nicolson.

Elvander, N. 1967. *Intreseeorganisationern i dagens Sverige*. Lund: CWK Gleerup.

Emmerich, Gustavo Ernesto. 1994. "Argentina: los partidos políticos y las ciudadanía ante la reforma constitutional." In Silvia Dutrénit and Leonardo Valdés, eds., *El fin de siglo y los partidos políticos en América Latina*. Mexico City: Instituto de Investigaciones Dr. José María Luis Mora, Universidad Autónoma Metropolitana Unidad Iztapalapa.

Epstein, Leon D. 1967. *Political Parties in Western Democracies*. London: Pall Mall.

Ergas, Yasmine. 1982. "1968–79—Feminism and the Italian Party System: Women's Politics in a Decade of Turmoil." *Comparative Politics* 14, 3: 253–280.

Erro, Davide G. 1993. *Resolving the Argentina Paradox: Politics and Development, 1966–1992*. Boulder: Lynne Rienner.

Essen, Josef. 1986. "State, Business and Trade Unions in West Germany After the 'Political Wende.'" *West European Politics* 9 (April): 198–214.

ETUI (European Trade Union Institute). 1985. *The Trade Union Movement in Italy: CGIL-CISL-UIL*. Brussels: ETUI.

Eyerman, Ron, and Andrew Jamison. 1991. *Social Movements: A Cognitive Approach*. University Park: Pennsylvania State University Press.

Faxén, K.-O., C.-E. Odhner, and R. Spånt. 1989. *Lönebildningen i 90-talets samhällsekonomi*. Stockholm: Rabén och Sjögren.

Feijoó, María del Carmen, and Marcela María Alejandra Nari. 1994. "Women and Democracy in Argentina." In Jane S. Jaquette, ed., *The Women's Movement in Latin America: Participation and Democracy*, 2d ed. Boulder: Westview.

Ferrante, Massimo. 1998. "Transizione di regime e interessi imprenditoriali in Italia." *Rivista Italiana di Scienza Politica* 28, 1: 81–118.
Finer, S. E. 1958. *Anonymous Empire*. London: Pall Mall.
Fisher, J. 1996. *British Political Parties*. London: Prentice-Hall.
Fishman, Robert. 1990. *Working-Class Organization and the Return to Democracy in Spain*. Ithaca, NY: Cornell University Press.
Foweraker, Joe. 1994. "Popular Political Organization and Democratization: A Comparison of Spain and Mexico." In Ian Budge and David McKay, eds., *Developing Democracy*. London: Sage.
Frantzich, Stephen E. 1989. *Political Parties in the Technological Age*. White Plains, NY: Longman.
Fredriksson, B., and A. Gunnmo. 1978, 1985, 1992. *Våra fackliga organisationer*, 3d, 6th, and 7th eds. Stockholm: Rabén and Sjögren.
Frei, Matt. 1995. *Getting the Boot: Italy's Unfinished Revolution*. New York: Times Books.
Fronk, Katka. 1999a. "Air Pollution Drops Dramatically." *Prague Post*, 28 April–4 May: A2.
———. 1999b. "Patients' Group Warns Doctors Not to Strike." *Prague Post*, 15 September (Internet edition at www.praguepost.cz).
The Funding of Political Parties in the United Kingdom. Cm 4057-I (Report and Appendixes); and Cm 4057-II (Oral Evidence). London: HMSO.
Funk, Nannette, and Magda Mueller, eds. 1993. *Gender Politics and Post-Communism*. New York: Routledge.
Galli, Giorgio, and Alfonso Prandi. 1970. *Patterns of Political Participation in Italy*. New Haven: Yale University Press.
Galnoor, Itzhak. 1982. *Steering the Polity: Communication and Politics in Israel*. Beverly Hills: Sage.
Gardawski, Juliusz, et al. 1999. *Rozpad Bastionu?* [The Fall of the Bastion?] Warsaw: Instytut Spraw Publicznych.
Garner, R., and R. Kelly. 1998. *British Political Parties Today*. London: Macmillan.
Garvía, Roberto. 1995. "Corporatism, Public Policy and Welfare: The Case of the Spanish Blind." *Journal of European Public Policy* 2, 2: 243–259.
George, Aurelia. 1988. "Japanese Interest Group Behavior: An Institutional Approach." In J. A. A. Stockwin, ed., *Dynamic and Immobilist Politics in Japan*. London: Macmillan.
Gibson, Edward L. 1996. *Class and Conservative Parties: Argentina in Comparative Perspective*. Baltimore: Johns Hopkins University Press.
Gidlund, G. 1989. "Folkrörelsepartiet och den politiska styrelsen: SAPs organisationsutveckling." In K. Misgeld, K. Molin, and K. Åmark, eds., *Socialdemokratins samhälle 1889–1989: SAP och Sverige under 100 år*. Stockholm: Tiden.
———. 1991. "Public Investments in Swedish Democracy—Gambling with Gains and Losses." In M. Wiberg, ed., *The Public Purse and the Political Parties: Public Financing of Political Parties in Nordic Countries*. Helsinki: Finnish Political Science Association.
Gillespie, Richard. 1990. "The Break-up of the 'Socialist Family'. Party Union Relations in Spain, 1982–89." *West European Politics* 13, 1: 47–62.
Gilljam, M., and S. Holmberg. 1995. *Väljarnas val*. Stockholm: Norstedts juridik.
Golan, Galia. 1971. *The Czechoslovak Reform Movement: Communism in Crisis 1962–1968*. London: Cambridge University Press.

———. 1973. *Reform Rule in Czechoslovakia: The Dubcek Era 1968–1969*. London: Cambridge University Press.
Golden, Miriam. 1986. "Interest Representation, Party Systems, and the State: Italy in Comparative Perspective." *Comparative Politics* 18, 3: 279–301.
González Casanova, Pablo. 1970. *Democracy in Mexico*. Trans. Danielle Salti. New York: Oxford University Press.
Grabowska, Miroslawa, and Ireneusz Krzeminski, eds. 1991. *Bitwa o Belweder* [The Battle for Belweder]. Warsaw: Mysl.
Grant, Wyn. 1990. *Pressure Groups, Politics and Democracy in Britain*. London: Philip Allan.
Gray, Virginia, and David Lowery. 1996. *The Population Ecology of Interest Representation: Lobbying Communities in the American States*. Ann Arbor: University of Michigan Press.
Greenwood, Justin. 1997. *Representing Interests in the European Union*. London: Macmillan.
Groux, Guy, and Rene Moriaux. 1989. *La C.F.D.T.* Paris: Economica.
———. 1996. "The Dilemma of Unions Without Members." In Anthony Daley, ed., *The Mitterrand Era: Policy Alternatives and Political Mobilization in France*. Basingstoke, England: Macmillan.
Gunther, Richard. 1980. *Public Policy in a No-Party State*. Berkeley: University of California Press.
———. 1992. "Spain: The Very Model of the Modern Elite Settlement." In John Higley and Richard Gunther, eds., *Elites and Democratic Consolidation in Latin America and Southern Europe*. Cambridge: Cambridge University Press.
———. 1997. "Managing Democratic Consolidation in Spain: From Consensus to Majority in Institutions." In Metin Heper, Ali Kazancigil, and Bert A. Rockman, eds., *Institutions and Democratic Statecraft*. Boulder: Westview.
Hagård, B. 1966. *Socialdemokratien och fackföreningsrörelsen*. Stockholm: Forum för Borgerlig Debatt, No. 3.
Hagevi, M. 1994. "Hur röstar de kristna." *Frisinnad Tidskrift* 65, 10: 22–32.
Halfmann, Jost. 1989. "Social Change and Political Mobilization in West Germany." In Peter J. Katzenstein, ed., *Industry and Politics in West Germany: Toward the Third Republic*. Ithaca, NY: Cornell University Press.
Hall, Peter. 1990. "The State and Dirigisme." In Peter Hall, Jack Hayward, and Howard Machin, eds., *Developments in French Politics*. New York: St. Martin's.
———. 1992. "The Movement from Keynesianism to Monetarism: Institutional Analysis and British Economic Policy in the 1970s." In Sven Steinmo, Kathleen Thelen, and Frank Longstreth, eds., *Structuring Politics*. Cambridge: Cambridge University Press.
Hamann, Kerstin. 1997a. "The Pacted Transition to Democracy and Labour Politics in Spain." *South European Society and Politics* 2, 2: 110–138.
———. 1997b. "The Legislative Process and Interest Groups in Spain." Paper presented at the Midwest Political Science Association meeting, Chicago, Illinois, April.
———. 1998a. "Civil Society and the Democratic Transition in Spain." *Perspectives on Political Science* 27, 3: 135–141.
———. 1998b. "Spanish Unions: Institutional Legacy and Responsiveness to Economic and Industrial Change." *Industrial and Labor Relations Review* 51, 3: 424–444.
———. 1999. "Federalist Institutions, Voting Behavior, and Party Systems in Spain." *Publius: The Journal of Federalism* 29, 1: 111–137.

---. 2000. "Linking Policies and Economic Voting: Explaining Reelection in the Case of the Spanish Socialist Party." *Comparative Political Studies* 33, 8: 1018–1048.
Hamilton, Nora. 1982. *The Limits of State Autonomy: Post-Revolutionary Mexico.* Princeton: Princeton University Press.
Hancock, M. Donald. 1998. "Part Five: Sweden." In M. Donald Hancock et al., *Politics in Western Europe*, 2d ed. Chatham, NJ: Chatham House.
Hansard Society. 1993. *Making the Law: The Report of the Hansard Society Commission on the Legislative Process.* London: Hansard Society Publications.
Hansen, Roger D. 1971. *The Politics of Mexican Development.* Baltimore, MD: Johns Hopkins University Press.
Hansson, D. 1999. "Partier och intresseorganisationer i Sverige." Paper presented at the 12th Nordic Political Science Association meeting, Uppsala, August.
Harari, Ehud. 1980. "The Institutionalization of Policy Consultation in Japan: Public Advisory Bodies." In Gail Lee Bernstein and Haruhiro Fukui, eds., *Japan and the World.* London: Macmillan.
Haungs, Peter. 1981. *Parteiendemokratie in der Bundesrepublik Deutschland.* Berlin: Colloquium Verlag.
Hellman, Judith Adler. 1983. *Mexico in Crisis*, 2d ed. New York: Holmes and Meier.
Henig, S. 1979. "The United Kingdom." In S. Henig, ed., *Political Parties in the European Community.* London: George Allen and Unwin.
Hennis, Wilhelm. 1961. "Verfassungsordnung und Verbandseinfluss. Bemerkungen zu ihrem Zusammenhang im politischen System der Bundesrepublik." *Politische Vierteljahresschrift* 2: 23–35.
Hermansson, J. 1993. *Politik som intressekamp: Parlamentariskt beslutsfattande och organiserade intressen i Sverige.* Stockholm: Norstedts Juridik.
Hernández Rodríguez, Rogelio. 1998. "The Partido Revolucionario Institucional." In Mónica Serrano, ed., *Governing Mexico: Political Parties and Elections.* London: Institute of Latin American Studies, University of London.
Hesse, Joachim Jens, and Thomas Ellwein. 1992. *Das Regierungssystem der Bundesrepublik Deutschland.* Opladen: Westdeutscher Verlag.
Hipsher, Patricia L. 1996. "Democratization and the Decline of Urban Social Movements in Chile and Spain." *Comparative Politics* 28, 3 (April): 273–298.
Hollingsworth, J. Rogers. 1997. "Continuities and Changes in Social Systems of Production: The Cases of Japan, Germany, and the United States." In J. Rogers Hollingsworth and Robert Boyer, eds., *Contemporary Capitalism: The Embeddedness of Institutions.* Cambridge: Cambridge University Press.
Horne, James. 1988. "Politics and the Japanese Financial System." In J. A. A. Stockwin, ed., *Dynamic and Immobilist Politics in Japan.* London: Macmillan.
Howell, Christopher. 1992. *Regulating Labor: The State and Industrial Reform in Post-War France.* Princeton: Princeton University Press.
Hrebenar, Ronald J. 1997. *Interest Group Politics in America*, 3d ed. Armonk, NY: M. E. Sharpe.
---. 2000. *The New Japanese Party System.* Boulder: Westview.
Hrebenar, Ronald J., Matthew J. Burbank, and Robert C. Benedict. 1999. *Political Parties, Interest Groups and Political Campaigns.* Boulder: Westview.
Hrebenar, Ronald J., and Clive S. Thomas, eds. 1987. *Interest Group Politics in the American West.* Salt Lake City: University of Utah Press.
---. 1992. *Interest Group Politics in the Southern States.* Tuscaloosa: University of Alabama Press.

———. 1993a. *Interest Group Politics in the Midwestern States*. Ames: Iowa State University Press.
———. 1993b. *Interest Group Politics in the Northeastern States*. University Park: The Pennsylvania State University Press.
http://www.saco.se. SACO (Swedish Confederation of Professional Associations) Internet site.
http://www.tco.se. TCO (Swedish Confederation of Professional Employees) Internet site.
Huizer, Gerrit. 1970. "Peasant Organization in Agrarian Reform in Mexico." In Irving Louis Horowitz, ed., *Masses in Latin America*. New York: Oxford University Press.
Hunter, Kennith G., Laura Ann Wilson, and Gregory G. Brunk. 1991. "Societal Complexity and Interest Group Lobbying in the American States." *Journal of Politics* 53: 488–502.
Iniciativa Social y Estado de Bienestar. n.d.a. "La participación ciudadana." Electronic version at http://www.geocities.com/CapitolHill/Lobby/2973/participacion.html.
———. n.d.b. "Evolución del asocianismo en España." Electronic version at http://www.geocities.com/CapitolHill/Lobby.2973/evolucion.html.
Inoguchi, Takeshi, and Tomoaki Iwai. 1987. *Zoku giin' no kenkyu: jimintoo seiken o gyujiru shuyakutachi* [A Study of Tribal Parliamentarians: Those Who Lead the LDP]. Tokyo: Nihon Keizai Shimbunsha.
Ippolito, Dennis S., and Thomas G. Walker. 1980. *Political Parties, Interest Groups and Public Policy: Group Influence in American Politics*. Englewood Cliffs, NJ: Prentice-Hall.
Janicki, Mariusz. 1998. "Zwiazkokracja." *Polityka* (Warsaw), 12 December.
Janos, Andrew C. 1970. "Group Politics in Communist Society: A Second Look at the Pluralistic Model." In Samuel P. Huntington and Clement H. Moore, eds., *Authoritarian Politics in Modern Society: The Dynamics of One-Party Systems*. New York: Basic.
Jewell, Malcolm E., and David M. Olson. 1988. *Political Parties and Elections in American States*. Chicago: Dorsey.
Johnson, Chalmers. 1982. *MITI and the Japanese Miracle: The Growth of Industrial Policy: 1925–1975*. Palo Alto: Stanford University Press.
Johnson, John J. 1958. *Political Change in Latin America: The Emergence of the Middle Sectors*. Stanford: Stanford University Press.
Jordan, A. G., and J. J. Richardson. 1987. *Government and Pressure Groups in Britain*. Oxford: Clarendon.
Jordan, G., and W. A. Maloney. 1992. "What Is Studied When Pressure Groups Are Studied?" British Interest Groups Project, Working Paper Series No. 1. Aberdeen (Scotland), University of Aberdeen.
Jowitt, Kenneth. 1991. "The Leninist Extinction." In Daniel Chirot, ed., *The Crisis of Leninism and the Decline of the Left*. Seattle: University of Washington Press.
Katz, Elihu, et al. 1992. *Leisure in Israel: Changes in the Forms of Cultural Activity 1970–1990*. Jerusalem: Guttman Institute for Applied Social Research.
Katz, R. 1986. "Party Government: A Rationalistic Conception." In F. G. Castles and R. Wildenmann, eds., *Visions and Realities of Party Government*. Berlin: de Gruyter.
Katz, Richard S., and Peter Mair. 1995. "Changing Models of Party Organization and Party Democracy." *Party Politics* 1: 5–28.

Katzenstein, Peter J. 1989. "Stability and Change in the Emerging Third Republic." In Peter J. Katzenstein, ed., *Industry and Politics in West Germany: Toward the Third Republic*. Ithaca, NY: Cornell University Press.

Kaufman, Robert R. 1989. "Economic Orthodoxy and Political Change in Mexico: The Stabilization and Adjustment Policies of the de la Madrid Administration." In Barbara Stallings and Robert R. Kaufman, eds., *Debt and Democracy in Latin America*. Boulder: Westview.

Keefe, William J. 1991. *Parties, Politics, and Public Policy in America*, 6th ed. Washington, DC: CQ.

Kenney, Padraic. 1999. "The Gender of Resistance in Communist Poland." *American Historical Review* 104, 2 (April): 399–425.

Kesselman, Mark. 1996a. "French Labor Confronts Technological Change: Reform That Never Was?" In Anthony Daley, ed., *The Mitterrand Era: Policy Alternatives and Political Mobilization in France*. Basingstoke, England: Macmillan.

———. 1996b. "Does the French Labor Movement Have a Future?" In John Keeler and Martin Schain, eds., *Chirac's Challenge: Liberalization, Europeanization, and Malaise in France*. New York: St. Martin's.

Key, V. O., Jr. 1964. *Politics, Parties and Pressure Groups*, 5th ed. New York: Thomas Y. Crowell.

Kirkpatrick, Evron M. 1971. "Toward a More Responsible Two Party System: Political Science, Policy Science, or Pseudo-Science?" *American Political Science Review* 65: 965–990.

Klačová, Eva, and Jan Příkryl. 1996. "Living on the Edge Is Difficult." *Ekonom*, 4–10 January: 11–13; reprinted in *Federal Broadcast Information Service* (FBIS) EEU–96–010, 16 January 1996: 13.

Klatt, Hartmut. 1993. "German Unification and the Federal System." In Charlie Jeffrey and Roland Sturm, eds., *Federalism, Unification and European Integration*. London: Frank Cass.

Klaus, Václav. 1997. *Renaissance: The Rebirth of Liberty in the Heart of Europe*. Washington, DC: Cato Institute.

Knight, Jack. 1992. *Institutions and Social Conflict*. New York: Cambridge University Press.

Koopman, Ruud. 1995. *Democracy from Below: New Social Movements in West Germany*. Boulder: Westview.

Korbonski, Andrzej. 1971. "Bureaucracy and Interest Groups in Communist Societies: The Case of Czechoslovakia." *Studies in Comparative Communism* 4, 1 (January): 57–79.

Kramer, Ralph. 1981. *Voluntary Agencies in a Welfare State*. Berkeley: University of California Press.

Krauss, Ellis, and B. L. Simcock. 1989. "Politics and Policymaking." In Takeshi Ishida and Ellis S. Krauss, eds., *Democracy in Japan*. Pittsburgh: University of Pittsburgh Press.

Kropp, Sabine. 1997. "Interessenpolitik." In Oscar W. Gabriel and Everhard Holtmann, eds., *Handbuch Politisches System der Bundesrepublik Deutschland*. München: Oldenbourg Verlag.

Kusin, Vladimir V. 1972. *Political Groupings in the Czechoslovak Reform Movement*. New York: Columbia University Press.

———. 1978. *From Dubcek to Charter 77: A Study of "Normalization" in Czechoslovakia, 1968–1978*. Edinburgh: Q Press.

———. 1979. "Challenge to Normalcy: Political Opposition in Czechoslovakia,

1968–77." In Rudolf L. Tokés, ed., *Opposition in Eastern Europe*. London: Macmillan.
Labour Party. 1997. *Labour Party Conference Guide*. London.
Lane, J.-E., and S. O. Ersson. 1994. *Politics and Society in Western Europe*, 3d ed. London: Sage.
Lange, Peter, and Marino Regini. 1989. "Conclusions: The Italian Case Between Continuity and Change." In Peter Lange and Marino Regini, eds., *State, Market and Social Regulation: New Perspectives on Italy*. Cambridge: Cambridge University Press.
Lange, Peter, George Ross, and Maurizio Vannicelli. 1982. *Unions, Change and Crisis: French and Italian Union Strategy and the Political Economy, 1945–1980*. London: George Allen and Unwin.
Lanza, Orazio. 1991. "L'agricoltura, la Coldiretti e la DC." In Leonardo Morlino, ed., *Costruire la democrazia: Gruppi e partiti in Italia*. Bologna: Il Mulino.
Lanzalaco, Luca. 1990a. *Dall'impresa all'associazione: Le organizzazioni degli imprenditori: La Confindustria in prospettiva comparata*. Milan: Franco Angeli.
———. 1990b. "Pininfarina, President of the Confederation of Industry, and the Problems of Business Interest Associations." In Raimondo Catanzaro and Raffaella Y. Nanetti, eds., *Italian Politics: A Review*, Vol. 4. London: Pinter.
———. 1993. "Interest Groups in Italy: From Pressure Activity to Policy Networks." In Jeremy J. Richardson, ed., *Pressure Groups*. Oxford: Oxford University Press.
LaPalombara, Joseph. 1964. *Interest Groups in Italian Politics*. Princeton: Princeton University Press.
———. 1987. *Democracy, Italian Style*. New Haven: Yale University Press.
Larsson, T. 1993. *Det svenska statsskicket*. Lund: Studentlitteratur.
Lawson, Kay, ed. 1980. *Political Parties and Linkage: A Comparative Perspective*. New Haven: Yale University Press.
Lawson, Kay, and Peter H. Merkl, eds. 1988. *When Parties Fail: Emerging Alternative Organizations*. Princeton: Princeton University Press.
Leal, Juan Felipe. 1986. "The Mexican State, 1915–1973: A Historical Interpretation." In Nora Hamilton and Timothy F. Harding, eds., *Modern Mexico: State, Economy, and Social Conflict*. Latin American Perspectives Volume 1. Beverly Hills: Sage.
Leff, Carol Skalnik. 1998. *The Czech and Slovak Republics: Nation Versus State*. Boulder: Westview.
Lehman-Wilzig, Sam N. 1992. *Wildfire: Grassroots Revolts in Israel in the Post-Socialist Era*. Albany: State University of New York Press.
Lehmbruch, Gerhard. 1982. "Introduction: Neo-Corporatism in Comparative Perspective." In Gerhard Lehmbruch and Philippe C. Schmitter, eds., *Patterns of Corporatist Policy-Making*. Beverly Hills: Sage.
Leibholz, Gerhard. 1952. *Der Strukturwandel der Moderns Demokratie*. Karlsruhe: Müller.
Leonardi, Robert, and Douglas A. Wertman. 1989. *Italian Christian Democracy: The Politics of Dominance*. New York: St. Martin's.
Leonardy, Uwe. 1993. "Federation and the Länder in German Foreign Relations: Power-Sharing in Treaty-Making and European Affairs." In Charlie Jeffrey and Roland Sturm, eds., *Federalism, Unification and European Integration*. London: Frank Cass.
Levitsky, Steven. 1998. "Crisis, Party Adaptation and Regime Stability in

Argentina: The Case of Peronism, 1989-1995." *Party Politics* 4, 4 (October): 445-470.
Lewin, L. 1988. *Ideology and Strategy: A Century of Swedish Politics.* New York: Cambridge University Press.
———. 1992. *Staten och de organiserade intressena.* Stockholm: Rabén and Sjögren.
———. 1994. "The Rise and Decline of Corporatism: The Case of Sweden." *European Journal of Political Research* 26, 1: 59-79.
Lidové noviny. 1995. Prague, 23 September: 3. Reprinted in FBIS EEU-95-194, 6 October 1995: 7-8.
Lieberman, Sima. 1986. *Labor Movements and Labor Thought.* New York: Praeger.
Liebert, Ulrike. 1995a. *Modelle Demokratischer Konsolidierung.* Opladen: Leske and Budrich.
———. 1995b. "Parliamentary Lobby Regimes." In Herbert Döring, ed., *Parliaments and Majority Rule in Western Europe.* New York: St. Martin's; Frankfurt: Campus Verlag.
Linz, Juan J. 1964. "An Authoritarian Regime: Spain." In E. Allardt and Y. Littunen, eds., *Cleavages, Ideologies and Party Systems.* New York: Academic Bookstore.
Ljungberg, C. J., ed. 1991. *Till bröders hjälp. Socialdemokratin, makten och miljarderna.* Stockholm: Timbro.
LO (Swedish Trade Union Confederation). 1945, 1967, 1976, 1984, 1990, 1997. Annual Reports. Stockholm.
Lösche, Peter. 1993. "Problems of Party Campaign Financing in Germany and the United States: Some Comparative Reflections." In Arthur B. Gunlicks, ed., *Campaign and Party Finance in North America and Western Europe.* Boulder: Westview.
Lowery, David, and Virginia Gray. 1995. "The Population Ecology of Gucci Gulch, or the Natural Regulation of Interest Group Numbers in the American States." *American Journal of Political Science* 39: 1-29.
Lowi, Theodore J. 1979. *The End of Liberalism: The Second Republic of the United States,* 2d ed. New York: W. W. Norton.
Luna, Matilde. 1995. "Entrepreneurial Interests and Political Action in Mexico: Facing the Demands of Economic Modernization." In Riordan Roett, ed., *The Challenge of Institutional Reform in Mexico.* Boulder: Lynne Rienner.
Luža, Radomír. 1973. "Czechoslovakia Between Democracy and Communism." In Victor S. Mamatey and Radomír Luža, eds., *A History of the Czechoslovak Republic 1918-1948.* Princeton: Princeton University Press.
Magstadt, Thomas M. 1998. "Flawed Democracies: The Dubious Credentials of NATO's Proposed New Members." *Cato Institute Policy Analysis,* No. 297: 17. Washington, DC: Cato Institute.
Mahood, H. R. 2000. *Interest Group Politics in American National Politics: An Overview.* Upper Saddle River, NJ: Prentice-Hall.
Mainwaring, Scott. 1994. "Political Parties and Democratization in Brazil and the Southern Cone." Reprinted in Jorge I. Domínguez, ed., *Parties, Elections, and Political Participation in Latin America.* New York: Garland.
Mainwaring, Scott, and Timothy R. Scully, eds. 1995. *Building Democratic Institutions: Party Systems in Latin America.* Stanford: Stanford University Press.
Mair, Peter. 1993. "Myth of Electoral Change and the Myth of Traditional Parties." *European Journal of Political Research* 24: 121-133.

Maisel, L. Sandy. 1999. *Parties and Elections in America: The Electoral Process*, 3d ed. Lanham, MD: Rowman and Littlefield.
———, ed. 1990. *The Parties Respond: Changes in the American Party System*. Boulder: Westview.
Maloney, W. A., G. Jordan, and A. M. McLaughin. 1994. "Interest Groups and Public Policy: The Insider/Outsider Model Revisited." *Journal of Public Policy* 14, 1: 17–38.
Maloney, William A., and Grant Jordan. 1998. "The Interest Group–Political Party Connection: The British Experience." Paper presented at the annual meeting of the Western Political Science Association, Los Angeles, California, March.
Mamatey, Victor S. 1973. "The Development of Czechoslovak Democracy, 1920–1938." In Victor S. Mamatey and Radomír Luža, eds., *A History of the Czechoslovak Republic 1918–1948*. Princeton: Princeton University Press.
Manzetti, Luigi. 1993. *Institutions, Parties, and Coalitions in Argentine Politics*. Pittsburgh: Pittsburgh University Press.
Maravall, José María. 1978. *Dictatorship and Political Dissent*. London: Tavistock.
Martinelli, Alberto. 1980. "Organised Business and Italian Politics: Confindustria and the Christian Democrats in the Postwar Period." In Peter Lange and Sidney Tarrow, eds., *Italy in Transition: Conflict and Consensus*. London: Frank Cass.
Martinelli, Alberto, and Luca Lanzalaco. 1994. "L'organizzazione degli interessi impreditoriali e il sistema politico. La logica dell' influenza." In Alberto Martinelli, ed., *L'azione collettiva degli imprenditori italiani*. Ivrea: Edizioni di Comunit.
Martínez, Robert E. 1993a. "The Business Sector and Political Change in Spain: Apertura, Reforma, and Democratic Consolidation." In Richard Gunther, ed., *Politics, Society, and Democracy: The Case of Spain*. Boulder: Westview.
———. 1993b. *Business and Democracy in Spain*. Westport, CT: Praeger.
Martinez Lucio, Miguel. 1991. "Employer Identity and the Politics of the Labour Market in Spain." *West European Politics* 14, 1: 41–55.
Martínez Rodríguez, Antonia. 1998. "Parliamentary Elites and the Polarisation of the Party System in Mexico." In Mónica Serrano, ed., *Governing Mexico: Political Parties and Elections*. London: Institute of Latin American Studies, University of London.
Mattina, Liborio. 1993. "Abete's Confindustria: From Alliance with the DC to Multiparty Appeal." In Stephen Hellman and Gianfranco Pasquino, eds., *Italian Politics: A Review*, Vol. 8. London: Pinter.
Mayhew, David R. 1986. *Placing Parties in American Politics*. Princeton: Princeton University Press.
McCarthy, John, and Mayer Zald. 1977. "Resource Mobilization and Social Movements: A Partial Theory." *American Journal of Sociology* 82: 1212–1241.
McDonough, Peter, Samuel H. Barnes, and Antonio López Pina. 1984. "Authority and Association: Spanish Democracy in Comparative Perspective." *Journal of Politics* 46, 3: 652–688.
McGuire, James. 1995. "Political Parties and Democracy in Argentina." In Scott Mainwaring and Timothy R. Scully, eds., *Building Democratic Institutions: Party Systems in Latin America*. Stanford: Stanford University Press.
———. 1997. *Peronism Without Perón: Unions, Parties, and Democracy in Argentina*. Stanford: Stanford University Press.
McKean, Margaret. 1977. "Pollution and Policymaking." In T. J. Pemple, ed., *Policymaking in Contemporary Japan*. Ithaca, NY: Cornell University Press.
McKenzie, R. T. 1955. *British Political Parties*. London: Heinemann.

Medding, Peter Y. 1972. *Mapai in Israel: Political Organization and Government in a New Society.* Cambridge: Cambridge University Press.
Merkl, Peter H. 1988. "The Challengers and the Party System." In Kay Lawson and Peter H. Merkl, eds., *When Parties Fail: Emerging Alternative Organizations.* Princeton: Princeton University Press.
Meyer, Marshall W., and Lynne G. Zucker. 1989. *Permanently Failing Organizations.* Newbury Park, CA: Sage.
Meynaud, Jean. 1962. *Les Groupes de pression en France.* Paris: Armand Colin.
Michaels, Albert L. 1967. "Mexican Politics and Nationalism from Calles to Cárdenas." Philadelphia: Unpublished dissertation, University of Pennsylvania.
Miliband, Ralph. 1969. *The State in Capitalist Society.* London: Winfield and Nicholson.
———. 1977. *Marxism and Politics.* London: Oxford University Press.
Miller, Charles. 1987. *Lobbying Government: Understanding and Influencing the Corridors of Power.* Oxford: Basil Blackwell.
Milner, H. 1990. *Sweden: Social Democracy in Practice.* Oxford: Oxford University Press.
Montero, José R., Francisco J. Llera, and Mariano Torcal. 1992. "Sistemas electorales en España: una recapitulación." *Revista Española de Investigaciones Sociológicas* 58: 7–56.
Moran, Dennis. 1998a. "Czech Corporations in the Giving Mood." *Prague Post,* 26 August (Internet edition at www.praguepost.cz).
———. 1998b. "Agriculture's Year of Angst." *Prague Post,* 30 December: A5–6.
Morawski, Witold, ed. 1994. *Zmierzch Socjalizmu Panstwowego* [The Dusk of State Socialism]. Warsaw: PWN.
Morehouse, Sarah McCally. 1981. *State Politics, Parties, and Policy.* New York: Holt, Rinehart and Winston.
———. 1997. "Interest Groups, Parties and Policies in the American States." Paper presented at the annual meeting of the American Political Science Association, Washington, D.C., September.
Moreno, Luis. 1997. *La federalización de España.* Madrid: Siglo XXI.
Morlino, Leonardo. 1991. "Conclusioni: La relazione tra gruppi e partiti." In Leonardo Morlino, ed., *Costruire la democrazia: Gruppi e partiti in Italia.* Bologna: Il Mulino.
———. 1995. "Consolidation and Party Government in Southern Europe." *International Political Science Review* 16, 2: 145–167.
———. 1998. *Democracy Between Consolidation and Crisis: Parties, Groups, and Citizens in Southern Europe.* New York: Oxford University Press.
Needler, Martin. 1971. *Politics and Society in Mexico.* Albuquerque: University of New Mexico Press.
Newell, James J., and Martin Bull. 1997. "Party Organisations and Alliances in Italy in the 1990s: A Revolution of Sorts." *West European Politics* 20, 1: 81–109.
Newton, Michael T. (with Peter J. Donaghy). 1997. *Institutions of Modern Spain.* Cambridge: Cambridge University Press.
Nownes, Anthony. 2001. *Pressure and Power: Organized Interests.* Boston: Houghton-Mifflin.
Öberg, P.-O. 1994. *Särintresse och allmänintresse: Korporatismens ansikten.* Uppsala: Acta Universitatis Uppsaliensis.
Odom, William E. 1976. "A Dissenting View on the Group Approach to Soviet Politics." *World Politics* 28, 4 (July): 542–567.

O'Donnell, Guillermo. 1973. *Modernization and Bureaucratic-Authoritarianism: Studies in South American Politics.* Berkeley: Institute of International Studies, University of California.

———. 1996. "Delegative Democracy." In Larry Diamond and Marc F. Plattner, eds., *The Global Resurgence of Democracy,* 2d ed. Baltimore: Johns Hopkins University Press.

Oldweiler, Cory. 1998. "Pig Farmers' Feeble Stand." *Prague Post,* 18 November: A1.

Olivecrona, G. 1968. *Hur väljarna vanns: Ett politiskt reportage.* Stockholm: Wahlström och Widstrand.

Olson, Mancur. 1971. *The Logic of Collective Action.* Cambridge: Harvard University Press.

———. 1982. *The Rise and Decline of Nations: Economic Growth, Stagflation, and Social Rigidities.* New Haven: Yale University Press.

Orenstein, Mitchell. 1996. "The Failures of Neo-Liberal Social Policy in Central Europe." *Transition* 2, 13 (28 June): 16–20.

Orenstein, Mitchell, and Raj M. Desai. 1997. "State Power and Interest Group Formation: The Business Lobby in the Czech Republic." *Problems of Post-Communism* 44, 6 (November-December): 43–52.

Ost, David. 1988. "Indispensable Ambiguity: Solidarity's Internal Authority Structure." *Studies in Comparative Communism* 21, 2 (summer): 189–201.

———. 1990. *Solidarity and the Politics of Anti-Politics: Reform and Opposition in Poland Since 1968.* Philadelphia: Temple University Press.

Paddock, Joel, and Allan J. Cigler. 1997. "The Interest Group Sources of Political Party Activism." Paper presented at the Western Political Science Association, Los Angeles, March.

Padgett, L. Vincent. 1966. *The Mexican Political System.* Boston: Houghton Mifflin.

Padgett, Stephen. 1993. "Party Democracy in the New Germany." In Stephen Padgett, ed., *Parties and Party Systems in the New Germany.* Brookfield, VT: Dartmouth Publishing.

Pallarés, Francesc, José Ramón Montero, and Francisco José Llera. 1997. "Non Statewide Parties in Spain: An Attitudinal Study of Nationalism and Regionalism." *Publius* 27, 4: 135–170.

Panebianco, Angelo. 1988. *Political Parties: Organization and Power.* Cambridge: Cambridge University Press.

Pankow, Wlodzimierz. 1993. *Work Institutions in Transformation.* Warsaw: Friedrich Ebert.

Pasquino, Gianfranco. 1988. *Istituzioni, partiti, lobbies.* Bari: Laterza.

———. 1989. "Unregulated Regulators: Parties and Party Government." In Peter Lange and Marino Regini, eds., *State, Market and Social Regulation: New Perspectives on Italy.* Cambridge: Cambridge University Press.

Pemple, T. J. 1977. *Policymaking in Contemporary Japan.* Ithaca, NY: Cornell University Press.

Pemple, T. J., and Keiichi Tsunekawa. 1979. "Corporatism Without Labor? The Japanese Anomaly." In Philippe C. Schmitter and Gerhard Lehmbruch, eds., *Trends Toward Corporatist Intermediation.* Beverly Hills: Sage.

Penn, Shana. 1994. "The National Secret." *Journal of Women's History* 5 (winter): 54–69.

Pérez, Sofía A. 1997. *Banking on Privilege.* Ithaca, NY: Cornell University Press.

Pérez-Díaz, Víctor. 1993. *La primacia de la sociedad civil.* Madrid: Alianza.

Petersson, O. 1994. *Swedish Government and Politics*. Stockholm: Publica.
Petracca, Mark P., ed. 1992. *The Politics of Interests: Interest Groups Transformed*. Boulder: Westview.
Pierre, J., and A. Widfeldt. 1992. "Sweden." In R. S. Katz and P. Mair, eds., *Party Organizations: A Data Handbook on Party Organizations in Western Democracies, 1960–1990*. London: Sage.
———. 1994. "Party Organizations in Sweden: Colossuses with Feet of Clay or Flexible Pillars of Government?" In R. S. Katz and P. Mair, eds, *How Parties Organize: Change and Adaptation in Party Organizations in Western Democracies*. London: Sage.
Pizzorno, Alessandro. 1993. *Le radici della politica assoluta*. Milano: Feltrinelli.
Poguntke, Thomas. 1995. "Parties and Society in Western Europe: Declining Linkage?" Paper presented at the conference Party Politics in the Year 2000, Manchester, United Kingdom, January.
Poiré, Domínguez, and Alejandro Poiré, eds. 1999. *Toward Mexico's Democratization: Parties, Campaigns, and Public Opinion*. New York: Routledge.
Purcell, Susan Kaufman. 1975. *The Mexican Profit-Sharing Decision*. Berkeley: University of California Press.
Radio Free Europe/Radio Liberty Newsline (RFE/RL). 1999. Vol. 3, No. 101, 5 May (Internet edition at www.rferl.org).
Ramet, Sabrina Petra. 1991. "The Catholic Church in Czechoslovakia, 1948–1991." *Studies in Comparative Communism* 24, 4 (December): 377–394.
Reed, Steven R. 1981. "Environmental Politics: Some Reflections on the Japanese Case." *Comparative Politics* 13, 3: 253–268.
Regini, Marino, and Ida Regalia. 1997. "Employers, Unions and the State: The Resurgence of Concertation in Italy?" In Martin Bull and Martin Rhodes, eds., *Crisis and Transition in Italian Politics*. London: Frank Cass.
Reuter, Konrad. 1991. *Fîderalismus. Grundlagen und Wirkungen in der Bundesrepublik Deutschland*, 4th ed. Heidelberg: Decker and Müller.
Rhodes, Martin. 1997. "Financing Party Politics in Italy: A Case of Systematic Corruption." In Martin Bull and Martin Rhodes, eds., *Crisis and Transition in Italian Politics*. London: Frank Cass.
Richardson, Bradley M., and Scott C. Flanagan. 1984. *Politics in Japan*. Boston: Little, Brown.
Richardson, Jeremy, J. 1995. "The Market for Political Activism: Interest Groups as a Challenge to Political Parties." *West European Politics* 18: 116–139.
Ridley, F. F., and Justin Greenwood, eds. 1998. "The Regulation of Lobbying." Special Issue of *Parliamentary Affairs* 51, 4 (October).
Ridley, F. F., and G. Jordan, eds. 1998. *Protest Politics: Cause Groups and Campaigns*. Oxford: Oxford University Press.
Riksdagen i siffror [The Swedish Parliament in Figures]. 1996–1997. Published by the Swedish Parliament (Riksdag).
Riksdagens Faktablad [Fact Sheets of the Swedish Parliament]. 1994–1995. No. 10, December 1994. Published by the Swedish Parliament (Riksdag).
Rix, Alan. 1988. "Bureaucracy and Political Change in Japan." In J. A. A. Stockwin, ed., *Dynamic and Immobilist Politics in Japan*. London: Macmillan.
Rock, David. 1987. "Political Movements in Argentina: A Sketch from Past and Present." In Monica Peralta-Ramos and Carlos H. Waisman, eds., *From Military Rule to Liberal Democracy in Argentina*. Boulder: Westview.

———. 1993. *Authoritarian Argentina: The Nationalist Movement, Its History, and Its Impact.* Berkeley: University of California Press.
Rodríguez, Josep A. 1992. "La política de las organizaciones de intereses médicos." *Revista Española de Investigaciones Sociológicas* 59: 121–160.
Rohde, David W. 1991. *Parties and Leaders in the Post-Reform House of Representatives.* Chicago: University of Chicago Press.
Ronit, Karsten, and Volker Schneider. 1998. "The Strange Case of Regulating Lobbying in Germany." *Parliamentary Affairs* 51: 559–567.
Rose, Richard. 1985. *Politics in England.* London: Macmillan.
Rose, Richard, and Thomas T. Mackie. 1988. "Do Parties Persist or Fail? The Big Trade-Off Facing Organizations." In Kay Lawson and Peter H. Merkl, eds., *When Parties Fail: Emerging Alternative Organizations.* Princeton: Princeton University Press.
Rosenberg, Jonathan. Forthcoming. "Latin America." In Clive S. Thomas, ed., *A Handbook of Research and Literature on Interest Groups.* Westport, CT: Greenwood.
Rothstein, B. 1996. *The Social Democratic State: The Swedish Model and the Bureaucratic Problem of Social Reforms.* Pittsburgh: Pittsburgh University Press.
———. 1998. "Breakdown of Trust and the Fall of the Swedish Model." Paper presented at the annual meeting of the American Political Science Association, Boston, Massachusetts, September.
Rush, M. 1990. "Parliament and Pressure Politics: An Overview." In M. Rush, ed., *Parliament and Pressure Politics.* Oxford: Clarendon.
Rutland, Peter. 1993. "Thatcherism, Czech-Style: Transition to Capitalism in the Czech Republic." *Telos* 94: 103–130.
Ryden, David K. 1996. *Representation in Crisis: The Constitution, Interest Groups and Political Parties.* Albany: State University of New York Press.
Sagardoy, Bengoechea, Juan Antonio, and David León Blanco. 1982. *El poder sindical en España.* Barcelona: Planeta.
Salisbury, Robert H. 1970. *Interest Group Politics in America.* New York: Harper and Row.
———. 1979. "Why No Corporatism in America?" In Philippe C. Schmitter and Gerhard Lehmbruch, eds., *Trends Toward Corporatist Intermediation.* Beverly Hills: Sage.
———. 1984. "Interest Representation: The Dominance of Institutions." *American Political Science Review* 78: 64–76.
———. 1994. "Interest Structures and Policy Domains: A Focus for Research." In William Crotty, Mildred A. Schwartz, and John C. Green, eds., *Representing Interests and Interest Group Representation.* Washington, DC: University Press of America.
Samstad, James G., and Ruth Berins Collier. 1995. "Mexican Labor and Structural Reform Under Salinas: New Unionism or Old Stalemate?" In Riordan Roett, ed., *The Challenge of Institutional Reform in Mexico.* Boulder: Lynne Rienner.
SAP (Swedish Social Democratic Party). 1975. *Utveckling av organisation och verksamhet. Rapport från arbetsgruppen i organisationsfrågor.* Stockholm: Tiden. Organizational Report to the 26th Social Democratic Party Congress.
———. 1945, 1967, 1976, 1984, 1990, 1997. Annual Reports. Stockholm.
Särlvik, B. 1983. "Coalition Politics and Policy Output in Scandinavia: Sweden, Denmark and Norway." In V. Bogdanor, ed., *Coalition Government in Western Europe.* London: Heineman Educational Books.

Saxonberg, Steven. 1999. "Václav Klaus: The Rise and Fall and Re-emergence of a Charismatic Leader." *East European Politics and Society* 13, 2: 391–418.

Schain, Martin. 1985. "Conditional Support for Communist Local Governments in France: Alienation and Coalition Building." In Philip Cerny and Martin Schain, eds., *Socialism, the State, and Public Policy in France*. New York: Methuen.

Schattschneider, E. E. 1942. *Party Government*. New York: Farrar and Rinehart.

———. 1960. *The Semisovereign People: A Realist's View of Democracy in America*. New York: Holt, Rinehart and Winston.

Schlesinger, Joseph. 1966. *Ambition and Politics: Political Careers in the United States*. Chicago: Rand McNally.

Schlozman, Kay Lehman, and John T. Tierney. 1986. *Organized Interests and American Democracy*. New York: Harper and Row.

Schmidt, Manfred. 1979. "Does Corporatism Matter?" In Philippe C. Schmitter and Gerhard Lehmbruch, eds., *Trends Toward Corporatist Intermediation*. Beverly Hills: Sage.

Schmitter, Philippe C. 1979. "Still the Century of Corporatism?" In Philippe C. Schmitter and Gerhard Lehmbruch, eds., *Trends Toward Corporatist Intermediation*. Beverly Hills: Sage.

Scott, Ruth K., and Ronald J. Hrebenar. 1984. *Parties in Crisis*. New York: John Wiley.

Self, P., and H. Storing. 1962. *The State and the Farmer*. London: Allen and Unwin.

Selle, Per. 1997. "Parties and Voluntary Organizations: Strong or Weak Ties?" In Karre Strøm and Lars Svåsand, eds., *Challenges to Political Parties: The Case of Norway*. Ann Arbor: University of Michigan Press.

Seton-Watson, R. W. 1965. *A History of the Czechs and Slovaks*. Hamden, CT: Archon.

Share, Donald. 1989. *Dilemmas of Social Democracy*. New York: Greenwood.

Skilling, H. Gordon. 1966. "Interest Groups and Communist Politics." *World Politics* 18, 3 (April): 435–451.

———. 1976. *Czechoslovakia's Interrupted Revolution*. Princeton: Princeton University Press.

———. 1981. *Charter 77 and Human Rights in Czechoslovakia*. London: Allen and Unwin.

———. 1983. "Interest Groups and Communist Politics Revisited." *World Politics* 36, 1 (October): 1–27.

Skilling, H. Gordon, and Franklyn Griffiths. 1971. *Interest Groups in Soviet Politics*. Princeton: Princeton University Press.

Smith, Denis Mack. 1959. *Italy: A Modern History*. Ann Arbor: University of Michigan Press.

Smith, W. Rand. 1998. *The Left's Dirty Job*. Pittsburgh: University of Pittsburgh Press.

Smith, William C. 1990. "Democracy, Distributional Conflicts and Macroeconomic Policymaking in Argentina, 1983–89." *Journal of Interamerican Studies and World Affairs* 32, 2 (summer): 1–42.

Snow, Peter G. 1996. "Argentina: Politics in a Conflict Society." In Howard J. Wiarda and Harvey F. Kline, eds., *Latin American Politics and Development*, 4th ed. Boulder: Westview.

Snow, Peter G., and Luigi Manzetti. 1993. *Political Forces in Argentina*, 3d ed. Westport, CT: Praeger.

Solomon, Susan Gross, ed. 1983. *Pluralism in the USSR: Essays in Honor of H. Gordon Skilling.* London: Macmillan.
Sousa, David J. Forthcoming. "The Responsible Party Model and Interest Groups." In Clive S. Thomas, ed., *A Handbook of Research and Literature on Interest Groups.* Westport, CT: Greenwood.
Spotts, Frederic, and Theodor Wieser. 1986. *Italy: A Difficult Democracy.* Cambridge: Cambridge University Press.
Staniszkis, Jadwiga. 1991. *The Dynamics of the Breakthrough in Eastern Europe.* Berkeley: University of California Press.
Stephens, John D., and Michael Wallerstein. 1991. "Industrial Concentration, Country Size, and Trade Union Membership." *American Political Science Review* 85, 3: 941–954.
Sternberger, Dolf. 1952–1953. "Der Staat der Gegenwart und die wirtschaftlichen und ausserwortschaftlichen Interessentengruppen." In *Kölner Zeitschrift für Soziologie,* Vol. 5. Köln: Opladen.
Stockwin, J. A. A., ed. 1988. *Dynamic and Immobilist Politics in Japan.* London: Macmillan.
Story, Dale. 1986. *The Mexican Ruling Party: Stability and Authority.* New York: Praeger.
Streek, Wolfgang. 1992. *Social Institutions and Economic Performance: Studies of Industrial Relations in Advanced Industrial Economies.* London: Sage.
Strøm, Karre, and Lars Svåsand, eds. 1997. *Challenges to Political Parties: The Case of Norway.* Ann Arbor: University of Michigan Press.
Suleiman, Ezra. 1987. *Private Power and Centralization in France: The Notaires and the State.* Princeton: Princeton University Press.
Swedish Election Study. 1968 and 1994. Göteborg: Swedish Social Science Data Service.
Tarrow, Sidney. 1989. *Democracy and Disorder: Protest and Politics in Italy, 1965–1975.* New York: Oxford University Press.
———. 1998. *Power in Movement: Social Movements and Contentious Politics.* Cambridge: Cambridge University Press.
Thelen, Kathleen. 1991. *Union in Parts: Labor Politics in Postwar Germany.* Ithaca, NY: Cornell University Press.
Thermeanius, E. 1933. *Sveriges politiska partier.* Stockholm: Hugo Gebers förlag.
Thomas, Clive S. 1998. "Interest Group Regulation Across the United States: Rationale, Development and Consequences." *Parliamentary Affairs* 51, 4 (October): 500–515.
Thomas, Clive S., ed. 1993. *First World Interest Groups.* Westport, CT: Greenwood.
Thomas, Clive S., and Ronald J. Hrebenar. 1995. "The Interest Group–Political Party Connection: Toward a Systematic Understanding." Paper presented at the annual meeting of the American Political Science Association, Chicago, Illinois, September.
———. 1999a. "Interest Groups in the States." In Virginia Gray, Russell L. Hanson, and Herbert Jacob, eds., *Politics in the American States: A Comparative Analysis,* 7th ed. Washington, DC: CQ.
———. 1999b. "Toward a Comprehensive Understanding of the Political Party–Interest Group Relationship in the American States." Paper presented at the Western Political Science Association, Seattle, March.
Tilly, Charles. 1984. "Social Movements and National Politics." In Charles Bright and Susan Harding, eds., *Statemaking and Social Movements.* Ann Arbor: University of Michigan Press.

———. 1986. *The Contentious French: Four Centuries of Popular Struggle.* Cambridge: Harvard University Press.

Truman, David B. 1971. *The Governmental Process*, 2d ed. New York: Alfred A. Knopf.

Tucker, Aviezer, et al. 1997. "The Czech Transition: Politics Before Economics." *Journal of Social, Political, and Economic Studies* 22: 407–416.

Ullmann, Hans-Peter. 1988. *Interessenverbände in Deutschland.* Frankfurt Main: Suhrkamp Verlag.

Uslaner, Eric M., ed. 1993. *American Political Parties: A Reader.* Itasca, IL: F. E. Peacock.

Valiente, Celia. 1995. "The Power of Persuasion: The Instituto de la Mujer in Spain." In Dorothy McBride Stetson and Amy Mazur, eds., *Comparative State Feminism.* Thousand Oaks: Sage.

———. 1997. "The Feminist Movement in Post-authoritarian Portugal and Spain (1974–1997)." Paper presented at the American Political Science Association meeting, Washington, D.C., August.

Von Beyme, Klaus. 1969. *Interessengruppen in der Demokratie.* München: Piper Verlag.

Walker, Jack L. 1991. *Mobilizing Interest Groups in America.* Ann Arbor: University of Michigan Press.

Wallace, William V. 1976. *Czechoslovakia.* Boulder: Westview.

Ware, Alan. 1988. *Citizens, Parties and the State.* Princeton: Princeton University Press.

Widfeldt, A. 1999. *Linking Parties with People? Party Membership in Sweden 1960–1997.* Aldershot: Ashgate.

Wiggins, Charles W., Keith E. Hamm, and Charles G. Bell. 1992. "Interest-Group and Party Influence Agents in the Legislative Process: A Comparative State Analysis." *Journal of Politics* 54, 1 (February): 82–100.

Wilkie, James W. 1967. *The Mexican Revolution: Federal Expenditures and Social Change Since 1910.* Berkeley: University of California Press.

Williamson, Peter J. 1989. *Corporatism in Perspective: An Introductory Guide to Corporatist Theory.* London: Sage.

Wilson, Frank. 1987. *Interest Group Politics in France.* Cambridge: Cambridge University Press.

Wilson, Graham K. 1990. *Interest Groups.* Oxford: Blackwell.

Wolchik, Sharon L. 1981. "Elite Strategy Toward Women in Czechoslovakia: Liberation or Mobilization?" *Studies in Comparative Communism* 14, 2–3 (summer–autumn): 123–142.

———. 1991. *Czechoslovakia in Transition: Politics, Economics and Society.* London: Pinter.

Wolfsfeld, Gadi. 1988. *The Politics of Provocation: Participation and Protest in Israel.* Albany: State University of New York Press.

Woodall, Brian, and Nobuhiro Hiwatari. 1988. *Inside Japan's Leviathan: Decision-Making in the Government Bureaucracy.* Berkeley: Institute of Governmental Studies, University of California, Working Paper 88-19.

Wootton, Graham. 1985. *Interest Groups: Policy and Politics in America.* Englewood Cliffs, NJ: Prentice-Hall.

Woronoff, Jon. 1986. *Politics: The Japanese Way.* London: Macmillan.

Wozniak, Lynne. 1992. "The Dissolution of Party-Union Relations in Spain." *International Journal of Political Economy* 22, 4: 73–90.

Wright, Gordon. 1981. *France in Modern Times*, 3d ed. New York: Norton.

Yanaga, Chitoshi. 1968. *Big Business in Japanese Politics.* New Haven: Yale University Press.
Yanai, Nathan. 1981. *Party Leadership in Israel: Maintenance and Change.* Ramat Gan: Turtledove.
Yishai, Yael. 1991. *Land of Paradoxes: Interest Politics in Israel.* Albany: State University of New York Press.
———. 1995. "Interest Groups and Political Parties: The Odd Couple." Paper presented at the annual meeting of the American Political Science Association, Chicago, August–September.
———. 1997. "Legislators and Interest Groups: Some Observations on the Israeli Scene." *Journal of Legislative Studies* 3: 89–111.
———.1998. "Regulation of Interest Groups in Israel." *Parliamentary Affairs* 51: 568–578.
Yonish, Steven. 1998. "Impact of Associational Life on Mass Linkages to the American Party System." Paper presented at the annual meeting of the American Political Science Association, Boston, August–September.
Zariski, Raphael. 1993. "Italy: The Fragmentation of Power and Its Consequences." In Clive S. Thomas, ed., *First World Interest Groups.* Westport, CT: Greenwood.
———. 1998. "Part Four: Italy." In M. Donald Hancock et al., *Politics in Western Europe,* 2d ed. Chatham, NJ: Chatham House.
Zeigler, L. Harmon. 1983. "Interest Groups in the States." In Virginia Gray, Herbert Jacob, and Kenneth N. Vines, eds., *Politics in the American States: A Comparative Analysis,* 4th ed. Boston: Little, Brown.
———. 1988. *Pluralism, Corporatism and Confucianism: Political Association and Conflict Regulation in the United States, Europe and Taiwan.* Philadelphia: Temple University Press.
———. 1992. "Interest Groups." In M. Hawkesworth and M. Kogan, eds., *The Encyclopedia of Government and Politics,* Vol. 1. London: Routledge.
———. 1993. *Political Parties in Industrial Democracies.* Itasca, IL: F. E. Peacock.
Zeigler, L. Harmon, and Michael Baer. 1969. *Lobbying: Interaction and Influence in American State Legislatures.* Belmont, CA: Wadsworth.
Zeigler, L. Harmon, and Wayne G. Peak. 1972. *Interest Groups in American Society,* 2d ed. Englewood Cliffs, NJ: Prentice-Hall.
Zeigler, L. Harmon, and Hendrik van Dalen. 1976. "Interest Groups in the States." In Herbert Jacob and Kenneth N. Vines, eds., *Politics in the American States: A Comparative Analysis,* 3d ed. Boston: Little, Brown.
Zeller, Belle. 1954. *American State Legislatures,* 2d ed. New York: Thomas Y. Crowell.
Živnustková, Alena. 1995. "Unions Say It's Time to Speak Up." *Prague Post,* 11 April: A3; reprinted in *Federal Broadcast Information Service* (FBIS) EEU–95-188, 8 May 1995.

The Contributors

Andrew Appleton is associate professor of political science at Washington State University, where he teaches courses in comparative politics and political parties. He has published articles on political parties and party organizations in a number of journals such as *Comparative Politics, Party Politics,* and *West European Politics.* He is working on a book about local political organizations in France.

John Constantelos is assistant professor of political science at Grand Valley State University in Michigan. His research focuses on the politics of adjustment to European integration. He has written on French and Italian business responses to Economic and Monetary Union and the Single European Act.

Robert K. Evanson is associate professor of political science and former associate dean and department chair at the University of Missouri–Kansas City. He earned his doctorate at the University of Wisconsin–Madison. He has published numerous articles on Soviet, Russian, Czech, and Czechoslovak politics.

Winand Gellner is professor and chair of the Department of Political Science at the University of Passau in Bavaria, Germany, and visiting professor at the University of Miami in Ohio, John E. Dolibois European Centre, Luxembourg. His research and publications are in the areas of comparative politics and political communications.

Kerstin Hamann is assistant professor of political science at the University of Central Florida. Her research focuses on Spanish politics, especially political parties, interest groups, elections, and regional elections and patterns of coalition formation. She has also published articles and book chapters on democratic transitions in southern Europe and Central America.

Ronald J. Hrebenar is professor of political science at the University of Utah. His research focuses on interest groups, political parties, public policy, and Japanese politics. He has published several books and articles including *Interest Group Politics in America* (3d ed., 1997), *Political Parties, Interest Groups and Political Campaigns* (coauthored, 1999) and *Japan's New Party System* (2000). He was a Fulbright scholar in Japan during 1982–1983.

Diane E. Johnson is a Ph.D. student in the Political Science Department at the University of California, Santa Barbara. Her research interests center on the Southern Cone region of South America, especially Argentina. Her current work is on the effect of technological change on media-state relations and its implications for democracy.

Grant Jordan is professor of politics, University of Aberdeen, Scotland. His interests focus on public policymaking and interest groups. His major publications include *Government and Pressure Groups in Britain,* with J. J. Richardson (1987); *Engineers and Professional Self-Regulation* (1992); and *The Protest Business,* with W. A. Maloney (1997).

Thomas M. Magstadt is adjunct professor of political science at the University of Missouri–Kansas City. He earned his doctorate at the Johns Hopkins School of Advanced International Studies. He chaired two political science departments and was a Fulbright scholar in the Czech Republic. He has authored two books and numerous articles on comparative and international politics.

William A. Maloney is a reader in politics, University of Aberdeen, Scotland. His publications include *Managing Policy Change in Britain,* with J. J. Richardson (1995); *The Protest Business,* with Grant Jordan (1997); and *The European Automobile Industry: Multi-Level Governance, Policy and Politics,* with A. M. McLaughlin (1999).

David Ost is professor of political science at Hobart and William Smith Colleges in Geneva, New York, and a frequent visiting professor at Central European University in Warsaw and Budapest. He has authored several works on Eastern European and comparative politics.

John D. Robertson is professor of political science at Texas A&M University where he teaches courses on comparative politics and research methods. His research and publications focus on the political economy and institutions of advanced industrial democracies. During 1988–1989 he was a Fulbright scholar at the University of Trier in Germany.

Jonathan Rosenberg is associate professor of political science at the University of Alaska, Fairbanks. He teaches comparative politics, political economy, international political economy, and Latin American politics. He has written on the Cuban political economy, the institutionalization of postrevolutionary regimes, economic sanctions, and the politics of oil in Alaska.

Clive S. Thomas is professor of political science at the University of Alaska–Juneau. His publications include works on interest groups, the legislative process, and U.S. state politics. He is director of the University of Alaska Legislative Internship Program, has been a volunteer lobbyist, and teaches seminars on lobby organization and tactics. During 1997–1998 he was a Fulbright senior research scholar in Brussels studying U.S. interest groups operating in the European Union.

Anders Widfeldt is a lecturer in Nordic politics in the Department of Politics and International Relations of the University of Aberdeen, Scotland. He was previously with the Department of Political Science at Göteborg University in Sweden.

Yael Yishai is professor of political science at the University of Haifa, Israel. Her publications include works on interest groups, political parties, and public policymaking in Israeli politics.

Index

Agnelli, Gianni, 128
Agrarian Party (Sweden), 65
Agricultural interests: in Argentina, 230; in Czech Republic, 198, 204–205; in France, 52, 61; in Germany, 103, 106; in Italy, 129–130; in Japan, 157, 160; in Spain, 177, 183
Agudat Israel (Israel), 143, 144, 147
Alemán, Miguel, 256, 258
Alfonsín, Raúl, 234, 236, 237, 239, 240, 242, 243
Alfonsinismo, 234
Ambiguity: centrality of, 226–227; concept in Poland, 213, 219–221; consequences of, 221; indispensable, 215–216
Andreotti, Giulio, 123
Appleton, Andrew, 27–44
Argentina: agricultural interests in, 230; Alfonsinismo in, 234; Argentine Feminist Organization, 237; Argentine Industrial Union in, 231, 234, 240; Argentine Rural Society in, 231, 234; austerity in, 234; authoritarian government in, 229, 231; business interests in, 235; capital accumulation model in, 236; categorizing party-group relations in, 244–245; Catholic Action in, 233; Catholic Church in, 233, 236; centralization in, 239; changes in interests in, 235–236; Christian Democratic Party in, 233; clientelism in, 238; Confederación General de Trabajo in, 231, 234, 240; corporatism in, 238; democracy in, 229, 231, 234, 236, 238, 241–244; Dignity and Independence Party in, 236; dual political system in, 238; economic crises in, 231, 234; economic reform in, 237; executive branch role, 233–234; Front for a Country in Solidarity in, 235; General Economic Confederation in, 231, 234, 240; groups and national executive in, 229, 238–241; human rights in, 236, 237; interest groups development in, 231–233; Justicialist Party in, 229, 231, 233, 235, 239; labor unions in, 231; military regimes in, 231, 233, 234; Mothers of the Plaza de Mayo, 237; Movement of Third World Priests in, 233; movimientismo in, 239, 240; National Autonomist Party in, 230, 231; neoliberalism in, 235, 237; Noninvolvement Model in, 245; "painted faces" in, 236; party/group separation in, 229; party-interest group relations in, 229–245; Peronist University Youth in, 233; policymaking in, 241–244; political culture in, 229; political development in, 233; political party development in, 230–231; presidential policies in,

339

234–235; privitization in, 235; Process of National Reorganization in, 234; Purple Band in, 233; Radical Civic Union in, 229, 231, 233, 234, 239; repression of parties/groups in, 229; Spring Plan in, 234; student groups in, 233; subsidies in, 235; Union for University Opening in, 236; Union of the Democratic Center in, 237; University Reform movement in, 233; women's groups in, 237
Argentine Industrial Union, 231, 234, 240
Argentine Rural Society, 231, 234
Association of the Homeland Expelled and Deprived Germans, 109
Associations; agricultural, 65; artisan, 49–50; auxiliary, 124; charity, 148; consumer cooperatives, 63; development of, 50–52; employer, 57, 107; grassroots, 53; industrial, 160; monopoly, 49; parent-teacher, 59–60; peak, 47, 65, 126, 160, 197, 231, 235; professional, 42, 52, 66, 145, 160–161, 183; recreational, 63; religious, 120, 161; sports, 63, 66, 184; temperance, 66; trade, 160, 167. *See also* Interest groups; Organizations.
Auroux Laws, 56
Austria, 48
Aznar, José María, 182

Balad (Israel), 143, 144
Begin, Menachem, 143
Berlusconi, Silvio, 120
Blair, Tony, 27, 29, 31, 35, 116
Bremer, Fredrika, 65–66
Britain: all-party subject groups in, 34; bureaucratic access in, 27; business interests in, 47; centralized political system in, 44; changes in party politics in, 28–30; Confederation of British Industry, 27; confrontational tactics in, 43; Conservative Party in, 27, 30, 35, 40, 41, 42, 44; Constituency Associations in, 30; contacts with Parliament in, 32, 34, 38–40; Cooperation/Ideological Model in, 41; Countryside Alliance in, 5, 9; Integration/Strong Partisan Model in, 40–41; interest groups links in, 38–40; Labour Party in, 2, 27, 28, 29, 30, 34, 35, 42; Liberal Democrats in, 5–6, 28; media use in, 43; National Farmers Union in, 27, 42; National Union of Conservative and Unionist Associations in, 30; New Labour Party in, 27, 28, 29, 31, 41; party annual conferences, 30, 32, 33–34*tab;* party funding in, 34; party-interest group relations in, 2, 27–44; political influence in, 38, 39, 39*tab,* 40; professional associations in, 42; Pro-Life Alliance in, 42; public opinion in, 43; Referendum Party in, 42–43; Scottish Nationalists in, 5–6, 35; service-sector in, 29; Social Democrats in, 28; social movements in, 27; social structure in, 29; Thatcherism in, 29; Trade Union Congress in, 27; trade unions in, 28, 29, 30, 31, 35, 44; unions in, 2, 42; Winter of Discontent in, 29
British Legion, 2
Bryan, William Jennings, 86
Bujak, Zbigniew, 217
Business interests: in Argentina, 235; in Britain, 37, 41, 43, 44, 47; in Czech Republic, 198, 199, 202–204; in France, 47, 57–58; in Germany, 47; in Japan, 159–162; in Mexico, 258–259; in Spain, 177–178, 182; in United States, 47

Calles, Plutarco Elías, 254
Camacho, Manuel, 258
Cárdenas, Cuauhtémoc, 260, 262, 264
Cárdenas, Lázaro, 254–255, 256, 257
Carli, Guido, 128
Catholic Action, 120, 122, 123, 233
Center Alliance (Poland), 214, 221
Center Party (Germany), 109
Center Party (Sweden), 65, 67, 73
Centre des Démocrates Sociaux (France), 56
Centrist Party (France), 46
Charter of Amiens (1906), 50, 55
Choisir (France). *See* Interest groups.

INDEX 341

Christian Democratic Party (Argentina), 233
Christian Democratic Party (Italy), 119, 120, 124, 127, 129
Christian Democratic Party (Sweden), 64, 74
Christian Democratic Union (Germany), 103, 105, 106
Christian National Union (Poland), 214, 221, 225–226
Christian Social Union (Germany), 103, 105, 106
Civic Democratic Party (Czech Republic), 196–197, 199, 202, 203, 205, 207
Civic Forum (Czech Republic), 196–197
Clean Government Party (Japan), 158, 159, 161
Clientela, 119, 120
Clientelism, 119, 132, 238
Clinton, Bill, 116, 212
Coldiretti (Italy), 129
Colors: changing nature of, 213, 215–216
Colosio, Luís Donaldo, 261, 262
Communion and Liberation (Italy), 123
Communist Party (Czech Republic), 194
Communist Party (France), 46, 50, 53, 54–55, 59, 61
Communist Party (Italy), 120, 123
Communist Party (Sweden), 65
Competition/Rivalry Model, 20–21, 284
Confagricoltura (Italy), 129
Confapi (Italy), 126
Confartigianato (Italy), 126
Confcommercio (Italy), 126
Confederación General de Trabajo (Argentina), 231, 234, 240
Confédération des Syndicats Libres (France), 56
Confédération Française Démocratique du Travail (France), 54–55
Confédération Françcaise des Travailleurs Chrétiens (France), 51, 56
Confédération Générale des Cadres (France), 57
Confédération Générale du Travail (France), 50, 54–55

Confédération Générale du Travail Unitaire (France), 50
Confederation of British Industry (UK), 27
Confederation of Mexican Workers, 248, 251, 255, 259, 260, 261, 262
Confederazione nazionale dell'artigianato (Italy), 126
Confesercenti (Italy), 126
Confindustria (Italy), 120, 126, 127, 128
Conflict/Confrontation Model, 21, 284
Conservative Party (UK), 27, 40; agricultural interests, 42; centralization of, 30; income, 35, 44; relations with business, 41, 44
Constantelos, John, 119–137
Constituency Associations (UK), 30
Cooperation/Ideological Model, 20, 282; in Britain, 41; in France, 61; in Israel, 148; in Italy, 123, 128; in Mexico, 250; in Sweden, 77; in United States, 79, 91
Corporatism, 11; in Argentina, 238; in Czech Republic, 201; in France, 49; in Japan, 155, 163–164; in Mexico, 247, 248–253, 259–261; party, 247, 248–253; role of parties in, 75; societal, 163; in Sweden, 63, 64, 75–76; as variant of individualism, 49; without labor, 163–164
Council for Economic and Social Agreement (Czech Republic), 198
Countryside Alliance (UK), 5, 9
Couseil Nationale du Patronnat Français (France), 51, 57
Czech Agriculture Chamber, 198
Czech-Moravian Chamber of Trade Unions, 197
Czech Republic: agricultural interests in, 198, 200, 204–205; Association of Entrepreneurs in, 199, 201; business interests in, 198, 199, 202–204; centralization in, 207; Civic Democratic Party in, 196–197, 199, 202, 203, 205, 207; Civic Forum in, 196–197; civil society in, 194; Communist Party in, 194; corporatism in, 201; corruption in, 203, 204, 208; Council for Economic and Social Agreement in, 198, Czech

Agriculture Chamber in, 198; Czech-Moravian Chamber of Trade Unions in, 197; Czech Social Democratic Party in, 196–197, 207; decision-making in, 193; democracy in, 193; deregulation in, 203; economic liberalization in, 203; economic paternalism in, 203; economic problems in, 198; environmental issues in, 205; European Union and, 204, 206; First Republic, 194; Green Party in, 201, 205, 208; health care in, 200, 206; hegemonistic party system in, 207; interest advocacy in, 195, 196; interest groups in, 197–198, 201; labor relations in, 202; Movement for Moravian and Silesian Self-Rule in, 201; multinational corporations in, 194; "normalization" in, 196; organized labor in, 199, 201–202; party domination in, 198–206; party-interest group relations in, 193–209; Party of Entrepreneurs, Tradesmen and Farmers, 201; Petka in, 194; pluralism in, 196; policymaking in, 193, 201–206, 207; political background, 194–196; political culture in, 193; political opposition in, 194; political parties in, 193, 196–197; "Prague Spring" in, 196; privatization in, 203; protectionism in, 204; Separation/Pragmatic Involvement Model in, 208; subsidies in, 201, 203, 205, 207; Third Republic, 194; trade unions in, 201, 202; Union of Industry and Transport in, 198; Velvet Revolution in, 196; "within-put" sector in, 194
Czech Social Democratic Party, 196–197, 207

de Gaulle, Charles, 45
De la Madrid, Miguel, 259
De la Rúa, Fernando, 237, 241
Democracy: compliant, 141–142, 149; consensual, 188; conservative, 164; delegative, 243; federal, 106; institutionalized, 243; liberal, 1, 6, 16–18, 155, 175; limited, 238; neocorporatist liberal, 107; nonliberal, 142; parliamentary, 106; representative, 48; social, 63, 143; spectator, 169
Democratic Party of the Left (Italy), 120, 126
Democratic Party (US), 79, 87, 95
Democratic Socialist Party (Japan), 158, 166
Dempsey, Brian, 37
Díaz Ordaz, Gustavo, 259
Domei (Japan), 160
Dumas, Roland, 58
Dyba, Karel, 202

Ecclestone, Bernie, 35
Echevarría, Luís, 259
Economic: coordination, 107; development, 254; efficiency, 107; integration, 128; liberalization, 203, 264; nationalism, 256; paternalism, 203; policy, 108, 143, 182; reform, 181, 237; stability, 188
Economy: export-based, 101, 107; political, 108–109, 110
Environment Party (Sweden), 64
European Union, 42; Common Agricultural Policy, 106; effects on domestic politics, 52; interest groups and, 46; policy processes, 52; protection against, 46; supranational challenges of, 46
Evanson, Robert K., 193–209

Falbr, Richard, 199
Fanfani, Amintore, 123, 127
Federal Campaign Act of 1971 (US), 87
Fédération des Conseils des Parents d'Eléves (France), 59
Federation of German Employers' Associations, 105
Federation of German Industry, 102
Federation of Young Italian Communists, 123
Federconsorzi (Italy), 129
Fernández de Cevallos, Diego, 262
Force Ouvriére (France), 54–55
Fox, Vicente, 249, 262, 263
France: advocacy in, 46; agricultural interests in, 52, 61; ambiguous relations in, 45; associational life in, 52, 54, 58, 62; Auroux Laws in, 56; *autogestion* in, 53, 55, 57; business

interests in, 47, 57–58; Centre des Démocrates Sociaux in, 56; Centrist Party in, 46; Choisir in, 60; Communist Party in, 46, 50, 53, 54–55, 59, 61; Confédération des Syndicats Libres in, 56; Confédération Française Démocratique du Travail in, 54–55; Confédération Franççaise des Travailleurs Chrétiens in, 51, 56; Confédération Générale des Cadres in, 57; Confédération Générale du Travail in, 50, 54–55; Confédération Générale du Travail Unitaire in, 50; Cooperation/Ideological Model in, 61; corporatism in, 49; Couseil Nationale du Patronnat Français in, 51, 57; decentralization of state activities in, 52, 54, 62; Deferre reforms in, 53; direct action in, 48, 50, 51; education in, 59–60; electoral laws in, 51, 53; Elf-Aquitaine scandal, 58; employers organizations in, 51, 57, 58; Force Ouvriére in, 54–55; four waves of associational development in, 50–52; fragmentation of interest group system, 47, 48; Front National in, 56, 59; Gaullist Party in, 46, 53; General Will in, 48, 49; Integration/Strong Partisan Model in, 61; labor movement in, 50; Le Chapelier Law, 49–50; legislation and parties/groups, 49–50; modernization of political system in, 52–54; Movement Républicain Populaire in, 56; National Assembly in, 46, 51; neocorporatism in, 47; neoliberalism in, 58; nonoccupational groups in, 58–60; nonpartisan groups in, 47, 54; occupational interest groups in, 54–58; parent-teacher associations in, 59–60; Parti Socialiste Unifié in, 54–55; party-interest group relations, 45–62; political culture in, 48–49; political decisionmaking in, 60; Popular Front government in, 50, 51; privatization in, 58; professional associations in, 52; *recentrage* in, 55–56; Socialist Party in, 46, 50, 52, 53; student groups in, 59; suspicion of interest groups in, 47; syndicalism in, 54–55; teachers union in, 59; trade unions in, 46, 47, 49, 50, 54–57; triangular relationships in, 47; understanding relations in, 46–48; Union Française d'Associations de Combattants et Victimes de Guerre in, 58–59; unitary character of, 48–49; veterans groups in, 58–59; women's groups in, 60

Franco, Francisco, 175, 177, 178, 186
Frasyniuk, Wladyslaw, 217
Fredrika Bremer Association (Sweden), 65–66
Free Democrats (Germany), 103
Freedom and Peace movement (Poland), 224
Freedom Union (Poland), 214, 222
Front for a Country in Solidarity (Argentina), 235
Front National (France), 56, 59

Gardini, Raul, 132
Gaullist Party (France), 46, 53
Gellner, Winand, 101–117
General Accord of Trade Unions (Poland), 214
General Economic Confederation (Argentina), 231, 234, 240
General Workers' Union (Spain), 175, 177, 178, 180, 182, 186
German Industrial and Trade Conference, 105
German Trade Union Federation, 105
Germany, 11; agricultural interests in, 103, 106; Alliance for Jobs in, 108; Alliance '90/Greens in, 103; associational life in, 101, 105, 112; Association of the Homeland Expelled and Deprived Germans, 109; authoritarian government in, 102; Basic Law in, 103; business interests in, 47; campaign financing in, 114; Center Party in, 109; Christian Democratic Union in, 103, 105, 106; Christian Social Union in, 103, 105, 106; dependencies between parties and groups in, 109–110; direct control by groups, 109; economic coordination in, 107;

economic policy in, 108; European Union and, 115; export-based economy in, 101, 107; external factors in party-group relations, 115; Federation of German Employers' Associations in, 105; Federation of German Industry, 102; Free Democrats in, 103; German Farmers Association, 106; German Industrial and Trade Conference in, 105; German Trade Union Federation in, 105; Green Party in, 101, 109; Ideological Model in, 110; independence of parties and groups in, 110; institutionalized bargaining in, 101; institutional reform in, 107; interest groups in, 104–106; internal factors in party-group relations, 106–109; *Konzertierte Aktion* in, 108; media in, 113; neocorporatism in, 101; Noninvolvement Model in, 111; occupational groups, 104–106; One Party Leaning/Neutral Involvement Model in, 110–111; parliamentary/governmental dimensions of party-group relations, 111–113; Partisan Model in, 110; party control of groups in, 110; party-interest group relations in, 101–117; Party of Democratic Socialism in, 103; party-system domination model in, 110; peak associations in, 48; pluralist model in, 110; policy process in, 108; political decentralization in, 106–107; political economy in, 101, 107, 108–109, 110; political parties in, 102, 103–106, 108; Pragmatic Model in, 111; recent party-groups relations in, 102–103; Reich Association of German Industries in, 102, 111; Reichsverband in, 103; Social Democratic Party in, 103, 105, 106, 108, 110; Social Democrats in, 5–6; social movements in, 101, 108, 109; state electoral lists in, 114; structure of federal system, 107; unification and, 109; Weimar Republic in, 102; as welfare state, 107

Go, Italy! Party, 120

Goldsmith, James, 43
Gompers, Samuel, 86
Gonzalez, Felipe, 181–182
Gorbachev, Mikhail, 196
Green Party (Czech Republic), 201, 205, 208
Green Party (Germany), 101, 109
Green Party (Mexico), 252
Green Party (Sweden), 64
Gurupu (Japan), 167, 168, 169
Gush Emunim (Israel), 146
Gutiérrez, Antonio, 180
Gyo-Ho (Japan), 162–163

Habad (Israel), 150
Hadash (Israel), 143, 144
Hague, William, 35
Hamann, Kerstin, 175–191
Harding, Matthew, 35
Haskins, Christopher, 35
Hata, Tsutomu, 158, 170
Havel, Václav, 196
Herut Party *See* Likud Party.
Histadrut (Israel), 145, 148
Historic Compromise of 1976 (Italy), 125
Hosokawa, Morihiko, 158
Hrebenar, Ronald J., 155–172
Hungary, 205

Imperial Rule Assistance Association (Japan), 164
Institutional Revolutionary Party (Mexico), 247, 249, 250, 251, 253–255, 256–257, 262, 263
Integration/Strong Partisan Model, 20, 281; in Britain, 40–41; in France, 61; in Israel, 147–148, 153; in Italy, 123; in Mexico, 250; in Spain; in Sweden, 77
Interest groups: agricultural, 122, 200, 204–205; anomic, 48; autonomy of, 139, 152, 175; bureaucratic contact and, 38–40; business, 122, 126–129, 199, 202–204; characteristics of, 17–18, 276; competitive, 12–13; conflicts in, 72–75; defining, 4–9; development of, 18, 51, 277; economic, 145, 176; environmental, 184, 205, 222; formal, 8; fragmented, 47, 48, 120; gay and lesbian,

184; goals of, 5, 277; group leadership and, 277–278; health care, 200, 206; human rights, 237; ideology of, 277; industrial, 160; leadership in, 18; local, 58; nonoccupational, 58–60; nonpartisan, 2, 47, 54; occupational, 104–106; partisan, 11, party-affiliated, 122; peace, 224; policy process and, 152; political party dependence on, 17, 29, 276; postmaterialist, 122, 130–131; protection of special interests and, 49; public, 145, 146; religious, 184; state-controlled, 185; student, 233; transformational effect of, 48; veterans,' 58–59; women's, 60, 65–66, 222, 224–225, 237. *See also* Associations; Organizations.

Israel: Agudat Israel in, 143, 144, 147; Arab parties in, 143, 144; Association Law in, 142; Balad in, 143, 144; centralization in, 140–141; changes in, 139; charity associations in, 148; civil society in, 153; as compliant democracy, 141–142, 149; Cooperation/Ideological Model in, 148; Coordinating Office of the Economic Associations in, 145; decisionmaking in, 140, 152; defense expenditures in, 141; determinants of party-group relations, 149–151; economic policy in, 143; Extension Law in, 145; Gush Emunim in, 146; Habad in, 150; Hadash in, 143, 144; Histadrut in, 145, 148; as ideological society, 141; immigrant associations in, 146; individualism in, 150; Integration/Strong Partisan Model in, 147–148, 153; interest groups in, 143, 144–146; kibbutz movement in, 147; Labor Federation in, 147; Labor Party in, 140, 142, 143, 149; Likud Party in, 140, 142, 143, 149; Manufacturers' Association in, 145; Meretz in, 143; monetary policy in, 141; National Religious Party in, 143, 144; as non-liberal democracy, 142; parentela relations in, 147, 153; party-interest group relations in, 139–154; Party Law in, 142; Peace Now in, 146; political background, 140–142; political changes in, 150; political parties in, 140, 142–144; politics of confrontation in, 149; privitization in, 141; professional associations in, 145; provision of social services by parties in, 140; public interest groups, 145, 146; public sector in, 141; Ra'am in, 143, 144; religious parties in, 5; Revisionist Party in, 143; Separation/Pragmatic Involvement Model in, 154; settlement movements in, 146; Shas in, 143, 144; Shinui in, 143, 144; social democracy in, 143; standard of living in, 150; statist orientation in, 140; as welfare state, 141; women's groups in, 145, 150; Yisrael Ahat in, 142–143; Zionism and, 141, 147

Italian Association of Christian Workers, 124
Italian Confederation of Workers' Unions, 124, 126
Italian General Confederation of Labor, 124, 125
Italian Social Movement, 120
Italian Union of Women, 123
Italian Women's Center, 122
Italy, 11; agricultural interests in, 129–130; antifascist resistance in, 124; business interests in, 126–129; Catholic Action in, 120, 122, 123; Christian Democratic Party in, 119, 120, 124, 127, 129; clientela in, 119, 120, 132; Coldiretti in, 129; Communion and Liberation in, 123; Communist Party in, 120, 123; Confagricoltura in, 129; Confapi in, 126; Confartigianato in, 126; Confcommercio in, 126; Confederazione nazionale dell'artigianato, 126; Confesercenti in, 126; Confindustria in, 120, 126, 127, 128; Cooperation/Ideological Model in, 123, 128; corruption in, 119; Democratic Party of the Left in, 120, 126; economic integration in, 128; environmental groups in, 130–131; European Union and, 122; expulsion of communists, 120; Federation of Young Italian Communists, 123;

Federconsorzi in, 129; formal institutions in, 120; fragmented groups in, 120; Go, Italy! Party in, 120; Historic Compromise of 1976, 125; independent political action in, 127; institutions in, 120, 122; Integration/Strong Partisan Model in, 123; interest group fragmentation in, 122; Italian Association of Christian Workers in, 124; Italian Confederation of Workers' Unions in, 124, 126; Italian General Confederation of Labor in, 124, 125; Italian Social Movement in, 120; Italian Union of Women, 123; Italian Women's Center in, 122; labor markets in, 125; labor movements in, 123; Liberal Party in, 120, 128; National Alliance in, 120; National Association of Italian Partisans, 122; neofeminist groups in, 130; Northern League in, 120; Opening to the Left in, 127–128; parentela in, 119, 120, 124, 129, 130; party auxiliary organizations in, 122–124; party dominance in, 119–137; party-group history in, 120–122; party-group links in, 120; party-interest group relations in, 119–137; partyocracy in, 120; patterns of party-group relations, 122–124; pluralism in, 120, 132; political opposition in, 120; political representation in, 120; political stability in, 119; Popular Movement in, 123; Popular Party in, 120; postmaterialist groups in, 130–131; recession in, 128; Republican Party in, 120; Separation/Pragmatic Involvement Model in, 128; Social Democratic Party in, 120; Socialist Party in, 120, 124; state interventions in, 129; Tangentopoli scandal in, 119, 122, 132–133; trade unions in, 124–126; transformism in, 120; Workers' Statute, 128

Japan, 11; agricultural interests in, 157, 160; antiwar/antinuclear groups in, 161–162; bureaucracy in, 157, 164–165; business interests in, 159–162; Clean Government Party in, 158, 159, 161; closed economy in, 163; Confucian tradition in, 163; conservative democracy in, 164; "convoy system" in, 162–163; corporatism in, 155, 163–164; decision-making in, 163; Democratic Socialist Party in, 158, 166; Domei in, 160; economic conglomerates in, 156; First Postwar Party System, 157; *gurupu* in, 167, 168, 169; Gyo-Ho in, 162–163; historical background, 156–157; Imperial Rule Assistance Association in, 164; industrial conflict in, 160; industrial groups in, 160; industrial law system in, 162–163; interest groups in, 159–162; Japan Socialist Party in, 158; Keidanren in, 159, 160, 167; Keizai Doyukai in, 159; labor movement in, 160; labor relations in, 159; leftist organizations in, 161–162; Liberal Democratic Party in, 156, 157, 158, 163, 165–166, 170; Meiji government in, 156–157; military regime in, 157; Mitsubishi in, 156, 157; Mitsui in, 156, 157; New Frontier Party in, 158, 170; Nikkerien in, 159; party funding in, 167–168; party-group connections in, 165–168; party-interest group relations in, 155–172; policymaking in, 168–169, 170–171; political culture, 155; political economy in, 162; political instability in, 164; political parties in, 157–159; political power in, 159–162; political realignment, 169–170; professional associations in, 160–161; protectionism in, 162–163; protest parties in, 158; religious associations in, 161; Rengo in, 160; Renmei in, 159, 160; role of bureaucracy in, 162–165; Second Postwar Party System, 157, 159; social movements in, 159–162; state role in, 155–156; Tokugawa Shogunate in, 156, 157; trade groups in, 160; unions in, 160; women's groups in, 161; yakuza in, 161; *zaibatsu* in, 156, 160; Zenchu in, 160; Zenno in, 160; "zoku" politics in, 166

Japan Socialist Party (Japan), 158
Johnson, Diane E., 229–245
Jordan, Grant, 27–44
Jospin, Lionel, 59
Justicialist Party (JP, Argentina), 229, 231, 233, 235, 239

Kaifu, Toshiki, 167
Keidanren (Japan), 159, 160, 167
Keizai Doyukai (Japan), 159
Kihara, Teiko, 161
Klaus, Václav, 193, 198, 201, 202, 204, 205, 207
Kohl, Helmut, 103
Krzaklewski, Marian, 213, 214, 219, 220, 226
Kwasniewski, Aleksander, 214, 220, 225, 226

Labastida, Francisco, 262
Labor: direct action and, 51; markets, 72, 75, 125; mobilization, 125; movements, 83; strikes, 50; unrest, 50
Labor Party (Israel), 140, 142, 143, 149
Labour Party (UK), 27, 28, 29; business plan, 37; income, 31, 34–35, 36–37*tab*, 38, 44; membership in, 31; organizational elements of, 30–31; relations with unions, 42; sponsors, 37*tab*; trade union relations, 31
Labuda, Barbara, 225
Lafontaine, Oskar, 103
Landsorganisationen (Sweden), 63, 65, 69, 71, 72, 73, 74, 76
Le Chapelier Law (France), 49–50
Left Party (Sweden), 65, 69
Liberal Democratic Party (Japan), 156, 157, 158, 163, 165–166, 170
Liberal Democrats (UK), 5–6, 28
Liberal Party (Italy), 120, 128
Likud Party (Israel), 140, 142, 143, 149
Lobbies, 3, 8, 57
Locke, John, 48
López Portillo, José, 259

McConnell, David, 34
McGhee, Alan, 37
Madison, James, 49, 84
Magstadt, Thomas M., 193–209

Maloney, William A., 27–44
Mapai Party: *See* Labor Party (Israel).
Menem, Carlos Saúl, 235, 236, 239, 240, 241, 242, 243
Meretz (Israel), 143
Mexico: agrarian reform in, 254, 255, 259; business interests in, 258–259; class conflict in, 249; commitment to development in, 257; Confederation of Mexican Workers in, 248, 251, 255, 259, 260, 261, 262; Cooperation/Ideological Model in, 250; corporatism in, 247, 248–253, 259–261; corruption in, 259; decisionmaking in, 249; economic crisis in, 260; economic development in, 250, 254; economic liberalization in, 264; economic nationalism in, 256; electoral reform in, 261, 264; foreign debt crisis in, 250, 259; Green Party in, 252; industrialization in, 257; Institutional Revolutionary Party in, 247, 249, 250, 251, 253–255, 256–257, 262, 263; Integration/Strong Partisan Model in, 250; Labor Industrial Pacts in, 257, 258; labor movement in, 251, 252; middle sectors in, 257–258; National Autonomist Party in, 258, 263; National Confederation of Popular Organizations in, 249, 251, 261; National Peasant Confederation in, 248, 251, 256, 260, 261, 262; National Solidarity Program in, 260–261; neoliberalism in, 249, 250, 259, 260; party dominance in, 253–256; party-interest group relations in, 247–265; peasant sector in, 251, 252; political economy in, 248; political stability in, 249, 250, 254, 259; popular sector in, 248–249; private sector in, 258–259; public sector employment in, 257–258; separation of powers in, 251; Social Democratic National Democratic Front in, 260; social movements in, 252; Sonora Dynasty in, 254; Zapatista Army of National Liberation in, 252
Mitterrand, François, 56, 57
Miyazawa, Kiichi, 170

Montague, Michael, 35
Movement for the Republic (Poland), 214, 221, 222
Movement of Third World Priests (Argentina), 233
Movement Républicain Populaire (France), 56
Movements: environmental, 9, 27, 109; labor, 50, 65, 123, 160; social, 9–10 See also Social movements.
Movimientismo, 239, 240
Municipal Workers' Union (Sweden), 70, 73
Mussolini, Benito, 120

National Alliance (Italy), 120
National Association of Farmers (Sweden), 65
National Association of Italian Partisans, 122
National Autonomist Party (Argentina), 230, 231
National Autonomist Party (Mexico), 258, 263
National Confederation of Popular Organizations (Mexico), 249, 251, 261
National Farmers Union (UK), 27, 42
National Labor Confederation (Spain), 177
National Organization of the Spanish Blind, 183
National Peasant Confederation (Mexico), 248, 251, 256, 260, 261, 262
National Religious Party (Israel), 143, 144
National Solidarity Program (Mexico), 260–261
National Union of Conservative and Unionist Associations (UK), 30
Neocorporatism, 47, 63
Neoliberalism, 58, 235, 237, 259, 260
Netanyahu, Binyamin, 143, 151
New Democracy Party (Sweden), 64
New Frontier Party (Japan), 158, 170
New Labour Party (UK), 27, 28, 29, 31, 41
Nikkerien (Japan), 159
Noninvolvement Model, 283–284

North American Free Trade Agreement (NAFTA), 260
North Atlantic Treaty Organization (NATO), 196–197, 224
Northern League (Italy), 120
Norway, 13, 44

Occhetto, Achille, 126
Olszewski, Jan, 222
Organization for Economic Cooperation and Development (OECD), 205
Organizations: auxiliary, 122; charitable, 178; community, 46; distrust of, 48; economic, 145; employers, 51; flanking, 122; formal, 7; grassroots, 260; housing, 63; as institutions, 7; intersectoral, 258; labor, 177; labor market, 75; local, 46; national, 58, 68; neighborhood, 178, 184; nongovernmental, 225; nonpartisan, 178; policy-influencing, 7; politically independent, 66; professional, 184; representative, 88*tab;* umbrella, 58, 145, 159; voluntary, 63; welfare, 148–149; white-collar, 54–57; women's, 179. See also Associations.
Oslo Accords, 143, 146
Ost, David, 211–227
Ozawa, Ichiro, 159, 170

Parentela, 119, 120, 124, 129, 130, 147, 153
Parti Socialiste Unifié (France), 54–55
Party-interest group relations; in Argentina, 229–245; in Britain, 2, 27–44; campaign financing and, 85; Competition/Rivalry Model, 20–21, 284; Conflict/Confrontation Model, 21, 284; constitutional provisions and, 276–277; contemporary level of development and, 273–274; Cooperation/Ideological Model, 20, 282; corporatism and, 75–76; in Czech Republic, 193–209; decentralization of government and, 274–275; determinants of, 16–18, 272, 278–279; Dominant Party Model, 281–282; effect on policymaking, 271, 285–288; effect on representation, 271, 285–288; effects on politi-

cal systems, 90–96; electoral cooperation and, 92; electoral system and, 275–276; external factors in, 115; factors shaping, 82–85, 269–270; forms of, 270, 279–285; in France, 27–44; general theory of, 271–272, 288–289; in Germany, 101–117; government frameworks and, 83–84; groups as auxiliary units to parties in, 45–46; Integration/Strong Partisan Model, 20, 281; internal factors in, 106–109; in Israel, 139–154; in Italy, 119–137; in Japan, 155–172; keys to, 46–48; legal provisions and, 276–277; in Mexico, 247–265; national experiences and, 22; Noninvolvement Model, 283–284; overall significance of, 287–288; parliamentary/governmental dimensions, 111–113; party strength and, 95–96; party system and, 275; patterns of change in, 88; patterns of socioeconomic development and, 273; in Poland, 211–227; policymaking and, 274–275; political culture and, 48–49, 82–83, 273; political science perspective, 10–12; political structures and, 16–17; political system development and, 16; postwar patterns of, 122–124; recent trends in, 270–271; Separation/Pragmatic Involvement Model, 20, 282–283; in Spain, 175–191; study of, 1–23; in Sweden, 2, 63–78; types, 20–21; in United States, 2, 79–98
Partyocracy, 120
Party of Democratic Socialism (Germany), 103
Party X (Poland), 214, 222
Peace Now (Israel), 146
Peel, Jonathan, 34
People's Party Liberals (Sweden), 65, 66
Perón, Juan Domingo, 231, 232, 239, 240, 243
Peronist University Youth (Argentina), 233
Petka (Czech Republic), 194
Pininfarina, Sergio, 128
Pinochet, Agosto, 212

Pluralism: competitive, 238; oligopolistic, 132; political, 264
Poland: abortion rights in, 225; Catholic nationalist movements in, 225–226; Center Alliance in, 214, 221; centrality of ambiguity in, 226–227; Christian National Union in, 214, 221, 225–226; coalition tendency in, 223; concept of ambiguity in, 213, 219–221; environmental groups in, 222; Freedom and Peace movement in, 224; Freedom Union in, 214, 222; General Accord of Trade Unions in, 214, 223; interest groups in, 211–213; Movement for the Republic in, 214, 221, 222; party-interest group relations in, 211–227; Party X in, 214, 222; peace movement in, 224; Polish Peasant Party in, 214; Polish Socialist Party in, 214; Polish United Workers' Party in, 212, 215, 217, 218, 222; political parties in, 211–213; Radio Maria in, 225–226; Social Democracy of the Polish Republic in, 215; Social Movement in, 215, 220; social movements in, 211–213; Solidarity in, 211; Solidarity of Labor Party in, 215, 222; trade unions in, 213, 215–216; Union of the Democratic Left in, 215; women's groups in, 222, 224–225
Policy: development, 92–93; economic, 108, 143, 182; participants, 7; promotion, 92–93; public, 7, 48
Polish Peasant Party, 214
Polish Socialist Party, 214
Polish United Workers' Party, 212, 215, 217, 218, 222
Political: action, 7; decentralization, 106–107; decisionmaking, 60; development, 274; economy, 108–109, 110; pluralism, 264; Polish United Workers' Party in, 215; pragmatism, 92–93; process, 11; representation, 120
Political parties: "big player" definition, 5–6, 43–44, 101, 103–106; business donations to, 67; cartelization of, 143, 144; class base, 73; in decisionmaking, 103; decline in, 12; defin-

ing, 4–5; establishment of groups by, 139; free organization of, 175; funding, 34–38, 167–168; goals of, 5; ideologically diluted, 51; influencing, 38–40; as interest groups in disguise, 139; loss of power, 139; nature of, 17; old-style, 139; provision of social services by, 140; regional, 201; religious, 143, 144; single interest, 42–43; state subsidies for, 67, 68; use of groups for own purposes, 47; weak, 51. *See also* Party-interest group relations.
Popular Alliance (Spain), 177, 179–181, 181
Popular Movement (Italy), 123
Process of National Reorganization (Argentina), 234
Pro-Life Alliance (UK), 42
Purple Band (Argentina), 233

Ra'am (Israel), 143, 144
Rabin, Yitzhak, 143
Radical Civic Union (Argentina), 229, 231, 233, 234, 239
Referendum Party (UK), 42–43
Reform: agrarian, 254, 255, 259; economic, 181, 237; electoral, 261, 264; institutional, 107
Reich Association of German Industries, 102, 111
Reichsverband (Germany), 103
Rengo (Japan), 160
Renmei (Japan), 159, 160
Republican Party (Italy), 120
Republican Party (US), 79, 87, 91, 95
Revisionist Party (Israel), 143
Rico, Aldo, 236
Robertson, John D., 101–117
Roosevelt, Franklin, 86
Rosenberg, Jonathan, 247–265
Rousseau, Jean-Jacques, 48
Rural People's Federation (Sweden), 65

Sainsbury, David, 35
Saito, Eishiro, 167
Salinas de Gortari, Carlos, 259, 260, 261, 262
Savary, Alain, 59–60
Schiller, Karl, 108
Schröder, Gerhard, 103, 106, 111

Sectors: agricultural, 157; banking, 127; energy, 127; health, 163; industrial, 127, 163; interest groups and, 8; party-group relations over, 54; popular, 248–249; public, 72, 73, 141; service, 29, 73; third, 148
Separation/Pragmatic Involvement Model, 20, 282–283; in Czech Republic, 208; in Israel, 154; in Italy, 128; in Spain, 181, 182, 184, 190; in Sweden, 77; in United States, 79, 91
Shas (Israel), 143, 144
Shinui (Israel), 143, 144
Smith, Adam, 48
Social: Catholicism, 54–55, 56; change, 140; emancipation, 102; pacts, 188; stability, 188; welfare, 8, 181
Social Democracy of the Polish Republic (Poland), 215
Social Democratic National Democratic Front (Mexico), 260
Social Democratic Party (Germany), 5–6, 103, 105, 106, 108, 110
Social Democratic Party (Italy), 120
Social Democratic Party (Sweden), 63, 64, 65, 67, 68, 69, 70, 73, 74, 76, 77
Social Democrats (UK), 28
Socialist Party (France), 46, 50, 52, 53
Socialist Party (Italy), 120, 124
Social Movement (Poland), 215, 220
Social movements: alternative, 109; elements of, 9–10; farmers, 65; in Germany, 101, 108, 109; pensioners, 201; in Poland, 211–213; self-help, 115; settlement, 146
Solidarity of Labor Party (Poland), 215, 222
Solidarity (Poland), 211; ambiguity and, 213, 215–216, 219–221; central organization of, 215; character of, 212, 216–221; during Communist era, 216–221; Electoral Action, 213, 214; in power, 218–219
Spain: agricultural interests in, 177, 183; associational life in, 175; authoritarian regime in, 178, 185; business interests in, 177–178, 182; charitable organizations in, 178; Civil War, 176; consolidation period in, 179–181; decisionmaking in,

178; democracy in, 175; democratic transition in, 179–181; economic crisis in, 181; economic policies in, 182; economic reform in, 181; European Union and, 191; federalization in, 191; General Workers' Union in, 175, 177, 178, 180, 182, 186; Integration/Strong Partisan Model in; interest groups in, 175, 176–177, 183–184, 185–188; Law of Associations in, 178; Law of Collective Bargaining in, 178; legalization of parties in, 176; National Labor Confederation in, 177; National Organization of the Spanish Blind, 183; party-interest group relations in, 175–191; pluralism in, 178; policymaking in, 188–190; political parties in, 175, 176–177, 185–188; Popular Alliance in, 177, 179–181, 181; professional associations in, 183; Separation/Pragmatic Involvement Model in, 181, 182, 184, 190; Spanish Communist Party in, 175, 177, 178, 180; Spanish Confederation of Employers' Organizations in, 175, 182; Spanish Socialist Workers' Party in, 175, 177, 179–181, 180, 182, 184, 186; support for democratic transition in, 175–176; Syndical Organization in, 177; underground unions in, 178; Union of the Democratic Center in, 177, 179–181, 181; unions in, 175, 179–181–180; as welfare state, 181; women's groups in, 181, 183; Workers' Commissions in, 175, 178, 180, 182; Workers' Statute in, 180, 189
Spanish Communist Party, 175, 177, 178, 180
Spanish Confederation of Employers' Organizations, 175, 182
Spanish Socialist Workers' Party, 175, 177, 179–181, 180, 182, 184, 186
Suárez, Adolfo, 179–181
Sweden: Agrarian Party in, 65; agricultural interests in, 65; associational life in, 63; Center Party in, 65, 67, 73; centralization of government in, 64; Christian Democratic Party in, 64, 74; class base in, 73; commissions of inquiry in, 75–76; Communist Party in, 65; confrontational political climate in, 77; Cooperation/Ideological Model in, 77; corporatism in, 63, 64, 75–76; decentralization of power in, 64; Environment Party in, 64; in European Union, 64, 78; fragmentation of party system in, 64; Fredrika Bremer Association in, 65–66; Free Church movement in, 65, 74; government, 64; Green Party in, 64; Integration/Strong Partisan Model in, 77; interest group conflicts, 72–75; interest groups membership in, 68–72; labor market in, 72, 75; labor movement in, 65; labor organizations in, 2; Landsorganisationen in, 63, 65, 71, 72, 73, 74, 76; Left Party in, 65, 67, 69; legislation in, 75; Liberal Party in, 67; Municipal Workers' Union in, 70, 73; National Association of Farmers in, 65; New Democracy Party in, 64; party financial support in, 67–68; party-interest group relations in, 63–78; party loyalty in, 74; partyness of government in, 63, 75; People's Party Liberals in, 65, 66, 73–74; policymaking process in, 64, 75, 76, 77; political party-interest group relationships in, 2; politics in, 64; professional associations in, 66; public sector in, 72, 73; Rural People's Federation in, 65; Separation/Pragmatic Involvement Model, 77; service sector in, 73; Social Democratic Party in, 63, 64, 65, 67, 68, 69, 70, 73, 74, 76, 77; socialist parties in, 2; sports movement in, 66; Swedish Agricultural Association in, 65; temperance movement in, 66; trade unions in, 63, 65; union clubs in, 71; wage structure in, 72; "War of the Roses" in, 73; welfare state, 73; women's groups in, 65–66
Swedish Agricultural Association, 65
Swedish Confederation of Professional Associations, 66

Swedish Confederation of Professional Employees, 66
Switzerland, 48
Syndical National des Instituteurs (France), 59
Syndical Organization (Spain), 177

Tangentopoli scandal, 119, 122, 132–133
Thatcher, Margaret, 29, 40
Thomas, Clive S., 1–23, 79–98, 269–291
Trade Union Congress (UK), 27
Transformism, 120
Tyminski, Stan, 214, 222

Union for University Opening (Argentina), 236
Union Française d'Associations de Combattants et Victimes de Guerre (France), 58–59
Union Nationale des Associations de Parents d'Eléves de l'Enseignement Libre (France), 59, 60
Union of the Democratic Center (Argentina), 237
Union of the Democratic Center (Spain), 177, 179–181, 181
Union of the Democratic Left (Poland), 215
Unions: "bread and butter," 54–55; in Britain, 28, 29, 30, 31, 35, 42; Catholic, 54–55; docile, 164; in France, 46, 47, 49, 50; in Italy, 124–126; in Japan, 160; labor, 175, 179–181; private sector, 72, 160; public sector, 72, 160, 166; in Sweden, 65; trade, 30, 31, 35, 42, 44, 46, 47, 49–50, 54–57, 124–126, 201; underground, 178
United States, 205; access to policymaking in, 81; business interests in, 47; campaign finance in, 85; Christian Coalition in, 87, 91; Cooperation/Ideological Model in, 79, 91; Democratic Party in, 2, 79, 87, 95; effect on political systems of party-group relations, 90–96; election funding, 86, 87; electoral cooperation in, 92; Federal Campaign Act of 1971, 87; federalism in, 83, 84; free enterprise system, 83; government framework in, 83–84; Greenback-Labor Party, 91; labor movement in, 83; legalism in, 83; Moral Majority in, 87; nature of party system in, 84; party control of government in, 95; party-group competition in, 81, 93–95; party-interest group relations in, 2, 79–98; party membership in, 86; party system in, 95; patterns of party-group relations, 86–88; policy development in, 92–93; political action committees in, 81, 85, 87, 89, 90; political culture in, 82–83; political development in, 79; Populist Party in, 91; pragmatism in, 79; Republican Party in, 79, 87, 91, 95; role of individualism on party-group relations, 82–83; separation of powers in, 83; Separation/Pragmatic Involvement Model in, 79, 91; state party-groups relations, 88–90; statutory provisions/regulations in, 84–85; Workingman's Labor Party in, 91
University Reform movement (Argentina), 233

Velásquez, Fidel, 256, 257, 259, 264

Walesa, Lech, 215, 217, 218, 219, 220
Widfeldt, Anders, 63–78
Workers' Commissions (Spain), 175, 178, 180, 182

Yishai, Yael, 139–154
Yrigoyen, Hipólito, 231, 239, 243

Zapata, Emiliano, 252
Zapatista Army of National Liberation (Mexico), 252
Zedillo Ponce de León, Ernesto, 262
Zeman, Milos, 197, 199, 202, 204, 207
Zenchu (Japan), 160
Zenno (Japan), 160
Zionism, 141, 147

About the Book

This benchmark study of the political party–interest group relationship—crucial in shaping the characteristics of democratic political systems—provides an in-depth analysis of the connection between special interests and political parties across thirteen democracies: Argentina, Britain, the Czech Republic, France, Germany, Israel, Italy, Japan, Mexico, Poland, Spain, Sweden, and the United States.

Clive S. Thomas is professor of political science at the University of Alaska–Juneau. His publications include *First World Interest Groups: A Comparative Perspective* and *Politics and Public Policy in the Contemporary American West*.